Swaps, Restitution and Trusts

AUSTRALIA
LBC Information Services
Sydney

CANADA and USA
Carswell
Toronto Ontario

NEW ZEALAND
Brooker's
Auckland

SINGAPORE and MALAYSIA
Sweet & Maxwell Asia
and Kuala Lumpur

Swaps, Restitution and Trusts

Alastair Hudson
LLB LLM Ph.D.
Barrister, Lincoln's Inn
Lecturer in law, Queen Mary and
Westfield College, University of London

LONDON
SWEET & MAXWELL
1999

Published in 1999 by
Sweet & Maxwell Limited of
100 Avenue Road
Swiss Cottage
London NW3 3PF
http://www.smlawpub.co.uk

Printed in Great Britain by MPG Books Ltd,
Bodmin, Cornwall

No natural forests were destroyed to make this product;
Only farmed timber was used and replanted

A CIP catalogue record for this book
is available from the British Library

ISBN 0421 65650 6

Preface

The author has worked in the derivatives markets as legal counsel and as a finance professional, retaining a particular interest in the law of restitution. In that time the author developed the view that existing private law rules relating to financial transactions did not meet the particular circumstance of commercial transactions nor did it accord closely with established regulatory principles, such as suitability. This book therefore seeks to analyse the *Westdeutsche Landesbank v. Islington* litigation, together with the other local authority swaps cases, in so far as they impact on these issues.

The book analyses the case of *Westdeutsche Landesbank v. Islington L.B.C.* and its ramifications for the swaps markets. In particular the book advances the thesis that claims in relation to restitution of money arising in relation to financial transactions ought to be founded on a notion of suitability. Further, the book highlights three key issues arising from the Islington litigation. First, that the courts failed to take into account the nature of swaps and their necessary allocation of risks between counterparties. Secondly, the problems created for the law of restitution by English law's conception of money as tangible property rather than as intangible choses in action held in electronic bank accounts. Thirdly, the problem of taking security in financial transactions as a result of the decision of the House of Lords and by using standard market contracts as currently constituted. The underlying theme of the book is the conflict between the attitudes of traditional trusts lawyers and the proponents of the emerging principle of restitution of unjust enrichment. The book sets out new models for problems of equitable proprietary claims and unjust enrichment claims based on suitability for future cases, based on existing case law and by employing other techniques such as common intention constructive trusts, the doctrine of severance and the doctrine of undue influence.

In the preparation of this broad-ranging study of the law of trusts, the law of restitution of unjust enrichment, the author has gleaned an enormous amount from others and would like to express his appreciation to the following people. In particular, thanks to Prof. Barry Rider for his vital guidance and support. The author has also benefited enormously from discussions of particular issues raised in this book with academic colleagues, especially Dr Mads Andenas, Dr Geraint Thomas, Prof. Roger Cotterell, Dr Joanna Benjamin, Prof. Gerard McCormack, Michael Bryan and Joanne Scott, in particular; and legal practitioners in the derivatives markets Edward Murray (Allen & Overy, and ISDA), Jeffrey Golden (Allen & Overy, and ISDA), Schuyler Henderson (Baker & McKenzie), and Satayajit Das (TNT, Australia). I would also like to thank Prof. Peter Birks for encouraging comments made on drafts of some of the ideas which make up this book.

ALASTAIR HUDSON Ph.D.
QUEEN MARY AND WESTFIELD COLLEGE
MILE END

NOVEMBER 1998

Addendum

Abstract of the text, and a new addition

This book analyses the case of *Westdeutsche Landesbank v. Islington L.B.C.* and its ramifications for the swaps markets. In particular, the book advances the thesis that claims in relation to restitution of money arising in relation to financial transactions ought to be founded on a notion of suitability. The aim of this addendum is to take account of the House of Lords' decision in *Kleinwort Benson v. Lincoln City Council* ("*Lincoln C.C.*"),[1] the few changes it makes to the law, as recounted in the remainder of this book, and also its impact on the development of the law relating to the restitution of money transferred in commercial transactions. Given the lateness of the decision, it has not been possible to alter the detail of the text, other than to add these few words. As Professor Burrows has said: "it is no exaggeration to say that one could write a book on the restitutionary consequences of the decision in *Hazell's* case".[2] As Lord Goff fears, such a book will grow in length as a result of this addition to the case law. I rue that remark as I craft this addendum to a book that was a long time in coming, in any event. There is much to say and I fear I have not said it all.

The main concern of this book, within the central remit of analysing the development of the law of restitution in the banking context, is to highlight three key issues arising from the *Islington* litigation. First, that the courts failed to take into account the nature of swaps and their necessary allocation of risks between counterparties. Secondly, the problems created for the law of restitution by English law's conception of money as tangible property rather than as intangible choices in action held in electronic accounts. Thirdly, the problem of taking security in financial transactions as a result of the decision of the House of Lords and by using standard market contracts as currently constituted.

The underlying theme of the book then is the conflict between the attitudes of traditional trusts lawyers, and the proponents of the emerging principle of restitution of unjust enrichment. The book sets out new models for problems of equitable proprietary claims and unjust enrichment claims based on suitability for future cases and on existing case law by employing other techniques such as common intention constructive trusts, the doctrine of severance and the doctrine of undue influence.

In looking at this new decision in *Lincoln C.C.* there is a feeling that it is a significant move towards the development of a principle of restitution on the ground of unjust enrichment in English law. The point is made later in this book that the detail of the speeches in *Westdeutsche Landesbank v. Islington* ("*Islington*") disclosed a conflict between a traditional trusts lawyers' approach to matters of restitution, which is ideologically opposed to the newer thinking based on reversing unjust enrichment. That battle is refought in *Lincoln C.C.*, this time with Lord Goff speaking on behalf of restitution lawyers for the majority and Lord Browne-Wilkinson responding with a strong dissenting judgment.

The facts in *Lincoln C.C.* are those common to the local authority swaps cases

---

[1] [1998] 4 All E.R. 513.

[2] "Swaps and the friction between common law and equity" [1995] R.L.R. 15.

taken on direct appeal from Langley J., as discussed in chapter 1.[3] The facts arose out of the attempt by the bank to recover moneys paid to the respondent local authorities under interest rate swap agreements. The claim for such recovery was based on a contention that those payments had been made under a mistake of law. The mistake of law claimed was as to the capacity of local authorities to enter into such agreements. That local authorities did not have that capacity was subsequently confirmed by the House of Lords in *Hazell.* There were two important issues considered by the House of Lords in *Lincoln C.C.*: first, whether a plaintiff can rely on a mistake of law to found a claim for restitution, and, secondly, whether there ought to be any distinction in restitutionary terms between part-performed and fully-performed transactions.

The majority decision in Lincoln C.C.

Two issues arose on the *Lincoln C.C.* appeal. First, the whole court agrees that restitution should be available for mistake of law. A further more controversial question was whether (a) a settled understanding of the law or (b) honest receipt of money by the payee should be a defence to such an action.

Lord Goff, speaking for the majority, held as follows:

> ...the rule that there could be no restitution of money paid under a mistake of law was no longer a part of English law;
>
> it is not a part of English law that payments made under a settled understanding of the law among market participants, which is subsequently held to be incorrect, is irrecoverable ;
>
> there is no principle that money paid under a contract void an initio is irrecoverable because the contract had been fully performed before the contract was declared, or understood to be, void.

Analysis of the dissenting position

The powerful central point made by Lord Browne-Wilkinson in his dissenting speech was that at the time of the payments made under the swaps transactions, it was a settled analysis of the then existing law that local authorities could enter into the swaps transactions. Therefore, it was said that there was no operative mistake on the minds of the banks. Rather, the banks were proceeding on the basis of an understanding of the law *at that time.* Lord Browne-Wilkinson rejected the proposition that there could be retrospective mistake of law activated by a subsequent change in the law. In his Lordship's view the parties to a contract ought to be able to rely on there being closure of their contractual arrangements such that subsequent judicial decisions ought to have no place. The risks for contracting parties was that no transaction would ever be capable of being deemed complete on the basis that a subsequent change in the law may yet have caused it to be declared void. Therefore, the law was created, in Lord Browne-Wilkinson's terms, in 1991 with the decision in *Hazell.* Lord Goff took the opposite view that the role of the court is to declare what the law has always been, *i.e.* at the time when the contracts were created pre-*Hazell.* On this view, a judicial decision may have retrospective effect on transactions entered into at an earlier date.

[3] Considered pp.9 *et seq.*, below.

This writer cannot agree with Lord Browne-Wilkinson's position that there was in logic no mistake, neither in relation to local authority interest rate swaps nor in general terms. The banks were under the impression that local authorities could enter into the transactions whereas, as the House of Lords declared in *Hazell*, local authorities could not enter into such transactions. The operative mistake in the local authority swaps cases was not based on law settled by a court but rather on a mistaken assumption among the swaps community as to the capacity of local authorities to enter into interest rate swaps in relation to what a court *would say if it were ever appraised of the issue at some time in the future.* The House of Lords in *Hazell* were not saying that there had been new events or new legislative intervention which meant, for the first time, that local authorities could not enter into such transactions. Rather, the House of Lords was declaring that local authorities *had never had capacity* to enter into such transactions. Therefore, the banks *had been* operating under a mistake on entering into the transactions.

The House of Lords considered the possibility of a claimant relying on a perception of "settled law" to found an action on mistake of law. Quoting Lord Denning, Lord Browne-Wilkinson found that "[t]he practice of the profession in these cases is the best evidence of what the law is - indeed it makes the law". The disturbing ramifications of market practice making law are considered below. The question will always be whether or not there is sufficient agreement in the market as to suggest that there is a clear view of the law. Given the troubled state of the law relating to derivatives in the wake of decisions like that in *Islington*, and the very disturbing pattern of slavish reliance on the terms of standard market contracts (which were designed in any event to be modified on a case-by-case basis), it is at least unlikely whether there could be said to be settled opinion in any event. It is something to be grateful for that the court decided that reliance on a settled view of the law would found a claim based on mistake of law. Perhaps a middle course would be to rely on such a defence only where the mistake is based on a judicial decision, and not the advice of a professional.

The context of risk

To disallow the parties from relying on restitution for mistake of law disables the parties from relying on the risk allocation provisions in their contracts. This argument carries us onto the roundabout considered below that, if it was *ultra vires* the local authorities entering into the interest rate swap, there can be no argument that there was any contract in the first place. This argument is countered in this book by saying that it ought to have been open to the parties to rely on the doctrine of severance to preserve their risk allocation decisions, and that the doctrine of common intention constructive trust ought to be employed to impose an equity on both parties to respect those risk allocation and security provisions.[4] Failure to recognise such provisions increases systemic risk in financial markets and makes the conduct of global financial business both more complex and riskier (that is, for economies involved as well as for the financial institutions).

[4] See the extended discussion in Chapter 12, *The Suitability Approach.*

What is the test for this mistake of law?

There is a necessary element missing from the House of Lords' decision —what is the appropriate measure of a mistake suitable for invoking this principle? In other words, should the plaintiff be entitled to rely on a mistake of law in all cases where the lawyer considers the law to be *x*, when it is in fact *y* according to a subsequent decision of a court. In considering the breadth of the test for mistake, the issue arises whether one ought to be able to include being badly advised by one's lawyers that the law does, or does not, permit a course of action. Similarly, must the mistake obtain only to capacity and ability to contract, or could it be said to be a mistake of law as to the tax law impact of a transaction for one or other of the parties?

It would seem unsatisfactory for Party A to be deprived of the benefits of a transaction entered into bona fide by A, simply on the ground that Party B had been negligently advised as to the tax impact of the transaction. To permit B to rescind the contract in such circumstances would have two effects: first, it gives B an option to terminate which would have required a very different pricing structure for a derivative product, and, secondly, it introduces a level of uncertainty into contractual dealings where otherwise valid contracts might be avoided on grounds of some unanticipated inconvenience to one or other of the parties.

If the categories of acceptable mistake are to be limited, there is a need for better guidance. It might be that legal incapacity is the sole category of suitable mistake. However, there are further issues as to the regulatory classification of transactions which may run to incapacity, or may simply impose an unexpected cost on the parties. Fundamentally, the issue must revolve around whether or not the mistake is mutual or simply unilateral. Unilateral mistake clearly offers greater potential for unfairness between contracting parties, whereas mutual mistake offers both parties reason for rescinding their agreement.

The clearest advice for contracting parties in financial contracts is to include in their agreements, their conduct of business documentation, and their transaction confirmations, some statement as to the expectations of the parties on entering into the transaction. The point is made in this book and in *The Law on Financial Derivatives* that standard market contracts are not sufficient in their current form to make sufficient statement as to the parties' underlying intention and to make plain those factors which are operative on the parties in creating (or in purporting to create) contracts.

There are only brief clues in the speeches as to the factors which may and may not be taken into account. In overruling the mistake of law rule, Lord Goff considers[5] the words of Sir William Evans's, author of the "Essay on the action for money had and received"[6] which first criticised the mistake of law concept, where he said:

> "... no man shall, under the pretence of ignorance of the law, excuse himself from the performance of his own obligations, or acquire an advantage, or avoid a detriment, when he has omitted using the means ordained by law for those purposes."

It is suggested that this goes only part way towards answering the question "what

[5] [1998] 4 All E.R. 513 at 527.

[6] Published originally in 1802 but reproduced at [1998] R.L.R. 1.

will found a mistake of law?". Lord Hoffmann considered, in outline, the nature of mistake and expressed reservations about "a robust, commonsense definition of a mistake" which would not account satisfactorily for Lord Browne-Wilkinson's difficulties with retrospectivity.[7] The question turns, in his Lordship's view, on whether or not it was possible to ascertain the truth or falsity of any proposition. This itself begs the question as to the forms of proposition which are material.

Inadequacy in assessing risk allocation between the parties

As considered in detail in the subsequent text,[8] the point which is not given much attention in any of the local authority swaps cases is that the swaps documentation signed by the parties provided expressly for a representation that both parties have the capacity to enter into the contract and to perform all their obligations under the contract.[9] Where this representation fails, the contracts provided that a failure in respect of such a representation is an event of default under the contract, leading to a right in the non-defaulting party to termination. In *Islington*, Hobhouse J. was alone among the judges who heard the *Islington* litigation in addressing the point in the context of the doctrine of mistake between the parties as to the capacity of one of them.[10] He found "[t]here is no evidence or allegation in either case that the relevant bank was mistaken as to any actual fact."[11] However, he did find that there had been a mistake as to the local authorities' capacity to perform under the swaps contracts. It was said that that mistake as to capacity stemmed from a mistake as to the interpretation of the Local Government Act 1972.

As set out above, what remains unclear as a result of *Lincoln C.C.* is the question *what exactly constitutes a mistake* and whether risk allocation provisions could play any part in this. There is, for example, a distinction between an *assumption* that something is the case and a *mistake* as to whether or not something is the case. The view propounded by Hobhouse J. in *Islington* would seem to suggest that that was not a case involving a mistake because the parties were acting on an assumption as to the validity of their contracts. This assumption view suggests that the risk was not considered and therefore was not, in any sense, an active factor which impacted on the parties. As considered elsewhere in this book, that view is in any event unsatisfactory in that it fails to acknowledge that in all the local authority swaps cases the documentation effected between the parties constituted an explicit assessment of the risks of such incapacity. It is not clear therefore the nature of the mistake which can be relied upon.

The primary submission for the banks in *Islington* was that there were mistakes of fact operating on the mind of their employees in dealing with the local authorities: specifically, that they thought local authorities were capable of entering into swaps agreements. Hobhouse J. decided from the outset that he would not consider questions relating to the state of mind, nor any possible mistake in the mind, of the employees of the banks. Therefore, the issue of mistake

---

[7] [1998] 4 All E.R. 513 at 552.

[8] See, in particular, pp.63 *et seq.*

[9] As discussed above in Chapter 4, this provision is common to the ISDA terms and also to the BBAIRS terms for swaps and OTC derivatives dealings more generally.

[10] [1994] 4 All E.R. 890 at 931.

[11] *ibid.*

was rapidly dismissed.[12] As set out in the ensuing text in *Problems of Credit and Security*,[13] the courts' determination to ignore the substantive terms of the agreements mean that the parties are not able to allocate risks, nor is the market able to control the systemic risks in the derivatives marketplace. Were it definitively the case that netting or hedging arrangements could never be included, at law or equity, as being within the contemplation of the parties, then this would have included some acknowledgment of the contractual intentions of the parties.

The role of the advising lawyer

The issue which arises in *Lincoln* is as to the role of the lawyer who provides advice. The swaps markets are a good example of a situation in which there is a good deal more law settled by professional practice, than is decided by the courts. Celebrated firms of solicitors, eminent barristers, and laudable trade organisations (like the International Swaps and Derivatives Association ("ISDA"), the Financial Law Panel and the British Bankers' Association ("BBA")) continue to attempt to isolate and resolve the vast majority of problems which are posed up by the products generated by commercial parties.

There is a tendency then for these lawyers to "make law" in that the market follows the opinions of these lawyers. As Lord Goff held, the markets had proceeded to do business with local authorities on the basis of "assumption ... based on practical grounds, rather than on advice about the legal position."[14] The opinions of these lawyers typically support the legal validity of market practice - or, even to the extent that they raise caveats, they are read with blinkers so as to appear wholly supportive of market practice. This, beyond mere cynicism on the part of this writer, is a pernicious, lazy and downright dangerous practice. There is a tendency within the financial institutions themselves to ignore potentially real problems. In this writer's view, in such situations, banks are not operating under mistake of law, rather they are rightly victims of their own sloppy business practices in failing to isolate and examine all the applicable legal risks. For them, the urge to make money is irresistible: the management of risk is a cost that is to be controlled like other costs.

The other problem which arises from this is more academic perhaps: in short, is a situation created in which sections of the market are sealing themselves off from the operation of law so that the law under which they operate is entirely their own law. These markets operate as an autopoietically-closed system into which there are not inputs from mainstream jurisprudence until a non-market player, such as a local authority, refuses to sign up to the prevailing orthodoxy and insists on outsiders in courtrooms sitting in judgment on financial innovation. This is always a risk - like other risks it can be measured and managed. The derivatives markets are beginning to mature. Their legal analysis and practice must similarly mature.

---

[12] [1994] 4 All E.R. 890 at 905, *per* Hobhouse J.

[13] See below pp.78 *et seq.*

[14] [1998] 4 All E.R. 513 at 539.

Contents

Table of Cases

Table of Statutes

Part I

The nature of derivatives

Chapter 1

Introduction

1–01 This book is sustained principally by the analysis of one decided case concerning financial derivatives: *Westdeutsche Landesbank Girozentrale v. Islington L.B.C.*[1] (hereafter "*Islington*"). This is perhaps the most difficult of the decided local authority swaps cases dealing with the restitution of money passed under a contract subsequently found to have been void *ab initio* and the availability of compound interest in such circumstances.[2] The structure of the book is to consider first the nature of financial derivatives, secondly the legal analysis of financial derivatives, thirdly the specific context of the "local authority swaps cases", fourthly the attitude of the High Court and Court of Appeal to the issues raised in *Islington*, and fifthly the various approaches adopted by the members of the House of Lords in *Islington*. Finally, this book considers the development of the law of restitution in these commercial contexts and suggests a new model approach for effecting restitution of money and other property in the context of financial transactions.

The argument

1–02 The central contention of this book is that it is impossible for parties to retain a proprietary interest in property transferred under a commercial contract which is found to be void *ab initio*, as a result of the majority decisions in the House of Lords in *Islington*. The restatement of the core rules of equity in the speech of Lord Browne-Wilkinson in *Islington*[3] have created a test for the allocation of equitable title in property which is based solely on the conscience of the defendant to any claim. It is submitted that this concentration on knowledge of a factor which ought to affect a person's conscience is not the most appropriate mechanism for allocating personal and proprietary claims in the context of commercial and financial transactions. In particular, Lord Browne-Wilkinson held that a proprietary remedy will only be imposed in circumstances where the defendant has knowledge of the factor which is alleged to impose the office of trustee on him as opposed to strict liability.[4] It is submitted that these principles restrict the potential intervention of equity to such a narrow range of cases that the

---

[1] [1996] 1 A.C. 669; [1996] 2 W.L.R. 802; [1996] 2 All E.R. 961.

[2] The decided cases encompass a number of issues ranging from the capacity of local authorities to issues surrounding the Gaming Act and restitution of money. The principal cases are: *Hazell v. Hammersmith and Fulham* [1991] 1 All E.R. 545, HL; *Westdeutsche Landesbank Girozentrale v. Islington L.B.C.* [1994] 4 All E.R. 890, *per* Hobhouse J., CA; and reversed on appeal [1996] AC 669, HL.; *Kleinwort Benson v. Sandwell Borough Council* [1994] 4 All E.R. 890, *per* Hobhouse J.; *Kleinwort Benson v. Birmingham City Council* [1996] 4 All E.R. 733, CA, on appeal from Gatehouse J., (unreported); *Kleinwort Benson v. South Tyneside M.B.C.* [1994] 4 All E.R. 972, *per* Hobhouse J.; *Morgan Grenfell v. Welwyn Hatfield DC and others* [1995] 1 All E.R. 1, *per* Hobhouse J.; and *Credit Suisse v. Allerdale B.C.* [1997] Q.B. 306; *Kleinwort Benson v. Glasgow C.C.* [1997] 4 All E.R. 641.

[3] [1996] 1 A.C. 669 at 698 *et seq.*

[4] Birks, "The Burden on the Bank" in *Restitution and Banking Law*, (Rose ed., Mansfield Press, 1998), p. 189.

mutual intentions of parties to commercial contracts will frequently not be enforced by either the rules of common law or of equity.

1–03 The core of this argument, as developed below, is that the courts' failure to enforce the credit enhancement and risk allocation provisions of the contracts and standard form agreements between the commercial parties to the swaps contracts, produced inequitable results between those parties, circumscribed the efficacy of English law in the context of financial agreements, and introduced further risk to financial markets by rendering otiose the terms of those standard form agreements.

1–04 In the context of financial derivatives contracts, it was the expectation of the parties that, even if their agreements should have proved to be unenforceable in whole or in part, the contractual terms of those agreements would regulate the manner in which unperformed, part-performed and executed contracts should be unwound.[5] The failure of equity to give effect to those expectations introduces further uncertainty to commercial contracts by displacing the parties' previous understanding of their agreement. In effect, the commercial context of financial derivatives became the battleground for an ideological conflict between the rules of equity and the emerging principles of restitution.[6]

1–05 The swaps cases have been broadly interpreted by many of the commentators as a conflict between the codes of equity and the emerging law of restitution.[7] Indeed, this was the attitude of Lord Browne-Wilkinson to the issues argued in front of him.[8] However, these analyses have failed to consider the impact of these decisions for the banking lawyer. Aside from the, admittedly important, issues of equitable proprietary claims and claims for restitution of unjust enrichment, are more general issues which impact on commercial parties of the effectiveness of market standard contracts, the entitlement to specified property under collateral agreements and physically-settled transactions, and the availability of compound interest in cash-settled transactions. For the derivatives lawyer, and anyone using the ISDA Master Agreement[9] or the BBAIRS terms for interest rate swaps[10] and other financial derivatives products, the impact of the swaps litigation remains problematic.

1–06 The core concern of this book, aside from examining the courts' approaches to the local authority swaps cases, is to consider the appropriate principles for effecting restitution of amounts paid under financial transactions. The book contrasts traditional equity and trusts law principles with the more

[5] International Swaps and Derivatives Association, *ISDA Multicurrency Master Agreement 1992* (ISDA, New York & London, 1992); and British Bankers Association, *British Bankers Association Interest Rate Swap Terms* (BBA, London, 1987).

[6] Birks, "Trusts raised to avoid unjust enrichment: the *Westdeutsche* Case" [1996] R.L.R. 3.

[7] *ibid.*

[8] [1996] A.C. 669 at 708, considering Birks, "Restitution and Resulting Trusts", in *Equity: Contemporary Legal Developments* (Goldstein ed., Jerusalem, 1992), p. 335. These issues are considered below in greater detail in *Conflicts between Traditional Equity and the Law of Restitution*, Chapter 7.

[9] International Swaps and Derivatives Association, *ISDA Multicurrency Master Agreement 1992* (ISDA, New York & London, 1992).

[10] British Bankers Association, *British Bankers Association Interest Rate Swap Terms* (BBA, London, 1987), which are expressed as taking effect between parties contracting interest rate swaps in London without need to include the terms explicitly in any contractual agreement.

progressive field of restitution of unjust enrichment and restitution for wrongs in the context of the local authority swaps cases.[11]

The problem in outline

1–07 The commonplace use of standard market contracts, particularly in the area of financial derivatives, sought to remove uncertainty and to control systemic risk by standardising the terms of over-the-counter agreements. As considered in *The Structure of Financial Derivatives Products* below,[12] the derivatives markets have sought to minimise the most serious risks facing their U.S. $50 trillion market place[13] by standardising the manner in which those risks are allocated and managed in legal documentation. Among these risk management terms are provisions for the termination of contracts in a manner which reduces the systemic effect of payments being required immediately and in gross amounts, while also reducing the immediate financial pressure on the parties to a contract on the happening of one of the termination events specified in the contract. In the application of the ultra vires principle in the case of local authorities seeking to contract interest rate swaps,[14] the English courts have chosen to consider these contracts to be simply unenforceable *ab initio*: as though they had never existed. As a result, the markets' attempts to introduce effective, consensual, ad hoc regulation by standardised documentation and market practices of the derivatives markets[15] have been rendered ineffective. The issues considered in this book revolve around the ramifications of this joint application of the *ultra vires* rule and traditional principles of equity in relation to proprietary rights for commercial parties acting in global financial markets.

1–08 It is submitted that there should be created a separate stream of principles to give effect to the underlying aims of equity and common law with the need to effect restitution in the context of financial transactions such as those in the swaps cases. Specifically in the context of commercial standard form contracts, this goal would be best achieved by means of the development of equitable and common law principles based upon the express allocation of risk between commercial parties and the "suitability" of the financial transactions entered into between them. It is contended that the use of these principles, in the manner set out below in the "suitability approach",[16] would give effect to the broader, desirable policies of providing certainty in financial contracts, reducing systemic risk, and preventing the indirect enforcement of unsuitable financial contracts.

1–09 The English principles of Equity were formulated primarily to regulate the conduct of family trusts and rights in homes from the eighteenth century and beyond. The norms which were created in respect of the availability of proprietary

---

[11] As to the nature of restitution in this context see Birks, "Misnomer" in *Restitution, Present and Future: Essays in Honour of Gareth Jones* (Cornish, Nolan, O'Sullivan and Virgo, eds., Hart Publishing, Oxford, 1998), p. 1; and the rejoinder by Tettenborn, "Misnomer: A Response", in Cornish, Nolan, O'Sullivan and Virgo eds., *op. cit.*, p. 31.

[12] Chapter 2.

[13] As estimated by the International Swaps and Derivatives Association ("ISDA"), *ISDA News*, December 1997.

[14] *Hazell v. Hammersmith and Fulham L.B.C.* [1992] 2 A.C. 1; [1991] 2 W.L.R. 372; [1991] 1 All E.R. 545.

[15] This development has been primarily in the form of the ISDA standard form master agreement, International Swaps and Derivatives Association, *ISDA Multicurrency Master Agreement 1992* (ISDA, New York & London, 1992).

[16] Set out in Chapter 12, *Suitability—a new model?*

rights and compound interest were orientated around domestic, factual situations. As Lord Browne-Wilkinson himself pointed out in *Target Holdings v. Redferns*,[17] those "traditional trusts rules" sit uncomfortably with the complex, cross-border markets of the late twentieth century.

1–10 In moulding the principles of equity, it is important to recognise context. The development of equitable principles in relation to commercial transactions has seen a greater "concretisation" of the tests used by the courts and a movement away from the application of general principle to this context. Recent cases, such as *Royal Brunei Airlines Sdn Bhd v. Tan*[18] and *Islington*, have typified a judicial desire to impose stricter rules on the nature of equitable responses than are suggested by the list of core equitable principles reproduced in *Snell's Principles of Equity*[19] where vaguely poetic and normative prescriptions such as "coming to Equity with clean hands" have long formed the lifeblood of the equitable counterpoint to the rigours of the common law. Indeed, areas of the common law such as the tort of negligence have seen an ever greater relaxation of principles, as indicated by cases such as *Caparo v. Dickman*[20] and rules as the common law and equity appear to be moving in opposite directions. The question then arises as to the need to re-frame some of these equitable remedies such as knowing receipt and dishonest assistance in terms of strict liability.[21]

1–11 The further development is the growth of adherents to the principle of restitution of unjust enrichment among the commentators, to the chagrin of traditional equity lawyers. The stage was set in *Islington* for a disagreement between the progenitor of the modern law of restitution, Lord Goff, and the new equity lawyer's broom of Lord Browne-Wilkinson. These two had taken different approaches to the appropriate use of equity and of trusts implied by law in decisions such as *Tinsley v. Milligan*.[22] The notion of a law based on reversing unjust enrichment has been developed by Birks in a number of publications.[23] Indeed, his work is considered in close detail by the House of Lords in determining which ideological route is to be favoured in deciding the swaps cases. Much of the later discussion in this book takes up the threads of these distinctions and segregates them out into a series of different "approaches" to factual circumstances such as those raised by *Islington*.[24] The approach of Lord Browne-Wilkinson was to apply the traditional law of trusts, whereas the unjust enrichment lawyers have developed a new approach set out in the *radical restitution approach* in Chapter 11.[25]

1–12 Birks has referred to there being little difference between the speeches of Lords Goff and Browne-Wilkinson in the interpretation of the equitable and restitutionary techniques available in *Islington*.[26] Indeed, Birks is somewhat dismissive of the extent of any change to the law of restitution introduced by Lord

---

[17] [1996] 1 A.C. 421; [1995] 3 W.L.R. 352; [1995] 3 All E.R. 785.

[18] [1995] 2 A.C. 378; [1995] 3 W.L.R. 64; [1995] 3 All E.R. 64; [1995] 3 All E.R. 97, PC.

[19] Baker and Langan, *Snell's Principles of Equity* (29th ed., Sweet and Maxwell, London, 1990).

[20] [1990] 2 A.C. 605.

[21] See, for example, Smith, "Tracing and Electronic Funds Transfer", in *Restitution and Banking Law* (Rose ed., Mansfield Press, Oxford, 1998), pp. 120, 125; Birks, "Equity in the Modern Law: An Exercise in Taxonomy" (1996) 26 U.W.A.L.R. 1 at 72.

[22] [1994] 1 A.C. 340; [1993] 3 W.L.R. 126; [1993] 3 All E.R. 65.

[23] Beginning with *Introduction to the Law of Restitution* (Oxford, 1989).

[24] See in particular Chapters 7, 8 and 9.

[25] *The emerging principle of unjust enrichment.*

[26] Birks, "Trusts raised to avoid unjust enrichment: the Westdeutsche Case" [1996] R.L.R. 3.

Browne-Wilkinson.[27] It is submitted, however, that the opposed speeches in *Islington* should be seen as the battleground for three factions of lawyers to consider the position of equitable proprietary remedies. Their various approaches to the problem at hand are symptomatic of their factional attitudes.

1–13 The first approach to the issues appealed to the House of Lords is identified as being a conservative "*restitution approach*" as set out in the speech of Lord Goff.[28] Strictly speaking Lord Goff's dissent is only partial—he dissents only on the question of whether or not compound interest should be made available, deciding that it should provide justice between the bank and the local authority. Lord Goff preserved the approach of the classical restitution lawyer in looking at problems of restitution of mistaken payments from the analysis of existing precedent and the need to achieve a "just result" by means of reversing unjust enrichment.[29]

1–14 The second approach, the "*equity approach*", is a modern trusts lawyer's view propounded by Lord Browne-Wilkinson's leading speech. Contrary to Lord Goff's imprecation that the appeal was not the opportunity to restructure the conceptual underpinnings of the applicable principles of equity and restitution,[30] Lord Browne-Wilkinson decided to undertake exactly such an exercise of revision and ideological restructuring.[31] As a result of his Lordship's extensive coverage, the nature and availability of resulting trusts is limited and the availability of proprietary remedies under constructive trusts is redrawn. Lord Browne-Wilkinson began his judgment with a quasi-legislative account of the "relevant principles of trusts law".[32] This passage in the speech is "quasi-legislative" in that it seeks to reform (or clarify, according to your view of the older precedents) the basis upon which trusts law operates. The detail of these fundamental principles is considered in greater detail below in *The Primacy of Equity*.[33] However, at this juncture it is necessary to stress simply that the new code is both purportedly comprehensive in its account of the basics of trusts law and controversial in the detail of some of its revision.[34]

1–15 The third approach is dubbed in this book a "*commercial common sense approach*" and was exemplified by the partially dissenting speech of Lord Woolf, finding some support in the speech of Lord Goff. This approach typified the attitude of a commercial lawyer seeking to isolate the way in which equitable remedies were, and ought to have been, available in commercial situations. It asserted that the expectations of commercial people ought to have been reflected in the principles which the courts will apply in cases like the interest rate swap litigation.

1–16 As mentioned above, this book identifies two further, extra-judicial approaches. The fourth approach then is the "*radical restitutionary approach*" which is typified by the work of Birks,[35] Chambers,[36] Smith,[37] and Mitchell[38] as

---

[27] Birks, "Trusts raised to avoid unjust enrichment: the Westdeutsche Case" [1996] R.L.R. 3.

[28] This is considered below in the *Restitutionary Approach*.

[29] [1996] A.C. 669 at 695.

[30] *ibid.* at 682.

[31] *ibid.* at 705 *et seq.*

[32] *ibid.*

[33] Chapter 10, below.

[34] [1996] A.C. 669 at 705 *et seq.*

[35] Principally Birks, *Introduction to the Law of Restitution* (Oxford, 1989).

[36] Chambers, *Resulting Trusts* (Oxford, 1997).

[37] Smith, *The Law of Tracing* (Oxford, 1997).

[38] Mitchell, *The Law of Subrogation* (Oxford, 1994).

set out below.[39] This approach identifies as its core principle effecting restitution of unjust enrichment by subtraction of that enrichment. Much of this academic discussion is considered expressly by their Lordships in *Islington*—for the most part this radical approach fared badly before the House of Lords, a fact acknowledged by Birks himself, in so far as it proposed the use of resulting trusts to achieve restitution.[40] The House of Lords instead favoured the approach taken by Swadling which propounded a more conservative use of constructive trusts.[41]

1–17 The thesis which underpins this book makes up the fifth approach and is dubbed the "*suitability approach*". This approach is a fusion of existing common law, equitable and generally restitutionary principles, some of which were not considered by the courts in *Islington*, and is also based on a close analysis of the true nature of financial derivatives (both in general and specifically of the type considered in the swaps cases). The fundamental premise of the fifth approach is that broader policy considerations require the development of a code of equitable and restitutionary principles which observe the contractual intentions of commercial parties, particularly where those contractual arrangements are based upon standard market contracts dealing both with the management of general systemic risk and specific risks between the parties. It is contended that standard market contracts for over-the-counter derivatives transactions seek to standardise and manage risk. Recent case law has identified the need to develop principles which are capable of dealing with modern commercial transactions.[42] It is submitted that three particular areas demanding such evolution of principle are the allocation of rights in property dealt with by commercial parties, the creation of credit support contracts,[43] and agreements as to the allocation of specific commercial risks between parties.

1–18 The book proceeds on the basis that the decided cases have not analysed swaps contracts in the way in which their substance demands that they be considered.[44] The adoption of an implied understanding of a swap as being a single, executory contract[45] rather than an amalgam of separate payment obligations has led the courts to treat all swaps as capable of simple rescission and restitution by payment of money and simple interest. Further, the courts have considered all swaps to be identical transactions even though the substance of each contract was materially different.[46] For the rapidly developing derivatives markets, these unsophisticated analyses of complex, idiosyncratic transactions will continue to hamper the availability of proprietary rights, credit support and other risk management techniques in future cases.

---

[39] Chapter 9.

[40] Birks, "Trusts raised to avoid unjust enrichment: the Westdeutsche Case" [1996] R.L.R. 3 at 15.

[41] Swadling, "A New Role for Resulting Trusts?" (1996) 16 L.S. 110, esp. 124–125, considering *Ayers v. South Australian Banking Co.* (1871) L.R. 3 P.C. 548.

[42] See Lord Browne-Wilkinson in *Target Holdings v. Redferns* [1996] 1 A.C. 421; [1995] 3 W.L.R. 352; [1995] 3 All E.R. 785.

[43] Such as guarantees, mark-to-market collateral agreements and other mechanisms considered below in *Problems of Credit and Security* in Chapter 4, *Issues of Finance and Law*.

[44] This issue is considered in detail in *Swaps Pricing Models* below.

[45] An analysis preferred in older cases concerned with foreign exchange contracts: *Re British Continental Bank* (1922) 2 Ch. 575; *Lisser and Rosencranz's Claim* (1923) 1 Ch. 976; *Bank of India v. Patel* [1982] 1 Lloyd's Rep. 506.

[46] For example, in *Kleinwort Benson v. Sandwell B.C.* [1994] 4 All E.R. 890, *per* Hobhouse J., and *Guinness Mahon v. Kensington and Chelsea R.L.B.C.* [1998] 2 All E.R. 272.

1–19 Indeed, the nature of the property at issue as money held in electronic bank accounts[47] is not considered at all by the courts.[48] As considered below in *The Concept of Money*,[49] the understanding of the property at issue as being a series of mutual obligations manifested by complex choses in action would require a different approach to that taken by the courts in the swaps cases. Similarly, the provision for set-off of reciprocally-owed payments on each swap payment date, and provision for set-off in the event of bankruptcy, were not taken into account in considering the contingent nature of those choses in action. Consequently, the issue as to availability of proprietary rights over such choses in action and of compound interest of such value is not related to the nature of the modern financial world beyond English law's attachment to the concept of money as a tangible item of property.

1–20 Further, this book considers the detailed structure of swaps and other derivatives products from their inception (in their modern form) in the early 1980s cross-currency swap and parallel loan swap structures, to the use of credit derivatives and complex equity swaps in the late 1990s. At the core of the formation of a swaps transaction is a pricing mechanism which is built on costing the cash flow which makes up each individual payment obligation. Swaps are subject to a segmental analysis of their structure rather than being taken as a single executory contract which is provided by the seller for a one-off fee. That is, the seller will fix a price as though selling each individual payment obligation as a separate contract. The final price for the swap is the aggregate of those separate prices for each payment. As such a swap is, in essence, more akin to a series of financial forwards[50] or options than to the single, executory contract envisaged by Woolf L.J.[51] and Lord Templeman in *Hazell* as set out immediately below.[52]

The background to the local authority swaps cases

1–21 It is a truth universally acknowledged that derivatives are "difficult". The approach of the courts in the swaps cases is to cluster round a single definition of the interest rate swap provided by Woolf L.J. in the Court of Appeal *Hazell*[53] in the following terms:

> "[An interest rate swap is] an agreement between two parties by which each agrees to pay the other on a specified date or dates an amount calculated by reference to the interest which would have accrued over a given period on the same notional principal sum assuming different rates of interest are payable in each case. For example, one rate may be fixed at 10% and the other rate may be equivalent to the six-month London Inter-Bank Offered Rate (LIBOR). If the LIBOR rate over the period of the swap is higher than the 10% then the party agreeing to receive 'interest' in accordance with LIBOR

---

47 Considered below under *The Concept of Money* in Chapter 4, *Issues of Finance and Law*.

48 Smith, "Tracing and Electronic Funds Transfer" in *Restitution and Banking Law* (Rose ed., Mansfield Press, Oxford, 1998), p. 120.

49 Chaper 4

50 As defined in more detail below in *The Structure of Financial Derivatives Products*, Chapter 2; see also Satyajit Das, *Swaps and Derivative Financing*, (2nd ed., Irwin, 1994), pp. 14–17.

51 [1990] 2 Q.B. 697 at 739 and [1990] 3 All E.R. 33 at 63.

52 *Hazell v. Hammersmith and Fulham L.B.C.* [1992] 2 A.C. 1; [1991] 2 W.L.R. 372; [1991] 1 All E.R. 545.

53 [1990] 2 Q.B. 697 at 739 and [1990] 3 All E.R. 33 at 63.

will receive more than the party entitled to receive the 10%. Normally neither party will in fact pay the sums which it has agreed to pay over the period of the swap but instead will make a settlement on a 'net payment basis' under which the party owing the greater amount on any day simply pays the difference between the two amounts due to the other."

1–22 There is a tendency to consider the transactions in *Islington* as being one-off transactions, contracted with a long expiry date. There are two problems with this view. First, it does not take into account the various possible analytical approaches to interest rate swaps.[54] Secondly, it fails to appreciate the simple fact that there were a number of separate contracts involved in joint appeals at first instance. Indeed Hobhouse J. spends much of his judgment explaining the context of those various transactions.

1–23 There are joined appeals of Westdeutsche Landesbank Girozentrale proceeding against the London Borough of Islington ("*Islington*")[55] and Kleinwort Benson proceeding against Sandwell Borough Council ("*Sandwell*").[56] There is another important group of appeals which proceeded on a parallel course but raised slightly different points of law as to the availability of defences. Two of these appeals were brought by Kleinwort Benson against Birmingham City Council ("*Birmingham*")[57] and against South Tyneside Metropolitan Borough Council ("*South Tyneside*").[58] All this is apart from the cases on capacity of local authorities to enter into transactions, *Hazell v. Hammersmith and Fulham*[59] ("*Hazell*") and the contracts for differences cases, *Morgan Grenfell v. Welwyn Hatfield D.C. and others*[60] ("*Welwyn*").

The context of local authority funding

1–24 A word should be said about local authority funding to set the scene.[61] At a time of rigorous rate-capping, the local authorities in the United Kingdom were seeking alternative means of raising finance or of manipulating existing financial arrangements. Given that interest rate swaps were, at the material times, off-balance sheet instruments, finance directors were able to use them without any requirement to declare them in annual accounts. This created a potential hidden source of extra funding.

1–25 The interest rate swap enabled authorities to hedge the risk associated with their interest repayments and to speculate on interest rate movements at the same time. Many of the interest rate swaps that were used were "deep discount" swaps which enabled the authorities to receive a lump sum, in effect a loan, which was repaid by calibrating the periodical swaps payments owed between them and the banks to repay the capital sum over time. This raised extra debt funding outside the limits of the rate cap. What is important about the swaps that were

[54] As considered in detail in Chapter 3, below.

[55] [1994] 4 All E.R. 890, *per* Hobhouse J., CA; [1996] A.C. 669, HL.

[56] [1994] 4 All E.R. 890, *per* Hobhouse J. The *Sandwell* action did not proceed beyond first instance.

[57] *Kleinwort Benson* v. *Birmingham City Council* [1996] 4 All E.R. 733, CA, on appeal from Gatehouse J., (unreported).

[58] *Kleinwort Benson* v. *South Tyneside M.B.C.* [1994] 4 All E.R. 972, *per* Hobhouse J.

[59] [1991] 1 All E.R. 545, HL.

[60] [1995] 1 All E.R. 1, *per* Hobhouse J.

[61] For accounts of the same passage of litigation see *Westdeutsche Landesbank Girozentrale v. Islington L.B.C.* [1994] 4 All E.R. 890, *per* Hobhouse J. For a brief account of the background to the litigation see McKendrick "Local Authorities and Swaps: Undermining the Market?" in *Making Commercial Law: Essays in Honour of Roy Goode* (Cranston ed., Oxford, 1997), pp. 201 *et seq.*

used by the local authorities is that they were "deep discount" swaps which contained an element of loan, rather than straightforward vanilla interest rate swaps as the market would ordinarily understand them.[62]

1–26 These arrangements collapsed when some authorities' speculation on interest rate movements meant that they ended up owing even more money under their debt portfolios than they had owed originally. The deleterious impact on the finances of the London Borough of Hammersmith and Fulham led to the litigation which caused the House of Lords to rule that these products were *ultra vires* United Kingdom local authorities.[63] It was the auditor for the authority which commenced the action. *Hazell* became the lead case, which was unfortunate given that Hammersmith and Fulham had entered into more interest rate swap transactions than all of the other 77 local authorities in the United Kingdom put together. It was generally accepted during that litigation that Hammersmith and Fulham was speculating in the main when it entered into those products.[64] This suspicion has surrounded derivatives ever since their promulgation as a highly volatile, complex and expensive form of risk management or portfolio enhancement in the early 1980s.[65]

1–27 There were a number of interest rate swaps outstanding between local authorities and the financial institutions before the litigation commenced in 1990 around Hammersmith and Fulham's entry into the market place. Lord Templeman found that there had been about 400 swaps entered into by 77 out of the 450 local authorities at that time. However, in relation to Hammersmith and Fulham,

> "[b]y 31 March 1989 the council had entered into 592 swap transactions and 297 of these were still outstanding. The total notional principal sum involved in all the transactions entered into by the council amounted in the aggregate to £6,052m ... These figures distort the position because some swap transactions were a hedge against others. But there is no doubt that the volume of swap business entered into by the council was immense. The council's actual borrowing on that date amounted to £390m, its estimated expenditure for the year ending 31 March 1989 was £85.7m and its quoted budget for that year was £44.6m."[66]

In the context of such a massive exposure compared to such a small level of borrowing and of expenditure, it would have been extremely surprising if the House of Lords had not decided the way it did. Otherwise, it would have fallen to the ratepayers of the borough to make good those amounts owed to the banks.[67] It is

---

[62] For a more detailed discussion of the operation of interest rate swaps see Hudson, *The Law on Financial Derivatives* (2nd ed., Sweet & Maxwell, 1998), generally; or for a briefer account see Hudson, "The Legal Aspect of Financial Derivatives", *Business Law Review*, October 1996, 199, pp.199–201.

[63] *Hazell v. Hammersmith and Fulham* [1991] 1 All E.R. 545.

[64] *ibid.* at 553, *per* Lord Templeman; *Westdeutsche Landesbank Girozentrale v. Islington L.B.C.* [1994] 4 All E.R. 890, *per* Hobhouse J.; and *Morgan Grenfell & Co Ltd v. Welwyn Hatfield District Council and others* [1995] 1 All E.R. 1, *per* Hobhouse J. generally.

[65] Indeed the literature in defence of the derivative as a useful tool of prudent financial management is still being produced. See most recently Merton Miller, *Merton Miller on Derivatives* (Wiley Investment, 1997). For a more conservative approach and some suggestions for more prudential regulation, see Hudson, *The Law on Financial Derivatives* (2nd ed., Sweet & Maxwell, 1998), Chapter 11.

[66] *Hazell v. Hammersmith and Fulham* [1991] 1 All E.R. 545 at 552, *per* Lord Templeman.

[67] Always presuming that anyone remained living in the borough after the removal of services and exponential rise in local rates.

also significant to note that this particular authority had entered into far more of these transactions than all of the other authorities put together.[68]

1–28 On this basis, the authorities themselves, the financial institutions and the Audit Commission came to the view that local authorities would be able to enter into interest rate swaps for debt management purposes. Indeed, it would seem to be logical that derivatives should be used to control exposure to movements in interest rates in the same way that umbrellas are carried to guard against rain.[69] It is submitted that the only possible reading of this litigation and the speech of Lord Templeman in the House of Lords in *Hazell*[70] is that the courts were concerned to guard against a particular risk to local authorities generally rather than to deal with a specific failure on the part of one individual local authority to act prudently in the management of its finances.

Islington: the deep discount swap

1–29 The Islington transaction is the prime example of the use of the deep discount swap to achieve off-balance sheet funding for the authority.

Back-to-back structure

1–30 The transactions entered into between Westdeutsche and Islington were arranged through an intermediary financial institution (Morgan Grenfell) seeking to match the authority's needs with a lender's available liquidity. In the early days of the swaps markets, all transactions were arranged by financial institutions who found two parties with equal and opposite requirements.[71] The commercial nature of the structure is important. Given that swaps are transacted with the primary aim of managing risk, the allocation of risks is central feature of the negotiations and documentation. None of the courts in the swaps litigation paid any attention to the painstakingly crafted documentation.[72]

---

[68] What is not clear is what would have happened if the lead case had involved a local authority which could have demonstrated that it was using interest rate swaps solely for the purposes of managing the cost of funding its debt. What is frequently forgotten is the breadth of the legislation that was at issue. Under section 111(1) of the Local Government Act 1972:

"... a local authority shall have power to do anything (whether or not involving expenditure, borrowing or lending of money or the acquisition or disposal of any property or rights) which is calculated to facilitate, or is conducive or incidental to, the discharge of any of their functions."

[69] The case of *Brane v. Roth* (Indiana Court of Appeals) 590 NE 2d 587 (Ind App 1 dist 1992) is instructive in this context. In that case a director was held liable in negligence for failing to protect the company against movements in interest rates by the use of interest rate swaps. This case illustrates perhaps the counter-view that where there is an exposure to market movements, the law ought to require market participants to act prudently in the use, rather than the avoidance, of financial derivatives. In respect of the growing context of prudence measured by reference to market usage, see the comments of Hoffmann J. that the duties of a trustee with reference to the proper investment of a trust fund are to be considered in the light of "current portfolio theory", in *Nestle v. National Westminster Bank* (June 29, 1988) [1993] 1 W.L.R. 1260, commented on in Underhill and Hayton, *Law of Trusts and Trustees* (Butterworths, 1995), 5p.99, also noted in Hayton and Marshall, *Commentary and Cases on the Law of Trusts and Equitable Remedies* (Sweet & Maxwell, 1996), pp. 595–7.

[70] [1992] 2 A.C. 1.

[71] This was particularly true of the early currency swaps which were transacted to avoid exchange controls. Party A in country A needed the currency of country B. Financial institutions would locate a Party B in country B who needed currency A. Both parties would borrow in their own currency and then, in effect, assign their rights to the moneys borrowed in favour of the other party—literally a "swap". The intermediary would take a fee. The net result was the acquisition of funding in another currency without breaching exchange controls.

[72] The implications of this omission are considered in detail below.

1–31 Hobhouse J. found that Westdeutsche's employee considered "commercial and solvency risk" on entering into the transaction—he did not look to the "legal risk" of entering into this arrangement with a United Kingdom local authority. It emerges from the judgment that there were "two contracts ... They were essentially back-to-back contracts."[73] This back-to-back arrangement, although it is not made explicit in the judgments, refers to the use of the intermediary Morgan Grenfell in setting up the deal. Under one contract Westdeutsche was the fixed rate payer at a rate of 7.5 per cent and Islington paid a floating rate of sterling LIBOR. On the second contract, Westdeutsche paid a floating rate of sterling LIBOR to and Morgan Grenfell paid 7.74 per cent to Westdeutsche.[74] The originally mooted transaction was four times the size of the deal that was ultimately brokered. Morgan Grenfell matched Westdeutsche's preparedness to lend the lump sum, and manage the authority's interest rate risk, with Islington's desire to borrow.

1–32 The contracts were "on the BBAIRS terms with a notional principal amount of £25 million".[75] However, there was a difference from the normal BBAIRS terms in that "it did not acknowledge any contemplation by the floating rate payer that the fixed rate payer might have any back-to-back agreement with another party".[76] The importance of this deviation is that a hedging agreement has been held not to be expressly within the contemplation of the parties to the main contract.[77]

Payment netting

1–33 While the judgments do not disclose the detailed terms of the contracts, we are told that "the contract only imposes a liability to pay net sums and that was all that was actually paid".[78] This tells us that payment netting was in place between the parties.[79] That is, while the floating rate and fixed rate payers owed each other amounts in gross on the same date, the contracts provided that only the party owing more that it was owed should pay a net amount equal to that surplus to the other party. This is a significant part of structuring this interest rate swap. Only one payment is ever actually made although two amounts are owed. It is therefore possible that on some occasions no surplus amount will be owed where the gross obligations set-off exactly. The manner in which this interest rate swap was priced meant that it would have required a large movement in sterling interest rates to achieve that result.

---

[73] [1994] 4 All E.R. 890 at 901, *per* Hobhouse J.

[74] The result of this mismatching was that Westdeutsche received a "turn" of 0.24% to encourage it to enter the transaction. It is assumed that Morgan Grenfell received either a flat fee or, more likely, its own turn priced into the product.

[75] The use of the British Bankers Association standard terms for interest rate swaps is unusual given the more general use of International Swaps and Derivatives Association ("ISDA") standard terms and the fact that Westdeutsche and Islington had signed a modified form of the ISDA 1987 Master Agreement for this type of transaction.

[76] [1994] 4 All E.R. 890 at 905, *per* Hobhouse J.

[77] *Kleinwort Benson v. Birmingham C.C.* [1996] 4 All E.R. 733, CA.

[78] [1994] 4 All E.R. 890 at 905, *per* Hobhouse J.

[79] It is important to distinguish "payment netting" during the life of transactions from "close-out netting" which occurs on the termination of the contractual agreement between the parties on bankruptcy or the happening of some other event of termination.

Analysis of the deep discount structure

1–34 There was an important further facet to these transactions. Most interest rate swaps involve only a payment of income amounts which are calculated by reference to a fixed notional amount—as discussed above. However, to give the local authorities the lump sum injection of cash they needed, a deep discount payment was made to the local authority. This peculiar feature, it is submitted, marks this transaction out from the norm in any event. As Hobhouse J. explained it:[80]

> "... each [agreement] provided for the fixed rate payer to pay to the floating rate payer on the commencement date, 18 June 1987, an additional sum of £2.5m. Under the scheme of the contracts this was expressed to be the first of the fixed rate payments and it was calculated against a discount in the later fixed rate payments. If there had been no discount, the appropriate fixed rate of interest for the ten-year period would have been 9.43% pa. £2.5m represented the advancement of periodic semi-annual payments of 1.93% pa on £25m over ten years."

Loan or swap?

1–35 One analysis of this structure could clearly be that a loan is made to the authority which is then repaid by structuring the level of the periodical payments. However, Hobhouse J. held that:

> "The contracts did not purport to be and were not expressed as contracts of loan but simply as interest rate swap contracts. This feature was vital to the reason of Islington for entering into the swap contract."[81]

There is a paradox here. The upfront payment by Westdeutsche is accepted as having been the *sine qua non* of the transaction for Islington. Without that payment, there would have been no deep discount swap. As discussed above, the local authority's primary motivation was obtaining debt funding within a debt management package. The authority was keen to avoid breaching the rate cap by borrowing more money directly—any influx of new money had to be packaged as something other than a loan. What is not clear is why Hobhouse J. is necessarily prepared to accept this assertion of form over substance. It appears to have been agreed between the parties that the structure was a swap not a loan. Had the parties contended otherwise, the contract would have been void as offending the rate-capping provisions—leading to penalties on the local authority and, potentially, the councillor's personally.

1–36 It is accepted in the House of Lords, where the point was not a point at issue, that there are loan-like features in this deep discount structure. In the speech of Lord Goff, the following, revealing passage arose:

> "I incline myself to the opinion that a personal claim in restitution would not indirectly enforce the ultra vires contract, for such an action would be unaffected by *any of the contractual terms governing the borrowing*, and moreover would be subject (where appropriate) to any restitutionary defences ... *the lender* should not be without a remedy."[82] [author's emphasis]

And later in the same speech:

---

[80] [1994] 4 All E.R. 890 at 901, *per* Hobhouse J.

[81] *ibid.*

[82] [1996] 2 All E.R.961 at 972–3.

> "... the fixed rate payer may make an upfront payment to the floating rate payer, and in consequence the rate of interest payable by the fixed rate payer is reduced to a rate lower than the rate which would otherwise have been payable by him. *The practical effect is to achieve a form of borrowing* by, in this example, the floating rate payer through the medium of the interest rate swap transaction."[83] [author's emphasis]

The important point made by Lord Goff is that the transaction entered into in this situation was, in reality, a form of borrowing packaged as an interest rate swap. The purpose of the transaction was to obtain preferential rate funding more than to manage existing debt. There can be little doubt that the deep discount payment does bear striking similarities to a loan. It is an amount of money paid by one party to another, on the basis that that other will make repayments of that amount periodically—some of those repayments being made by set-off of other obligations. It would appear that analysis accords with the basic definition of a loan. Indeed, rather than the contracts looking like they were not a loan, *the very purpose* of the arrangement was to acquire lump sum funding for the authority in a way that would appear to elude legislation governing local authority funding. However, Hobhouse J. accepts, without more, that the money was not intended as a loan—despite the "vital feature" of the deep discount payment.[84]

1–37 There can be little doubt that the structure does include the typical characteristics of an interest rate swap.[85] However, the *Islington* litigation is therefore something of a chimera for derivatives lawyers. It relates to a one-off transaction which is used only rarely in the modern market place. Where its principles come into importance are with reference to payment of compound interest, provision of collateral, and contracts dealing with physically settled products. The *Islington* decision has broader ramifications for the derivatives lawyer (as well as general commercial lawyers) beyond its own limited facts.

The *Sandwell* structure—complete and incomplete swaps

1–38 There are two significant distinctions between the following structures and the *Islington* case. The most important difference between the *Islington* and *Sandwell* claims is that there is no deep discount payment made in the *Sandwell* swaps. The other difference is that, rather than there being a single swap, there are four separate interest rate swap transactions entered into between Sandwell and Kleinwort Benson. Sandwell had entered into a total of 50 interest rate swap transactions with various financial institutions between 1983 and 1987. All of these transactions were apparently made on the basis of the standard BBAIRS terms.[86]

1–39 Amounts payable under the four transactions at issue were calculated by reference to a notional amount of £5 million with a five-year maturity period. Kleinwort Benson paid a fixed rate of 11.75 per cent semi-annually. Sandwell paid a floating amount calculated by reference to the sterling LIBOR rate on a quarterly basis. This mismatch between payments dates complicates the payment

[83] [1996] 2 All E.R. 961 at 965.

[84] *ibid.* at 965.

[85] Although it is not apparent from the cases as reported which risks were sought to be managed by the use of the swap—nor whether they had some alternative, speculative strategy.

[86] See generally [1994] 4 All E.R. 890 at 907 *et seq.*, *per* Hobhouse J.

netting position.[87] When payments are owed on the same dates, a single amount was to be paid on a net basis. The first swap had expired before the writ was served. With reference to the second swap, amounts payable were calculated by reference to a notional amount of £5 million. Kleinwort Benson paid a fixed rate of 10.3125 per cent semi-annually. Sandwell paid a floating amount calculated by reference to the BBAIRS sterling settlement rate on a semi-annual basis. The swap had a maturity of 10 years. The second swap had also expired before the writ was served.

1–40 The third and fourth swaps were made on nearly identical terms and were to expire in 1996. Therefore, they were only part performed at the time when the writ was served and when judgement was handed down. Kleinwort Benson paid fixed rates of 11.42 and 10.25 per cent semi-annually respectively under the third and fourth swaps. Sandwell paid a floating amount calculated by reference to the sterling LIBOR rate on a semi-annual basis. These amounts were calculated by reference to a notional amount of £5 million. Before the initial payment was made under the third swap, the parties entered into a "reverse swap". This was really a further separate contract which provided for the precise inverse of the third swap—enabling the parties to exit the transaction without making a disposal of it. The precise reason for this is not clear. It might have been to avoid capital gains tax consequences. However, Kleinwort Benson were required to make net payments to Sandwell as a result of relevant market movements. The fourth swap was similarly reversed, with payments being made only one way. Therefore, there were six swaps entered into in total. The last two swaps were entered into to terminate the transactions.

1–41 There are therefore fundamental structural dissimilarities between the transactions. Yet, the general legal issues were decided in predominantly the same way.

What *Islington* decided

1–42 Before considering the detail of the *Islington* litigation, it would be useful to set out, briefly, the main points of the decisions in all three courts which considered the issues. In particular, it is important to note that there were many more issues raised in front of Hobhouse J. than were appealed ultimately to the House of Lords. Further, it is important to analyse the facts that were found by Hobhouse J. and accepted by the Court of Appeal and the House of Lords in turn.

The decision at first instance[88]

1–43 The broadest range of issues considered by any of the courts were the issues raised at first instance before Hobhouse J. His Lordship held that the doctrine of failure of consideration should be understood to be a doctrine of absence of consideration.[89] In the light of the partial performance of the purported contracts, the case was not one of absence of consideration because the failure had

[87] As considered below, this mismatching aspect to the transactions raises a broader issue with reference to Hobhouse J.'s analysis of the payment structure. His Lordship considers each payment to be properly analysed as a repayment of an earlier amount. Where payments are made, strictly, on separate days, then it is possible to consider the latter payment in time to relate to the "earlier payment". However, as considered [below] it is not clear that this repayment analysis will always be compelling.

[88] [1994] 4 All E.R. 890.

[89] Relying in part on *Woolwich v. IRC* [1993] A.C. 70; [1992] 3 W.L.R. 366; [1992] 3 All E.R. 737.

not been total. Given absence of consideration, moneys received by Islington were held on trust for Westdeutsche because it would be unconscionable to allow the authority to retain title in that money. Finally, there was no defence of change of position available to the authority because Islington had already ring-fenced the money which it would owe to Westdeutsche. As a result of the foregoing, compound interest was therefore payable.

1–44 A single, precise *ratio decidendi* of Hobhouse J.'s decision is difficult to isolate. The reason for the decision appears to be a belief that it was in some way wrong for the payee to retain moneys which would not have been paid to them if the contract had been known to have been invalid.[90] The rationale given for the decision straddles a number of different possible analyses, as indicated by the following passage:

> "The plaintiff is entitled to recover that sum either as money had and received by the defendant to the use of the plaintiff or as money which in equity belongs to the plaintiff and which it is entitled to trace in the hands of the defendant and have repaid it out of the present assets of the defendant. The basis of the plaintiff's claim, whether at common law or in equity, is that the defendant has been unjustly enriched at the expense of the plaintiff and that in conscience the defendant must repay to the plaintiff, save in so far as it has already done so, the sum which it received from the plaintiff. The right to restitution arises from the fact that the payment made by the plaintiff to the defendant was made under a purported contract which, unknown to the plaintiff and the defendant, was *ultra vires* the defendant and wholly void."[91] [author's emphasis]

The core conviction in this judgment is the obligation borne by Islington to make some repayment to the bank. What is not immediately apparent from that passage is whether the remedy granted is meant to be based on the restitution of unjust enrichment or the application of equitable principle in the sense outlined by Lord Browne-Wilkinson, and whether it is personal or proprietary in character. Clearly, all four of those concepts are present in that passage. What appears from the judgment, as considered in more detail on a category by category basis below,[92] is that his lordship was reasoning in a teleological way. Having decided on the end-point, his Lordship progressed through all the possible arguments which would lead to the desired conclusion.

1–45 The judgment has enormous scope and covers an enormous number of factual and legal issues. However, the more closely it is analysed the more difficult it becomes to unearth a binding, consistent rationale for that result. The following chapter considers some of the issues of principle which arise: for example, Hobhouse J.'s award of a remedy on grounds of money had and received is a personal remedy, as defined by Lord Goff, whereas the equitable remedy awarded as a result of an equitable tracing claim was proprietary in nature. Further, the claim as allowed, while having a basis in both equity and common law, is

---

[90] Leggatt L.J. comes to his judgment by looking to a central equitable premise: "Any system of law, and indeed any system of fair dealing, must be expected to ensure that Islington do not profit by the fortuity that when it became known that the contract was ineffective the balance stood in their favour. In other words, in circumstances such as these they should not be unjustly enriched." [1994] 4 All E.R. 890 at 967.

[91] [1994] 4 All E.R. 890 at 955.

[92] As considered in Chapter 6, below.

nevertheless held to be a restitutionary response to some unjust enrichment, thus raising many of the doctrinal questions addressed in Chapter 5 below.[93]

The Court of Appeal[94]

1–46 Counsel for Westdeutsche in the Court of Appeal relied heavily upon the decision of the House of Lords in *Sinclair v. Brougham*.[95] Indeed, as Leggatt L.J. found, the House of Lords in *Sinclair v. Brougham* held in the banks' favour with respect to all of the components of Westdeutsche's claim in equity. Following Hobhouse J. at first instance, Leggatt L.J. held that in equity the money paid under the deep discount payment and the interest payments remained the property of Westdeutsche throughout the life of the transaction on the basis that the mere receipt by Islington of money which, in the opinion of the Court of Appeal, "was not theirs, constituted them fiduciaries".[96] Consequently, Westdeutsche's equitable right in relation to the money held by Islington remained the property of Westdeutsche by means of an equitable charge; and given that Islington was solvent, Westdeutsche was entitled to "recover in full".[97] The Court of Appeal affirms the decision of Hobhouse J.

House of Lords—(in outline)[98]

1–47 The House of Lords was unanimous in holding that neither the lump sum nor any of the interest amounts were to be held on resulting trust. Further, it was unanimous in holding that there would not be constructive trust imposed over the money on the basis that the local authorities did not know that the money had been advanced to them under a void transaction and therefore their consciences had not been affected. At most there was a personal claim in restitution for the amount of money transferred under the void agreement together with simple interest.[99]

1–48 The restatement of the core rules of equity in the leading speech of Lord Browne-Wilkinson in *Islington* created a test that a proprietary claim in constructive trust will only be imposed in circumstances where the defendant has knowledge of the factor which is alleged to impose the office of trustee on him, thus affecting his conscience.[100] Similarly, a proprietary claim based on resulting trust will only obtain where a purported express trust of an equitable interest has failed to allocate the whole of that interest, or where an equitable interest is created by dint of contribution to the purchase price of property.[101] It is submitted that these principles restrict the potential intervention of equity to such a narrow range of cases that the mutual intentions of parties to commercial contracts will frequently not be enforced by either the rules of common law or of equity.

1–49 The decision of the majority is most clearly set out in the speech of Lord Browne-Wilkinson:

---

[93] *Equity and Modern Financial Techniques.*

[94] [1994] 4 All E.R. 890 at 960, *et seq.*

[95] [1914] A.C. 398.

[96] [1994] 4 All E.R. 890 at 969, *per* Leggatt L.J.

[97] *ibid.*

[98] [1996] 1 A.C. 669.

[99] Lord Goff and Lord Woolf dissented on the availability of compound interest: the former asserting that it ought to have been available on the grounds of justice, the latter asserting that commercial people would expect that it would be made available.

[100] [1996] 1 A.C. 669 at 709.

[101] *ibid.* at 705–707, 711–16.

"... a claimant for restitution of moneys paid under an *ultra vires*, and therefore void, contract has a personal action at law to recover the moneys paid as on a total failure of consideration; he will not have an equitable proprietary claim which gives him either rights against third parties or priority in an insolvency; nor will he have a personal claim in equity, since the recipient is not a trustee."[102]

1–50 Lord Browne-Wilkinson held in *Islington* that there could be no retention of any rights in the deep discount payment by the bank[103] because both parties intended that there be an outright transfer of that sum to the authority. Lord Browne-Wilkinson rejected the possibility of a proprietary interest based on constructive trust on the ground that the English model of constructive trust is institutional in nature, operating in response to the trustee's knowledge of some factor which ought to impact on his conscience sufficiently to warrant the imposition of such a constructive trust. On the facts of *Islington* it was found that the authority did not have knowledge of the status of the contract until it was declared to be *ultra vires* by the courts.

1–51 However, at that point there is another impact on the authority's conscience: it had already agreed with the bank that it would be bound by the termination provisions in its swap agreement (including calculation of interest and netting of transactions). It is submitted that this prior agreement ought to be sufficient to cause the authority to be bound by those terms of the swap contract with regard to the amount owed under the agreement. Similarly, such common intention as to termination and proprietary rights in assets transferred by arm's length market participants should be enforced by equity through the common intention constructive trust. In the event, the weakness of the market standard contracts for over-the-counter derivatives is that they do not cater sufficiently for retention of title in property.[104] This shortcoming is particularly important in the case of physically-settled transactions and transactions annexed to deep discount payments where title to the specific property transferred is what is required commercially by the parties, rather than the receipt of the cash equivalent value of that property in a designated currency.

1–52 The issue which then arises is: how can a void contract be given effect to in part? First, it is clear from *Re Goldcorp*[105] that if a contract is avoided by election of the parties, and property transferred under that contract can still be identified, a constructive trust will be imposed over that identifiable property. Therefore, there is a difference between the enforceability of a voidable contract and a void contract as a result of *Islington*.[106] Secondly, it is submitted that it would be possible to sever the termination provisions from the economic provisions of the swap contract.[107] One important issue arising in this context is why severance had not been available with reference to the *Sandwell* litigation[108] where some of the contracts had been performed. The further issue is whether some of the payments made between the parties could be treated as settled (thus supporting a mutual debts analysis) or whether they are to be required as part of a single (executory) contract which had not been fully performed until the final payment had been made.[109]

---

[102] [1996] 1 A.C. 669 at 714; [1996] All E.R. 961 at 996.

[103] As considered in *Background to the Swaps Cases*, p.9 above.

[104] There is clearly an issue for ISDA and for the BBA to redraw its standard contracts to take account of this deficiency in counterparty protection.

[105] [1995] A.C. 74; also Worthington, above.

[106] It is accepted that in *Islington* the property was no longer identifable because the bank account into which the property had been paid had subsequently been run overdrawn on a number of occasions.

[107] This issue is considered in more detail below in Chapter 12, *Suitability Approach, Severance.*

[108] The joined appeal with *Islington* at first instance: [1994] 4 All E.R. 890.

[109] On this issue see Hudson, *Amicus Curiae*, November 1997, Vol. 2, p. 27.

Chapter 2

The structure of financial derivative products

2–01 Before pursuing the detail of the decisions in *Islington* and the other local authority swaps cases, it is important to dissect and analyse the component parts of the financial derivatives which were at issue: principally interest rate swaps. This section considers the broad range of derivatives transactions which are contracted in the over-the-counter markets to advance a thesis that swaps ought properly to be considered as made up of other derivatives, namely forward contracts and options. Whereas the local authority swaps cases restricted themselves to the analysis of interest rate swaps, to understand the component parts of a swap transaction it is necessary to understand, first, how the products evolved, and, secondly, how options and forwards contracts form an essential part of the building blocks of a swap. This chapter considers the genesis and interrelationship of the various products, whereas Chapter 3, *The Legal Analysis of Swaps*, considers the role of swaps pricing models on the structure of the products and the concomitant impact on the numerous potential legal analyses of swaps transactions.

2–02 One of the initial tasks will be definition of the many variations on three central themes that make up the financial derivatives firmament,[1] followed by an analysis of the structure of those products as understood both by lawyers and market participants. While this section is aimed principally at introducing the subject matter considered by the House of Lords in *Islington* and by the other courts in the local authority swaps cases, it will also consider some of the more exotic derivatives products which have become used in a widespread context. The products which were considered by the various manifestations of the House of Lords, Court of Appeal and the High Court throughout the local authority swaps cases are now somewhat antiquated. However, the basic legal analyses of even the complex[2] products is based on the same analyses which were prevalent in the marketplace during the contracting of the products which led to the litigation at issue. Therefore, it is important in forming a picture of the impact of the swaps litigation to consider newer developments such as "credit derivatives" while also looking at some of the new techniques which have been developed around long-established products.

2–03 The primary characteristic of all financial derivatives is the payment of cashflows between contracting parties. The status of cash flow has established a

---

1 Namely options, forwards and swaps.

2 The term "complex" is used here not to denote a level of difficulty but rather to describe a product which builds on comparatively straightforward techniques to construct a structured, or "complex", financial product to meet more specific hedging or speculative goals.

pre-eminence in business school theory over the last decade.[3] Title to capital assets is less important to the banker in most situations than the entitlement to receipt of cash flow or the likely generation of cash flow by commercial activity.[4] In this context the derivative seeks to enhance cash flow or to protect contracting parties against exposure to risks associated with their cash flow. The commercial attraction of well-established instruments such as the share and the bond are the cash flows that will be generated by the dividend or the coupon respectively. Newer innovations over the last decade such as asset securitisation have sought to use entitlement to a large number of cash flows, for example repayment streams owed to building societies in relation to domestic mortgages, to create a single asset which can be sold for a lump sum to investors in return for the future cash flow.[5]

2–04 For a corporate counterparty, the central purpose of the derivative instrument is risk management. For many financial institutions the risk management function is the primary purpose for hedging market exposures. The use of the derivative enables the treasurer to minimise the company's exposure to the risk of movements in underlying rates and prices. For the banking institution, the risks faced cover a broad spread of issues from the economic movements in the marketplace to credit risks on counterparties' default, insolvency, the failure of management systems and procedures to facilitate complex derivatives transactions. Credit risk itself subdivides into settlement risk and counterparty risk. Settlement risk is the risk that the counterparty will default or fail to perform its obligations under the contract. Counterparty risk is the more general risk that the counterparty will cease to be able to perform due to insolvency or some similar factor.

What is a "derivative"?

2–05 Before attempting to define and explain each product in detail, it would be as well to attempt a definition of the term "derivative". The term is not susceptible to precise definition: it can be considered to be the collective term for the range of products discussed in the following sections which have been developed by financial markets in the late 1980s and 1990s. A derivative product is a financial product which derives its value from an underlying financial product. For example, an option to buy a share at some point in the future is a financial product derived from the underlying share. Similarly, a swap on an interest rate is a product derived from the underlying loan. Hence the term "derivative".

---

[3] In the context of interest rate swaps see, for example, Copeland and Weston, *Financial Theory and Corporate Policy* (3rd ed., Addison Wesley, 1988) p.656 *et seq.*; see generally Brealey and Myers, *Principles of Corporate Finance* (4th ed., McGraw Hill, 1991), esp. pp.627–652 in relation to derivatives hedging products; and generally Smith and Walter, *Global Financial Services* (Harper & Row, 1990), pp.564 *et seq.*

[4] Whereas capital assets form useful security for lending and other transactions, and are also important factors in considering the net worth of a client for credit assessment purposes, modern banking has come to concentrate on cash flow as the most important factor in the establishment of its global business.

[5] See, for example, Wood, *Title Finance, Derivatives, Securitisations, Set-off and Netting*, (Sweet & Maxwell, 1995), pp.41 *et seq.*; Haynes, "*Asset Securitisation*", CWG Hart Workshops, Institute of Advanced Legal Studies, London, 1998).

Derivative strategies: why enter into a derivative?

2–06 The derivative market as we understand it in the late 1990s grew out of the exchange control avoidance. The modern context of the market is more complicated than straightforward regulatory avoidance. Estimates of the size of the derivatives markets across the world are somewhere in the region of U.S. $55 trillion at the time of writing.[6] While there is still some regulatory avoidance use in the derivative, the modern uses are roughly fourfold: speculation, hedging, asset liability management and arbitrage.

2–07 The general assumption surrounding the use of derivatives is that they are being used with straightforward speculative intention. The core of the swaps cases was the commercial intentions of the local authorities to improve their debt exposure while generating some collateral income. The approach taken by Lord Templeman in *Hazell v. Hammersmith and Fulham* was that the contracts were used by the authorities with "no other interest than seeking to profit from interest rate fluctuations".[7] One issue which has arisen out of this understanding that derivatives are primarily speculative is whether they constitute contracts for differences which are void under the Gaming Act 1845. This issue was examined by Hobhouse J. in *Morgan Grenfell v. Welwyn and Hatfield D.C.*[8] It was held that interest rate swaps are not void gaming contracts on the basis that they are used for a commercial purpose in connection with section 63 of the Financial Services Act 1986. However, his Lordship was not able to reach this conclusion before finding that they have "at least potentially a speculative character deriving from the fact that the obligations of [parties] are to be ascertained by reference to a fluctuating market rate which may be higher or lower than the fixed rate at any time".[9]

2–08 Derivatives, in particular options, enable the contracting parties to assume a trading position on the anticipated movements of financial markets in the future. By acquiring an option to buy a share at a given time in the future for a given price, the buyer is able to speculate on the level of those markets in the future. Similarly, the seller is speculating that the price to be paid for the security under the option is greater than the price of acquiring that security in the market. The basic technique of acquiring some ability to acquire an asset at a speculative price other than the spot price[10] in the market is common to all derivatives when they are being used for speculative purposes. At each time a payment is required to be made under a transaction there is a risk that that payment will be greater or less than the price payable in the open market.

2–09 The other side to the derivative is the risk management function. Where a party has an exposure to United Kingdom interest rates, a derivative can be used to generate an amount of income which will offset any loss suffered from movements in interest rates. This matching of income and risk is known as "hedging". Usually a hedge will be achieved by constructing a derivative product which will increase in value if the underlying risk generates a loss. For example, a rise in interest rates may generate a loss in increased interest charges on bank debt,

---

[6] See Henderson speaking on December 8, 1997 at *Legal, Accounting and Control Challenges of Credit Derivatives*, IBC; *ISDA News*, (London, ISDA, December 1997).

[7] [1991] 1 All E.R. 545 at 549.

[8] [1995] 1 All E.R. 1.

[9] [1995] 1 All E.R. 7.

[10] The "spot price" is the price at which a standard unit of an asset, security or currency is trading at any given time on the market.

whereas an equity product might rise in value inline with increased rates. Buying into the latter in sufficient quantities will offset the cost of the former.

2–10 Clearly there are complex issues of selection of the appropriate product to create the hedge and also of measuring the size of the anticipated risk and the corresponding size of the derivative product constructed to meet it. It is at this level that the derivative becomes a particularly complicated instrument seeking to measure anticipated market movements, volatility coefficients and related projected cash flows. The hedge is a benign instrument in its purpose: the aim is to reduce risk rather than to create it. However, there is also the risk that the market will move such that the hedge generates a cost or that it fails to cover the underlying market risk exactly. There are legal, regulatory and accounting issues often in terms of the hedge itself. At the commercial level there is the risk that the hedge will not operate in the manner anticipated at the time of its creation. All of these factors contribute to make a hedge a 'risk bearing' instrument, albeit one with a conservative commercial purpose.[11]

2–11 Derivatives are also used as part of portfolio management. Where an entity has exposure to a given market sector, derivatives are used within that mix to hedge against market movements. Swamy defines "asset liability management" as "the process by which a bank or institution monitors its portfolio of assets and liabilities to control company-wide interest rate exposure".[12] Within this scope comes an analysis of the time of payments of obligations, sensitivity to market movements, and the predicted volatility of related underlying markets. The derivative can be used to anticipate future movements. A management strategy will use derivatives whose movements will match and set-off (to the extent possible) substantive positions within the portfolio.

2–12 The final use, "arbitrage", concerns the exploitation of mismatches in market movements to generate profit. For example, movements in one rate may take some time to filter through to related markets. In the intervening period there will be a window in which that mismatch can be exploited to profitable effect. The commonest form of arbitrage is therefore a dissonance between events and market prices. Strategic use of derivatives can position market participants to acquire assets or cash settlement when such mismatches do arise, rather than waiting for the physical market itself to move. Arbitrage is also possible in other contexts. Regulatory arbitrage is the practice of using derivative products to establish a position whereby a favourable regulatory regime or treatment applies to a transaction rather than an unfavourable one. Similarly, arbitrage obtains in respect of substantive legal principles[13] whether in respect of favourable tax treatment or ensuring a preferable legal analysis.

2–13 As considered in greater detail below, capital markets arbitrage is one of the primary motivating factors behind the pricing of swap-related derivatives in

---

[11] One issue which arises with hedging transactions at this level is whether or not they could be said to constitute insurance contracts, in that they oblige one party to pay an amount of money to another party should a given contingency happen. It is submitted that the same analysis would apply here as applies in respect of *Morgan Grenfell v. Welwyn & Hatfield D.C.* [1995] 1 All E.R. 1 that the contract would be formed with a commercial purpose under section 63 of the Financial Services Act 1986. Furthermore, it is submitted that most derivatives do not fall within the categories of 'insurable interest' set out particularly in classes 14, 15 and 16 in Schedule 2 to the Insurance Companies Act 1982. The proximity of many of these products to insurance in literal analytical terms indicates the commercial nature of hedging transactions.

[12] Swamy, *Derivative Instruments* (revised edition., Konoshi & Dattatreya ed., Irwin, 1996), p.47.

[13] As opposed to the rules of self-regulatory organisations or of rules established by subordinate legislation and regulatory diktat.

particular and complex derivatives in general. In many situations a company will be able to borrow money more cheaply from one market (perhaps its domestic loan market) than from another (perhaps the eurobond market). Therefore, there is an arbitrage between its comparative cost of funding. In seeking to borrow in a currency other than that of its host state, that company can use derivatives to arbitrage the differential between its cost of funding across the two markets by use of currency swaps or interest rate swaps.[14] Therefore arbitrage can take place on a number of levels and in a number of contexts. It can be straightforwardly speculative by enabling the construction of a strategy in anticipation of market movements. Alternatively, it can use static market anomalies, such as different costs of funding between markets, to generate preferential funding. These possibilities form an essential part of the structuring and pricing of financial derivative products.

Understanding swaps

Historical development—the early parallel loan swaps

2–14 The currency swap, one of the earliest of the modern derivatives, first emerged as a method of eluding national exchange controls. Where companies sought to conduct business overseas, they had to contend with restrictions on the amount of a foreign currency which they were allowed to borrow and on the amount of currency which they were entitled to export from the jurisdiction in which they were organised. The solution was offered by rudimentary currency swaps. Where A, a Swiss manufacturer, needed to borrow U.S. dollars to transact business in the USA, and B, a U.S. manufacturer, needed to borrow Swiss Francs to transact business in Switzerland, both would be prevented from conducting business above a certain size by exchange control. Therefore, intermediary banks would organise that A would borrow Swiss francs in Switzerland and that B would borrow U.S. dollars in the USA. A and B would then swap the rights in the money borrowed with one another such that A and B both received the money they needed without needing to breach domestic exchange controls. The first such swap was reputed to have been contracted between IBM and the World Bank on this basic structure.[15]

2–15 The currency swap continued to be a useful instrument even after the abolition of United Kingdom exchange control in 1979 because it enabled domestic borrowers to make use of more advantageous loan terms available to borrowers in a different currency. The factors to be taken into account were whether more advantageous loan terms would still confer an advantage after the costs of putting the swap transaction into operation had been met. For example, a German company could borrow Deutschemarks in Germany more cheaply than an American company. Principally this would be because the German company would be better known to German banks who could therefore make a better assessment of its credit worth. The same would be true *mutatis mutandis* for a U.S. company in the USA. Where the German company required U.S. dollars, it would be easier to have the German company borrow Deutschemarks and the American company borrow U.S. dollars in their own jurisdictions and then simply swap the sums of money. As the markets have progressed, the effective cost of these transactions has reduced and therefore conducting such a deal is now a cost-efficient means of reducing the way in which foreign currency debt is obtained.

---

[14] These strategies are explained in greater detail below.

[15] See on this Das, *Swaps and Derivative Financing* (2nd ed., Irwin, 1994), pp.14–17.

2–16 The shortcomings of these early swaps was that the intermediary bank would have to find two counterparties with equal and opposite funding requirements. The commercial problems of finding such parties were only exceeded in terms of complication by the detail of the negotiations and the legal documentation to make these transactions effective. For this technique to establish itself in the marketplace there needed to be a more malleable format. The banks developed the practice of acting as a warehouse for these transactions after the removal of exchange controls. Banks realised that they could often acquire foreign exchange at a lower rate of funding than their corporate clients. Therefore, it became easier for the bank to borrow the money and enter into the exchange of currency amounts with the corporate itself—without the need to use the third party. This greatly increased the volume of business possible. Furthermore, the banks started to leverage from their foreign exchange businesses by combining the lending function and the currency swap function into one transaction. Profit was made by the dual means of a lower cost of funding for the bank in the money markets and pricing a profit into the rate at which currency was provided to the client.

2–17 The swap markets grew as a result of increased volatility in interest rates and in financial markets generally. The U.S. markets grew particularly fast as a result of low interest rates producing low returns on investments.[16] There was therefore an enthusiasm to exchange rates of interest into more attractive packages by means of swaps and also to invest in high yield, low quality investments (junk bonds) to produce better overall returns. The introduction of the Bank for International Settlements (BIS) capital adequacy accord controlled the ability of financial institutions to act as intermediaries in swap transactions.[17] This confusion of circumstances encouraged development in the market place of a more sophisticated and generic form of swap.

2–18 The next development was the interest rate swap. These early currency swaps had the physical delivery of the currency as an essential part of its structure. However, a currency swap which centres on interest rate movements, will be differently structured because the parties are not required to enter into the money markets to deliver currency. It became clear that, rather than simply swapping large amounts of cash, corporate clients could swap their interest rate streams from fixed to floating rates (or vice versa) by use of the same technique. However, the capital cost of doing the business was reduced (by removing the need to transfer whole loan amounts in favour simply of amounts of interest) while generating a reasonable rate of return.

2–19 This development of interest rate swaps was at the expense of the currency swap market. Foreign exchange markets still use the swap mechanism in a high volume, low-specific format. The other uses of derivatives have developed in a manner which requires much more focus from credit professional, lawyers and particularly financial engineers. While the products themselves are distinct, in the manner which will be set out below, there is a great deal of interchange between categories. The driving force behind the markets is the need to construct products which both maximise return and meet the commercial requirements of the client base. Therefore, while different derivatives products appear to have no structural similarities (other than a vague one in their reference to an underlying financial product), they are organised in separate departments and used to achieve common commercial goals.

---

[16] Konoshi and Dattatreya, *Derivative Instruments* (revised edition., Konoshi & Dattatreya ed., Irwin, 1996), pp.1–19.

[17] Das, *Swaps and Derivative Financing* (2nd ed., Irwin, 1994), p.17.

Interest rate swaps

2–20 The modern form of swap is an exchange of cash flows between parties. The following example is a common form of strategy in a market in which interest rates are considered likely to rise over the longterm. Where A plc is borrowing money at a floating rate of LIBOR + 100bp (that is, 100 basis points above the London inter-bank offered rate at any given time), it will wish to guard against future increase in interest rates. There are two reasons for this. First, it will want to avoid the cost of higher interest rates. Secondly, it will wish to be able to calculate with certainty its future cash out-flow in interest rate payments in forming its medium and long-term corporate strategy. Therefore, it will seek to swap its floating rate debt for fixed rate debt.

2–21 Thus, where A has an existing debt obligation under which it is required by the loan contract to make payments of LIBOR + 100bp calculated by reference to the size of the loan. If B Bank agrees to put in place an interest rate swap, B Bank will pay that amount of LIBOR + 100bp to A so that A can satisfy its ordinary debt interest obligations. A will pay B a fixed rate of interest in return plus a spread, which makes up B's fee. B relies on having a lower cost of funding than A for this transaction to generate a profit. A's expectation is that LIBOR + 100bp will be higher than the fixed rate of interest it is paying to B.

2–22 It is important to point out at this stage that several issues arise, all of which will be considered in greater detail below. First, the parties owe each other the full amount of the payments calculated by reference to the actual debt. Therefore, there are mutual debts owed between the parties. Secondly, these mutual debts are owed, usually, simultaneously on a series of payment dates throughout the life of the transaction.[18] Thirdly, while there are mutual debts owed, the parties only actually *pay* a single, net amount between them being the difference between the amounts owed. Fourthly, the negotiations between the parties as to the economic terms of their agreement and manner in which those terms are priced, are based on a segmental analysis of contract, rather than on a single executory contract approach. The impact of this particular concern is considered below with respect to Swap Pricing Models.

2–23 A brief word should be said about the status of the bank under this type of transaction. At first blush it would appear that A gains and B loses on the transaction. A number of points should be made to demonstrate why the transaction is not entirely to B's disadvantage. First, A and B may simply have different views on the direction in which interest rate will move in the future such that each party is taking a view of the risk of rate movements. Secondly, B can probably borrow money in the money markets more cheaply that A. This may be because B has a better credit rating and is better known in the market place. More likely B will be borrowing in bulk across all of its banking business and therefore can acquire funds more cheaply on a volume basis in the money markets than A can acquire through occasional retail borrowing. Thirdly, in pricing the transaction B will include a spread (or profit margin) in the level of the fixed rate which A will pay to B throughout the life of the transaction.

2–24 The fourth criterion relates to the hedging strategy of B and necessitates a three-dimensional view of the manner in which B runs its derivatives business. The interest rate swap market grew out of the parallel and back-to-back loan structures discussed elsewhere in this section. Those structures required two

---

[18] In the type of transaction considered in this example, those swap payment dates will mirror the payment dates for interest on the underlying loan.

parties to be brought together to transact business on an equal and reciprocal basis. In that way banks have intervened in that structure by replacing the need for two arm's length parties with equal and opposite requirements by making up one side of the bargain itself. In the modern context, banks can be considered to be warehouses for cash flows of this sort. Where A requires LIBOR +100bp, B should be able to use its available pool of assets and generate a cash flow (or aggregate of cash flows) equivalent to LIBOR + 100bp which can be passed on to A. Therefore, the management of B's business should aim to produce a balanced "swap book" whereby business is transacted which is capable of offset across transactions.

2–25 The following example explains the way in which this is achieved. C plc seeks to issue bonds to the market to raise finance. Due to its credit rating, the market requires a coupon of 8 per cent to be paid on those bonds to ensure a sufficient subscriber base. C wishes to enter into an interest rate swap with B Bank to lower its effect cost of funding this debt. B agrees to pay the 8 per cent coupon to C in return for the floating rate of LIBOR + 200bp calculated by reference to the total size of the bond issue. B is therefore receiving an inflow of 8 per cent which it believes will match its obligation to A.[19] B will calculate the aggregate of its outflows and inflows across the swap book on (at least) a daily basis to ensure that all obligations are matched by amounts owing, together with a required margin of profit. To the extent that there are positions which are not matched by reciprocal, arm's length transactions, B Bank will enter into hedging transactions of its own. This is achieved by contracting derivatives with other financial institutions such that its obligations are hedged with acceptable modelling predictions and liquidity requirements.

2–26 The day-to-day operation of the swaps market is dependent on this three-dimensional view of the use of derivatives products. One of the commonest criticisms of the English courts' treatment of these products is that each transaction is seen as being a distinct contract unrelated to these other interlinked obligations. This theme is resumed in the context of *Swap Pricing Models* below in the context of the factors which the parties necessarily take into account in assessing the size and nature of payments to be made between the parties. It is important to indicate that the majority of swaps transactions are not transacted by reference to specific amounts of debt and do not require that the whole of those amounts of money are transferred. Rather, swap payments are calculated by reference to notional amounts of money. The size of this notional amount may bear reference to some existing obligation but it is not necessarily linked directly to it. There is no general rule in this context, only a need to examine each situation on a case-by-case basis.

Caps, Collars and Floors

2–27 The buyer of an interest rate swap assumes obligations under a loan transaction; the risk the buyer bears is that the rate which it is required to pay will rise. Therefore there is a need for the buyer to restrict the bounds within which that rate will be payable. A "cap" is a derivative product which places a ceiling on the maximum interest rate which a counterparty will have to pay under a swap. In short it restricts the economic downside of floating interest rates.[20] The cap

---

[19] Often this form of swap is contracted as a part of the bond issue between the issuer and one of the lead managers. That it is embedded in the underlying bond issue leads to it's being described as an "embeddo" in market parlance.

[20] The cap is purchased for a lump sum which makes the arrangement commercially similar to a lump-sum insurance premium.

operates in normal circumstances by the seller of the cap undertaking to pay the obligations of the buyer to the extent that they exceed the threshold identified by the cap contract. On occasions an interest rate swap will incorporate a cap structure so that the buyer is never required to make payments beyond a given threshold. The buyer acquires the rights under the cap contract on payment of a premium to the seller. The willingness of the bank to enter into the transaction is predicated on its belief that rates will not rise beyond the level established in the contract and on the level of premium paid to it from which it can generate a profit and hedge its potential exposure.

2–28 A floor is the same in principal as a cap but it exists to guard against interest rates that fall too low. The risk that that client bears is that the interest rate which it is required to pay will rise. A floor is a derivative product which places a barrier on the minimum interest rate which a counterparty will receive under a swap transaction. In short it restricts the economic downside of floating interest rates. The need to guard against a rate falling too low is more often used in respect of currency swaps where the rate of interest received from holding a particular currency is necessary to maintain a profit margin. The bank assumes the risk of paying the client's interest obligation when the interest rate falls below the threshold level set in the transaction. The willingness of the bank to enter into the transaction is predicated on its belief that rates will not fall below the level established in the contract.[21]

2–29 A cap or a floor is capable of analysis as a series of options or forwards on interest rates.[22] In pricing terms, as considered below, a cap in relation to each payment date denotes an ability in the floating rate payer to pay no more than a maximum amount by calling on the cap. There is such an ability in respect of each payment date. The single cap agreement will be priced by reference to the cost of such an option or forward in respect of each separate payment.[23] The legal analysis of a cap is that it is an obligation assumed by the financial institution selling it, to pay[24] the interest of the purchaser when that interest climbs above a predetermined rate. Caps are used to hedge floating interest rate exposures. If the exposure in relation to the interest rate swap leads to a loss, the counterparty is able to ensure that the loss grows beyond a given level.[25]

2–30 A cap can be analysed as a series of European-style put options under which the buyer has acquired the right to sell to the other party a succession of interest rate equivalents at given dates. An alternative analysis is that the buyer has an option to receive an amount of money equal to the excess of the interest rate over the cap level. Therefore, to price the cap, the deal is treated by the trader as a series of put options on each of the payment dates, each of which has a specific value against expected interest rates at that time. The aggregate of these option

[21] A "collar" is a combination of cap and floor which ensures the investor against the interest rate payable or receivable moving outside the given range of interest rates. This structure might be used, for example, by a company which needs to be able to predict their cost of funding with relative certainty. The cap-floor combination supplies the certainty needed for strategic planning purposes. The structure for a collar is a combination of that for the cap and the floor transaction.

[22] Perhaps it is better analysed as a forward related to an interest rate given the obligation on the parties neither to pay nor to receive amounts in excess of the limit expressed by the cap or floor contract.

[23] Das, *Swaps and Derivative Financing* (2nd ed., Irwin, 1994), p.119.

[24] Or to meet the obligation represented by such interest.

[25] There are other factors which make the combination of "caps" and "floors" attractive. The credit worth of a counterparty may lead to a view that its status makes it unsuitable for too great an exposure to interest rates. The addition of a cap-floor combination lowers the risk of the transaction in return for a premium outlay. The result is the "collar".

amounts is then given its present value to ascertain the upfront premium that has to be paid. Further, it could be said that a cap is a contingent obligation to pay an ascertainable amount of money to a counterparty. That contingent obligation is the movement of the applicable rates through the identified threshold level. The analysis of the cap as a series of options is not always the only possible legal construction of the arrangement. The counterparty that buys the cap is not required to elect to exercise the options for the bank to become obliged to pay out under the cap transaction. That is, unless one interprets the situation as an automatically exercised put option.

2–31 The issue then is whether the implicit involvement of options theory in the pricing of the cap has any effect on the *legal* analysis of the parties' relationship. If the matter of pricing is not discussed explicitly between the parties, it is difficult to see that there could be any implied term in the cap transaction that it be treated as an option without it being specifically documented as an option. For example, the implied term that the option is automatically exercised could be implicitly inferred into the contract. The question would arise whether a cap that was not priced as a series of options, but rather by some other method[26] would alter the legal analysis. If a cap *could* be analysed for legal purposes as an option, could that analysis be displaced by evidence that the instrument has been ascertained in another way.

2–32 The further similarity between the cap and the segmented option is the payment mechanism. The buyer of the cap pays a premium for the contract. The contract is entitled to be called in where rates move outside the range specified in the agreement at the times specified in the cap agreement. In this way the cap is very similar to the option. The conceptual issue is whether the cap is closer to an option (which grants an ability to enjoy a benefit) or to a forward (which obliges the provision of the benefit). If the contract is better expressed as an option in financial terms it would appear to be an option which is automatically exercised, given that it obliges the seller to make good the buyer's interest rate obligations beyond a certain level. In legal terms, however, it appears closer to a forward in that it requires the seller to make payment. The non-lawyer, financial analyst would not see it as a forward because there is not necessarily a guarantee that a payment will be made unless the contingency of suitable rate movement is satisfied, regardless of the obligation on the seller should the contingency occur.[27]

Options

2–33 The option is a familiar technique in commercial contracts and even in relation to buying and selling homes.[28] In financial derivative terms the concept is no different and its subject matter can relate to an option to buy or sell shares, commodities, bonds or even the right to be paid or to pay money at a particular rate of interest ("swaptions" below). There are two forms of option: the "call option" and the "put option". A call option gives the purchaser the right, but not the obligation, to call for delivery of the underlying instrument at a given price on a given date (or one of a number of given dates). A put option gives the purchaser

---

26 For example, as a series of forwards or bullet swaps.

27 See, for example, Das, *Swaps and Derivative Financing* (2nd ed., Irwin, 1994), p.119.

28 See, for example, real property cases such as *London and South Western Rly Co. v. Gomm* (1882) 20 Ch. D. 562 and *Pritchard v. Briggs* [1980] Ch. 338.

the right, but not the obligation, to sell the underlying instrument at a given price on a given date (or one of a number of given dates).

2–34 There is a very important distinction between cash-settled and physically-settled options. All that a cash-settled option gives the buyer is a debt equal to the difference between the market price of the underlying security and option price for the same security, in a specified currency payable on a specified date. There is no right to any specific property created by that option in itself.[29] The physically-settled option will give rights to receive property of a given type[30] at a given date delivered in a given manner. There are no proprietary rights in any given securities in the normal course of events,[31] only a personal claim in contract for performance of the contract[32] or a personal claim at common law in contract for money damages representing the value of the securities contracted for.

2–35 Bond options are options to purchase bonds at a price at a date in the future. They do not have a factor priced into them to cope with an interest rate movement in their price. Rather a bond option enables the holder to benefit from a movement in ordinary interest rates against the interest rate that is payable on the bond, affecting the price of the bond directly.[33] A movement in interest rates generally makes the interest rate (or coupon) that is payable on a bond, more or less attractive. Therefore, bond options enable the investor to hedge against movements in interest rates by using an instrument which is more or less valuable relative to interest rates without actually including that rate in its price, or alternatively to speculate on those same movements.

2–36 Equity, or Share, options fall into two basic categories: cash settled options and physically settled options. The former is predicated on a requirement for the cash equivalent of an option which is in-the-money at the expiration date. The latter entitles the purchaser of the option to receive or to sell (as appropriate) the given quantity of the underlying share. Currency options are options to purchase a given quantity of a currency at a price at a date in the future. A currency option enables the holder to benefit from a movement in the interest rate attached the relevant currency against the interest rate that is payable on taking out debt in that currency. The currency option operates as a means of hedging against movements in the underlying currency.

2–37 Complex option positions can involve bundling options together to form complex structures aimed at the achievement of particular financial goals. Depending on a party's view of the future movements of the market, it will choose to go "short" on a particular underlying security. Going "short" means contracting to supply more securities than you own and, more importantly,

---

29 As considered below, there may be come credit enhancement documentation which seeks to provide proprietary rights in certain circumstances but such an arrangement must necessarily be only collateral to the option contract, or even completely outside it.

30 Alternatively, many physically-settled contracts in fact permit the buyer to elect between cash or physical settlement even where the contract is avowedly for physical settlement by common intention.

31 Without segregation of assets subject to a trust, *Re Goldcorp* [1995] 1 A.C. 74.

32 It would seem that specific performance will not give equitable rights in the property in this instance (*cf.*: *Chinn v. Collins* [1981] A.C. 533, *per* Lord Wilberforce; *Oughtred v. IRC* [1960] A.C. 206) given the decision of the Privy Council in *Re Goldcorp* [1995] 1 A.C. 74, that property must be segregated so as to be certain before imposition of a trust or other equitable device. In circumstances where the seller is still solvent, there would appear to be no problem with forcing performance of the contract. Unless the intended subject matter cannot be obtained in which case the doctrine of frustration or breach of contract would be preferable, it is submitted, rather than proprietary rights over property which cannot be provided for the buyer's enjoyment in any event.

33 The price on a bond being the inverse of the interest coupon payable on that bond against prevailing market rates.

promising to supply those securities at a rate lower than the cost of acquiring those securities in the market. This position assumes that the market value of those securities will fall before the obligation to supply them is required to be performed. Selling short as part of a portfolio of investment generates risk and possible return.[34] Combining put and call options can create a different form of product which resembles different derivatives structures. It grants the ability to exit and enter markets. Buying and selling vertical spreads, made up of combined short and long positions on the same security, enables complex strategies to be formed on the guaranteed acquisition and sale prices of a security against market movements.

Options to enter into a swap ("swaptions")

2–38 A swaption is an option to enter into a swap at a future date. Instead of a series of payment dates by which payments are calculated as amounts of interest, the swaption entitles the investor to enter into a swap transaction on given terms. These terms would require the seller to effect a particular structure which would be activated by the buyer when the underlying interest rate markets move in a given direction to a given level at which point the swap would be profitable for the buyer. The principal difference between the swap and the swaption is the fixing of a strike level for the swaption which governs whether or not it can be exercised, whereas an interest rate swap is necessarily effective from the time when it is sold.

The link between options, forwards and swaps

2–39 At one level, the option is completely different from a swap. Aside from the issue of whether or not the parties are obliged or simply entitled to make payment, the option is a one-off ("single-shot") agreement whereas the swap contains a series of mutual payments. However, both constitute hedging or speculative positions on the same underlying markets. In both transactions there are payments of money between the parties. The buyer of an option makes a fixed rate, premium payment to the seller—akin to the fixed rate payment in a swap. In return the seller will be obliged to make a payment or transfer a security dependent upon movements in market rates. This is akin to the floating rate payment under a swap. For regulatory arbitrage purposes options and swaps are frequently repackaged one as the other to elude restrictions on conduct of business. Alternatively, there is scope to arbitrage the funding costs of one type of product against the comparative costs of the other.

2–40 Some commentators see certain types of swaps as complex options. The equity swap is a right to receive a rate of return calculated by reference to a market's performance. In economic terms that is similar to a right to receive a series of options which each pay a single amount by reference to the performance of a given underlying market. The issue of whether this seeming similarity is one of form or of substance is an issue which the courts have failed to consider. Lord

[34] By contrast, the seller may go "long" on a particular security. This means agreeing to buy securities at a given price. The assumption is that the market value of those securities will be greater than the agreed future purchase price. Where the market price is higher, the option entitles the buyer to acquire securities at a discount to their market value and then sell them at a profit. Again, as a portfolio investment, this derivative enables the buyer to take a speculative or hedging position on the movement of markets against which it can arbitrage the difference between the option price and the open market price if its position turns out to be correct.

Templeman's analysis of the interest rate swap in *Hazell*[35] failed to consider this possible, analytical possibility. The more difficult question in relation to swaps would have been whether or not a package of separable options would have been held *ultra vires* the local authorities, whereas options to buy premises or agreements to attachment of earnings orders in respect of unpaid rent would appear to be perfectly lawful transactions for such a body. In each situation, the authority is acquiring an entitlement to payment of a future cash flow which is dependent upon the other party's ability to pay at any time and the movement of variable indicators such as interest or housing management costs.[36]

Synthetic options

2–41 If a bank owns a quantity of a security and a put option over the same quantity of that security, it has something which is a cash-settled call option in all but name. The put option will be in-the-money where the price of the underlying instrument falls below the put option strike price; and the underlying security will be sold at a profit where its true market value rises. This profit structure is very similar to that of a call option. This combination is a "synthetic call option". Similarly, if an institution is long a call and short a put where both have the same expiration date, the institution is, in effect, long a synthetic instrument. The use of these synthetic relationships enable clients of financial institutions to maximise their assets in circumstances where they stand exposed solely to an upward or downward movement in a market in the underlying instrument. The aim of the synthetic option is to transform this position into a "heads you win, tails you win" situation.

2–42 The relationship between an underlying instrument and an option, where they form a synthetic position, might have an effect on the appropriate hedging strategy: whether it deals with the positions as separate exposures or as a composite risk. However, the legal analysis may well be different from the commercial appraisal. Whether there is in fact a call option in legal terms under a single contract or distinct transactions with a community of commercial purpose is a difficult mixture of fact and law.

Forwards and futures

2–43 The forward is an obligation to make a payment or delivery at a given price on a given date (often in a given place) in the future. The future is the same structure organised on an exchange. The sense in which the term "forward" will be used in this context refers solely to transactions which are contracted off-exchange, or "over-the-counter". It is possible to analyse a forward as being made up of two options: one a call option sold to a party to demand payment or delivery and on the other hand a put option which entitles the other party to make the

---

[35] [1992] 2 A.C. 1.

[36] While many of the swap structures common in the derivatives market currently are becoming more commoditised (for example, "vanilla" interest rate swaps and currency swaps) the equity derivative market is, by its nature, open to more exotic structures. The plethora of equity products that are traded on a broad range of stock and futures exchanges are more difficult to package into commoditised structures. The structure of debt derivative products is more homogenous than the equity derivative products that are traded and regulated on equities markets. There are more customised features about equity derivatives.

payment or delivery in return for payment. A swap is, by one analysis,[37] a series of forward contracts to pay or to receive an amount of money on a particular date according to the movement in a chosen interest rate. Therefore, a swap could, by extension, be analysed as a series of put and call options to receive or to pay an amount of money on a particular date, with reference to a particular interest rate.[38] Derivatives products are all rights or obligations to pay or to receive sums of money by reference to a floating indicator, whether that be an interest rate, a share index, or the price of a bond or commodity index.

2–44 A forward conveys the right to purchase or sell a specified quantity of an asset at a fixed price on a fixed date in the future. In exchange traded futures contracts, which are a standardised form of forward contract, the quantity of the underlying asset to be delivered per contract is fixed, as is the underlying financial instrument or index, the minimum price movement for the contract and the life of the contract. In a forward agreement, these elements are at large for negotiation between the parties.[39]

The link between the products

2–45 The links between the products are explored more closely in the following chapter. The central points are two. First, it is common for a single commercial purpose which cannot be achieved by using one form of product, to be achieved by using a combination of other derivatives. Therefore, there is fluidity between the products. Secondly, the pricing of swaps transactions is predicated, as explored in the following chapter, on the analysis of swaps as being made up of options and forwards.

---

[37] See the discussion in *Swaps Pricing Models* below.

[38] Das, *Swaps and Derivative Financing* (2nd ed., Irwin, 1994), pp.80–88.

[39] The prices are quoted as an amount (100) less the implied interest rate on that instrument. Therefore, the price of a futures instrument moves in inverse correlation to movements in interest rates. This inverse movement against interest rates, makes forwards (and particularly exchange traded futures contracts) the ideal instrument to hedge against movements in interest rates. If interest rates falls and the price of futures therefore rises, there is an inverse correlation that means a movement in one will be compensated by an opposite movement in the other. As a result, one is a useful instrument in hedging a movement in the other.

Chapter 3

The legal analysis of swaps

Swaps pricing models

3–01 One element of the swaps market which was not considered in any of the swaps cases was the mechanics behind the products. While there has been some discussion of the commercial purposes behind the swaps used by the local authorities, there was no consideration in any of the judgments as to the financial structuring issues in putting those products in place or as to the legal analysis propagated by the documentation. The issues of documentation and of legal analysis are considered separately. This section considers the manner in which swaps are priced. In short, there are two basic elements in pricing swaps: the first is to consider them as made up of separate financial forwards in the manner considered above; and the second is to consider them as afecting capital markets arbitrage.

The financial forwards element

3–02 The financial futures approach sees each separate swap payment as an obligation to pay an amount of money on a given date calculated by reference to a rate of interest and a notional capital sum. On each payment date there are two financial forwards: one owed by the floating rate payer and the other owed by the fixed rate payer. The payment netting provisions mean that only the surplus represented by the difference between the two amounts owed reciprocally.[1] Thus, rather than attempting to price the swap on a single contract approach, the transaction is divided up into segments.

3–03 The swap is an integrated financial instrument made up of a number of distinct segments. Each payment date is treated as a distinct financial product for pricing purposes. This process is generally known as "financial engineering".[2] From the point of view of the financial engineer each segment must receive a separate pricing analysis according to its commercial underpinning. Das refers to this segmental approach as the "decomposition" of the swap.[3] The pricing for a swap based on a commercial need to recalibrate a debt obligation combines interest rate forwards, FRAs and possibly vanilla interest rate swaps.[4] A contingent contract[5] would have an element of the option priced into it as though it included an independent option. Similarly, the structuring of currency swaps are made up of a series of long-term foreign exchange contracts, or options to acquire foreign currency. In either case, there may be features which ensure that there are levels above which and below which performance of the swap contract is restricted: such elements are priced as though independent caps, collars and floors.

---

[1] As considered below this means that there is a possibility that, if the amounts set off exactly, no amount will actually be owed at all.

[2] Das, *Swaps and Derivative Financing* (2nd ed., Irwin, 1994), p.114.

[3] *ibid.* at pp.113 *et seq.*

[4] Where the transaction is particularly complex.

[5] Such as a barrier swap, which is contingent on the specified index reaching a given level before any payments are required to be made.

3–04 Each of these individual components has its own pricing methodology. In pricing a swap, the applicable forward and option prices on the prevailing capital markets are incorporated into the structure. Currency swaps adopt the price of options contracts on the foreign exchange markets. In considering the price of options and forwards the familiar Black–Scholes Option Pricing Model is adopted as for open market contracts.[6] Similarly, the put-call parity will be included to account for the mathematical relationship between forward contracts and options. Therefore, the ultimate price assigned to the swap contract is the result of an aggregation of the distinct prices of each of these market instruments. Indeed Das describes swaps as being "portfolios of forward and option contracts" rather than single executory contracts.[7]

Capital markets arbitrage element

3–05 The second mechanism for pricing swaps is the use of capital market arbitrage calculations. Given that the use of swaps is often to arbitrage the funding possibilities between different financial markets, the comparative costs of transacting in different markets is an important factor in pricing these products.[8] Given the anomalies which markets generate, there will always be scope for arbitrage. Tax regulation, capital adequacy regulation and other general financial regulation impact on the transaction costs of swaps. Similarly, perceptions of risk attached to particular markets will impact on pricing decisions. Volatile markets attract higher prices in accordance with the return required to offset the increased risk that is taken. The term 'markets' in this context can refer to geographic markets, to particular financial sectors, or a specific form of index or exchange. Added to this is the perception of any particular market participant within such market. As considered above, perception of credit worth and cost of funding may be have an effect on the value of the derivative and therefore on the pricing of a derivative in respect of a specific counterparty.

3–06 An example of swap arbitrage would occur in the following circumstances. Suppose that A plc can borrow floating rate loan funding at LIBOR and fixed rate bond funding at 6 per cent. Similarly, B plc can borrow floating rate loan funding at LIBOR + 100bp[9] and fixed rate bond funding at 7 per cent. There is therefore a respective difference in funding cost of 100bp and 1 per cent respectively: there is clearly a large differential between these differences which are not untypical in capital markets. A wishes to pay a floating rate but can only pay a fixed rate to bond investors. B wishes to pay a lower floating rate than it is able to obtain in the market. A structured, capital arbitrage solution would operate as follows.[10] The parties would borrow in the markets which best suit them and swap their respective borrowings through an intermediary bank. The cost to A of paying 6 per cent to the bond market can be swapped for the floating rate A wishes to pay for its debt (LIBOR). The fixed rate paid to the bond investors can be obtained from B where B pays a floating rate (via the intermediary bank) and receives A's floating rate of funding (LIBOR) which it passes to its own lenders. As a result, A pays its preferred

---

[6] See, for example, Brealey and Myers, *Principles of Corporate Finance* (5th ed., McGraw Hill, 1995), pp.503 *et seq.*, expressed as $[N(d_1) \times P] - [N(d_2) \times PV(EX)]$.

[7] Das, *Swaps and Derivative Financing* (2nd ed., Irwin, 1994), p.119.

[8] *ibid.* at pp.126 *et seq.*

[9] "bp" being a "basis point", or one one-hundreth of a single percentage point of an interest rate.

[10] This example draws on a more complex worked hypothetical situation suggested by Das, *op. cit.*, pp.131–133.

floating rate interest and receives a higher rate from B. B has a comparatively high debt cost; A has a much lower debt cost. B prefers to pay A's debt cost. B in turn receives a floating rate which matches much of its obligations to its own lenders, thus reducing its own effective cost of funding.

3–07 On a net basis, both parties are closer to their preferred cost of funding than is possible in the marketplace in which it is commercially required to borrow by means of ordinary loan. The role of the intermediary bank would have been to bring these two parties together and set up parallel transactions. In the swaps cases which make up the bulk of this book, intermediary investment banks brought together lending institutions and the local authorities who needed either debt funding or debt management (or both). In the modern market place the intermediary would not necessarily need to introduce the parties but might take the risk of both transactions by "warehousing" both sides of the deal and setting the separate deals off in its own swap book.[11] These arbitrage considerations are then priced into the transaction.

The core importance of the pricing models

3–08 Two centrally important points for the context of the swaps cases emerge from the foregoing analysis of swap modelling and pricing. The first is that swaps are not contracted between the parties on the basis of a single figure generated by reference to a single executory contract. Rather, each transaction is treated as made up of a number of segments which are priced separately such that a final total is reached on the basis of the calculated cost of a series of mutual obligations. It is impossible to overemphasise the importance of the manner in which these markets conduct their business. To apply everyday rules of common law and equity without reference to the detailed factual process of creating these contracts is to overlook the risks which are considered and which are allocated as part of the transaction. Similarly, in deciding whether or not part-performed contracts can be considered differently from wholly unperformed contracts is dependent upon a financial analysis of those contracts as made up of distinct debts which are documented as part of a larger transaction.[12]

3–09 The second point is the integral involvement of the hedging transaction within the context of creating the main transaction. The cost of hedging is necessarily priced into main transaction.[13] The availability and cost of suitable hedging material impacts directly on the price which is charged to the buyer by means of the level of pricing that is fixed in the swap contract. The operation of the entire market is predicated on the parallel loan structure whereby market liquidity is ensured by a balance of transactions which offset with each other such that swaps books held by financial institutions are capable of being balanced and satisfactorily hedged. To deny the nexus between the hedge and the underlying contract is to ignore not only market practice but also the swathe of prudential regulation which requires that financial institutions effect netting and maintain capital adequacy ratios.

---

[11] This reluctance to introduce the parties to one another might arise in the situation of a house bank jealous of its proximate status to the client but reluctant to assume any more lending exposure to the counterparty.

[12] *Guinness Mahon v. Kensington & Chelsea R.L.B.C.* [1998] 2 All E.R. 272; *Kleinwort Benson v. Sandwell Borough Council* [1994] 4 All E.R. 890, Hobhouse J.

[13] *Kleinwort Benson v. Birmingham City Council* [1996] 4 All E.R. 733, CA.

3–10 As considered in the remainder of this book, the English courts have sought to analyse each swap contract as a distinct legal entity which is separate from all of the other contracts entered into between those parties and the hedging transactions which are contracted as a direct consequence of them. This fits into the neat English law model which demands direct connections between contracts for losses caused by one to be capable of account in respect of another. However, it also constitutes a blindness as to both the actual functioning of financial markets and, more significantly, the necessarily prudent functioning and risk management capabilities of those same relationships.

The future development of swaps

3–11 Whereas the foregoing discussion of swap pricing models involves a great deal of complex mathematics in its application, the building blocks of the analysis are not complicated. The core of any derivatives pricing structure is that it looks at the component parts of the transaction rather than at the totality of the transaction.

3–12 The growth of new markets has introduced some new strands to the analysis of the financial derivative. Foremost among the developments is the "credit derivative". At the time of writing the credit derivative is a novel form of open market instrument which has yet to have a standard form market contract developed for it[14] and market participants are only beginning to explore the regulatory, legal and accounting issues which surround these products.[15] The theory behind the credit derivative is that it is priced according to the credit worth of a "reference entity", rather than according to a fixed or floating rate market indicator. The aim of the credit derivative is to provide a means of hedging exposure to the credit worth of a particular entity or market sector. The seller of the derivative agrees to pay a cash flow to the buyer. The buyer is obliged to make reciprocal payment, usually, in the event that the credit worth of the reference entity deteriorates.

3–13 The aim of the credit derivative is to provide a means for investors in, for example, the publicly issued debt of a particular reference entity, to hedge their exposure to that entity failing to pay by selling credit derivatives. Alternatively, the credit derivative provides investors the ability to speculate on the credit worth of particular reference entities or on a particular market sector. The investor receives a return which is priced according to the credit worth of the reference entity. The calculation of this credit worth factor generates the mathematical complication and is dependent upon the type of structure used.

3–14 The structure can operate in a number of ways. First, the parties could agree to a swap structure in which seller pays a fixed rate and buyer pays a floating rate. The floating rate will be close to zero unless the reference entity's credit worth deteriorates. Secondly, the parties could structure the agreement as an option where seller pays a lump sum premium (possibly in instalments) and thus buys the option to receive a cash sum from the buyer calculated in accordance with the credit worth of the reference entity.

3–15 The credit swap takes two forms. The first is the "total return swap" under which the total return of a bank loan or credit-sensitive is exchanged for a fixed rate cash flow or, more usually, a floating rate cash flow linked to an

[14] ISDA published a Credit Derivatives confirmation in March 1998, limited to credit swaps.

[15] See "An Introduction to the Legal Accounting and Control Challenges of Credit Derivatives", chaired by Hudson, London, December 8, 1997 (materials IBC, 1997).

indicator such as LIBOR. Typically there will not be any exchange of principal amounts or change of ownership of any assets. Some commentators consider this structure to be a form of synthetic security or synthetic loan in that it achieves the same cash flow effect as a security or loan by means of the swap structure.[16] A total return swap will be cash settled.

3–16 The alternative formulation is the "default swap" under which a premium, lump sum payment is swapped for an amount contingent on a specified credit event where the size of that floating amount is calculated by reference to that credit event. Default swaps are created in connection with a single reference entity or a range of reference entities. The forms of credit event will span a spectrum from bankruptcy and events close to insolvency, to cross default by associated entities or cross acceleration of other forms of public or private debt. In many cases reference is made to downgrading by credit ratings agencies or the performance of specified financial criteria such as gearing or interest coverage. The default payment is therefore linked to a specific performance on an underlying security or loan. Some commentators describe this as a "binary pay-off".[17]

3–17 Option or forward structures are orientated around a number of types of "credit-linked note" in which financial institutions have tended to assert their copyright. The notes aim to link the return on the note to the credit-related performance of the underlying security or loan. There is therefore a bicameral means of calculating the value of the security: first, the performance of the issuer and, secondly, the credit performance of the underlyer and the redemption value of that underlyer. A credit option gives the buyer the ability to buy an asset which is linked to performance of the underlyer. The result of using either product is to create a sophisticated hedging position linked to the credit performance of the underlying asset or liability.

3–18 The underlying pricing structure is the same as for a vanilla option or swap. Each payment is considered separately and priced according to its status as a forward or swap. Into this pricing mechanism is a factor to account for the credit worth of the reference entity and its associated volatility. There is no difference from a vanilla product in pricing in such a factor to account for credit worth. However, the value of that factor may differ given the centrality of the credit worth element to the transaction. The credit derivative is a complex market instrument which contains enormous mathematical complication, above and beyond vanilla products. There are issues surrounding its proximity to a contract of insurance, given that it is an obligation to make a payment in the event that a given risk produces a given financial exposure. The appropriate categorisation for the credit derivative for regulatory capital purposes is similarly complicated. It is not clear whether or not the credit derivative ought to receive a capital weighting equivalent to an equity, debt or commodity product. Despite that complication the core analysis remains the same: the product is priced according to is constituent segments and not its totality.

3–19 One further point is made as to "tax derivatives"—a novel form of derivative which seeks to arbitrage differences in tax regulations either between jurisdictions or different forms of transaction within a single tax jurisdiction. The tax derivative is rarely considered as a stand-alone form of product because it is usually transacted as one of the products already discussed but with a commercial

---

[16] See Whittaker and Kumar, "Credit Derivatives—A Primer" in *Derivative Instruments* (revised edition, Konoshi and Dattatreya eds, Irwin, 1996), pp.595 *et seq.*

[17] See the discussion of binary options above for an example of binary payments. Commentators include Whittaker and Kumar, "Credit Derivatives—A Primer" in *Derivative Instruments* (revised edition, Konoshi and Dattatreya eds, Irwin, 1996), pp.595 *et seq.*

purpose which is orientated around tax avoidance. It is submitted that, further to the preceding point that a financial derivative is properly analysed according to the way in which it is created and priced (that is by reference to its constituent segments), any court presented with a tax derivative would look to its substance as a series of segments rather than at the tax efficient form of its totality.

3–20 For example, where a series of payments for goods or services generate a liability to tax on each occasion that such payment is made, the tax–efficient solution would be to tie those payments up into one single, larger contract which provided that no payment obligation was to be treated as expired unless all payments were made. This would be a series of forwards or options packaged as a single swap. The commercial aim would be to delay the liability to tax until the end of the contract.[18] Applying the principle in *Furniss v. Dawson* it is contended that the court would look at such a repackaging of a commercial transaction and consider it to contain an artificial step or as a structure which is properly analysed in accordance with its structure as a series of individual forwards or options rather than an executory contract. Therefore, while many analysts favour the single, executory contract approach, it is contended that the pragmatic view of the courts ought to be to look to the substance of its pricing and payments rather than to its contractual form.

Six legal analyses of swaps and other derivatives

3–21 While the preceding explanation of the development of financial derivatives in the market place has emphasised the segmental approach to pricing and hedging strategies, the available legal analyses do not necessarily observe the commercial logic of those same structures. The following discussion aims to categorise the legal analyses. What emerges from that discussion is that the courts have favoured analyses which are in conflict with the commercial underpinnings of the derivative. The ensuing analysis of the swaps cases will then examine these analyses in more detail, isolating the problems associated both with failing to apply the standard market contracts and the implied preference for the single, executory contract approach.

The legal nature of derivatives

3–22 The fundamental question revolves around the very nature of the derivative product. As considered in outline in the introduction and in greater detail below, the swaps cases have not addressed the express issue of the workings of interest rate swaps in particular or of financial derivatives in general. The standard market contracts, particularly the ISDA Master Agreement[19] and related documentation, are premised on an understanding of the legal nature of the products which that documentation seeks to mould. In particular the "single contract approach" of the ISDA Master Agreement,[20] which aims to achieve systemic stability by providing for set-off across the complete range of derivatives

---

[18] Some tax structures using "perpetual stock instruments" sought to use single, executory contracts which would never expire, thus purportedly never generating a charge to tax. The Special Commissioners have held that such a structure will be effective where there is a genuine commercial purpose in the transaction.

[19] ISDA, *ISDA Multicurrency Master Agreement* (ISDA, 1992).

[20] *ibid.* s.1(c).

contracts entered into between commercial parties, constitutes an ideological understanding of the risks associated with financial derivatives in the marketplace.

3–23 This analysis of the risks in the market place, considered above[21] informs a prudent attempt to introduce informal regulation of the over-the-counter markets. However, the real questions behind the correct legal analysis of the products are masked by the sleight of the signature hand that gives effect to the contracts. The impact of the swaps cases is the unspoken decision that the courts will not enforce such contracts at all where there is an event of incapacity. It remains to be seen what will happen in relation to the other events of default, isolated above in Chapter 2, and whether English law will seek to enforce mandatory rules such that the standard market documentation will be considered to be ineffective or inapplicable. Within this discussion of the nature of derivatives, therefore, there is a core question of the manner in which the products are to be categorised. A number of the potential remedies available under English law will be applicable to some types of derivatives agreement but not to others. Therefore, the unresolved question of how to analyse derivative products constitutes the first problem for a lawyer seeking to set in place a broad range of derivative transactions.

3–24 The initial question is probably whether or not a series of distinct derivative transactions contracted between the same parties constitutes one composite agreement or a number of separate agreements. A tentative answer, based on the case law,[22] must be that they are entirely separate agreements. Even where a hedging contract is entered into as part of a composite transaction, it would appear that the courts intend it to constitute an entirely separate set of legal relations. This area is set out in greater detail below. However, this prima facie view, which Atiyah places at the heart of the classical understanding of English contract law, is that a contract is based on the enforcement of some undertaking to be performed at some point in the future.[23] That elides easily into an understanding of the interest rate swap as being made up of one central obligation, rather than a number of distinct, mutual debts.

3–25 There are six separate, potential analyses of the manner in which these contracts are performed set out below. Their underpinnings can be briefly put. Hobhouse J. has held that a single payment made under a swap constitutes a repayment of an earlier amount paid under the same agreement. Perhaps unconsciously this places the nexus on individual payment obligations rather than on the generality of amounts owed ("the repayment analysis"). Alternatively, therefore, these distinct payments might be said to be separate debts and obligations which are necessarily bound together as one set of legal relations under an overarching contract ("the mutual debts analysis"). This analysis of swaps transactions analyses them as obligations owed reciprocally between the counterparties.

3–26 However, the more common understanding of the contracts, and the one propounded by most common law and civil code forms of standard agreement,[24] is to view the swap as a contract which is to be performed over time where performance is related to the occurrence of some event in the future ("the executory contract analysis"). Therefore, the size of any payments would depend on a series of contingencies: such as the movement in interest rates. The basic

---

[21] In Chapter 2, *The Structure of Financial Derivatives Products.*

[22] See, for example, the decision of the Court of Appeal in *Kleinwort Benson v. Birmingham C.C.* [1996] 4 All E.R. 733; *Guinness Mahon v. Kensington & Chelsea R.L.B.C.* [1998] 2 All E.R. 272; and the decision of the House of Lords in *Kleinwort Benson Ltd v. Glasgow City Council* [1997] 4 All E.R. 641.

[23] Atiyah, *The Rise and Fall of Freedom of Contract* (Oxford, 1979).

[24] For example, ISDA, *ISDA Multicurrency Master Agreement* (ISDA, 1992), s.1(c).

analytical question can therefore be summarised as a question whether structured derivatives like swaps are one composite transaction (a single contract to pay a series of amounts) or a number of separate transactions (such as individual options or forwards).

Classifying claims and remedies

3–27 There are subtle distinctions to be made between types of claims and remedies which are available in relation to the range of derivatives products which have been discussed above in *The Structure of Financial Derivatives Products*.[25] In practice, claims in this area will tend to fall into three categories: claims arising out of contract (consent), claims arising out of tort and wrongs other than torts[26] (wrongs), and claims arising on the basis of profit made by means of some unconscionable act by one or other of the parties or enriching one party as a result of some unjust factor (unjust enrichment).

3–28 For the most part, in practice, claims arising out of consent will tend to settle—unless one of the parties has become insolvent. This is because the market tends to shy away from litigation that will result in the payment of damages when the parties can usually come to a financial compromise between themselves. This preserves the market free from interference by regulators or the courts. Where a financial institution is dealing with a valued client, it will generally not wish to sour that relationship by pushing matters to court. Where the issue arises between two financial institutions, the parties will generally prefer to go to arbitration where the claims and remedies can be defined between themselves. Alternatively, the parties will seek to avoid the publicity associated with litigation and attempt to reach some financial compromise between themselves. Therefore, claims based on consent arise only rarely, usually associated with some wrong, while the parties remain solvent.

3–29 Claims based on wrongs will generally revolve around a claim which, in the context of derivatives, connects to the category of "suitability". Generally a claim in suitability based upon a wrong will be brought by a non-financial institution seeking a remedy from a bank which, allegedly, wrongly sold it a particular derivative product. The wrong might fall into one of a number of established categories: (1) that the bank made a misrepresentation as to the nature of the derivative; (2) that the bank ought to have given better advice as to the effect of the derivative, implying negligence or misstatement; (3) that the derivative itself was unsuitable for the purpose for which it was acquired, implying negligence or misstatement; (4) that the derivative itself was simply unsuitable for the purchasing institution in all the circumstances, implying misstatement; or (5) that some mistake on the part of the seller was made which caused the derivative to be unsuitable.

3–30 The claim in unjust enrichment based on suitability would be a claim (1) to recover specific property; (2) to acquire specific property; (3) to order payment of money in compensation for some loss; or (4) to impose responsibility on the defendant in respect of some loss. The restitutionary basis of suitability is considered in more detail below in *suitability approach*. In short, it is said that the generation of profits from unsuitable financial products (that is, unsuitable in the

[25] Chapter 2.

[26] See, for example, the discussion as to the nature of claims for dishonest assistance and knowing receipt: for example Birks, "Misnomer" in *Restitution, Present and Future: Essays in Honour of Gareth Jones* (Cornish, Nolan, O'Sullivan and Virgo eds., Oxford, Hart Publishing, 1998), p.1.

context of being formed subject to some unjust factor) would constitute unjust enrichments in the hands of the seller which it would be appropriate to resolve by the application of some restitutionary remedy. There is some potential overlap between the factual basis of some of the claims in wrongs and these claims in unjust enrichment. However, the claim in unjust enrichment based on suitability of the product would be based on restitutionary principles or on equity. The two separate approaches in the context of the swaps cases, and, in particular, based on the speeches in the House of Lords in *Islington*, are set out in detail below. In short, the claim for suitability would be orientated around some unjust factor requiring a restitutionary response or (In Lord Browne-Wilkinson's terms) the application of an equitable remedy on grounds of unconscionability. It is the contention of the *suitability approach* that the current development of those restitutionary and equitable principles will not accord with commercial requirements or the expectations of parties to financial transactions, requiring a development of the question of suitability in this context.

The Six Analyses

3–31 It is suggested that there are six ways of looking at the different types of derivative which we have already considered (the sixth is a peculiar exception). Most of the case law deals with interest rate swaps. Analyses 1 and 2 have arisen in the case law. Analyses 3 and 4 are the author's own conceptions which, it is suggested, would have been open to the courts had they looked at the derivatives before them in a different manner. Analysis 5 is one which is favoured in fact, although without any necessary reference to this legal analysis, by many financial engineers working in the derivatives field. Analysis 6 is unfortunately a part of English law, but, like an unattractive ornament, is something you would generally hope will sit quietly in a corner so that it can be ignored completely. The six analyses may be labelled as follows:

(1) Executory contract analysis;
(2) Repayment analysis;
(3) Mutual debt analysis;
(4) Condition precedent analysis;
(5) Financial forwards analysis; and
(6) Disjointed option analysis.

The aim of setting out these analyses in the ensuing discussion is to illustrate the point that the courts in the swaps cases have failed to apply equitable and restitutionary principles in a way which comprehends the commercial requirements of the material in front of them. The following analyses of swaps transactions, which are applicable to the other financial derivatives considered above, are the logically anterior questions to the judgments delivered in the swaps cases. Before the best restitutionary solution can be found, the commercial context requires closer examination. In moving towards the suitability approach set out in the conclusion to this book, it is necessary to identify that no single equitable remedial solution will be appropriate in all circumstances. Rather, it is necessary to apply the principles set out in the suitability approach to the precisely appropriate analysis of the contract at issue. Reliance simply on the vague outline set out in *Hazell*[27] prevented the courts from getting to the heart of the issue and

[27] *Hazell v. Hammersmith and Fulham* [1992] 2 A.C. 1; [1991] 2 W.L.R. 372; [1991] 1 All E.R. 545.

setting out the suitable way forward in future decisions relating either to derivatives specifically or financial contracts more generally.

3–32 For the derivatives lawyer the issue of the availability of set-off in the event that one of the parties becomes insolvent ("close-out netting") has been the most important issue in the framing of documentation. Therefore, the primary restitutionary issue has been the termination of contracts and the recovery of amounts of a specified currency calculated by reference to given contractual provisions. The following analyses grew out of the need to establish the availability of remedies akin to set-off, specific performance and rescission in the event of a contractual termination.[28] Since the introduction of the second edition of the ISDA form of contractual agreement in 1992, the English law position in relation to close-out netting has become clarified. It is now accepted that rule 4.90 of the Insolvency Rules 1986 operates as a substantive rule which provides for set-off on insolvency.[29]

3–33 It is suggested that no single analysis will have a claim to truth or validity in all situations. Rather, the particular context will have to be analysed to locate the appropriate response. In each case, some attempt is made to identify the situations in which each of these analyses would appear to represent the best fit. In some cases there will be only a narrow distinction between the use of mutual debts analysis and the financial forwards analysis, for example.

The Executory Contract Analysis

3–34 The executory contract analysis considers a swap to be one single agreement which is made up of a matrix of obligations. The contract is executory in that it is not to be considered as having been performed until its expiry date. An executory contract is one which is formed at the creation of the agreement but which requires performance to be made at some point in the future. The literal application of this approach would require that the payment of each obligation owed must be made before the contract can be said to have been performed. There is no possibility of part performance being said to effect performance of that part separate from the rest of the agreement.[30] Completion of all payments is the prerequisite of performance and not the making of any individual payment.

How many executory contracts?

3–35 There is a potentially difficult side issue in the area of executory contracts. That problem is created by the fact that it is possible to argue that a number of seemingly unrelated transactions entered into between two parties are to be treated as one, single contract if the logic of the ISDA Master Agreement is applied rigorously.[31] Indeed, that is the analysis which ISDA's lawyers would

---

[28] On this see Hudson, *The Law on Financial Derivatives* (2nd Ed., Sweet & Maxwell, 1998), pp.203–246.

[29] See on this Goode, *Principles of Corporate Insolvency Law* (2nd ed., Sweet & Maxwell, 1997), p.177. This analysis is supported by the decision of the House of Lords in *National Westminster Bank v. Halesowen Presswork and Assemblies Ltd.* [1972] A.C. 785; *Stein v. Blake* [1996] 1 A.C. 243; *Morris v. Rayners* (unreported) October 30, 1997.

[30] As suggested by *Guinness Mahon v. Kensington & Chelsea R.L.B.C.* [1998] 2 All E.R. 272 in that there was no discrimination made between completed, unperformed, and part-performed swaps by the Court of Appeal.

[31] *ISDA Multicurrency Master Agreement 1992*, s.1(c).

propound.[32] It is proposed to deal with this issue at the outset so that it can be put to one side for the remainder of the discussion.

3–36 It is probably the case that the existence of payment netting means that there is only one contract rather than two streams of contractual obligations when considering a single swap: the floating rate payments on the one hand and the fixed rate payments on the other. Whereas the ISDA Master Agreement seeks to set-off payment obligations across all derivatives transactions entered into between contracting parties, it is at least unlikely that a court would find that an interest rate swap transaction entered into in 1995 and an equity swap transaction entered into in 1997, would be capable of being considered together as one contract. The ISDA Master Agreement analyses all derivatives transactions entered into between two parties as being capable of set-off against one another. Therefore, whether or not the transactions are of different types, they are treated as being formed as part of one large contract (referred to a "the single agreement approach").[33] Despite this single agreement approach, those disparate transactions appear to be separate contracts. The swap transaction entered into in 1995 is not economically bound in with the equity swap created in 1997. These transactions will be created by different traders within each contracting party for different commercial purposes. Indeed, absent that assertion that they are one in the standard form master agreement, there would be no question but that they were separate agreements. However, the rigid application of the provisions in the documentation and the organisation of payments under both transactions would cause there to be only one net amount paid between the parties under the interest rate swap and the equity swap. Therefore, the argument raised by the single agreement approach would be that there is only one executory contract which obliges performance by reference to two, commercially distinct transactions.

3–37 The difficulty with following ISDA's single agreement analysis to its logical conclusion (*i.e.* that there is only one executory contract created across all of the parties' derivatives transactions) is two-fold. First, it is not clear at what time that executory contract would ever be performed and completed. By definition, it would appear that an "executory contract" must be capable of "execution". Rather, it would appear that the contract would be either in action or in abeyance waiting for new transactions to be created under its provisions. That is the way that the markets treat a master agreement—it is an agreement as to the "rules of the game" governing all of the contracts entered into by them, where each individual transaction is therefore to be considered as a separate playing of the game. Therefore, it is suggested that the better approach would be to consider each transaction as an individual executory contract for which it is possible to identify the expiry date. The master agreement should be considered to be a standard form of agreement which incorporates standardised terms into the individual transactions without binding commercially distinct agreements into one contract for legal-analytical purposes.[34]

---

[32] See, for example, Golden speaking at "*OTC Derivatives, the Legal and Regulatory Challenge*", May 31, 1997, London (IBC U.K. Conferences).

[33] See, for example, section 3 of the *ISDA Multicurrency Master Agreement* 1992, *op cit.*

[34] Alternatively, it could be said that there is only one "single agreement", as ISDA would define it, in relation to transactions which are actually subject to payment netting. Otherwise, there cannot be a presumption that there is one single contract rather than separate agreements because the parties are not *de facto* treating the transactions as being capable of set-off. While the reason for this failure to setoff comprehensively is often as a result of the practical difficulty of establishing operations systems which are capable of matching amounts owed under different currencies and in different jurisdictions.

3–38 Secondly, it is not clear on the terms of these agreements what happens if one form of derivative transaction (for example, an equity swap) becomes unenforceable under the regulatory regime governing one of the counterparties, in circumstances where there are a number of other types of transaction (for example, interest rate swaps) unexpired between them. It could be said that the ISDA approach requires the termination of all contracts, both interest rate swaps and equity swaps, because they are to be considered as one large, executory contract. This would appear to be contrary to the parties' intentions. As a result, it is likely that the parties would terminate, or seeking to repackage the void equity swaps, while maintaining the valid interest rate swaps. Again, the treatment of the transactions as being separate would seem to require that they are not treated as one, executory contract but rather as separate contracts.

Executory expectation

3–39 There will be situations in which the expectation of the parties will be that the contract is intended to be an executory one. For example, the creation of a 10–year interest rate swap between X bank and Y Ltd with the express purpose of altering the obligations which Y has in its long-term debt, would appear to fit in with the executory contract analysis in the following situation. Where Y is exposed to rises in interest rates over the life of a 10–year loan, Y would be seeking a contract which will ensure payments to it of that floating amount throughout the 10–year life of loan. Therefore, the obligation on X would be to make those payments in a way that makes performance over only a part of the 10–year period incompatible with Y's intentions on entering into the contract.

3–40 In many financial contracts, it is the guaranteed cash flow that is important. In the context of swaps embedded into public issues of debt, the swap is required to provide (often) fixed rate funding for the duration of the bond's life. Derivatives used in conjunction with asset securitisations also require that there be a certain receivable cash flow. Without the reliability of this continuing cash flow, the derivative is commercially useless. In these contexts there would be no performance at all in the absence of full performance. Atiyah locates the classical approach of the contract lawyer as being to favour the executory approach:

> "In modern times, lawyers and economists are accustomed to think of contracts—executory contracts for future performance—as devices for allocating the risks of future events. So prevalent is this viewpoint that it is commonly assumed that this is the sole function of contracts, and that every contract must necessarily allocate the risk of future events affecting its performance."[35]

He identified contracts as being "essentially risk-allocation devices, like simple bets".[36] The history of the derivative being seen as a bet has been part of the history of the swaps cases. The nature of the contracts underpinning interest rate swaps is that the transaction must generally remain executory prior to the occurrence of the risk. The problem is isolating the point at which the risk crystallises: whether that is at the payment of each obligation or at the ultimate expiry of the swap. In contract theory terms, the whole point of the transaction would be lost if the arrangement could not be made binding for the future.[37]

---

[35] Atiyah, *The Rise and Fall of Freedom of Contract* (Oxford 1979), p.176.

[36] *ibid.* at p. 3.

[37] *ibid.*

3–41 The issue is whether the promise-based, executory contract approach remains the best approach in ensuring the efficacy of that contract as a means of risk-allocation and of private planning. Modern contracts contain terms which enable variation and flexibility if these terms are given effect in the context of the over-the-counter derivatives markets where exactly such flexible response to change and risk is the essence of both the legal contract and the financial transaction.[38] In support of this instinctive[39] support of the executory contract analysis Lord Browne-Wilkinson identifies:

> "[t]he essence of the swap agreement is that, *over the whole term of the agreement*, each party thinks he will come out best: the consideration for one party making a payment is an obligation on the other party to make counter-payments *over the whole term of the agreement*."[40]

There is therefore an assumption that there has been a failure of consideration in the *Islington* litigation on the basis that an executory contract requires performance of all of the periodic payments before there has been any performance of the agreement.

The insolvency context

3–42 The most vexed issue in the insolvency context has been the feasibility of relying on contractual provisions to effect close-out netting.[41] The issue under the executory contract approach is whether or not liquidators are entitled to "cherry-pick" contracts which are in-the-money[42] for the insolvent entity, while repudiating simultaneously those contracts which will generate a loss.[43] There is a difficulty with seeking to close-out contracts which remain executory or require the creation of reverse transactions.[44] It is accepted that there is no difficulty in consolidating amounts owed so as to generate a single sum which is required to be exchanged between the parties. Complications arise where matured obligations are to be paid between the parties. In the context of swaps, matured obligations would appear to include periodical amounts where the reset date has been reached.

Remedies under executory derivatives contracts between solvent parties

3–43 Under an executory contract to exchange amounts of value between electronic accounts, the prime remedy of a willing party against a repudiating party is for damages equal to the contemplated loss suffered after exercise of the duty to mitigate loss. The measure of damages would often be any excess cost in replacing the contract in the market plus any special damages.[45] The damages may be predetermined by liquidated damage clauses, such as those represented by the ISDA termination provisions, in accordance with normal contractual

---

[38] See, for example, Atiyah, *The Rise and Fall of Freedom of Contract*, Atiyah (Oxford 1979), p.714.

[39] That is, without specific analysis.

[40] [1996] 2 All E.R. 961 at 993.

[41] See on this Goode, *Principles of Corporate Insolvency Law* (2nd ed., Sweet & Maxwell, 1997), pp.172–203; rule 4.90 of the Insolvency Rules 1986.

[42] That is, profitable at the date of expiration.

[43] See on this Goode, *Principles of Corporate Insolvency Law* (2nd ed., Sweet & Maxwell, 1997), p.178.

[44] For example, of the type executed in *Sandwell*, discussed below.

[45] The standard market contracts deal with situations like recovery of legal expenses (excluded under the ISDA code), the cost of unwinding hedges (generally held to be unenforceable by the Court of Appeal in *Kleinwort Benson v. Birmingham* [1996] 4 All E.R. 733), and the cost of replacement transactions.

principles. The appropriate remedy of a solvent party in the event of the repudiation by, or insolvency of, the counterparty is to rescind the contract. If the contract represented claims for debts both ways, then unquestionably the solvent party could not cancel its obligation to pay vested debts to the insolvent party and so full, reciprocal rescission would not be possible. In the event that the executory analysis is followed, rescission would be possible on the basis that the condition precedent to execution (completion of the transactions), had not been performed. This is the primary value of the executory analysis: it enables the parties to rescind across a wider section of payments. It is possible to exist from the totality of an agreement rather than relying on it being partially enforceable because it has been partly performed.

3–44 Where there is only a liability to make a net payment one way at the date of completion, due to set-off, the availability of reciprocity is altered and it may affect the suitability of rescission. At first blush, rescission is made simpler by the composite executory contract analysis because it makes calculation of the amounts to be repaid more straightforward. However, the incorporation of separate contracts into a single master agreement, makes it equally feasible to achieve rescission across the spread of swaps transactions on the basis of the ISDA "single contract approach" considered above.

The Repayment Analysis

3–45 The repayment analysis is one suggested by Hobhouse J. in analysing the set-off of amounts owed under individual transactions contracted under the derivative.

As Hobhouse J. held:

> "where there have been cross-payments in respect of the same swap, reverse payments pro tanto reduce or reverse the pre-existing equity. Since the payments were made pursuant to the same void transaction, they fall to be looked at together and there is no equity in respect of one payment independent of the equity in respect of the others."[46]

As considered below,[47] it is not obvious why the reverse swap is to be considered to be part of the original swap transaction rather than being an entirely separate swap transaction. A reverse swap is either a cancellation of a previous contract by the creation of its economic mirror, or a form of perfect hedge entered into separately so that the two cancel each other out from an economic standpoint. The better view must be that a reverse swap is a separate transaction which cancels out the original swap arithmetically.

3–46 The implications of the repayment analysis can be seen in the Court of Appeal decision in *Kleinwort Benson v. Birmingham City Council*[48] where the court was specifically asked to consider the availability of the defence of "passing on". The bank contended that the defence of passing on should be available to it on the basis that it had entered into further interest rate swap agreements with third parties to "hedge" its risk under the agreement with the local authority. It was this hedge that was said to constitute the passing on. The reason for that was the amount owed to the third party would be the inverse to that owed to or received from the local authority—the value of the hedge would be calculated to move in

[46] [1994] 4 All E.R. 890 at 937.

[47] In the discussion of the decision of the High Court.

[48] [1996] 4 All E.R. 733.

an opposite and roughly equal way to the value of the main contract. The Court of Appeal held that the hedging agreement was not a part of the main agreement with the local authority and therefore amounts paid under it would not attract the defence of passing on.

3–47 The decision of the Court of Appeal in *Birmingham* is predicated on the difficult proposition advanced by Hobhouse J. that, when reciprocal payments are made under an interest rate swap, "the later payment is treated as, *pro tanto*, repayment of the earlier sum paid by the other party".[49] There are three issues to confront here: two practical ones and a theoretical one. The first practical problem is that there are not usually two payments made—rather, payment netting applies and only one amount of money is transferred on a net basis. Therefore, there is a difficulty with saying that a single payment is a repayment of an amount which was never paid.

3–48 The second practical problem is whether the reference to a "*re*payment" made by Hobhouse J. means a payment which has in fact already been made or is simply an analytical device meant to connote some form of reciprocity. There is insufficient evidence available in the judgments to know whether or not there were *any* instances in which full payments were made reciprocally, and not on a net basis, such that the "repayment hypothesis" could have some grounding in fact. It seems unlikely that this was the case—it would be very exceptional for payment netting not to be used in the mature derivatives markets.[50] Even when dealing with illiquid assets, most derivatives contracts contain some formula by which a net amount can be calculated. The appointment of a calculation agent between the parties is done with exactly this in mind.[51] It is possible then that his Lordship meant to refer to payments made reciprocally but which were satisfied by the exchange of a single, net amount by the party that owed the surplus.

3–49 The theoretical question is then: how should an interest rate swap be analysed by the application of the structure proposed by Hobhouse J.? At one level there is a single contract under which the parties agree to make reciprocal payments which are reduced to single net amount and that net amount is paid across (as in the single executory contract analysis). However, many models for calculating the appropriate pricing structure of an interest rate swap would analyse that swap as a series of mutual debts to be made between the parties, all binding from the time of the creation of the "agreement" but to be considered as separately enforceable (considered below in the "mutual debts analysis"). Thus there would be no single executory contract in this latter approach, but rather a series of executory contracts which may or may not be performed. In either event, the proper analysis of the contract would not consider payments made under that contract to be *repayments* of one another. Payments under the contract are amounts payable one way calculated after set-off of simultaneous, reciprocal obligations.

---

[49] [1994] 4 All E.R. 890 at 929, *per* Hobhouse J. and affirmed at [1996] 4 All E.R. 733 at 738 *per* Evans L.J.

[50] As considered below in *Liquidity Risk,* financial institutions seek to remain liquid. It would therefore be an illiquid policy which required the total amount of an obligation be paid by A to B, when B owed a reciprocal amount under the same transaction. For that financial institution the impact on its capital adequacy position would be in respect of the gross amount of its obligation rather than the considerably smaller net amount. There is nothing in Hobhouse J.'s account of the facts to indicate that the parties were doing anything other than payment netting.

[51] As considered above the calculation agent is person, whether or not an agent of one of the parties, appointed to perform any necessary calculations of termination provisions, or of the level of appropriate indicies, by the parties.

3–50 However, an instructive example of the feasibility of the "repayment analysis" is observable from the *Sandwell* litigation. Under the interest rate swap entered into in that example, amounts payable under the four transactions at issue were calculated by reference to a notional amount of £5 million with a 5 year maturity period. The financial institution, Kleinwort Benson, paid a fixed rate of 11.75 per cent semi-annually. The local authority, Sandwell, paid a floating amount calculated by reference to the sterling LIBOR rate on a quarterly basis. It is potentially this mismatch which constituted the *re*payment referred to by Hobhouse J.

3–51 The mismatch between payments dates observable in *Sandwell*[52] complicates the payment netting position. The mismatching element of this swap structure raises a broader issue with reference to Hobhouse J.'s analysis of the payment structure. His Lordship considered each payment to be properly analysed as a repayment of an earlier amount. Where payments are made strictly on separate days, then it is possible to consider the latter payment in time to relate to the "earlier payment". However, it is not clear that this repayment analysis will always be compelling because in most swaps transactions payments will be made on the same day to enable payment netting to take place.

3–52 Therefore, the analysis based on "repayment" does not appear to operate on any basis of practical or theoretical fact, unless there is an express or *de facto* mismatch in the payment dates. As a result, its utility as a fiction appears to be similarly limited. It does not reflect any of the risk management or pricing-motivated analyses that form the parties' contractual common intention. It is therefore submitted that the repayment analysis, while accepted by the Court of Appeal[53] as a workable analysis, is not without difficulties in some situations and does not constitute a typical analysis of swaps transactions in most situations.

The Mutual Debts Analysis

3–53 The two analyses discussed above have acknowledged that over the life of a derivative transaction there are reciprocal payments made. The mutual debts analysis is predicated on the following construction of those payments: where periodical payments are required to be made by each party to a swap which will continue over time until expiry, each payment made by each party should be seen as a distinct contractual obligation. This approach, predicated on the existence of a distinct contract governing each payment between the parties where those payments are said to have no nexus with one another, runs counter to the approach taken by the ISDA form of master agreement. Evidently there will be situations where this approach will not be supportable on the facts. For example, in the hypothetical used above of X bank and Y Ltd seeking to manage Y's interest rate liabilities over a 10–year period, it would be impossible to sustain an analysis based on any reading of that contract other than that each payment over 10 years is aimed to manage the underlying interest rate risk. Therefore, there is a necessary nexus between the payments.

3–54 However, it would be possible to repackage those payments. Where the agreement is priced as a series of separate forwards compelling a fixed rate payment to acquire the forward (analogous to a payment of a premium) and a repayment of a floating amount calculated by reference to an interest rate, the individual

---

[52] *Kleinwort Benson v. Sandwell Borough Council* [1994] 4 All E.R. 890, *per* Hobhouse J.

[53] *Kleinwort Benson v. Birmingham C.C.* [1996] 4 All E.R. 733.

payments are linked to10–year debt but are not necessarily linked to one another. Thus it would be possible to create a structure in which the parties agreed to reciprocal payments on a one-off basis but which operate *de facto* at regular intervals.[54] In this way a 10–year debt obligation would be hedged by using a series of forward rate agreements which require one-off payments at given dates. The last of the forward rate agreements would have an effective settlement date approximately 10 years from its trade date. Clearly, this structure would be open to an analysis that its substantive purpose was to create an interest rate swap. However, there is nothing unusual in the creation of forward rate agreements with a long lead-time. Provided that the agreement was carried into effect in the manner which was set out in the documentation, there is no reason why it should be considered to be inefficacious.[55] As considered above in *The Structure of Financial Derivatives Products* it would be possible to repackage the swaps as options and the options as swaps. As such, the creation of a contractually sound structure is a feasible one.[56]

3–55 If the claims were reciprocal, obligations to pay debts would be for the gross nominal value of the debt owing to it. Under an executory contract to exchange money, the prime remedy of a non-defaulting party against a defaulting party is for damages equal to the contemplated loss suffered after exercise of the duty to mitigate because there could not be said to have been any performance at all without complete performance. Under the mutual debts analysis, a debt would generate in damages for breach of contract the amount of money required to put the counterparty in the position it would have occupied had the contract been performed because each separate payment obligation would be considered to have been performed separately and therefore completed separately. The measure of damages would often be any excess cost in replacing the contract in the market plus any special damages. The damages may be predetermined by liquidated damage clauses, such as those represented by the ISDA termination provisions, in accordance with normal contractual principles.

3–56 The attraction of the mutual debts analysis, however, is that the amounts which are owed are smaller than the amounts which would remain outstanding under an executory contract. For example, assume the following contractual structure. X bank agrees to make four payments in a floating amount to Y Ltd., calculated by reference to a notional amount. In return, Y undertakes to makes payments in a fixed amount calculated by reference to the same notional amount.

January 1X pays LIBOR to Y[Payment 1]
Y pays 9.00% to X
March 1X pays LIBOR to Y[Payment 2]
Y pays 9.00% to X
June 1X pays LIBOR to Y[Payment 3]
Y pays 9.00% to X
September 1X pays LIBOR to Y[Payment 4]
Y pays 9.00% to X

[54] Commercially this would offer flexibility to both client and bank, while enabling the bank to increase its spread. The ensuing composite product would be more sensitive to market movements and therefore offer the client a closer risk management tool.

[55] To take a *Furniss v. Dawson* [1984] A.C. 474 analysis of the issue, there would be no artificial step in this set of transactions because each contract is priced, performed and settled at market rates and at arm's length, with a valid commercial purpose in mind. Therefore, the mutual debts analysis would be a feasible one.

[56] This aspect of the analysis is similar to the Financial Forwards Analysis considered below.

The mutual debts analysis would record that when X made Payment 1, that obligation was executed and of no further interest in the analysis. In fact, X and Y would set-off amounts owed in relation to Payment 1, such that only one amount was eventually paid in satisfaction of the obligations. Where Y commits an event of default during February, the issue would arise as to the treatment of payments outstanding. A mutual debts analysis would enable the parties to ignore payments on June 1 and September 1, where the master agreement provided that they were to be considered as no longer owed. For set-off purposes, the amounts owed under Payment 2 would then constitute the final amounts necessary to be transferred between the parties. There would need to be no accounting for the amounts transferred under Payment 1 because the mutual debts analysis treats them as separate contractual obligations which have been completely performed and therefore of no further relevance.[57]

3–57 Therefore, the amounts ultimately owed between the parties would be considerably smaller than under the executory contract. The effect in terms of systemic risk would be a reduced pressure on the surviving assets of Y by reducing the size of both receivables and payables. Particularly where the purpose of the transaction is speculation or arbitrage, the courts would not be failing to effect the contractual intention of the parties to hedge an existing cash flow with a cash stream of equivalent time to expiry.

3–58 The appropriate remedy of a solvent party in the event of the repudiation by, or insolvency of, the counterparty to a cash-settled transaction is to rescind the contract. If the contract represented claims for debts both ways, then the solvent party could not cancel its obligation to pay vested debts to the insolvent party and so rescission would not be possible. Rescission requires it to be possible for the parties to be placed in the position they occupied previously. It is contended that the "mutual debts analysis" enables a cleaner form of rescission because you only have to cancel one of a number of debts. It would be said to be "cleaner" in the sense that performance is effected without measurement of the replacement cost of executed payments. On the other hand, the single executory contract approach contains complications because it makes rescission difficult in choosing between executed and non-executed payments.[58]

The Condition Precedent Analysis

3–59 The condition precedent analysis takes as its starting point the obligation that payment is only required, in connection with option and forward transactions in particular, where there is some condition precedent satisfied. In these circumstances that condition precedent would mean the movement of market rates such that payment was required to be made at the settlement date. In the case of the forward this would mean the compulsory payment made on the settlement date; in the case of an option which is in-the-money at the exercise date. In this way, the interest rate swap agreement can be read as being made up of a series of individual contracts all subject to a condition precedent. The floating rate payer would be required to make a payment in the event that the floating rate

---

[57] The approach of the courts in *Islington* was not to consider any of these questions. As contended below in *Suitability Approach; Severance* and suggested by Dillon L.J. in *Islington*, *op. cit.*, it should be possible to sever the many obligations under the swaps agreement and thereby treat performed obligations as terminated and concentrate instead on amounts still owed.

[58] On this see the questions raised, but not addressed, by Hobhouse J. with reference to the part-performed transaction in *Sandwell* which was not appealed.

has risen above the fixed rate (by reference to the applicable notional amount). Akin to a forward contract, there is an obligation to make a payment of money as the buyer of the product where rates have moved against your expectations.

3–60 The payment is said to be conditional on two bases. First, the floating rate payer only has to make a payment where the floating rate is greater than the fixed rate. Secondly, it is possible that the floating and fixed amounts would cancel each other out with the result that there was no amount to be paid—that is, the netting provision would lead to no payment being made due to a mathematically exact set-off. Due to the payment netting provision, the condition precedent analysis would say that there is only a 50:50 chance that one of the parties will have to make a payment in any event. Rather than payments being reciprocal, at least one party will not be required to make any payment on each reset date. Therefore, there is a bicameral condition precedent in any swap transaction, just as there is no obligation to make a payment under a cash settled forward where the forward is in the money.

Financial forwards analysis

3–61 The "executory contract analysis" maintains that interest rate swaps do not give rise to separate debts: whether or not ascertained debts and whether or not contingent. The financial forwards analysis suggests that complex transactions should actually be construed as being simple transactions packaged together.[59] In the mind of the trader, a swap is often analysed as a series of forward transactions. A "forward" is an obligation to pay an amount of money, on a given date, for a given product calculated by reference to market movements. A swap contract requires payments of interest on a series of dates, calculated by reference to interest rate movements. On each of the interest payment dates, it could be said, there is a forward payment. It is therefore problematic to decide whether a single executory contract (looked at across the complete series of payments) is really to be analysed according to the financial engineer's pricing model as a series of interest rate forwards. The question then is whether a forward itself would be a simple obligation or an executory contract. There would seem to be no reason why a forward should not simply be an obligation to pay a debt calculated by reference to interest rates at a given time—it is executory in the sense that it is only completed at the settlement date.[60]

3–62 The role of the set-off provision in market standard documentation may affect this analysis. By catering for the set-off of obligations, there is a presumption raised that each of the series of transactions is a reciprocal debt. The contract specifically approaches the individual transactions as standing separately and being capable of set-off. The approach of the documentation is usually to create a master agreement, which operates as an umbrella agreement. Each individual transaction is then expressly incorporated into that master agreement. There are therefore two possibilities. First, the swap is an executory contract which requires elements within it to be off-set to reach the final, payable amount. Secondly, it is a series of reciprocal debts which are capable of being set off individually under the terms of a central master agreement.

---

[59] There is a subtle distinction between the financial forwards analysis and the mutual debts analysis: the former analyses the swap as separate contracts whereas the latter sees the swap as made of linked choses in action.

[60] executory contract analysis is supported by analogy with foreign exchange: *Re British Continental Bank* (1922) 2 Ch. 575; *Lisser & Rosencranz's Claim* (1923) 1 Ch. 976; and *Bank of India v. Patel* [1982] 1 Lloyd's Rep. 506.

3–63 The form of the documentation would therefore suggest that the individual interest rate swaps must be considered to be separate contracts. The question remains whether or not they are individual debts or individual executory contracts. There is no reason, in principle, why they should be executory contracts. The more rational solution is that they are reciprocal debts linked by a master agreement for the purposes of set-off. The master agreement requires that money is paid by each of the parties. It does not require that a delivery of money is made by one party for the other to have to make the reciprocal payment. Either party could be sued for a debt on the basis that it fails to make any payment.

3–64 The only circumstance in which the payments are linked to one another is in the settlement procedure whereby each party agrees in the master agreement whether or not to set-off amounts owed to one another either on the same day or in the same currency. This is not the same as being reciprocal. The reciprocity arises from the obligation to pay floating rate being set-off against the fixed rate payment. The issue of debt or executory contract turns on the chose in action. If A fails to pay, B can sue for the payment. This does not exclude B's obligation to pay A under the parallel leg of the interest rate swap.[61]

3–65 The question of which analysis wins out might be decided on the basis of what the documents provide for in substance. The documents will usually provide for a series of reset dates on which payments are to be made. Alternatively, the better analysis of a particular contract might be one agreement which requires action on a series of dates. Market standard swaps contracts contain provisions for the early termination of the transaction, either because of the default of one or other of the parties, or as a result of the agreement of the parties. How does this early termination provision affect the definition of the swap contract? Is this the termination of an executory contract or the extinction of a chain of mutual debts? Early termination terminates all of the resulting transactions. This would seem to indicate a composite agreement requiring a series of payments. However, losses or gains flowing from terminated executory contracts would be categorised as ordinary debt. Therefore, there is little practical difference in the two analyses for this purpose.

3–66 The answer, it is suggested, will turn on the approach taken by the contracting parties. The intention of the trader is to mimic the forward transaction. If the aim of the parties is to create a series of forward transactions, that would appear to be the most appropriate solution to the issue of whether the interest rate swap is a series of forwards or composite executory contract.

The Disjointed Option Analysis

3–67 This final approach is included for the sake of completeness, rather than to advance any probable correctness in the analysis. It stems from the decision of the Court of Appeal in *Vandervell (No.2)*.[62] Of specific interest is the decision of

[61] An alternative analysis would maintain that, if the swap contract does create reciprocal obligations to pay debts, it would be for the gross nominal value of the debt owing to it. However, it is not clear why it would be for the gross nominal value rather than a contract for a stream of payments. The debt analysis turns on there being a chain of forward agreements, grouped in pairs. The gross nominal value is not the defining issue. As explained above, the deciding question is on what basis either party can sue.

[62] [1974] Ch. 269; [1967] 2 W.L.R. 87; [1967] 1 All E.R. 1.

Lord Denning M.R. and that of Lawton L.J.[63] who sought to resolve the long-running litigation surrounding the attempt by the (by then) deceased Mr Vandervell to bestow a chair of pharmacology on the Royal College of Surgeons.[64] An option to purchase shares had been created and was held on trust for Trust 1, but money was taken from Trust 2 by the trustees who had chosen unilaterally, and without provision in the trust deed, to resettle the shares on the trusts of Trust 2. The traditional analysis of these facts, it is contended, is that the shares would have come into Trust 1, further that the trustees could not resettle those shares without the power so to do under the terms of Trust 1, and in any event not without equitable title in the shares becoming vested in Trust 1 on exercise of the option.

3–68 However, it was held by the Court of Appeal that the option rights simply disappeared when the option was exercised, leaving a gap in the beneficial ownership of the shares. Therefore, the shares were said to pass directly to Trust 2 because that trust had provided the value for them.[65] It was held, further, that there would be an estoppel in favour of Trust 2 in any event because it was in reliance on the receipt of the shares that the money had been extended in the first place.[66] This approach cuts against the common understanding that exercise of the rights necessarily and simultaneously translates into rights in the shares which were the subject–matter of the option in favour of Trust 1 which had full title in those option rights.

3–69 The impact of this decision for the derivatives lawyer is as follows: on exercise, the rights represented by an option cease to exist. There would therefore be no automatic vesting of those rights in the subject–matter of the option (the underlying security or its cash settlement equivalent). Rather, those option rights would be said simply to vanish. It is not clear on that analysis how property rules would explain the acquisition of the beneficial interest in the underlying property by the buyer of the option. It would be more natural to expect that those rights would then attach to the property which is the subject–matter of the option. It would appear that there is an equitable interest in the underlying property provided that two things have occurred.

3–70 The first would be the condition precedent that the option is in-the-money (in the case of an automatically exercised option) or that the option has been exercise by the buyer. The equitable interest on this basis would arise by virtue of the right to sue on the option contract for specific performance,[67] provided that the premium had been paid.[68] The second condition would be that the property at issue would be identifiable as the property specifically the subject of that equitable interest.[69] In the majority of OTC derivatives transactions, this will not be the case. It would therefore be an issue as to whether or not the

[63] Some comment will be made below about the judgment delivered by Lawton L.J. However, it is important to bear in mind the comments of Stephenson L.J., sitting with some discomfort in the Court of Appeal on this matter, having some "difficulty ... in what I have not found an easy case" and his hope that the matter would be appealed to the House of Lords. Unfortunately, no appeal was forthcoming.

[64] See *Vandervell v. IRC* [1967] 2 A.C. 291, HL; and *White v. Vandervell Trustees Ltd* [1974] Ch. 269.

[65] *Re Vandervell's Trusts (No.2)* [1974] Ch. 269, *per* Lawton L.J.

[66] *ibid. per* Lord Denning.

[67] *Chinn v. Collins* [1981] A.C. 533, HL, especially *per* Lord Wilberforce at 548; see also *Oughtred v. IRC* [1960] A.C. 206.

[68] On this point see Hayton and Marshall, *Cases and Commentary on the Law of Trusts and Equitable Obligations* (Sweet & Maxwell, 1996), p.93, 72n, and *Oughtred v. IRC* [1960] A.C. 206, *per* Lord Cohen; and *Chinn v. Collins* [1981] A.C. 533, HL, *infra*, *per* Lord Wilberforce at 548.

[69] *Re Goldcorp (in receivership)* [1995] 1 A.C. 74 at 91, *per* Lord Mustill.

documentation or the credit support annexes made specific what would otherwise be purely personal causes of action in contract against the seller of the option.[70]

3–71 What is equally difficult to divine from the judgment of Lord Denning is precisely how the buyer of the option is then to acquire any rights in any property at all, if its contractual rights are said to have disappeared completely. On the facts of *Vandervell (No. 2)* there was a third party in whom the property was said to vest. However, in ordinary, bilateral transactions there will be no other person capable of asserting any rights in the property. Therefore, the rights of the buyer of the option would be said to disappear without their translation into rights in property or a right to sue the seller of the option for the cash equivalent of the property to have been transferred. It is contended that this analysis does not form part of the contractual understanding or intention of the parties to option contracts in the derivatives markets.

The particular problem of insolvency under these analyses

3–72 Set-off arises in two distinct situations for the derivatives lawyer. The first is in the context of payment netting, the second in the context of close-out netting. The reason why insolvency is considered in specific terms is that it is the primary concern for commercial parties in settling their documentation under derivatives transactions. Furthermore, as considered below in *Problems of Credit and Security*,[71] the impact of the decision of the House of Lords in *Islington* appears to preclude the retention of property rights, *inter alia*, on insolvency of one of the parties where the contract is held to be void.

3–73 Payment netting concerns the ability of parties to set-off amounts owed reciprocally in financial transactions. The standard provision for payment netting in the ISDA Master Agreement[72] provides that amounts shall be set off across potentially all forms of derivative transactions entered into between the same contracting parties. Usually this form of set-off will be restricted to transactions in the same currency although the only restriction on that provision in its market usage is the ability of the counterparties' electronic systems to cope with the demands of netting on that scale.

3–74 That this form of set-off by contractual agreement is permissible is not surprising. In the context of interest rate swaps, it was considered lawful by all courts in the *Islington* litigation.[73] While we are not given any of the detailed terms of the contracts, we are told that "the contract only imposes a liability to pay net sums and that was all that was actually paid".[74] This tells us that payment netting was in place between the parties.[75] That is, while the floating rate and fixed rate payers owed each other amounts in gross on the same date, the contracts provided that only the party owing more that it was owed should pay a net amount equal to that surplus to the other party.

---

[70] *Re Goldcorp (in receivership)* [1995] 1 A.C. 74 at 91, *per* Lord Mustill.

[71] In Chapter 4, *Issues of Finance and Law*.

[72] s.1(c).

[73] [1996] A.C. 669.

[74] [1994] 4 All E.R. 890 at 905, Hobhouse J.

[75] It is important to distinguish "payment netting" during the life of transactions from "close-out netting" which occurs on the termination of the contractual agreement between the parties on bankruptcy or the happening of some other event of termination.

3–75 This use of payment netting is a significant part of structuring this interest rate swap. Only one payment is ever actually made although two amounts are owed. It is therefore possible that on some occasions no surplus amount will be owed where the gross obligations set-off exactly. The manner in which this interest rate swap was priced meant that it would have required a large movement in sterling interest rates to achieve that result.

3–76 The second type of set-off, close-out netting, is the ability of set off amounts owed reciprocally on the insolvency of one of the parties.

Set-off on insolvency

3–77 The most vexed issue in the insolvency context for the derivatives lawyer has been the feasibility of relying on contractual provisions to effect close-out netting.[76] The issue under the executory contract approach is whether or not liquidators are entitled to "cherry-pick" contracts which are in-the-money for the insolvent entity, while repudiating simultaneously those contracts which will generate a loss.[77] There is a difficulty with seeking to close-out contracts which remain executory or requiring the creation of reverse transactions.[78] It is accepted that there is no difficulty in consolidating amounts owed so as to generate a single sum which is required to be exchanged between the parties. Complications arise where matured obligations are to be paid between the parties. In the context of swaps, matured obligations would appear to include periodical amounts where the reset date has been reached.

3–78 The term "set-off" is considered in a number of authorities. The Court of Appeal were required to consider that term in the context of cross-claims and set-off under section 28 of the Limitation Act 1939: thus "legal set-off". Lord Denning M.R. held:

> "These cross-claims must arise out of separate transactions[79] [i]f there is no separate transaction, but only opposing demands arising out *of the same transaction*, then no question of set-off, properly so called, arises."[80] [his Lordship's emphasis]

Hobhouse J., however, disagreed with the interpretation set out by Lord Denning in the context of a statute bar to a claim of set-off in respect of the first swap contract at issue in *Kleinwort Benson v. Sandwell B.C.*[81] The question then is, if that is the position with reference to legal set-off under statute, what is the position of equitable set-off? The discretionary nature of the defence of equitable set-off is seen clearly in *Hanak v. Green.*[82] The question with reference to set-off, in the opinion of Hobhouse J. is whether it is in accordance with equity on the facts of any particular case.[83]

3–79 With reference to the *Sandwell* case, the issue arose whether the transactions should be considered to be completely separate, or whether there was

---

[76] See on this Goode, *Principles of Corporate Insolvency Law* (2nd ed., Sweet & Maxwell, 1997), pp.172–203; rule 4.90 of the Insolvency Rules 1986.

[77] See on this Goode, *Principles of Corporate Insolvency Law* (2nd ed., Sweet & Maxwell, 1997), p.178.

[78] For example, of the type executed in *Sandwell*, discussed below.

[79] This returns to the core discussion of whether or not there are separate transactions in relation to payment netting.

[80] *Henriksens Rederi A/S v. PHZ Rolimpex* [1974] Q.B. 233 at 245.

[81] [1994] 4 All E.R. 890 at 945.

[82] [1958] 2 Q.B. 9.

[83] [1994] 4 All E.R. 890 at 945.

some nexus between the separate payments where they were made expressly in connection with one another. Thus, in the finding of Hobhouse J.:

> "Accordingly, the position was analogous to that of a running account between the two parties. Only one underlying transaction was involved—the first Sandwell swap contract. The successive payments merely altered the location and extent of the enrichment which existed from time to time. The earlier payments had long since ceased to give any cause of action to either party. They were merely part of the previous dealings between the parties which were relevant to ascertaining what, if any, cause of action either party had at a later date."[84]

In considering the "executory contract analysis" or "mutual debts analysis" dichotomy in the nature of the swaps contract, the issue arises which is the more effective approach when seeking to create a set-off on insolvency under the contract. Hobhouse J. found the following facts in relation to the position where there were a number of interrelated payments but some were made outside the limitation period:

> "Where there have been a whole succession of payments one way and the other in respect of a single underlying transaction, both equity and justice require that one should have regard to the totality of those payments and the resultant overall benefit and detriment and not have regard to some arbitrary cut-off point (*i.e.* in relation to the Limitation Act) unless there is some statutory provision which requires one to do so."[85]

It is submitted that this passage does not provide an answer to the issue that of the two analyses has greater utility. What it does indicate is that it is preferable to consider the totality of the payments made between the parties, rather than to separate those payments into mutual debts.

Close-out netting

3–80 This issue of matured obligations arose in the House of Lords' decision in *British Eagle International Airlines v. Air France*[86] where it was held that the divestment of an insolvent's assets was against the spirit of the bankruptcy laws. That case involved a clearing house scheme whereby airlines would net amounts owed between themselves on a regular basis. British Eagle went into liquidation still owing amounts under that agreement. It was held by the majority that to uphold British Eagle's obligations under that contractual clearing house arrangement would be to the disadvantage of the airline's other creditors and would therefore infringe the *pari passu* rule.[87] The decision of the House of Lords in *British Eagle* therefore suggested that executory contracts may not be rescinded on the insolvency of a counterparty, even if there is a clause to that effect in the

---

84 [1994] 4 All E.R. 890 at 941.

85 *ibid.*

86 [1975] 2 All E.R. 390, HL.

87 Goode has criticised this decision for failing to observe the commercial expectations of the parties: Goode, *Principles of Corporate Insolvency Law* (2nd ed., Sweet & Maxwell, 1997), p.182. In this, the House of Lords has acted similarly to *Islington* in imposing legal principle in a way which went against the parties' commercial understanding of their agreement.

contract, and provided that no asset has been transferred under the contract from the insolvent party.[88]

3–81 However, an express clause similar to that typically found in a derivatives document providing for rescission, it is suggested, has been held to be valid.[89] In the absence of a rescission clause, the position of the liquidator with reference to undertaking to perform the contract would be different, as in *Re Castle.*[90] In *Shipton Anderson & Co v. Micks Lambert,*[91] a buyer's right to rescind a commodity contract was upheld when the seller ceased payment under an express termination clause. It was at this level that the derivatives community rested uneasily over the question of close-out netting.

3–82 The position in relation to the right of set-off in company liquidations has been made clearer by the decision of the House of Lords in *Stein v. Blake*[92] where the provisions of rule 4.90 of the Insolvency Rules 1986 were upheld as being mandatory in circumstances where there were mutual debts between the parties[93] created before the person asserting set-off had notice of the insolvency of the liquidated party.[94]

Rule 4.90 of the Insolvency Rules 1986 provides:

> "(1) This rule applies where, before the company goes into liquidation there have been mutual credits, mutual debts or other mutual dealings between the company and any creditor of the company proving or claiming to prove for a debt in the liquidation. (2) An account shall be taken of what is due from each party to the other in respect of the mutual dealings, and the sums due from one party shall be set off against the sums due from the other. (4) Only the balance (if any) of the account is provable in the liquidation, Alternatively (as the case may be) the amount shall be paid to the liquidator as part of the assets."

3–83 The litigation in the wake of the BCCI collapse has generated a number of issues in relation to operation of set-off on insolvency. The decision of the House of Lords in *Morris v. Rayners Enterprises Incorporated*[95] considered rule 4.90 in the context of the ability of a borrower to seek to set-off its debt obligation to BCCI against a third party depositor with the bank. In particular this case concerned an attempt to use money in a tax efficient manner by borrowing on the security of a deposit, rather than simply using the money which constituted the deposit itself. In both joint appeals deposits were provided as security for loans to the respondent borrower.[96] The security documents purported to grant a proprietary interest in the deposit to BCCI by means of "a lien or charge".

---

88 The only qualification to this argument, under the executory analysis, is that no asset must have passed under the contract to the insolvent.

89 See, for example, *Ogdens v. Nelson* [1905] A.C. 109

90 [1917] 2 KB 725.

91 [1936] 2 All E.R. 1032.

92 [1996] 1 A.C. 243, *per* Lord Hoffmann; also the Court of Appeal in *MS Fashions Ltd. v. Bank of Credit and Commerce International S.A. (No.2)* [1993] Ch. 425, per Hoffmann J., affirmed at [1993] Ch. 439.

93 *Bank of Credit and Commerce International S.A. v. Prince Fahd Bin Salaman Abdul Aziz Al-Saud* [1997] B.C.C. 63.

94 *Stein v. Blake* [1996] 1 A.C. 243.

95 (Unreported) October 30, 1997.

96 An argument was raised in the second appeal that the deposit had pre-existed the loan and therefore ought to be dealt with differently from the other appeal where the deposit was created as part of the lending transaction.

Further, the documents asserted that there was no prior pledge over the "beneficial interest" in that deposit. Finally, the documents provided that the deposit would not be repayable to the depositor unless all of the liabilities of the borrower had been satisfied.

As Lord Hoffmann held in considering rule 4.90:

> "When the conditions of the rule are satisfied, a set-off is treated as having taken place automatically on the bankruptcy date. The original claims are extinguished and only the net balance remains owing one way or the other: *Stein v. Blake*. The effect is to allow the debt which the insolvent company owes to the creditor to be used as security for its debt to him. The creditor is exposed to insolvency risk only for the net balance."

This rule is clearly restricted to English law transactions and cannot control the private international law problems created by conflicting codes of insolvency law.[97] As Lord Hoffmann continued, the availability of mutual set-off in these circumstances is restricted to claims between contracting parties and not to claims in respect of third parties, for fear that this would "subvert the fundamental principle of *pari passu*" as established in *British Eagle*. On the facts of *Morris*, therefore, the separate legal personality of borrower and depositor could not be overlooked to give effect to set-off. As his Lordship held:

> "[The appellant] cannot manufacture a set-off by directing that the deposit be applied to discharge someone else's debt, even though it may, as between itself and the debtor, have a right to do so. This is the very type of arrangement which the House declared ineffective in *British Eagle*."

Therefore, the set-off must be clearly operational between two contracting parties specifically and cannot benefit the obligations owed by some third party to that set-off arrangement. This may have implications for margin-credit agreements in the derivatives area, which are considered below.

3–84 More generally, the impact of this decision on cross-default language is important. The ISDA form of cross-default considers defaults by a counterparty in the performance of a specific type of derivative transaction. In most situations, market participants widen this definition to include any acceleration of any debt-related or equity-related obligation of a counterparty or any associated entity specified as falling within the ambit of the provision. Where set-off is to be limited to obligations between contracting parties as a result of *Morris*, it would appear that the ISDA form of cross-default clause, expressed purportedly to take into account the obligations of parties who are not a party to the agreement, will not be able to take those obligations into account in calculating a final netted termination amount.[98]

3–85 Importantly for the cash-settled OTC derivatives markets, Lord Hoffmann is able to overcome the conceptual difficulty which founded the rule in *Re Charge Card Services Ltd.*[99] of taking a charge over a book debt held by the chargee. At one level Lord Hoffmann dismisses the much vaunted conceptual impossibility as being founded on the idea of there being a lien over a book debt in these circumstances.[100] However, an equitable charge over property is

---

97 See *In re Bank of Credit and Commerce International S.A. (No.10)* [1997] 2 W.L.R. 172.

98 The standard ISDA Master Agreement wording expressly includes specified transactions and specified entities.

99 [1987] Ch. 150.

100 See, for example, *Halesowen Presswork & Assemblies Ltd. v. National Westminster Ltd.* [1971] 1 Q.B. 1; [1972] A.C. 785, *per* Buckley L.J.

considered by his Lordship to grant the holder rights to resort to that property to satisfy some liability owed to it. This recourse can involve either the sale of an asset or the cancellation of some equity of redemption in respect of it. More particularly, a chose in action is accepted as being property capable of being the subject matter of a charge and therefore, it is said, there ought to be no problem with beneficiary of the charge being the debtor under that chose in action.

3–86 The resistance of the financial markets to seeking registration of charges in this context, considering that to be an unwelcome added cost of transacting, is subject to the proviso that charges granted by companies over book debts are registrable under sections 395 and 396(1)(e) of the Companies Act 1985. In the context specifically of dealings with bank deposits, it is "unlikely"[101] that there will be an obligation to register such charges.[102] This does not appear to remove the obligation to register charges created in connection with warrants over English companies. In the context of many equity derivative products, it is suggested, this problem may still be at large.

Specific OTC derivative situations

3–87 The arrangement in *Morris* mirrors many forms of derivatives credit support or margin-credit agreements where assets are pledged by Holding Co. to secure the performance of Subsidiary Co. in contracting derivatives with Seller. It is intended that title in property will pass to Seller where Subsidiary Co. fails to perform. What is important is whether there is a collateral agreement between Holding Co. and Seller for the provision of security which is separate from the master agreement and confirmation between Seller and Subsidiary Co.

3–88 The widespread use of margin-credit arrangements in the over-the-counter derivatives market carries problems of set-off with it.[103] Set-off under the master agreement has been considered above. What has not been considered is the ability of the parties to include the value of any margin-credit supplied within the scope of close-out netting. Seller should insist that property is transferred to Subsidiary Co. and that it is Subsidiary Co. which provides the credit support or margin-credit.

3–89 To maintain a tripartite structure creates difficulty in respect of set-off between the two contracting parties and the credit support provider. The courts have shown their reluctance to see consequential losses associated with hedging transactions as being linked to losses arising from the main derivatives transaction in *Kleinwort Benson v. Birmingham C.C.*[104] It is submitted that the same problems of establishing a nexus would obtain where Seller is seeking to enforce a set-off provision across the full range of derivatives contracted with Subsidiary Co., where only a part of that range of transactions is covered by the credit-margin or credit support agreement. This is despite the explicit assumption in the standard ISDA provision that close-out netting will take place across all derivatives transactions. The lack of contractual nexus would prevent such across-the-board netting being permitted.

3–90 Habitually the market place requires that the whole interest in any form of margin-credit is transferred to Seller with a contractual obligation to transfer to

---

[101] *Per* Lord Hoffmann, *op. cit.*

[102] *Northern Bank Ltd. v. Ross* [1990] B.C.C. 883, *per* Lord Hutton.

[103] This is a structure whereby party A requires B to deposit securities or cash in a form of escrow account such that A can have recourse to the value in that account where B fails to perform its obligations under the contract.

[104] [1996] 4 All E.R. 733; noted by Hudson, *Amicus Curiae*, November 27, 1997.

Subsidiary Co. the cash equivalent or assets equivalent to the margin-credit if all of Subsidiary Co.'s obligations are performed in full. Evidently this approach raises a number of commercial questions as to Subsidiary Co.'s willingness to transfer assets outright. Furthermore, there are a number of issues as to the manner in which the assets forming the margin-credit are to be valued and the manner in which the outstanding derivatives transactions are to be marked-to-market before their maturity.

3–91 The issue is considered below whether or not proprietary claims to margin-credit arrangements will be available in all derivatives transactions.

Matured and unmatured obligations

3–92 In the context of unmatured obligations, it is submitted that the appropriate analysis is to look at those obligations as reaching maturity at the time when the company becomes insolvent. This approach appears to be in-line with the principle that such unmatured debts be converted into matured debts available for set-off on liquidation.[105] It is further contended that where an unmatured debt is terminated by operation of some contractual provision, it is to be treated as matured as of the date applicable under that provision—whether the event of default is the counterparty's insolvency or some other cause. Thus, the use of termination events which terminate all transactions entered into between two parties, as with the ISDA Master Agreement, in themselves favour the application of the single contract approach.

3–93 The market standard form master agreements have the effect that, where the derivative instrument is properly analysable as a single executory contract, on the insolvent winding up of one of the parties, mutual executory contracts entered into before the insolvency petition can be terminated at market value. Where there is a provision in the master agreement to that effect, gains and losses on a series of terminated transactions can be set-off—subject to the counterparty nexus required by *Morris*. The standard provisions in the ISDA form of master agreement will operate to allow for netting on insolvency where there are two-way payments. It is advisable, from an insolvency perspective, that there be a requirement for notice precipitating termination rather than automatic termination under an appropriate event of default in the Master Agreement. One of the difficulties with automatic termination is that of establishing the correct mechanics to calculate the appropriate netted amount to be paid as at the termination date.

3–94 The provisions in the ISDA Master Agreement will further provide for set-off on the insolvency of one of the parties to a derivative instrument which provides for a contingent debt: for example, cash-settled options, caps and floors. Where it is the seller of the instrument that goes into insolvency, the value of the claim under the contract will be available for set-off. Where it is the buyer of the instrument that goes into insolvency, it is likely that the value of the instrument at termination will be available for set-off. However, where the value at termination cannot be ascertained or accelerated, it is likely that set-off will still be available provided that the master agreement does not attempt to divest the seller of its obligations to make payments under the agreement. As above, it is preferable that there be two-way payments and that there be a requirement for notice before termination.

3–95 Specific performance is not available for cash-settled, executory contracts in most circumstances because damages will be an adequate remedy. In the case

[105] *MS Fashions Ltd v. Bank of Credit and Commerce International S.A. (No.2)* [1993] Ch. 425, *per* Hoffmann J., affirmed at [1993] Ch. 439; see also Goode, *Principles of Corporate Insolvency Law* (2nd ed., Sweet & Maxwell, 1997), p.195.

of an insolvent counterparty, specific performance would be an impossibility in most practical circumstances in any event. The tidier analysis from the insolvency point of view is the composite executory contract view. The mutual debts analysis imports complications of performed and unperformed, and separately enforceable obligations.

3–96 The appropriate remedy for a solvent party in the event of the repudiation by, or insolvency of, the counterparty is to rescind the contract. If the proper analysis of the derivatives contract is that it represented claims for debts both ways, then unquestionably the solvent party could not cancel its obligation to pay vested debts to the insolvent party and so full, reciprocal rescission would not be possible. However, in the event that the executory analysis is followed, rescission would be possible on the basis that the condition precedent to execution, had not been performed.

3–97 The peculiarities of the ISDA Master Agreement complicate the picture with reference to close-out netting. There are a number of provisions which are not specifically recognised by English law. There is therefore a need to include a provision in the master agreement which provides for ineffective provisions to be deleted and for the remainder of the contract to continue in effect. The complication is clearly that a contract which has a part of its terms removed, will complicate the position as to rescission. Rescission in these circumstances is made simpler by the composite executory contract analysis because it makes calculation of the amounts to be repaid more straightforward. However, the incorporation of separate contracts into a single master agreement, makes it equally feasible to achieve rescission across the spread of swaps transactions.

3–98 The certainty of the netting position on swaps, collars, forwards and physically-settled options would be enhanced if full two-way payments were adopted. In the case of caps, floors and cash-settled options, the adoption of full two-way payments is essential.

Set-off on termination of agreement between solvent parties

3–99 Set-off provisions will be called into play in situations other than on liquidation of one of the counterparties. The range of events terminating a master agreement include pre-liquidation events where there is no eventual liquidation, such as credit downgrades, and other impacts on the legality, efficacy or commercial viability of the transactions entered into under it. An executory, cash-settled derivatives contract is an agreement to exchange amounts of value between electronic accounts, under which the prime remedy of a willing party against a repudiating party is for damages equal to the contemplated loss suffered after exercise of the duty to mitigate. The measure of damages would often be any excess cost in replacing the contract in the market plus any special damages.[106] The damages may be predetermined by liquidated damage clauses, such as those represented by the ISDA termination provisions, in accordance with normal contractual principles.

3–100 The appropriate remedy of a solvent party in the event of the repudiation by, or insolvency of, the counterparty is to rescind the contract. If the contract represented claims for debts both ways, then unquestionably the solvent party

[106] The standard market contracts deal with situations like recovery of legal expenses (excluded under the ISDA code), the cost of unwinding hedges (generally held to be unenforceable by the Court of Appeal in *Kleinwort Benson v. Birmingham* [1996] 4 All E.R. 733), and the cost of replacement transactions.

could not cancel its obligation to pay vested debts to the insolvent party and so full, reciprocal rescission would not be possible. In the event that the executory analysis is followed, rescission would be possible on the basis that the condition precedent to execution (completion of the transactions), had not been performed. This is the primary value of the executory analysis: it enables the parties to rescind across a wider section of payments. It is possible to exist from the totality of an agreement rather than relying on it being partially enforceable because it has been partly performed.

3–101 Where there is only a liability to make payment one way at the date of completion, due to set-off, the availability of reciprocity is altered and it may affect the suitability of rescission. At first blush, rescission is made simpler by the composite executory contract analysis because it makes calculation of the amounts to be repaid more straightforward. However, the incorporation of separate contracts into a single master agreement makes it equally feasible to achieve rescission across the spread of swaps transactions on the basis of the ISDA "single contract approach" considered above.

Chapter 4

Issues of finance and law

The legal context of risk

4–01 The globalised economy revolves around the exploitation and management of risk. Profit and loss arise from volatility in those markets. It is therefore a necessary part of financial transactions that there is risk. Both parties to such a contract enter into that arrangement on the basis that there are risks which may generate loss or which can be used to generate profit. Aside from risk of volatility in financial markets, there are risks specific to certain types of contracting. In the legal context there are two main forms of risk. First, regulatory risk: the risk that a regulator will seek to intervene in the use of some financial agreement between parties. Secondly, legal risk: the risk that a system of law will preclude the efficacy of a financial contract through the courts. The former refers to the control exercised by statutory or self-regulatory bodies. The latter concerns the application of the ordinary commercial and criminal law to the global financial markets.

4–02 The question which arises in this book, and which concerned the English courts in *Islington* is: how should equity deal with commercial risk? In the world of globalised, risk-inherent economic capital, the role of equity is more difficult to place than in a simpler time of Dickensian gentleman trading the stock of venture capital undertakings in the coffee houses of London. The decisions of the English Supreme Court and the House of Lords concerning interest rate swaps and other financial derivatives has served to highlight this difficulty.

4–03 The use of the equitable doctrine is clearly at its most comfortable when deciding on questions of fraud or trustee's breach of trust. Hence, the uncomfortable extension of the nature of fiduciary duties to encompass those situations which do not obviously fit within fraud or breach of an express trust but in which the courts have identified some unconscionable act. It is not in every commercial situation where the parties seek some remedy that there will be a clearly identifiable fraud or breach of trust. The issue must therefore be: should the principles be broadened to reflect commercial reality or is it the underlying policy of those principles that it is only in situations where there is fraud or breach of trust that the courts are prepared to intervene?

4–04 The development of a doctrine of unjust enrichment, for all that it remains in an embryonic form, suggests that there is to be some further category of claim and, possibly remedy, which is available in this context. As considered in greater detail in the *radical restitutionary approach* is that the doctrine of unjust enrichment has now been accepted as existing in English law[1] but that the nature and extent of that action is still at large.[2] What is particularly unclear in the commercial context, is the range of unjust factors which will trigger a remedy on grounds of unjust enrichment. Under the swaps contracts which the House of Lords held to be void in *Hazell* there was provision for orderly termination and

[1] *Lipkin Gorman v. Karpnale* [1991] 2 A.C. 548; and *Woolwich v. IRC* [1993] A.C. 70.

[2] See, for example, Burrows, *Understanding the Law of Obligations* (Hart, 1998), pp.42 *et seq.*

allocation of risks. It is not clear whether or not the frustration of those mutual intentions should constitute an unjust factor which should ground a claim for unjust enrichment.[3]

4–05 Rather, the courts concentrated on three main categories of restitutionary claim in the swaps cases: total failure of consideration, absence of consideration, and mistake. It was the House of Lords which paid least attention to the scope of these claims—Lord Goff choosing to say that these were not questions which fell strictly to be decided by the Judicial Committee which had been asked to consider the matter of compound interest alone. Indeed, the dividing line in the House of Lords appeared to be a simple conflict between the development of restitutionary principles to satisfy commercial expectations and the contextualisation of long-standing equitable principle. The issue is then whether or not remedies on grounds of unjust enrichment ought to be available in circumstances where there have been unacceptable risks taken by a party to a financial transaction or to reinforce the common contractual intentions of commercial parties in allocating specific risks that exist in their transactions.

Calculating risk in the creation of financial derivatives

4–06 In considering the role of risk in developing restitutionary remedies or in the operation of equity, it is worth remembering the way in which derivatives are used by financial institutions and end-users. A number of different entities will use derivative instruments in the current market place. The sophistication of the products has progressed from the deals such as the first swap between IBM and the World Bank where the interest rate and currency swap was established as a one-off transaction between large institutions with equal and opposite requirements for foreign currency. Derivatives are used by dealers as a hedging tool and a means of speculation. Borrowers use derivatives as a means of hedging exposure, providing access to a lower cost of funds and providing access to particular types of funding in the first place. Investors who enter the derivative markets use the products as a method of portfolio management, as hedging tools and as a means of speculating.

4–07 The central purpose of the derivative is risk management. As financial products and their markets become more and more volatile, the corporate treasurer is expected to be more and more sophisticated. The acquisition of funding at preferential rates is important in the globalised, downsized economy where management of risks can add to or detract from bottom line profitability. The use of the derivative enables the treasurer to minimise the company's exposure to the risk of movements in interest rates or currency prices. For the institution, the risks involved range from the economic to credit risks on counterparties' default or bankruptcy to the failure of management systems and procedures to cope with the detail of the transactions. As discussed above, the credit risk is something which is both priced into the price of the derivative transaction.[4] What is important for the legal context is to isolate the main risks and to enable market participants to establish suitable, legal means for their avoidance. Among the more important risks in this context are systemic risk, liquidity risk and credit risk.

---

[3] This point was untested throughout the swaps cases, the assumption appearing to be that the terms of the void contracts could have no influence on the case.

[4] See Chapter 3, *Swap Pricing Models*.

Systemic risk

4–08 Systemic risk is said to arise from the complex web of derivatives deals that are created between regular market participants.[5] As discussed earlier, participants in the market will enter into a transaction with one party and then seek to hedge the risk created with another party. Each market participant is therefore hedging risks with one another. Every transaction creates a hedging transaction which will in turn create more hedging transactions, and so on. Systemic risk constitutes the risk that, if one player in the market goes into insolvency and is unable to meet its payment obligation, this will introduce stress into the remainder of the market creating a risk that more players will be forced into a position where they are unable to meet their payment obligations because they have not been paid by the insolvent party. It is this "domino effect" which is the essence of systemic risk.

4–09 The market place has sought to introduce some protection against this form of total market risk by standardising market practices and standardising legal documentation. The work of ISDA and of the British Bankers Association (BBA), among others, has been to ensure that termination provisions, payment systems and netting provisions are both standardised and legally effective. This is the source of the derivatives market's particular concern about the decisions affecting local authorities. At one level, the finding in *Hazell* that local authorities were not capable to enter into interest rate swaps caused concern with reference to deals with local authorities. However, the greater disquiet has been caused by the manner in which English law has both failed to enforce the terms of those standard market contracts and the denial of proprietary remedies to market participants.

Liquidity Risk

4–10 The core concern which is posed by systems of insolvency law is the ability of a solvent party to a transaction to enforce the contract against an insolvent party. The risks are similar where one party is unable to perform under the agreement for reasons other than insolvency. While there is not the same risk of an inability to recover any money from the defaulting party, there is the risk that an open position is created by the hedge to the defaulted transaction, that the economic purpose for which the contract was created will be frustrated and that inability to receive payment will add to systemic risk. Where market participants are unable to perform, the risk posed by financial derivatives is a haemorrhaging of liquidity. The notion of liquidity is different from solvency, but the economic risks are similar. The aim of a treasury function within a trading company or bank is to provide liquidity without impacting on the solvency of the entity in one way or another. Liquidity means matching obligations with ability to pay. Derivatives markets aim to add to this pool of liquidity as well as to add speculative opportunities. Where payment in full under derivatives contracts is precluded by operation of law, there is an increased level of liquidity risk in the market place.

Credit Risk

4–11 The control of these risks lie in enforcing a due diligence review in all circumstances of a prospective market counterparty's credit status before signing conduct of business contracts, the taking of collateral and broader use of parental

---

[5] See, for example, Campbell and Picciotto, "Regulating Futures Markets", W.G. Hart Workshop, London 1998.

guarantees. However, there would be a need to establish the underlying legal efficacy of any credit support structure that is created.

4–12 There are credit risks associated simply with derivatives products themselves, aside from the credit risks associated with market counterparties. The strategies of companies entering into derivatives contracts are as risky as the movements in the markets themselves. There is an inherent danger if these products remain off-balance sheet. The markets need to know about the exposure of the counterparties with which they are dealing. Trade creditors need to know whether the company it is supplying can meet its obligations and banks need to know more about the risks involved in the companies to which they are lending money. Bound up with these commercial concerns, is a need for the markets to know whether or not credit support structures will be legally effective. Where the agreements created between the parties to manage these risks are held to be ineffective by the courts, there is a problem for the market place to assess their open credit risks, their liquidity and their capital adequacy.

4–13 As the use and understanding of derivative instruments has increased, the products have become "commoditised". That is to say, the increased use of standard forms (vanilla products) by financial institutions for their client base removes the requirement for extensive negotiation and detailed documentation by a clearer understanding of the available legal risks. The impact of court decisions that cut against common understandings of the position between parties adds to the uncertainty in financial markets.

4–14 The primary reason for focusing on OTC derivatives is that that is the area of the derivative markets which has shown the most grown and innovation. The bespoke nature of the products in this market, also mean that they can be tailored to specific clients and sold at a higher rate. It is also in the OTC market that the issues of credit and legal risk management are at the most important: most significantly centred on the risk of the failure of the counterparty to perform. In the case of structured financial arrangements with embedded options or warrants, credit risk is centred primarily on the credit-worth of the issuer of the bond or convertible security. This category of risk is better known as "inventory risk". The risks attributable to counterparty default when holding a bond are increased when there is an embedded derivative forming part of the structure.[6]

Risk equivalency

4–15 In pricing a standard financial derivative product, the credit risk component of the transaction would be calculated by reference to its risk equivalency, or some similar credit rating tool. "Risk equivalency" is the process by which the notional amount of a transaction is re-evaluated in the light of its specific financial or structural characteristics[7] to yield a figure which most accurately reflects the potential risk of the transaction. This is also referred to as the "loan equivalent exposure". Risk equivalency is necessary primarily because the derivative instruments are not funding transactions, like unsecured loans. The process adjusts the notional amount so that the actual and potential risks are appropriately quantified.

4–16 For example, an unsecured loan of U.S.$100 million represents a potential risk of U.S $100 million. An interest rate swap on a notional of U.S. $100 million with anticipated interest payments on current rates of U.S.$1 million, represents an

---

[6] As discussed in greater detail in Hudson, *The Law on Financial Derivatives* (2nd ed., Sweet & Maxwell, 1998), pp.253–265.

[7] Whether these characteristics are maturity, initial rate, frequency of payments, etc.

actual market risk of U.S.$1 million. All that is at risk is the interest payment of U.S.$1m and not the notional amount. The risk equivalency process involves the alteration of the notional amount to yield a risk equivalent exposure which is considered to be a suitable credit risk for the given counterparty.

4–17 The risk equivalency factor is then calculated by a twofold process. First, the risk factor is calculated to reflect the underlying movements in the rates or prices which govern the transaction. Calculating the risk factor is a combined process of measuring the underlying products rate movements over time and also the maturity of the proposed transaction. Secondly, that risk factor must be applied to the formula that is being used to calculate the price of the derivative instrument in question. The risk factor must be altered on a continuous basis through the life of the transaction to account for market movements or any added credit risks.

4–18 The business of performing these calculations is the subject of complex mathematical texts. Option pricing models such as the Black-Scholes Option Pricing Model and the Binomial Option Pricing Model are widely used in the derivatives markets and many credit calculation models use these fundamental techniques in quantifying risk factors.[8] While no model is perfect,[9] there is a sophisticated process at work of risk calculation in the model and of risk allocation in the standard form documentation.

Credit exposure of swaps: a worked example

4–19 There is no single agreed approach to the management of credit exposure to swaps. There are clearly differences between the requirements which the regulators will place on the institution and the institution's own credit perameters. Risk calculation methods have varying priorities: capital adequacy, pricing, counterparty credit, bank failure, systemic risk, and so forth.

4–20 The Bank for International Settlements has set out its two methods of calculating bank exposure to derivatives.[10] The Current Exposure Method ("CEM") concentrates on the replacement cost of the product (or mark-to-market value), together with a factor to account for future credit exposure. The Original Exposure Method ("OEM") focused on the future credit exposure without looking to the mark-to-market value. The mark-to-market value method is the method which is prevalent in the market among the financial institutions. It is also the approach taken in the credit support instruments discussed below.

4–21 The BIS has set out the manner in which banks are to allocate capital to cover their exposure to derivatives.

$$\text{Capital Ratio} = \frac{\text{k}}{(\text{MTM} + (\text{CEM}_{factor} \times \text{N}) \times \text{RW}}$$

where:
Capital ratio is an institution's target BIS ratio
k is the capital required to support a transaction
CEM_{factor} is the appropriate current exposure method factor
N is the notional amount of the swap
RW is the risk weighting.

The calculation of risks in this specific format belies an impression that swaps are

[8] See, for example, Banks, *The Credit Risk of Complex Derivatives* (Macmillan, 1994), generally.

[9] Calculation of risk according to a model will never predict earthquakes, political risk or calamities like the effect of asbestosis claims on the insurance market or losses generated by unsupervised traders.

[10] *International Convergence of Capital Measurement and Capital Standards*, BIS (1988).

simply about "taking risks". As the English courts have been quick to point out, derivatives will often be used simply for speculation. The courts also accept that derivatives can be applied for "useful purposes". There is a large amount of speculation inherent in these products even where they are used for risk management purposes. However, the speculation is in the form of risks being taken within clearly understood limits and not necessarily the taking of risks in a way that is recklessly akin to gambling. The corporate treasurer is seeking to manage market risk; the financial institution is seeking to construct a complex model within which that commercial goal can be achieved.
The next section considers the allocation of risks in documentary form.

OTC derivative contracts

4–22 The most important development in the law relating to over-the-counter derivatives has been the framing of standard market documentation by common endeavour of market participants through representative trade bodies.[11] The foremost in this field is the ever growing family of contracts produced by the International Swaps and Derivatives Association which has slowly adapted to cover the breadth of derivatives contracts which are contracted between private parties.[12] There are four aspects of the documentation which are of interest:

(1) the Confirmation;
(2) the Master Agreement (usually in a standard form);
(3) the Schedule to the Master Agreement; and
(4) Credit Support documentation

4–23 The aim of the following section is to outline some of the more important terms in the standard market documentation. In the light of the English courts' determination to ignore the terms of these contracts on the basis, it is assumed, that they were in any event *ultra vires* the local authorities in the swaps cases, it would not be profitable to dwell on them for too long. In the *suitability approach*, below, and in *Problems of Credit and Security*,[13] below, it is contended that it was neither necessary on principle to ignore the terms of the contract nor advisable in the interest of controlling systemic risk in financial markets. However, the structure of the contracts is also important in the context which this book will seek to develop as to the application of the principles in the swaps cases to financial market contracts in general.

4–24 Each separate transaction is contracted on the phone by traders. The traders prepare a deal ticket which evidences their understanding of the terms which they have transacted with their counterparty. At a later date[14] a written agreement is signed containing all of the terms agreed between the parties (a "confirmation"). The traders will not have agreed to all of the terms which are contained in the confirmation. Rather, the majority of those contracts will have been added by the parties' lawyers. It can take some weeks for these confirmations to be signed. In some cases (numerous, if in a minority) no confirmation is ever signed. The confirmation sets out all of the financial terms (agreed between the

[11] Most of these documents are based upon the English and American systems of law and therefore the civil code jurisdictions, principally France and Germany, have begun to develop their own contracts which incorporate their commercial codes in their entirety into the contract.

[12] The most important documents being ISDA, *Multi-currency Master Agreement 1992* (ISDA, 1992); ISDA, *User's Guide to the 1994 ISDA Credit Support Annex* (ISDA, 1994); ISDA, *Credit Support Deed* (ISDA, 1995); and ISDA, *Credit Support Annex* (ISDA, 1995).

[13] Chapter 4, *Issues of Finance and Law.*

[14] It is hoped not more than 24 hours later.

traders with some exceptions), payment conventions and accounts, governing law, and a large amount of risk allocation clauses concerning the status of the underlying security or currency concerned and the calculation of amounts to be paid (added by the lawyers usually).

4–25 The parties seek to deal with all of the risks at large between them across all of their many derivatives transactions in a single contract which seeks to incorporate all the separate confirmations under its umbrella by reference (the "master agreement"). The master agreement provides for payment netting and close-out netting. Importantly, it sets out all of the situations in which the broad spread of separate transactions under confirmations can be terminated. Attached to these provisions are the mechanisms by which that termination is to be carried out. Among the termination events is the failure of a group of standard representations relating to capacity to contract and to perform under the contract.[15]

4–26 The master agreement sets out standard provisions which are capable of adaptation, deletion or addition in a schedule to that agreement. The negotiation of such schedules typically takes months and can take years in many cases. Attached to the master agreement and schedule is often a credit support annex which provides a guarantee, a collateral (or "margin") agreement, or other credit support device. The master agreement will specify that the parties are liable to make all payments calculated under the confirmation and thereby links the obligation under each transaction into the broader web of transactions under the master agreement generally.[16] By specifying that all payments calculated by reference to the Confirmation are to be paid as a contractual obligation under the Master Agreement, it becomes easier to set off the amounts whereas the payments might otherwise be thought to be subject to different proper laws.

4–27 The ISDA Master Agreement specifies that it is a condition precedent of the formation of the contract under either the master agreement or the payment of any obligation under a confirmation, that there is no event of default, actual or potential, has occurred and is continuing at the time any such payment is made. This provision enables the parties to void the contract *ab initio* in the event that there is any hidden defect in the capacity or credit worth of the counterparty.[17] There is also a provision for the netting of payments which are either to be made in the same currency or in respect of the same derivatives transaction.[18] The parties' willingness to enter into this provision might be tempered by operational considerations which might make it impossible to net amounts properly across a spread of transactions or of different currencies.

4–28 The documentation will set out the manner in which the master agreement shall be terminated as a result of a "termination event" or an "event of default".[19] The mechanism for bringing the contract to a close is then provided at the discretion of the non-defaulting party in the case of a termination event. The usual mechanism is to provide for notice of termination to be provided by the non-defaulting party. This might be obviated by the agreement of the parties where they opt for automatic termination of their contractual relations.

4–29 These provisions dictate the manner in which payments made as a result of an early termination are to be made—reaching a single net sum rather than

---

[15] These provisions are set out below.

[16] ISDA, *ISDA Multicurrency Master Agreement,* (ISDA, 1992), s. 2(a)(i).

[17] *ibid.* at s. 2(a)(iii).

[18] *ibid.* at s. 2(c).

[19] ISDA, *ISDA Multicurrency Master Agreement* (ISDA, 1992), s. 6.

seeking to allocate specific proprietary rights. The ISDA terminology "Market Quotation" will apply where the calculation of those payment amounts is made with reference to price quotations obtained from a given number of market participants who are market makers in the appropriate product. "Market Quotation" is the amount which the market would require the non-defaulting party to pay on the date of termination to replace the terminated contracts. The alternative method is that of "Loss" which requires proof of the loss suffered by the non-defaulting party. While some forms of collateral loss are included within its purview, legal expenses are expressly excluded. The latter method is often easier to police although it does have problems of evidence in terms of loss and also in taking into account the full range of issues which can be included in the scope of loss. The cost of unwinding hedging transactions is one matter which the non-defaulting party would usually seek to include in its calculations, even the Court of Appeal has held that there is ordinarily no nexus between the main transaction and the hedging transaction.[20]

Allocation of risks in derivatives documentation

4–30 The English courts in the local authority swaps cases refused to consider the terms of the contracts entered into between the parties.[21] The core argument asserts that arguments based on risk allocation and suitability of product should not be dismissed because they are based on void contracts. As submitted above, the calculation of risk and the structuring of financial products to meet those risks are the foundations of the creation of financial derivatives. Furthermore, the attitude of the courts would appear to make it impossible to effect credit support for such transactions in circumstances where they are found to be founded on unenforceable contracts. It is contended below that it would be possible to adapt either equitable or restitutionary principles to give effect to the common intention of the parties.

4–31 The markets attempt to allocate risks generally by means of standard form documentation. In all cases, such documents are predicated on the basis that the parties can enter into the transactions which they purport to effect. The BBAIRS Agreement (British Bankers Association Interest Rate Swap standard terms)[22] provides as follows:

> "1. Representations and Warranties
>
> 1.1 Each party represents and warrants to other that:
>
> (i) it has full power and authority (corporate and otherwise) to enter into this Agreement and to exercise its rights and perform its obligations hereunder and has obtained all authorisations and consents necessary for it so to enter, exercise rights and perform obligations and such authorisations and consents are in full force and effect;
>
> (ii) the obligations expressed to be assumed by it under this Agreement are legal and valid obligations binding on it in accordance with their terms
>
> ...
>
> 5. Events of Default
>
> The occurrence of any one or more of the following circumstances in respect of either party ... shall be an Event of Default:

---

[20] *Kleinwort Benson v. Birmingham C.C.* [1996] 4 All E.R. 733.

[21] This discussion is amplified in *Problems of Credit and Security*, Chapter 4.

[22] Published by the British Bankers Association.

(i) failure by the Defaulting Party to pay any sum due and payable hereunder within three Business Days of receipt of written notice from the other party ... that such sum is overdue; or

(iv) any representation made or warranty given by the Defaulting Party pursuant to Clause 1 is or proves to have been materially incorrect or misleading when made."[23]

Therefore, the failure of a representation of ability to contract or to perform any payment obligation is a breach of the express terms of the contract which is capable of compensation in the contractually provided manner by the party which is unable to perform under the contract. It is not true to say, therefore, that there was no attempt to allocate risks under the express terms of these agreements. What is not clear from the facts of the judgments is whether or not there was any added credit enhancement provision available. It should noted that the BBAIRS terms were intended to be a default market standard agreement for market participants operating on the London inter-bank market.[24]

4–32 The ISDA (International Swaps and Derivatives Association) 1992 edition of the Multicurrency Master Agreement,[25] provides:

"1. Interpretation

(c) Single Agreement. All Transactions are entered into in reliance on the fact that this Master Agreement and all Confirmations form a single agreement between the parties (collectively referred to as 'this Agreement'), and the parties would not otherwise enter into any Transactions,

3. Representations

(a) Basic Representations

(i) Status. It is duly organised and validly existing under the laws of the jurisdiction of its organisation or incorporation and, if relevant under such laws, in good standing;

(ii) Powers. It has the power to execute this Agreement and any other documentation relating to this Agreement[26] to which it is a party, to deliver this Agreement and any other documentation relating to this Agreement that it is required by this Agreement to deliver and to perform its obligations under this Agreement and any obligations it has under any Credit Support Document to which it is a party and has taken all necessary action to authorise such execution, delivery and performance;

(iii) No Violation or Conflict. Such execution, delivery and performance do not violate or conflict with any law applicable to it, any provision of its constitutional documents, any order or judgment of any court or other agency of government applicable to it or any of its assets or any

---

[23] Clause 7 of the BBAIRS agreement then provides for "Compensation on Termination" whereby the Defaulting Party must fully indemnify the non-Defaulting Party from "any and all expense, cost, loss, damage or liability ... arising out of the termination of this Agreement pursuant to clause 5". There is amplification of the meaning of "loss" to include "without limitation ... any reasonable legal or out of pocket expenses". This would appear to capture the winding up of hedging transactions or the acquisition of a replacement transaction as out of pocket expenses.

[24] "5. ... With effect from 2nd September 1985 ... in the absence of clarification to the contrary, banks and brokers in the London interbank market will be assumed to be operating on BBAIRS terms for swaps of less than 2 years maturity within the defined categories."

[25] Published by ISDA.

[26] This would include the Credit Support documentation set out later in the Agreement and required to be specified precisely in the Schedule to the Agreement.

contractual restriction binding on or affecting it or any of its assets;

(iv) Consents. All governmental and other consents that are required to have been obtained by it with respect to this Agreement or any Credit Support Document to which it is a party have been obtained and are in full force and effect and all conditions of any such consents have been complied with; and

(v) Obligations binding. Its obligations under this Agreement and any Credit Support Document to which it is a party constitute its legal, valid and binding obligations, enforceable in accordance with their respective terms ...

5. Events of Default and Termination Events

(a) Events of Default. The occurrence at any time with respect to a party or any Credit Support Provider of such party or any Specified Entity of such party of any of the following events constitutes an ... Event of Default with respect to such party:

(iv) Misrepresentation. A representation made or repeated or deemed to have been made or repeated by the party or any Credit Support Provider of such party in this Agreement or any Credit Support Document proves to have been incorrect or misleading in any material respect when made or repeated or deemed to have been made or repeated ..."

In the event of such early termination, the non-defaulting party (on giving the necessary notice and allowing for any applicable grace period) is entitled to nominate a date on which the master agreement is to terminate. On that date, a single termination amount is to be calculated. That amount is a net amount representing the net position between the parties calculated either as the replacement cost of the terminated transactions[27] or with by reference to the loss suffered by the non-defaulting party. "Loss" in this context expressly includes a good faith estimate of "losses and costs ... including any loss of bargain, cost of funding ... loss or cost incurred as a result of its terminating, liquidating, obtaining or re-establishing any hedge or related trading position".[28] Also captured within the definition of "loss" are any costs associated with delivery of goods under physically-settled transactions.

4–33 Thus, the ISDA Master Agreement expressly deals with a broad range of events of default (including those relating to misrepresentations) and provides for a sophisticated mechanism terminating transactions and calculating appropriate levels of reparation and compensation. Clearly, there is an express mechanism for both calculating and allocating risks on the happening of a number of specified events. It is submitted that to overlook the impact of those standard market documents is to deny the risk allocation that is provided by the marketplace and by the individual, contracting parties.

The legal context of money

4–34 Central to the issue of deciding the swaps cases is the issue of the property which was involved in those cases. Earlier the distinction was drawn between

[27] Such values are calculated by reference to quotations from nominated market makers in those transactions.

[28] ISDA, *ISDA Multicurrency Master Agreement* (ISDA, 1992), s. 14.

cash-settled and physically-settled transactions. In the decided cases there was no issue of delivery of physical assets. The only situation in which delivery of specific property was an issue was in the deep discount swap cases where the extension of the original "loan" amount was essential.[29] As considered below, the resolution of the disputes by the English courts in these cases fail to appreciate the nature of the performance of the transactions and the intangibility of the property involved.

What is "money"?

4–35 The definition of "money" is a perennial problem for the lawyer. Indeed it is one that is so intrinsic to many legal conundra that it is rarely addressed explicitly at all. As set out in Mann's exhaustive *The Legal Aspect of Money*,[30] there is a real problem with achieving a comprehensive legal definition of the term. The term 'money' as used by economists and by bankers is equally difficult to pinpoint. In the mind of the derivatives professional, money divides between physical foreign exchange and "cash value equivalent". The notion of "value" is perhaps closer to money in this context. It is unusual for there to be real physical settlement of cash in financial transactions. Even at the level of currency swaps, it is usually an electronic transfer of amounts of a specific currency (whose value is calculated by reference to some market indicator) which takes place, rather than the reallocation of notes and coins. There is clearly a considerable amount of retail foreign currency business which is contracted through high street clearing banks but this is small beer compared to the money markets transactions and foreign exchange transactions which typically take place between financial institutions and the treasury departments of their corporate clients.

4–36 The use of electronic funds transfer is the reallocation of debts—that is, value held in electronic bank accounts is assigned to other accounts.[31] There is no physical settlement in the sense that is understood by the transfer of tangible chattels like sales of paintings at auction. The delivery of physically settled transactions in the foreign currency field (the for-ex markets) takes place at a virtual level—that is, no physical property ever exists nor is any transferred. Rather, amounts of value represented by electronic bank accounts are transferred. While there is generally an entitlement to claim delivery of notes and coins in respect of the value held in a bank account, it is rare for such delivery to take place.

4–37 Global capital operates at the level of the transfer of "equivalent value". It also operates at the level of arbitrage between different measurement mechanisms. An amount of sterling held in a bank account will have its market value altered from day to day, minute to minute as the value of sterling fluctuates in the market place. Sterling's market value will change according both to its value compared to competitor currencies and in relation to the interest rate which attaches to deposits of sterling in the money markets. Mann sought to develop a legal definition of "money". His definition is:

> "... the quality of money is to be attributed to all chattels which, issued by the authority of the law and denominated with reference to a unit of account, are meant to serve as universal means of exchange in the State of issue."[32]

---

[29] As set out with reference to the *Islington* litigation below.

[30] Mann, *The Legal Aspect of Money* (5th ed., Oxford, 1992).

[31] Smith, 'Tracing and Electronic Funds Transfer" in *Restitution and Banking Law* (Rose ed., Oxford, Mansfield Press, 1998), pp.120 *et seq.*

[32] Mann, *The Legal Aspect of Money* (5th ed., Oxford, 1992), p.8.

Mann deals specifically with chattels as attracting the quality of money. Either this definition is to be said to be defective because it does not include electronically held units of value, or, alternatively, electronically held units of value should be considered to be something other than "money" in legal terms.

4–38 Goode describes money as fungible in that any unit of account is capable of being exchanged for any other unit of account.[33] However, the issue remains that it does have to be segregated for trust or for tracing purposes before any proprietary claim can be established.[34] Thus, where a bank account goes overdrawn, the money that was held in that bank account is said to disappear.[35] This turns against the assertion made by Goode, that the nature of money is such that it ought not to matter which part of the fund is allocated subject to the proprietary base required to found an equitable tracing claim. The Court of Appeal has accepted that where a fund of identical units is impressed with a trust equal to 5 per cent of their total value, there is no requirement to segregate out a fund equal to that 5 per cent.[36] This decision, is however, in opposition to the speech of Lord Browne-Wilkinson in *Islington*[37] and the speech of Lord Mustill in *Re Goldcorp*.[38] As such there is a fundamental difficulty with deciding whether or not money is a form of property which, at English law, is required to be segregated in order for there to be a binding trust over it. Without the possibility of a binding trust, the efficacy of standard market means of taking security is negated.

4–39 The difficulty caused by these analyses of money, as Millett J. held in *Agip v. Jackson*,[39] is that it is impossible to maintain an action for tracing at common law where money was moved between accounts by means of "telegraphic transfer".[40] His Lordship held that the property which was being dealt with in *Agip* was really a transmission of electrons between computers which evidenced debts of money in the form of bank accounts. Similarly, the issues before the House of Lords in *Westdeutsche Landesbank v. Islington* were concerned with the payment, and sought-after repayment, of amounts of money represented by electronic bank accounts and telegraphic transfers. Indeed Lord Goff makes the following point early in his judgment:

> "... the basic question is whether the law can restore the parties to the position there were in before they entered into the transaction. I feel bound to say that, in the present case, *there ought to be no difficulty about that at all. This is because the case is concerned solely with money. All that has to be done is to order that each party should pay back the money that it has received*—or more sensibly strike a balance, and order that the party who has received most should repay the balance; and then to make an appropriate order for interest in respect of that balance. It should be as simple as that. And yet we find ourselves faced with a mass of difficult problems, and struggling to reconcile a number of difficult cases."[41] [author's emphasis]

It is as though the practical problem is so straightforward ("pay back the money")

---

[33] Goode, *Commercial Law* (2nd ed., Penguin, 1997), p.491.

[34] *Re Goldcorp* [1995] 1 A.C. 74 and *Boscawen v. Bajwa* [1996] 1 W.L.R. 328.

[35] *Boscawen v. Bajwa* [1996] 1 WLR 328; *Roscoe v. Winder* [1915] 1 Ch. 62.

[36] *Hunter v. Moss* [1994] 1 W.L.R. 452.

[37] [1996] A.C. 669.

[38] [1995] 1 A.C. 74.

[39] [1990] Ch. 265; affirmed at [1992] 4 All E.R. 385.

[40] [1990] Ch 265 at 279.

[41] [1996] 2 All E.R. 961 at 966.

and yet a number of issues of legal analysis arise concerning the proprietary and personal nature of the remedies, and the applicable codes of rules under which they should be awarded. Nothing but a stream of electrons passes between the banks as a result of telegraphic transfers.[42] The very nature of inter-bank clearing systems creates problems of identifying property.[43] The broader issues of property law involved in money laundering and tracing property in money is created by the very intangibility of the property involved.[44] The issue also arises: what constitutes a proprietary claim with respect to this type of property? Having the use of the property would connote an ability to earn compound interest on it. It is submitted that to arrive at any other measure of the proprietary rights attached to money would be too speculative because it is impossible to know how the money would have been invested if it had not been applied to the transaction between the bank and the local authority. In the context of financial contracts, compound interest is the appropriate measure of proprietary title. Therefore, the approaches of Lord Goff and Lord Woolf to award compound interest while expressly disavowing proprietary claims in *Islington*[45] appear to be counter-intuitive because the award would have been tantamount to a proprietary remedy.

4–40 It is in the House of Lords that much of the legalistic, as opposed to Lord Goff's common sense, problems with the case arise. Lord Browne-Wilkinson is not able to begin his analysis at the place where Millett J. in *Agip* places the modern performance of financial contracts by electronic transfer. Rather, there is a need to retreat into the history of money as a chattel—where the intrinsic worth of coins were equal to their face value. This requires Lord Browne-Wilkinson to begin with the analysis of the title to a stolen bag of coins, before progressing to consider the applicability of equitable tracing rules to deep discount and income payments made in *Islington.*[46]

Analysing cash-settled and physically-settled derivatives

4–41 A cash-settled derivatives transaction is one which is performed by the transfer of value equal to an amount of cash denominated in a given currency. In most cases, no cash will pass physically from hand to hand. Rather electronic accounts will record a recalibration of value. Similarly, a physically-settled transaction will not necessarily require physical transfer of assets, unless those assets are denominated in bearer form. Rather, property rights attaching to those assets will be transferred from one party to another. Where the assets are expressed to be bearer securities, but which are held subject to a global note held in a central depository, transfer of property rights in those assets will be affected by alteration of the register held by the custodian of that central depository.[47] Thus, value is transferred through some accounting mechanism.

4–42 In the case of commodity transactions, two possibilities obtain. Dealing on a futures exchange, acquisition of rights to physical amounts of a commodity which are in transit or to be transported physically, may be contracted by persons

---

42 *Agip v. Jackson* [1990] Ch. 265 at 286, *per* Millett J.; CA [1991] Ch. 547.

43 Oakley (1995) 54 C.L.J. 377.

44 Birks (1989) 105 L.Q.R. 258; Millett (1991) 107 L.Q.R. 71; Harpum, 50 C.L.J. 409; Goudling, [1992] Conv. 367; Swadling, All E.R. Rev. 259.

45 See below.

46 As Dworkin puts it in "A Matter of Principle" where those who want money are fetishists after "little green paper". See Elias, *Explaining Constructive Trusts* (Oxford, 1993), p.25. Even this analysis presumes that there is cash.

47 See Benjamin, *The Law of Global Custody* (Sweet & Maxwell, 1996).

who wish to acquire physical possession of commodities or by people who wish to speculate on the future value of the physical possession of those commodities. Dealing off-exchange, two possibilities obtain. First, a financial product may have its price linked to an underlying commodity to speculate on the value of that underlying commodity. Secondly, a financial product may have its price linked to an underlying commodity to manage a separate risk by creating a cash flow which moves in inverse manner to the risk which is sought to be managed. In the off-exchange examples, no physical transfer of the underlying commodity is effected. Rather, amounts of value pass between electronically held accounts. Where the underlying asset is an amount of a particular currency, physical transfer will not usually take place—rather, there will a recalibration of value between electronically held accounts. There is clearly little difference in practical terms between this form of settlement and cash settlement.

Specific features of the interest rate swap in this context

4–43 The operation of interest rate swaps perhaps requires one further level of analysis in this context.[48] Where the commercial purpose of the interest rate swap is to manage an exposure to interest rate movements,[49] the contracts require the payment of a floating amount by one party and the reciprocal payment of a fixed amount by the other party. In fact, these payments are then set-off such that only a single amount is paid between those parties. The buyer of the swap requires a cash flow to be paid to it which meets exactly its obligation to the lender which has created the interest rate risk. Therefore, the buyer of swap requires the full amount of value, or of money, to be paid to it, so that that amount can be passed on to its lender. In fact, the seller of the swap only pays a small proportion of the total amount which is required to satisfy the obligation to the lender. However, this small proportion is equal to the surplus which the buyer owes over the amount which it wishes to pay to its lender in interest payments, as a result of payment netting. Therefore, the substance of what is paid *de facto* is the difference (if any) between the real cost of the loan and the cost which the buyer is prepared to bear. The form of the payment is the transfer of value between electronically held accounts.

4–44 Where there is no surplus, the buyer is required to make a payment to the seller of the swap equal to the difference between the cost of servicing interest on the loan and the floating rate. The risk the buyer is taking is that, while its floating loan interest is advantageous, it is nevertheless required to make a payment to the seller which maintains the level of the debt cost at an artificially high level. As before, all that passes is that small proportion equal to the difference between the floating and fixed amounts. This does not match the description of the interest rate swap set out by Woolf L.J. in *Hazell*[50] as a mixture of floating and fixed rate payments made, seemingly, in gross.

4–45 The final irony of the interest rate swap is as follows. The buyer of the swap can only receive a given cost of funding. The market considers, given prevailing market conditions and the nature of the buyer's credit risk, that lenders should lend only at that cost of funding. Nevertheless, the seller of the interest rate swap is prepared to discharge that cost of funding in receipt for a cash equivalent cost of funding which the buyer considers will be lower than the cost of funding it

[48] Considered in Chapter 3.

[49] Rather than to achieve speculative return, in this instance.

[50] [1990] 2 Q.B. 697 at 739 and [1990] 3 All E.R. 33 at 63.

can achieve in the market. Therefore, the lender is prepared to grant a lower cost of funding via an interest rate swap, than it would be prepared to grant on a straightforward loan. Given the issues with the understanding of the property which is at stake in the interest rate swap, there then arises the problem of securing transfers and obligations surrounding that property.

Problems of credit and security

The impossibility of risk allocation in the swaps cases: (the source of the suitability approach)

4–46 The problem with the decision in *Islington* and all of the other swaps cases is that the courts ignore the *fact* that the parties *had allocated the risks of their transactions*. Leggatt L.J. considers that there is no substantive issue to consider on the facts of *Islington* when he held that:

> "The parties believed that they were making an interest rate swaps contract. They were not, because such a contract was *ultra vires* the local authority. So that they made no contract at all."[51]

Despite the exhaustive documentation created between the parties, the courts made no reference at all to any of the contractual terms agreed between them. Precisely why there was no such reference is not made clear. At one level it would appear that no argument was raised by counsel as to the efficacy of the risk allocation provisions. Perhaps this is an example of systemic closure: the practices of the financial markets not translating themselves to the legal environment. Indeed, the whole of the local authority swaps cases could be explained in autopoietic terms as the irritation between two separate, closed systems.[52]

4–47 A more sophisticated, or at any rate less cynical, means of approaching the issue would be to suggest that the terms of the contracts were of no relevance because the authorities were not capable of entering into them at all in any event. As a result, it would be appropriate to ignore any term within that contract on the basis that it had been found to be void. This would include, logically, terms dealing with credit risk management, as well as terms dealing with the creation of commercial interest rate swap obligations.[53]

4–48 That the contracts are of no importance in the context of the appeal emerges, from a close reading, of the speech of Lord Goff where his Lordship held that:

> "[Hobhouse J.] decided that the bank's right to restitution at common law arose from the fact that the payment made by the bank to the council was made under a purported contract which, unknown to both parties, was ultra vires the council and so void, no consideration having been given for the making of the payment."[54]

The issue is therefore one of restitution[55] in place of a purported contract which has been held to be void.

---

[51] [1994] 4 All E.R. 890 at 967.

[52] Teubner, *Law as an Autopoietic System* (Oxford, 1994).

[53] On this, see *Suitability Approach, Severance* below in Chapter 12.

[54] [1996] 2 All E.R. 961 at 965.

[55] Or the issue is one of the availability of equitable remedies, as in the speech of Lord Browne-Wilkinson.

4–49 However, the further question arises: would a guarantee be valid if it were annexed to that contract. That is, would the banks have been able to enforce the terms of any guarantee extended to them by the local authorities? What is not clear is whether the preclusion on entering into interest rate swaps must also be binding on any guarantee collateral to that agreement. If that were the case, it would follow that any credit support document attached to the interest rate swap agreement would be similarly void. Therefore, if the authorities had ring-fenced a particular bank account with an amount of money in it, held on trust for the banks contingent on the authorities' failure to perform under the main agreement, the banks would have had no recourse to that money. This would be despite the authorities' ability to pay amounts of money to banks acting at arm's length from them by way of interest or fees.

4–50 In considering whether or not proprietary claim ought to be available to the Westdeutsche in equity, Lord Goff said:

> "The immediate reaction must be—why should it? Take the present case. The parties have entered into a commercial transaction. The transaction has, for technical reasons, been held to be void from the beginning. Each party is entitled to recover its money, with the result that the balance must be repaid. But why should the plaintiff bank be given the additional benefits which flow from a proprietary claim, for example the benefit of achieving priority in the event of the defendant's insolvency?"

At this level is possible to say that a commercial party should only be entitled to recovery on the basis of a proprietary claim where there is some attempt to reserve to it some proprietary remedy. It is not this writer's contention that proprietary rights should always be awarded to commercial parties entering into financial transactions. However, the following words of Lord Goff contribute to the conclusion that it is not clear how the banks could have taken proprietary rights in the swaps litigation:

> "After all, [Westdeutsche] has entered into a commercial transaction, and so taken the risk of the defendant's insolvency, just like the defendant's other creditors who have contracted with it, not to mention other creditors to whom the defendant may be liable to pay damages in tort."[56]

The weakness with this reasoning is that Westdeutsche has not taken the risk of the authority's insolvency. Rather, it had sought to protect itself against the insolvency of the authority by means of the termination language in the contract and any credit support language it may have used.

4–51 Given the mutual determination of Lord Goff and Lord Browne-Wilkinson that there was no ground for the banks having a proprietary interest in any property held by the local authorities, the logical conclusion of their reasoning is that there would have been *no way in which the banks could have reserved to themselves any proprietary interest in the money paid to the local authorities.*

4–52 This alarming contention operates in the following way. If the banks are not able to enforce any credit support documentation against the authorities on the grounds that executing such documentation was beyond the powers of the authorities, they would have to seek to effect some other agreement ("the proprietary clause") between them and the authorities as to the title to the property. Where that proprietary clause forms a part of the interest rate swap

---

56 [1996] 2 All E.R. 961 at 968.

documentation, it would have been void on the grounds that the authorities did not have the powers to create such a provision.

4–53 The finding of their Lordships, unanimously, was that there was no reason for equity, common law, or any general principle of restitution to provide the banks with proprietary title to any property. Therefore, it is impossible for the banks to create a proprietary interest for themselves by means of contractual provision or guarantee. It is similarly impossible for them to rely upon operation of law—even express provisions in the documentation seeking to retain title appear to be of no efficacy. There is an elision of the laudable aim to protect bona fide third parties with the need to refrain from discouraging commercial parties to contracts under English law because they will not be able to obtain secured, proprietary interests in the property which they extend as part of their transacting.

4–54 There would have been only one route left available to them. With reference first to the deep discount swaps, that route would have been for the banks to hold the deep discount amounts[57] paid by them on trust for themselves should the authority fail to perform. The authorities' ability to use the money as required by their rate-capped position is thus complicated. It is difficult to see how there could have been retention of title where the contracts were held to be void and where the courts would not enforce such language. Express trust structures appear to be the only reliable method. Otherwise the parties would have had to enter into a stand-alone loan structure to allow the retention of title language to stand outwith the void swap documentation. However, that would simply have created an on-balance sheet, rate-capped loan which would have opened the authority up to surcharges. Therefore, there would be no effective, commercial means for the banks to have retained title in the money which they paid over.

4–55 At the time when the intention to pass title in the money to the authority was formed, the issue arises what risks were accepted and appropriated between the parties. Avowedly, neither party took the risk that the other party would be unable to perform the agreement (as set out in the BBAIRS and ISDA terms above). However, their agreement provided only for the payment of net amount to unwind the transaction and did not provide for any specific retention of proprietary title in the property passed.[58] Therefore, it is not proposed to consider the impact of the *Quistclose*[59] line of cases because there was no express retention of title as in those cases. The only point made on the area of *Quistclose* in the concluding ***suitability approach*** is that the contract was not performed, nor the deep discount payment used and repaid, in the manner envisaged by the parties at the time they formed their common contractual intention.

4–56 With reference to the vanilla interest rate swaps,[60] it would be simply impracticable to require that payments made under the periodic structure would be held on trust through the life of the agreement. The property forming the subject matter of that trust, value in electronic bank accounts, would be exhausted a number of times over thus removing all equitable tracing rights.[61] To require a static trust would again defeat the commercial purpose because the interest rate swap would be of no commercial efficacy at all. The use of language to create

---

[57] In *Islington.*

[58] *Re Goldcorp* [1995] 1 A.C. 74.

[59] *Quistclose Investments Ltd v. Rolls Razor Ltd (in liquidation)* [1970] A.C. 567.

[60] In *Sandwell.*

[61] *Roscoe v. Winder* [1915] 1 Ch. 62 and *Bishopsgate v. Homan* [1995] 1 WLR 31.

some charge over the property of the authority would similarly be void, annexed as it would be to the void interest rate swap contract.

4–57 Therefore, the practical commercial implications of the decision of the House of Lords is that it is impossible to retain title to any property or value passed in the conduct of a swap transaction which is subsequently found to be void. This result must indicate that the rationale behind the decision cannot be the correct approach in commercial contexts. The risk that is run is that the over-the-counter derivatives markets will simply seek to put themselves outwith the reach of English law so that they are able to achieve the commercial results they desire. The impact would be two-fold. As Lord Goff and Lord Woolf identify, there is a risk of the weakening of the lure of London, as the geographical encouragement to use English law, as a financial centre. The other impact is the inability of English law to regulate commercial transactions effectively where equity enforces not mandatory policy prescriptions but arcane delineations of principle appropriate to family trusts. While the majority approach of the House of Lords might be the better approach with reference to domestic mortgages and the subject matter of traditional trusts, it is submitted that it is not appropriate with reference to sophisticated financial transactions.

4–58 Martin joins the camp of commentators who identify in the bank satisfaction that they would pass title in the deep discount payment absolutely to Islington "and had been prepared to take the risk of insolvency".[62] There was, of course, no intention to take that risk absent effective netting provisions—as the BBAIRS and ISDA terms attest. The result is that property in the money passes even though the contract is void. If the contract is void *ab initio*, speaking simply logically, why should it have been effective to pass property in the money at all. This efficacy of the contract would appear to be in support of the original purpose of the contract, rather than returning the full property in the money to the bank to negate the commercial effect of the transaction.

4–59 It is therefore necessary to construct a model for the application of equitable and/or restitutionary principles which would provide a suitable result in accordance with established legal and equitable principle. This is attempted below in the *suitability approach*. First it is important to understand the detail of the approach of the courts in the swaps cases.

[62] Hanbury and Martin, *Modern Equity* (13th ed., Sweet & Maxwell, 1993), p.665.

Part II

The Central Legal Issues in *Islington*

Chapter 5

Equity and modern financial techniques

Law of finance and equity

5–01 As considered in the opening chapter, it is a truth universally acknowledged that derivatives are complicated. However, what the discussion of the interest rate swap cases misses is that they are, at root, very simple ideas, based on options, forwards and the quotidian idea of swapping.[1] Rather, it is the full implications of the courts' interpretations and analyses of those products that are complicated. The root cause of the problems considered in the swaps cases, and resulting from the swaps cases, is that these very new financial market products have raised very topical and intricate questions of the laws of trusts and of restitution of unjust enrichment. Complex subject–matter from the world of global finance has intruded on a seismic debate about the structure and future legal treatment of personal and proprietary rights to property.

5–02 The core of the problem is that the traditional rules relating to the availability of proprietary remedies sit uneasily in the commercial context. Principles which were created with family trusts in mind, do not respond well to the requirements and challenges of commercial contracts. As Lord Browne-Wilkinson said in *Target Holdings v. Redferns*[2]:

> "In the modern world the trust has become a valuable device in commercial and financial dealings. The fundamental principles of equity apply as much to such trusts as they do to the traditional trusts in relation to which those principles were originally formulated. But in my judgement it is important, if the trust is not to be rendered commercially useless, to distinguish between the basic principles of trust law and those specialist rules developed in relation to traditional trusts which are applicable only to such trusts and the rationale of which has no application to trusts of quite a different kind."

In-line with this acceptance of the need for equity to become relevant to commercial situations, it is contended that there is a need to develop specialist rules to treat cases such as those arising from the financial derivatives market, rather than to attempt to make new wine and old skins work together. It is somewhat ironic that Lord Browne-Wilkinson both sets out this call for the possible need for equity to adopt a new approach in the commercial context and then delivered the leading speech in the House of Lords in *Islington* in which the existing rules are consolidated in contradistinction to laying the groundwork for the development of such new commercial principles. At one level, it appears that equity is perhaps not best suited in its current composition to deal with commercial and financial situations.

5–03 There is a challenge for existing legal structures to consider the manner in which they interact with commercial transactions. From the earliest cases, the role

[1] On the nature of the different derivatives products see Chapter 2, above.
[2] [1996] 1 A.C. 421; [1995] 3 All E.R. 785 at 795.

of equity has been seen to be "to correct men's consciences for frauds, breach of trust, wrongs and oppressions."[3] It has therefore been concerned to mitigate the technical rigour of the common law with a moral code enforceable by the courts. As Mason summed up that development: "equitable principles were shaped with a view to inhibiting unconscientious conduct and providing for relief against it".[4] The problem facing equity is that it developed as a moral code responding to a cultural understanding of property rights in the seventeenth century which does not correlate exactly with the common contractual intentions of the parties to complex financial transactions at the end of the twentieth century.

5–04 Rather than focus on effecting the common intentions of commercial parties, one of the policy priorities for equity has been the "application of a broad standard in the invalidity of a transaction in which one party unconscionably takes advantage of the other, to create no injustice as between the parties ... but the consequential effect of that invalidity on third parties that is of more concern".[5] Broad–brush judicial principle places concern for innocent third parties high on the agenda. This can be discerned easily from the speech of Lord Templeman in *Hazell* where the situation of the innocent ratepayers of Hammersmith loomed large in the judicial mind when considering the validity of interest rate swap contracts entered into by the local authorities.

5–05 There is suspicion of the role of equity in commercial disputes. In considering the available remedies it is unsurprising that finance lawyers and bankers do not want to leave their well-being in the hands of equitable tracing, equitable compensation, constructive trusts and resulting trusts. As Mason puts it: "there is strong resistance, especially in the United Kingdom, to the infiltration of equity into commercial transactions ... [arising] from apprehensions about the disruptive impact of equitable proprietary remedies, assisted by the doctrine of notice, on the certainty and security of commercial transactions".[6] It is in response to these fears that those market places have sought to develop iron-clad documentation which allocates risks and imposes responsibilities in the event of a number of specified occurrences. The aim of the finance lawyer is the obviate the need to rely on litigation or the application of the courts' discretion.

5–06 As Lord Browne-Wilkinson held, there is a difficulty with the use of equitable remedies in commercial situations:

> "... wise judges have often warned against the wholesale importation into commercial law of equitable principles inconsistent with the certainty and speed which are essential requirements for the orderly conduct of business affairs."[7]

These principles are derived from older authorities such as *Barnes v. Addy*[8] as well as being discernible in more modern ones such as *Scandinavian Trading Tanker Co AB v. Flota Petrolera Ecuatoriana.*[9] For the finance lawyer, maintaining the distance between the counterparties and the courts is primary among the risk management function. The legal role is primarily a prophylactic one. However, it

---

[3] *Earl of Oxford's Case* (1615) 1 Ch. Rep. 1 at 7; 21 E.R. 485 at 486.

[4] Public lecture given at King's College London on March 10, 1997, reproduced at K.C.L.J. 8 (1997/98), at 1.

[5] Mason, K.C.L.J. 8 (1997/98), at 1, 2.

[6] Mason, K.C.L.J. 8 (1997/98), at 1, 5.

[7] [1996] 2 All E.R. 961 at 987.

[8] (1874) LR 9 Ch. App. 244 at 251, 255.

[9] [1983] 2 A.C. 694 at 703-4.

is clear that there will be situations in which the courts are required to impose its own principles in the resolution of disputes outwith the ambit of the documentation as the swaps cases have shown.

5–07 The growth of globalisation in the economy has led to a change in the way in which law is used. The availability of security and the certainty in remedies available are ever more important. The use of English law by commercial parties has become a growing part of the importance of the City of London in world of banking and finance. Its propitious location in the European time zones adds to its attraction, being placed between bedtime in Tokyo and breakfast in New York. This change in the nature of the global economy requires different things from the rules of equity which were developed to administer the property of private individuals and to ensure the proper behaviour of fiduciaries and trustees.

5–08 The concerns of commercial practice and the interaction with equity fall into two basic categories: taking security and obtaining remedies. These two concerns were considered above in relation to the pricing of financial derivatives. The pattern of concerns thrown up by these quotidian commercial issues mirrors, to some extent, the concern of equity between the availability of personal and proprietary remedies. The concern of the commercial negotiator is to be able to recover some specific property in the event that the contractual agreement is not performed in the way that performance is anticipated. It is within the expectation of bankers and their clients that money or value provided as part of transaction would otherwise be invested at commercial rates of return had the particular transaction not been created. Therefore, there is an inbuilt expectation that there will be some proprietary remedy available on termination of the transaction.

5–09 The problem is the intervention of some legal principle outwith the expectation of the parties: such as the avoidance of *ultra vires* interest rate swap contracts. As Robert Goff L.J. held:

> "It is of the utmost importance in commercial transactions that, if any particular event occurs which may affect the parties' respective rights under a commercial contract, they should know where they stand. The court should so far as possible desist from placing obstacles in the way of either party ascertaining his legal position, if necessary with the aid of advice from a qualified lawyer, because it may be commercially desirable for action to be taken without delay, action which may be irrecoverable and which may have far-reaching consequences. It is for this reason, of course, that the English courts have time and again asserted the need for certainty in commercial transactions—the simple reason that the parties to such transactions are entitled to know where they stand, and to act accordingly."[10]

5–10 The essence of commercial certainty is the minimal use of discretionary remedies. In that context, the decision of the majority of the House of Lords in *Islington* created a level of certainty in that there is little likelihood of a proprietary remedy being awarded outwith cases of fraud or breach of fiduciary duty with knowledge of that duty. However, certainty is obviated where the contractual common intentions of the parties are circumvented by the application of those same principles.

Leggatt L.J. in the Court of Appeal in *Islington* was moved by similar concerns:

> "... tempting though it may be to follow the path which Lloyd J. was inclined to follow in *the Afovos,*[11] we do not feel that it would be right to do so. The

[10] *Scandinavian Trading v. Flota Ecuatoriana* [1983] 2 W.L.R. 248 at 257.

> policy which favours certainty in commercial transactions is so antipathetic to the form of equitable intervention invoked by the charterers in the present case that we do not think it would be right to extend that jurisdiction to relieve time charterers from the consequences of withdrawal."[12]

Indeed, Lord Lloyd echoed in the House of Lords in *Westdeutsche Landesbank v. Islington L.B.C.* his own reluctance to intervene and apply fairness in commercial situations. The more complicated question is in deciding which form of commercial certainty ought to be enforced. In the swaps cases, it is not at all clear that commercial certainty would be promoted by failing to apply the understanding evidenced by the contractual, standard documentation.

Concretisation of equitable principles

5–11 One development in the principles of equity has been the increased rigidity of the tests that the courts are applying, particularly in commercial contexts. This tendency has been particularly discernible in the speeches of Lord Browne-Wilkinson in *Islington* and *Target Holdings*,[13] and in the speech of Lord Nicholls in *Royal Brunei Airlines v. Tan.*[14] In each of these cases there is a two-fold development: the solidifying of the appropriate test, and a restatement of the principles on which equity operates. Not only have the tests changed the law but they have moved it towards a greater level of certainty which typifies common law, rather than equitable principles. There is a reduced discretion in the courts to apply equitable remedies. Rather, the House of Lords is seeking to apply more tightly defined policy pronouncements.

5–12 Within the terms of the substantive tests that are being applied, however, there remains a broad brush approach to judicial control. While there is an intention to set out clear tests, the manner in which those tests are being applied goes beyond a simple application of those rules. One good example of this development appears in the decision of the Privy Council in *Royal Brunei Airlines v. Tan* which is considered at this stage as an introduction to the context of the use of equity in commercial situations.[15] The principle of dishonesty in *Tan* is broadened far beyond any of the more usual tests of whether or not a person is "dishonest" *strictu sensu.* The respondent in *Tan* was the managing director of a travel agency which was required to place money received from the sale of tickets for a particular airline on trust for the airline. Strictly, the travel agency was the trustee, whereas the respondent was found to be a third party to the arrangement—despite being the controlling mind of the agency. In breach of the trust, the respondent procured that moneys be paid from the trust account in discharge of the agency's own debts. The financial difficulties facing the agency worsened and in time, the travel agency went into insolvency. Therefore, the appellant sought to proceed against the respondent, Tan, for knowingly assisting in a breach of trust. The issue between the parties was whether "the breach of trust which is a prerequisite to accessory liability must itself be a dishonest and fraudulent breach of trust by the trustee".

5–13 The issue is stated most clearly in Lord Selborne L.C.'s dicta in *Barnes v. Addy*[16] distinguishing between "knowing receipt" and "knowing assistance". This

---

[11] [1980] 2 Lloyd's Rep. 469.

[12] *Scandinavian Trading v. Flota Ecuatoriana* [1983] 2 W.L.R. 248 at 258.

[13] *Target Holdings v. Redferns* [1996] 1 A.C. 421, [1995] 3 W.L.R. 352; [1995] 3 All E.R. 785.

[14] *Royal Brunei Airlines v. Tan* [1995] 2 A.C. 378.

[15] [1995] 2 A.C. 378.

is rendered as the difference between the liability of a person as "recipient" of trust property or its traceable proceeds, and the liability of a person as "accessory" to a trustee's breach of trust. The accessory liability is described as a form of "secondary liability" which arises in situations when there has been a breach of trust—as in *Royal Brunei v. Tan*.[17] That is, liability is asserted against some third party to the trust. Lord Nicholls was clear that the principle which is required to fix a third party to the trust with liability for a breach of that trust depends on whether or not that third party has acted "dishonestly". The particular issue in *Tan* was the purported honesty of the trustee travel agency and the alleged dishonesty of the third party, Tan. In Lord Nicholls view, the test for "acting dishonestly, or with a lack of probity, which is synonymous, means simply not acting as an honest person would in the circumstance. This is an objective standard."[18]

5–14 The interesting notion in this framing of the test is that "dishonesty" can be an *active* state of mind or alternatively a *passive* "lack of probity". It is suggested instead that this *active deceit* is the natural meaning of "dishonesty". The test of dishonesty developed by Lord Nicholls is therefore both strict and broader than a natural meaning of that term. Reckless risk-taking is considered to be a part of "dishonesty". This category appears to occupy a ground between fraud (necessarily *active deceit*) and negligent failure to appreciate risk (*passive unsuitability*).[19] It is contended that precluding a test of unconscionability, in favour of a broad test of dishonesty, does not sit comfortably with the natural meaning of the term chosen, *viz.* dishonesty. Despite the central assertion of the speech of Lord Browne-Wilkinson in *Islington*, which placed the notion of "conscience" at the centre of the principles of the new model of equity, Lord Nicholls expressly disavows a test of unconscionability—preferring instead a test based on the more specific, if stylised, category of dishonesty. The impact of this alteration to the test is that a far broader spectrum of activity is captured within the doctrine of dishonest assistance than had otherwise been the case in advance of the opinion of the Privy Council. The restatement of core principles, as with Lord Browne-Wilkinson in *Islington*, constitutes an arbitrary change in the law which was not anticipated by actors who made their choices and risk allocations in advance of judgment.

Equitable proprietary claims in banking transactions

5–15 This section focuses on the approach of the Court of Appeal and the High Court in *Islington* to the availability of equitable proprietary claims in favour of the banks in the local authority swaps cases. There are fundamental problems in relation to English law's attitude to proprietary claims in relation to money. Most specifically in relation to value held in electronic bank accounts which is loosely described as "money".[20] In terms of establishing proprietary claims to electronic money there is a need to distinguish between those claims which require the establishment of a property law claim ("following") and those which require the activation of the tracing process to identify some rights in substitute property

---

[16] (1874) L.R. 9 Ch. App. 244 at 251-252.

[17] [1995] 2 A.C. 378.

[18] [1995] 2 A.C. 378 at 386.

[19] These issues are considered further below in *Suitability Approach*, Chapter 12.

[20] See Chapter 4, *The Legal Context of Money*.

("tracing").[21] It appears that in relation to a direct recipient of property there is no requirement to rely on tracing to establish a property claim against money; as opposed to the situation where the defendant has interfered with the defendant's proprietary rights in some way.[22]

5–16 The approach to equitable tracing loomed large in the *Islington* appeal. At first instance, his Lordship followed the decision in *Chase Manhattan Bank NA v. Israel-British Bank (London) Ltd*[23] in the context of the possibility of permitting a common law remedy for money had and received alongside the existence of a fiduciary relationship. Thus, there was a mingling of common law and equitable claims. This mixture of claims and remedies from common law and equity runs contrary to the decision in *Stocks v. Wilson* [24] which Hobhouse J. did not apply on the basis that to allow the equitable remedy in this context would not lead to a *de facto* enforcement of the contract, which would be precluded by common law.[25] In the face of arguments concerning the availability of equitable tracing, and the appropriate remedy should that claim be upheld, Dillon L.J. held that "I find none of these matters relevant to the issue with which we are concerned": that is, the availability of compound interest.[26]

The need for a fiduciary relationship

5–17 In the opinion of Dillon L.J., "Islington was, on the true view that the swap agreement with Westdeutsche was ultra vires and void, a person in a fiduciary position from the outset, 18 June 1987 ..."[27] Relying the dicta of Lord Parker in *Sinclair v. Brougham*[28] where money is paid to a company to buy land which that company is not entitled to sell "the implied promise on which the action for money had and received depends would form no part of, but would be merely collateral to, the *ultra vires* contract". Therefore, the question arises whether or not Westdeutsche could have argued that the borrowing of money (represented by the deep discount payment) would have been a valid contract (if voidable under the rate-capping provisions) and therefore merely collateral to the interest rate swap agreement to pay and receive income amounts over time. In short: the authority was permitted to borrow money and therefore part of the deep discount swap would have been within Islington's capacity. The councillors might have been subject to surcharges and the loans made voidable by the rate-capping statute—significantly, though, the borrowing would not have been beyond the authority's capacity. Clearly this argument would depend upon some contention that the pricing of the lump sum repayments into the income payment streams was a form of set–off and did not prevent the interpretation of the contracts' being collateral one to another.

---

[21] On this division see Smith, *The Law of Tracing*, (Oxford, 1997).

[22] Smith, "Tracing and Electronic Funds Transfer" in *Restitution and Banking Law* (Rose ed., Mansfield Press, Oxford, 1998), pp.120, 131. *cf. Bank Tejarat v. Hong Kong and Shanghai Bank Corp* [1995] 1 Lloyd's Rep. 239, in which it was held that tracing was required in a claim for money had and received induced by fraud.

[23] [1981] Ch. 105.

[24] [1913] 2 K.B. 235.

[25] Indeed the blurring of the distinction between common law and equitable remedies in this litigation would seem to raise no objection to their complete elision in many contexts. See below, for example, in the context of what is said about the desirability of continuing to distinguish between common law tracing and equitable tracing.

[26] [1994] 4 All E.R. 890 at 966.

[27] *ibid.* at 964; applying *Sinclair v. Brougham* [1914] A.C. 398 at 420, *per* Viscount Haldane and *Re Diplock's Estate* [1948] Ch. 465 at 540.

[28] [1914] A.C. 398 at 440.

5–18 With reference to the availability of a tracing remedy in this context, Hobhouse J. summarised Lord Parker's approach in *Sinclair v. Brougham* by finding that:

> "the starting point must be some fiduciary relationship which sufficed to give rise to an equity but the relationship could arise simply from the circumstances in which the money was received."[29]

Therefore, there would be some fiduciary responsibility incumbent upon the recipient of the money under a loan transaction. This argument would not obtain in the *Sandwell* litigation in the same way that it could be said to obtain in the Islington context.[30] Similarly, the Court of Appeal in *Re Diplock's Estate* interpreted *Sinclair* as having decided that[31]:

> "... a sufficient fiduciary relationship was found [to have existed] between the depositors and the directors by reason of the fact that the purposes for which the depositors had handed their money to the directors were by law incapable of fulfilment."

Thus, an *ultra vires* contract should create the necessary fiduciary relationship in itself. On that basis, it would appear possible that there was a fiduciary relationship between the financial institutions and the local authorities. The remaining issue as considered in *Sinclair* is whether the appropriate remedy is a proprietary one or the award of an equitable charge.[32]

Tracing what—gross or net amount?

5–19 The issue then arises, what property can be traced where payments have been made in absolute discharge of the contractual obligations on a net basis? Value does not in fact pass as to the full extent of the obligation owed. Rather an amount representing the surplus owed after set-off is transferred. Therefore, it is important to decided whether tracing ought to have been permitted to the full extent of the obligation that has been discharged, or whether it should have been restricted to the net amount that it actually paid. As Hobhouse J. held:

> " ... where there have been cross-payments in respect of the same swap, reverse payments pro tanto reduce or reverse the pre-existing equity. Since the payments were made pursuant to the same void transaction, they fall to be looked at together and there is no equity in respect of one payment independent of the equity in respect of the others."[33]

Therefore, the equitable set-off relating to one payment should be held to apply throughout. This would appear to be in accordance with principle. Even though the gross obligation has been satisfied, only a net amount has been transferred. In line with restitutionary principles, it would be wrong for the restitutionary response to go beyond the size of the unjust enrichment. The unjust factor relates

---

29 [1994] 4 All E.R. 890 at 919, *per* Hobhouse J.

30 The further point, that is considered below, is: "what if the transaction concerns the transfer of some physical security or commodity which cannot be considered to be merely another payment of an income stream of money?" This concentration on the property as being identical and easily capable of amalgamation because it is all cash, does not wash.

31 [1948] Ch. 465 at 540.

32 *Sinclair v. Brougham* [1914] A.C. 398 at 444; see also *Re Guardian Permanent Benefit Building Society* (1882) 23 Ch.D. 440.

33 [1994] 4 All E.R. 890 at 937.

solely to the loss of the net amount. By definition, the payer has not lost the gross amount because it has set its own liability off against that asset. Similarly, there is no impact on conscience where there has been set-off, equal to the gross amount.

5–20 As Hobhouse J. expressly held, the personal claim in restitution will operate only on a net basis such that the claim cannot be asserted without at the same time giving credit for any payments received. Therefore, as a matter of the principle of unjust enrichment, the defendant could only have been said to have been enriched in the net sum and the enrichment has only been at the expense of the plaintiff in the net sum.[34] However, it is difficult to see why, in the context of deciding the equitable proprietary position as to net amounts, the reverse swap posited by Hobhouse J.[35] is considered to be part of the same transaction rather than being an entirely separate transaction. A reverse swap, as defined in the generality of the swaps litigation, constitutes one of two things. Either it is a cancellation of a previous contract by the creation of its economic mirror, or alternatively it is a form of perfect hedge entered into separately so that the two cancel each other out from an economic standpoint.

5–21 The better view in principle must be that a reverse swap is a separate transaction which cancels out the original swap arithmetically. If it were the activation of some termination provision (which on the facts it was not), then the original swap would have disappeared (which on the facts it did not). Further on the facts, the original swaps were still in existence at the date of service of the writs and therefore the reverse swaps can only be considered to be further agreements rather than cancellations on the original agreements. In allowing a proprietary claim in equity, Hobhouse J. also contravenes the principle as to the need to segregate a fund which is to be the subject of the equitable proprietary claim. As decided by the Privy Council in *Re Goldcorp*,[36] and supported by Lord Browne-Wilkinson in *Islington*,[37] it is not possible to impose a proprietary claim over a general bank account without the segregation of the particular property which is to be held on trust.[38]

Surviving equity

5–22 The difficulty in Hobhouse J.'s judgment in the context of the equitable remedy is that he is prepared to say that the rights in the value transferred by the banks has not disappeared and therefore must be said to continue in existence. As Hobhouse J. held:

> "The character of the equity upon which Westdeutsche relies is that in conscience Islington should repay the £2.5m to Westdeutsche out of the assets which Islington has. At no time since 1987 has Islington had insufficient assets to enable it to give effect to the equity. Therefore the equity has survived. Similarly, in terms of an equitable charge, there have throughout been assets which could be the subject of the charge."[39]

The argument therefore runs: you owe this amount and you still have this amount

---

[34] [1994] 4 All E.R. 890 at 941.

[35] See Birks, *Introduction to the Law of Restitution*, (Oxford, 1989), p.15.

[36] [1995] 1 A.C. 74.

[37] Considered below.

[38] See Moriarty, "Tracing, Mixing and Laundering" in *Laundering and Tracing* (Birks ed., Oxford, 1995), pp.73, 85.

[39] [1994] 4 All E.R. 890 at 940.

under your control, therefore you should pay the amount over. At first blush there is some attraction in this point of view. The bank has transferred £x and therefore should receive £x back after the contract has been held to be void. Given that the authority has the money set aside and is solvent, it should pay the amount.

5–23 It is possible that the problem in the swaps cases is exacerbated by the fact that the property involved is money. As considered above in *The Concept of Money*[40] one of the issues to arise out of this litigation is whether there ought to be any difference between cash-settled transaction and physically-settled transactions. In principle there is no reason why they should be considered differently. The analyses should apply on the basis of whether the facts give rise to proprietary or to personal rights, and nothing more. In saying that the authority has the requisite amount of money under its control, it is possible to say the debt is capable of being discharged. However, to the extent Hobhouse J. is granting a proprietary remedy it is not enough to say that the property held in one account is very similar to the property which was paid away under a mistake, and should therefore be handed over in discharge of an obligation to return such property, rather than in discharge of a personal obligation to pay an equivalent, non-specific amount of money.

5–24 Hobhouse J. purported to grant a proprietary remedy. First, he held that the property be held on an implied trust arising out of the impact on the recipient's conscience. Secondly, he held that:

> "Accordingly, Westdeutsche is entitled, subject to the defence of change of position, *to the equitable remedy of tracing* against Islington and, since Islington's assets are more than sufficient to satisfy any *equitable charge* upon them of £2.5m, to have an order that Islington pay that sum to Westdeutsche. In so far as it depends upon questions of law the conclusion in the Sandwell action must be the same."[41] [author's emphasis]

The detail of the order is therefore an order equivalent to an equitable charge in favour of the banks over the assets of the authorities. This is a proprietary claim in their favour. Therefore, the issue revolves around the identification of the specific money which is held by the authorities.

5–25 In accordance with authority there must be some identification of that property. While there is no need for writing for a valid trust over personalty,[42] the further issue is as to the certainty of subject matter under this trust. On the basis of *Re Goldcorp*[43] which suggests that the fund must be segregated for there to be sufficient certainty of subject matter.[44] Hobhouse J. is seeking to impose a trust on the property without that property being identifiable, having found expressly that the account into which the £2.5 million had been paid had gone overdrawn. As has been held in numerous recent cases, once an account goes overdrawn the property in that account is said to be no longer traceable.[45]

5–26 In *Re Goldcorp*,[46] a precious metals exchange went into insolvency. It had three categories of creditor, for the purposes of the litigation. The first category

---

[40] Chapter 4, *Issues of Law and Finance.*

[41] [1994] 4 All E.R. 890 at 940.

[42] *M'Fadden v. Jenkyns* (1842) 1 Ph. 153.

[43] [1995] 1 A.C. 74.

[44] Where shares are held to the order of the beneficiary on bare trust, there will not be a problem as to certainty: *Hunter v. Moss* [1994] 1 W.L.R. 452; [1994] 3 All E.R. 215.

[45] *Bishopsgate v. Homan* [1995] 1 W.L.R. 31.

[46] [1995] 1 A.C. 74.

had contracted with the insolvent that the insolvent would acquire quantities of precious metals on the clients' behalf and allocate specific property to their account (the allocated creditors). The second category of claimant were customers who had contracted that quantities of precious metals would be acquired on their behalf and that the insolvent would take physical delivery of the amount of metal purchased for them. In fact, the insolvent did not perform this obligation, opting instead to acquire amounts of metal sufficient to satisfy the normal calls made on it by its customers in any standard business period (the unallocated claimants). The third category of customer was a person who had contracted for the acquisition of a large quantity of a very specific and unusual type of gold coin (the evident purchase claimant). The evident purchase claimant sought to argue that the amount of that particular coin held by the insolvent must have been intended for him alone.

5–27 Lord Mustill, delivering the leading judgment of the Privy Council, held that because the coins had not been segregated to his account, they could not be said to have been held on trust for him and therefore there was no available equitable proprietary right. Similarly, the unallocated claimants could not support an equitable proprietary claim on the basis that no identifiable property had been segregated for their benefit. The allocated claimants were entitled to rely on proprietary claims in the insolvency because they had identifiable property segregated for their benefit.

5–28 On the facts of *Islington*, it is impossible for the banks to prove that the money still held by the authorities was the same money that had been paid to them at the outset. Indeed, it is found in *Islington* that the accounts had been run into overdraft on a number of occasions. In accordance with authority, that the account becomes overdrawn should automatically terminate the right to trace on the basis that the property no longer exists.[47] The only exception to this rule appears to be where the court orders an equitable charge over the assets of that recipient.[48] Otherwise the only possible remedy would be one based on subrogation,[49] or, as Hobhouse J. put it, the question would be "whether or not the principles recognised by Lord Parker analogous to subrogation could not be relied upon by Westdeutsche."[50] There is some similarity in approach with the swollen assets theory advanced by Lord Templeman in *obiter* remarks in *Space Investments*.[51]

Set-off

5–29 The term "set-off" is considered in a number of authorities. The Court of Appeal were required to consider that term in the context of cross-claims and set-off under section 28 of the Limitation Act 1939: thus "legal set-off". Lord Denning M.R. held:

> "These cross-claims must arise out of separate transactions[52] ... If there is no separate transaction, but only opposing demands arising out *of the same*

---

[47] *Roscoe v. Winder* [1915] 1 Ch. 62; *Bishopsgate v. Homan* [1995] Ch. 211.

[48] *Chase Manhattan N.A. v. Israel-British Bank (London) Ltd* [1981] 1 Ch. 105; *Space Investments Ltd v. Canadian Imperial Bank of Commerce Trust Co. (Bahamas) Ltd* [1986] 1 W.L.R. 1072, [1986] 3 All E.R. 75.

[49] See below in Chapter 9, see also Mitchell, *The Law of Subrogation* (Oxford, 1994) generally; and also Smith, *The Law of Tracing* (Oxford, 1997).

[50] [1994] 4 All E.R. 890 at 940.

[51] [1986] 1 W.L.R. 1072.

> *transaction*, then no question of set-off, properly so called, arises."[53] [his Lordship's emphasis]

Hobhouse J., however, disagreed with the interpretation set out by Lord Denning in the context of a statute bar to a claim of set-off in respect of the first *Sandwell* swap.[54] The question then is, if that is the position with reference to legal set-off under statute, what is the position of equitable set-off? The discretionary nature of the defence of equitable set-off is seen clearly in *Hanak v. Green*[55]. The question with reference to set-off, in the opinion of Hobhouse J. is whether it is in accordance with equity on the facts of any particular case.[56]

5–30 With reference to the *Sandwell* case, the issue arose whether the transactions should be considered to be completely separate, or whether there was some nexus between the separate payments where they were made expressly in connection with one another. Thus, in the finding of Hobhouse J.:

> "Accordingly, the position was analogous to that of a running account between the two parties. Only one underlying transaction was involved—the first Sandwell swap contract. The successive payments merely altered the location and extent of the enrichment which existed from time to time. The earlier payments had long since ceased to give any cause of action to either party. They were merely part of the previous dealings between the parties which were relevant to ascertaining what, if any, cause of action either party had at a later date."[57]

5–31 In considering the "executory contract analysis" or "mutual debts analysis" dichotomy in the nature of the swaps contract, the issue arises whether there is a difference between the analyses in considering the set-off position. Hobhouse J. found the following facts in relation to the position where there were a number of inter-related payments but some were made outside the limitation period:

> "Where there have been a whole succession of payments one way and the other in respect of a single underlying transaction, both equity and justice require that one should have regard to the totality of those payments and the resultant overall benefit and detriment and not have regard to some arbitrary cut-off point (*i.e.* in relation to the Limitation Act) unless there is some statutory provision which requires one to do so."[58]

It is submitted that this passage does not provide an answer to the issue which of the analyses has greater utility. What is does indicate is that it is preferable to consider the totality of the payments made between the parties, rather than to separate those payments. However, the separation of payments does not arise from some analysis of the structure involved but is concerned with some intervention of law.

---

52 This returns to the core discussion of whether or not there are separate transactions in relation to payment netting.

53 *Henriksens Rederi A/S v. PHZ Rolimpex* [1974] Q.B. 233 at 245.

54 [1994] 4 All E.R. 890 at 945.

55 [1958] 2 Q.B. 9.

56 [1994] 4 All E.R. 890 at 945.

57 *ibid.* at 941.

58 *ibid.*

Interest

5–32 There is an irony, as referred to above, that there should be difficulty with the availability of interest when it is held by Hobhouse J. that there is no underlying debt involved in these contracts. It would be better to talk about fixed and floating *income* payments rather than "interest". Income payments are therefore to be calculated on the basis that there is some sum of money which should be calculated by reference to the authorities' use of money which is owed to the banks on the basis of use of property owed under a court award.

The availability of compound interest

5–33 The issues taken to the Court of Appeal dealt only with the *Islington* litigation. The *Sandwell* litigation ceased after the High Court. Of the many issues raised before the High Court the only question before the Court of Appeal was whether or not Hobhouse J. was entitled to award compound interest to Westdeutsche.[59] The Court of Appeal recited Lord Templeman's definition of an interest rate swap in *Hazell v. Hammersmith and Fulham,*[60] set out above. Dillon L.J. then summarised the interest issue[61]:

> "*A fiortiori*, if interest rates at the time had been such that the first four six-monthly 'interest' payments had been paid by Westdeutsche as the fixed rate payer to Islington (instead of having actually been paid the other way round), Islington would have been bound to repay to Westdeutsche the total of the £2.5m *and the 'interest' payments (assumedly) paid by Westdeutsche to Islington*."

The questions which arise from this short passage are: what is meant by the treatment of the term "interest", *i.e.* does this imply a loan or that payments made are not payments of interest but payments which actually have some other form; and does this imply an executory or mutual debts analysis of the interest rate swap?

5–34 Hobhouse J. considered it to be "a logical argument" that the court should be concerned solely with the question whether or not the defendant was enriched and not be concerned with any collateral transaction into which one party had entered and with which the other party was in no way concerned. In his opinion this overlooked "the discretionary nature of the remedy ..., and the question whether it is just that the defendant should be ordered to pay interest to the plaintiff at a time when both the plaintiff and the defendant were labouring under a bona fide mistake and at a time when the plaintiff was not actually out of pocket."[62] It is clear that the decision as to interest is motivated by the same principles of equity as the decision as to the availability of a proprietary remedy. The decision to award compound interest emerges from the following passage:

> "There was no consideration for the making of the payment. The fact that the plaintiff's mistake was not a mistake as to any actual matter of fact does not preclude the plaintiff from recovery. The plaintiff's payment does not fall to be categorised as a voluntary payment. ... Since the plaintiff was entitled

---

[59] As part of the question about interest, was the question of the date from which the calculation of interest should run.

[60] [1992] 2 A.C. 1 at 24.

[61] [1994] 4 All E.R. 890 at 958.

[62] *ibid.* at 954.

to invoke equitable remedies against the defendant, it was entitled to ask the court to award it compound interest, not merely simple interest. In the exercise of my discretion I have ordered that the principal sum to be repaid by the defendant to the plaintiff with compound interest calculated at six-monthly rests from 1 April 1990 down to the date of this judgement."[63]

5–35 The availability of equitable proprietary rights in the property was said to lead to the availability of compound interest. The application of the equitable approach to the resolution of the dispute at both High Court and Court of Appeal level made this remedy possible. What remained unclear, as considered below, was whether this remedy was intended by their Lordships to be solely based on equity or whether their frequent reference to principles of restitution indicated some elision of the applicable concepts.

A pseudo-subrogation claim? Money used to discharge liabilities

5–36 The question arises whether the banks are entitled to say that they should be entitled to claim a restitutionary proprietary claim on the basis of subrogation. There are two possible contexts in which this contention could arise. The first is in relation to the deep discount payment made in *Islington* where that payment is put to use in the discharge of local authority obligations. The second is in relation to the vanilla interest rate swaps in *Sandwell* where the income payments made by the bank on a net basis are used by the authority in the discharge of a debt obligation or in its habitual income expenditure.[64]

5–37 The argument raised on behalf of Westdeutsche was that its money had been used to discharge the local authority's liabilities and, as such, it should have been entitled to be reimbursed on a restitutionary basis on a claim based on subrogation. As Hobhouse J. commented:

> "This argument has obvious attractions and satisfies a general concept of unjust enrichment. The recipient has had the benefit of the money. If he had not had the plaintiff's money he would have had to pay his creditor. Let him now therefore pay the plaintiff instead."[65]

It is difficult to see how this argument is different from subrogation. However, Hobhouse J. suggests that it is similar to a tracing remedy.[66] The primary obstacle is seen as been an evidential one.[67] What cannot be shown is the particular discharge of debts with the money advanced by Westdeutsche. The deep discount payments and the income payments were paid into general accounts and then disbursed in general expenditure. Those accounts were then run into overdraft.

5–38 The question is considered in the context of the authorities dealing with contracts of loan to persons without the requisite authority to borrow. In particular the dicta of Lord Parker in *Sinclair v. Brougham*[68] state that:

---

63 [1994] 4 All E.R. 890 at 956.

64 The difficulty in this regard is that local authority accounts are usually run to a nil balance. That is, all the money in the budget is spent. There will not necessarily be any discrimination between money used to discharge a particular obligation and money used in general, day-to-day expenditure. Following these sums is therefore a task incapable of strict proof.

65 [1994] 4 All E.R. 890 at 934.

66 *ibid.*

67 *Re National Permanent Benefit Building Society, ex p. Williamson* (1869) LR 5 Ch. App. 309; *Blackburn and District Benefit Building Society v. Cunliffe Brooks & Co* (1882) 22 Ch.D. 61.

68 [1914] A.C. 398 at 440.

> "... if the borrowed money be applied in paying off legitimate indebtedness of the company ... the lenders are entitled to rank as creditors of the company ... to the extent that the money has been so applied ... There appears to be some doubt as to whether this result is arrived at by treating the contract of loan as validated to the extent to which the borrowed money is so applied ... or whether the better view is that the lenders are subrogated to the rights of the legitimate creditors who have been paid off."

The evidential problem was therefore whether the money has been used to discharge a particular debt. The conceptual problem was whether this form of remedy required the partial performance of the void contract or relied instead upon general principles of subrogation. It is this writer's view that some form of reviving subrogation, in Mitchell's conception of that term, is the better approach. The availability of subrogation as a restitutionary remedy is considered below in *The emerging principle of unjust enrichment* (Chapter 11).

Defences

Change of position

5–39 Contrary to equity both parties sought to argue that they have changed position such that they should be entitled to receive moneys owed to them, but that they should not be required to make any payments. Hobhouse J. found that Islington had not changed its position because it had set aside a fund to meet its potential liability under the litigation.[69] Westdeutsche similarly argued that it had changed its position by entering in the agreement with the intermediary, Morgan Grenfell, under which it could make a loss in the future. Despite the finding that reverse swaps and original swaps are somehow linked[70], Hobhouse J. does not find a link between the main transaction and the transaction with the intermediary—even though they also mirror one another.[71] Nevertheless, despite the loss of bargain suffered by the financial institutions, Hobhouse J. held that[72]: "To assert that Westdeutsche will have made a loss through entering into the Morgan Grenfell contract is simply a speculation."[73]

5–40 The basis for the High Court's decision that the defence would not be available was that the authority in *Islington* had a fund set aside which would meet the obligation owed to Westdeutsche.[74] The existence of this fund was a prudent accounting action by the authority in seeking to set aside an amount equal to its potential liability in case there were a proprietary claim made out against it. It was this very prudence which brought on the authority's downfall because Hobhouse J. held that the authority was therefore capable of making the payment and should

[69] This decision is overruled by Dillon L.J., as considered below.

[70] See above.

[71] It is accepted that this mirroring might be apart from the necessary spreads paid between the financial institutions.

[72] [1994] 4 All E.R. 890 at 949.

[73] This is, presumably, an unintentional pun.

[74] As Hobhouse J. held: "Accordingly, as at the time the House of Lords delivered its decision [in *Hazell*], the defendant had set aside out of budgeted sums for the years 1989/90 and 1990/91 sums which in the aggregate were more than sufficient to meet the restitution liability which I have held was the consequence of the decision of the House of Lords. This is the end of the defendant's change of position argument on the facts. It had been planning to make payments to the plaintiff and it had been budgeted for them. It had expected the liability to make those payments to be a contractual liability." [1994] 4 All E.R. 890 at 953.

therefore be required to do so. This is despite the fact that a proprietary remedy could not be appropriate where the property involved had ceased to exist and that it traceable subject was not identifiable. On the basis of this prudent account it was held that there had not been "any significant alteration of the position of the defendant as a result of its having assumed that it was entitled to receive the sum of £2.5 million from Westdeutsche in the summer of 1987".[75]

5–41 Dillon L.J.'s response to this analysis of Islington's behaviour was brutally straightforward:

> "That [finding of Hobhouse J.] is factually wrong, however, in so far as it suggests that Islington had set money apart to make restitution to Westdeutsche. Islington never did any such thing, even in respect of the instalment which Islington would have had to pay to Westdeutsche under the swap arrangement, if it had been valid, on 18 December 1989 ... The most that Islington did was to credit such interest payments to a suspense account code; but that was a mere accounting entry, not supported by any actual fund, indicating a liability which Islington might have to meet."[76]

Therefore, an accounting entry will not be sufficient to suggest a restitutionary remedy *in se*.

5–42 It is against this background that we come to consider the manner in which the courts sought to deal with the specific legal issues in the local authority swaps cases.

---

[75] [1994] 4 All E.R. 890 at 953.

[76] *ibid.* at 963.

Chapter 6

Restitution for want of consideration

6–01 Given the very different approaches of the High Court and Court of Appeal, in accepting that a proprietary claim ought to have been available to the banks in the swaps cases, from the unanimous belief of the House of Lords that such a proprietary remedy would have been unjustified, it is proposed to analyse the attitudes of the different courts separately. By considering the approach of Hobhouse J. (and the less detailed judgments of their Lordships in the Court of Appeal), first, it is possible to see the motivations and the range of legal arguments extended by the parties more clearly. The speeches delivered in the House of Lords have in mind far greater questions of the economic impact of their decisions and the effect on the development of English law. The initial trial and the first appeal are more concerned with the issues arising simply between the parties (while mindful of the other claims for which *Islington* and *Sandwell* were test cases). This separation is also useful because the High Court and Court of Appeal considered themselves to be bound by the authority of *Sinclair v. Brougham*,[1] whereas the majority in the House of Lords were content to start afresh with a restatement of core principles unencumbered by precedent.[2]

Permissive proprietary approaches in High Court and Court of Appeal

6–02 There was a straightforward difference in approach between, on the one hand, the High Court and the Court of Appeal granting a proprietary interest to the banks and, on the other hand, a unanimous (on this point) House of Lords deciding that there could not be a proprietary interest granted to the banks under the terms of the swap agreements. As considered above in *Problems of Credit and Security*,[3] the approach taken by the majority of the House of Lords does appear to present some fundamental problems of taking security. This is identified as the principle practical problem with their Lordships' approach—leading to issues of systemic risk management. The decisions in the High Court and the Court of Appeal adopt a completely different approach. It is the further contention of this book, as set out in Chapter 4, that the attitude of the High Court and Court of Appeal are not ideal, in part because a number of analytical points were not taken before those tribunals.

6–03 Therefore, the following sections will analyse the judgments of the High Court and Court of Appeal in detail, before coming to the House of Lords. There were issues argued before the High Court which were not appealed—in short all of the *Sandwell* litigation and the restitution points arising in *Islington*.[4] Therefore,

---

[1] *Sinclair v. Brougham* [1914] A.C. 398.

[2] Lord Browne-Wilkinson in *Islington* [1996] A.C. 669.

[3] Chapter 4, *Issues in Finance and Law*.

[4] Although Lord Browne-Wilkinson did choose to re-open issues not strictly appealed to House of Lords.

the structure of the remainder of this book is predicated on the basis that there is a need to consider the approach of Hobhouse J. in the High Court before turning to other matters. The subsequent chapters[5] will consider the attitude of the three categories of judicial decision and then two further approaches are set out in Chapter 12.

The arguments before Hobhouse J.: a summary

6–04 The financial institutions were seeking to make proprietary claims to the moneys which they had advanced. Their arguments in outline were summarised by Hobhouse J. in the following way:

> "The proprietary claims made by the banks rest entirely upon the contention that equity would say that it was unconscionable that the councils should retain the moneys. Thus the banks submit that the present cases illustrate the principle of unjust enrichment and that both law and equity should recognise this and, further, that they disclose a sufficient fiduciary relationship between the recipient and the payer to give rise to equitable remedies."[6]

There were therefore four main grounds for the proprietary claim on the submission of the financial institutions: unconscionability giving rise to an equitable remedy; unjust enrichment giving rise to a common law remedy; unjust enrichment giving rise to an equitable remedy; and fiduciary relationship giving rise to an equitable remedy.

6–05 The core of the banks' claim is the availability of restitution as a result of payments made under a void contract, leading to a failure (or absence) of consideration. However, despite this core submission on behalf of the banks, we are told expressly that they did not seek to argue that the authorities were constructive or resulting trustees of the money. The approach of counsel for the banks was that they considered themselves bound by *Sinclair v. Brougham*. Therefore, their submission rested on the availability of an equitable charge on the basis of *Sinclair v. Brougham*.

The context for the decisions: Hobhouse J.

6–06 Having identified the detail of the issues brought at first instance in the Introduction, it is important to look at the organisation of the arguments before the High Court to understand the approach to the judgment itself.

Attitudes to mistake and intention on the facts

6–07 The primary submission for the banks was that there were mistakes of fact operating on the mind of their employees in dealing with the local authorities: specifically, that they thought local authorities were capable of entering into swaps agreements. Hobhouse J. decided from the outset that he would not consider questions relating to the state of mind, nor any possible mistake in the mind, of

[5] Chapters 8, 9 and 10.

[6] [1994] 4 All E.R. 890 at 916, *per* Hobhouse J.

the employees of the banks. Therefore, the issue of mistake was rapidly dismissed.[7]

6–08 There was a recital in the contract that "the floating rate payer had certain liabilities in respect of which it is obliged to pay interest at a fixed rate and wishes to exchange such obligations for obligations to make payments at a floating rate of interest." As Hobhouse J. commented on that term of the contract: "This recital purports to state that so far as Islington was concerned the contract was a hedging transaction. This was not in accordance with the facts."[8] The terms of the contract are thus ignored.[9] The courts throughout the swaps litigation have all ignored the terms of the standard market contracts which had been put before them. Rather than being simply the intentions of the parties in written form, these terms constitute the consensus of market participants as to the manner in which their business is to be conducted. The importance of standard market usage has been made clear in many regulatory and other analyses of this topic.[10] Brushing aside the statement in the contractual documentation that this is a hedging transaction does not assist systemic risk management.

6–09 As set out above in *Problems of Credit and Security*,[11] the courts' determination to ignore the substantive terms of the agreements mean that the parties are not able to allocate risks, nor is the market able to control the systemic risks in the derivatives market place. Were it definitively the case that netting or hedging arrangements could never be included, at law or equity, as being within the contemplation of the parties, then this would have included some acknowledgement of the contractual intentions of the parties.

Risk allocation

6–10 Westdeutsche argued that, through their agent, they had not voluntarily assumed the risk that the contracts would be unenforceable or void.[12] As such they contended that they ought to be entitled to restitution in reliance on this failure to allocate risk. Hobhouse J. held that 'there was no contemplation of the existence of any such risk and that no such risk was, as a matter of fact, voluntarily assumed'.[13] Two questions then arise, first, how to treat a risk which is not contemplated between the parties, and secondly, why the terms of the contracts between the parties which purported to allocate these risks were not deemed to contribute to a decision on this point?

6–11 The issue which would appear to arise at this juncture is whether the parties have accepted or allocated risks in such a way that one party ought to become a fiduciary in relation to that other as a result of the fruition of the risk. Where the risk has not been allocated, the appropriate response must be to return the property to the other contracting party.[14] The role of risk within the rules of equity is considered below with reference to the discussion of the *equity approach*,

---

[7] [1994] 4 All E.R. 890 at 905, *per* Hobhouse J.

[8] *ibid.*

[9] As set out above in *Problems with Credit and Security*, Chapter 4.

[10] Little, "An Overview of Regulation in the UK" in *Swaps and Off-Exchange Derivatives Trading* (Bettelheim, Parry and Rees eds., FT Law and Tax, London, 1996), pp.15 *et seq.*; Walker, "Financial Derivatives—Global Regulatory Developments" [1996] J.B.L. 66.

[11] Chapter 4.

[12] [1994] 4 All E.R. 890 at 906, *per* Hobhouse J.

[13] *ibid.*

[14] This obligation would be subject to the caveats set out in relation to the discussion of the suitability approach below in Chapter 12.

drawing on the speech of Lord Browne-Wilkinson. What his Lordship identified as the core part of the availability of a constructive trust would be the knowledge on the part of the constructive trustee of a factor which ought to impact on that person's conscience. Therefore, risk is only important in the context of constructive trusts generally where the risk is known by the constructive trustee to affect that person's conscience. However, the speech of Lord Nicholls in *Royal Brunei Airlines v. Tan*,[15] as discussed with reference to the *equity approach* below, clearly identified risk-taking as being capable of falling within a more general test of dishonesty in the case of a claim based on dishonest assistance in a breach of trust. Therefore, it is possible that certain categories of unacceptable risk-taking may fall within the scope of behaviour which will produce an equitable response. What is not considered in the judgment of Hobhouse J. is whether the nature of risk allocation in the swap agreements before him ought to have impacted on the equity which ought to have been made available in that case.

6–12 The further element of public policy which was identified in the swaps cases was that the court should always consider the competing equities of third parties to a transaction—particularly the creditors in an insolvency. What was not clear was the impact which the rights of third parties should have on a decision based on knowledge affecting conscience. The commercially attractive element of the *Sinclair v. Brougham*[16] and *Re Diplock*[17] approaches is that they look to the matter without the normative lens of "conscience". The issue is the *ex post facto* allocation of risks which ought to have been considered between the parties. In this context, impact on conscience may, exceptionally, become a factor—cases of fraud and conscious breach of fiduciary duty would be the most obvious examples of this. However, what is not apparent is why conscience ought to be the only factor in allocating proprietary rights in commercial transactions. The idea of risk is already catered for but not considered by Hobhouse J.

6–13 The restitutionary analysis of the void interest rate swap contracts would start from the point of seeking to isolate an unjust factor which has generated an unjust enrichment at the expense of the claimant for the benefit of the defendant.[18] In the general run of commercial cases it is suggested, where there is no demonstrable fraud, inappropriate risk-taking and unsuitability of the financial product are more useful tools for identifying unjust enrichment to plug the gap between contract and ordinary civil wrongs. The issue for the restitution approach is whether inappropriate risk-taking or unsuitability would constitute unjust factors in themselves. Where the risks have been purportedly agreed by contract between the claimant and the defendant, it would appear unjust to allow the defendant to elude the terms of their common intention and rely upon the use of the claimant's property despite their agreement having been held void. These issues were not raised in the proceedings before the High Court or the Court of Appeal. They are considered in greater detail below in the concluding chapter under the *radical restitutionary approach*[19] and the *suitability approach*.[20] As will be seen in more detail, the decision to award a proprietary claim was based on traditionally equitable grounds rather than on more modish restitutionary grounds.

---

15 [1995] 2 A.C. 378.

16 [1914] A.C. 398.

17 [1948] Ch. 465.

18 Birks, *Introduction to the Law of Restitution*, (Oxford, 1989); Smith, "Tracing and Electronic Funds Transfer" in *Restitution and Banking Law* (Rose ed., Mansfield Press, Oxford, 1998), p.120.

19 Chapter 11.

20 Chapter 12.

Voluntary assumption of risk

6–14 It is clear that neither party was found to have accepted the risks of the local authority's incapacity to perform the terms of the contract. As Hobhouse J. held: "If the facts were that these payments had been made with a conscious appreciation that the contracts were or might be void, that would normally suffice to negative any right of recovery."[21] Therefore, there was no *explicit* allocation of risks in his Lordship's view. However, the issue must be, with reference to a contract which was structured to take advantage of, or to control, risk, how could the question be dismissed so lightly. Rather, two questions which ought to have been considered were: why can those contractual terms not be considered as an *explicit* allocation of the risks, and second, what risks were assumed between the parties *implicitly*?

6–15 The *equity approach* and the *suitability approach* below consider whether common intention constructive trusts or estoppel offer useful mechanisms to enforce proprietary remedies in cases where the parties have demonstrated some form of agreement, even if that agreement is not strictly binding in its own terms. As considered above, Hobhouse J. identifies that the kernel of his judgment rests on a finding of unconscionability in allowing the local authority to retain the money for the life of the void contract. That money is subject to an implied trust—although the nature of that trust must be subject to some debate.[22] It is submitted that, within this consideration of the conscionability of retaining property passed under a contract void *ab initio*, there should be some analysis of the allocation of the risks taken by the parties.[23] In fact, all parties in *Islington* and *Sandwell* had contracted on the basis of legal opinions and statements of understanding of the capacity of the local authorities. There is no implication that the purpose of the contracts was to do anything which involved the taking of unnecessary, or purely speculative, risks.

6–16 The explicit risks dealt with by the contracts were that the local authorities represented their capacity and that the failure of such representation constituted a termination event under the contract. The procedure for termination was similarly allocated in the contract as providing for a single, net amount to be transferred between the parties. Therefore, it is not true to say that there was no allocation of these risks, as set out in the ISDA and BBAIRS provisions above.

The annuity cases

6–17 One comparison which was made at first instance with the interest rate swap cases was the old annuity cases. Much is made of the old annuities cases, where annuities were required to be registered under the Grants of Life Annuities Act 1777 as a result of the widespread usurious selling of annuities at that time. The early cases considered that all contracts not registered were void *ab initio*. As a result these cases gave rise to complete restitution on a claim for money had and received.[24] The similarities were that regular periodic payments were made and that those contracts would be held to be void where a registration formality had

---

[21] [1994] 4 All E.R. 890 at 934.

[22] As considered in Chapter 10.

[23] As a more general point, with reference to litigation under derivatives, of the suitability of the products themselves.

[24] *Byne v. Vivian* (1800) 5 Ves. 604; 31 E.R. 762; *Hoffman v. Cooke* (1801) 5 Ves. Jun. 623; 31 E.R. 772; *Bromley v. Holland* (1802) Coop. G. 9; 35 E.R. 458.

not been complied with. The leading case at the time was *Hicks v. Hicks*[25] where Lord Ellenborough C.J. held that:

> "... the sums paid on either side were money had and received by one party to the other's use. If the consideration of the annuity be money had and received, it must be money had and received with all its consequences; and therefore the defendant must be at liberty to set off his payments as such, on the same score."[26]

As Hobhouse J. held in *Islington*[27]:

> "*Hicks v. Hicks* also established the general principle that restitution must be mutual and that the nature of the remedy is a form of mutual restitutio in integrum, that is to say, putting the parties back into their original positions. This is an earlier example of the same principle as that applied in *Newbigging v. Adam*[28] in relation to the law of rescission, where Bowen L.J. stressed that there ought to be 'a giving back on both sides'."

6–18 The real issue is whether or not it is the whole of the transaction which requires to be unwound to achieve restitution, or simply the last outstanding payment. The mutual debts analysis[29] would suggest that it is only the last outstanding payment which is required to be repaid because all of the other debts would be considered to have been discharged. The approach of Hobhouse J. is to look to *Hicks* as providing necessarily for the rescission of an executory contract. The legal analysis in *Hicks* is similar to that for the claim for money had and received relating to interest rate swaps. There was money had and received: in the modern parlance, a personal claim in restitution arises in favour of the payer. However, there is a danger of applying Lord Ellenborough's words too literally. In the context of an annuity, money is paid to the payee in circumstances where the payee becomes the owner of that money subject to a contractual obligation to make reciprocal payments to the payer at a future date.

6–19 In *Islington,* there was an upfront payment which belonged to the payee absolutely from the time of the payment, subject to an obligation to make repayments of that capital amount in the future. The vanilla interest rate swap payments, as in *Sandwell,* were made in discharge of a currently existing obligation to pay amounts if income, rather than being made in consideration of some executory promise in relation to a lump sum.[30] Under an annuity contract, the payer acquires rights to receive a future cash flow. In the case of a vanilla interest rate swap, the payer has a pre-existing obligation to make income payments. There is simultaneous reciprocity under vanilla interest rate swaps where amounts are set off. There is not an acquisition of future cash flow.[31] In that context, there is no total failure of consideration. Rather, consideration in *Sandwell* was provided *as at that date in the manner required by contract.*

6–20 A further question arises: are the annuities considered in *Hicks* closer to swaptions[32] rather than to interest rate swaps? The issue arises whether the

---

[25] (1802) 3 East. 16, 102 E.R. 502.

[26] *ibid.*

[27] [1994] 4 All E.R. 890 at 923, Hobhouse J.

[28] (1886) 34 Ch.D. 582 at 595; [1886–90] All E.R. Rep. 975 at 984.

[29] Chapter 3, above.

[30] Where that lump sum may be properly explicable as a loan in any event, as considered below.

[31] On this basis the confusion of the Repayment Thesis appears to arise, as discussed in Chapter 2.

[32] Described in Chapter 2 as an option to enter into a swap transaction.

annuity acquires for the payer a right to receive a cash flow at some point in the future. The annuity is closer to an option than it is to a simple swap. Under the option, the payer acquires some right to receive a cash flow in the future. The size of that cash flow is calculated by reference to a movement in an underlying market indicator. There is no requirement that the payer continue to make payments once the annuity has matured. Therefore, there are not reciprocal payments over time. Rather, there is a stream of payments one way up to maturity, and then a stream of payments made the other way until the termination of the annuity. It is therefore submitted that the annuity cases ought not to be considered, in any event, as providing an exact match with the interest rate swap.

Executed and non-executed transactions

6–21 The argument was made by counsel for Sandwell that the first swap, which was completed before the facts giving rise to the litigation happened, should not be dealt with in a different way from the other swaps, simply because those others had not been completed. Reliance was placed on the annuity case of *Davis v. Bryan*[33] where an executrix had sought to recover money paid under an unregistered annuity by a testator on an action for money had and received. The primary limb of the judgment was that a purchaser in such a situation should not be allowed to wait and see whether or not a contract turns out to be profitable before deciding to affirm it by registration or other action.[34] Rather, the court would apply principles of "equity and good conscience". In distinguishing *Hicks*[35] it was held that it was not open to the person who had failed to affirm the transaction to seek to terminate it unilaterally. Furthermore, a contract, once terminated, was not capable of being rescinded. The particular aspect relating to unilateral termination of contracts by the person who had failed to register them was applied in further cases.[36]

6–22 The authority in *Sandwell* sought to argue that it should not be open to the bank to terminate all the transactions under their BBAIRS agreement on the basis that one of the contracts had already been performed. Further, that it should not be open to either side to disaffirm those contracts once they had commenced enforcement. Hobhouse J. decided that there was no point decided in *Davis* which would be of assistance to the authority in considering the *Sandwell* litigation.[37]

6–23 One point which arose specifically in *Sandwell*,[38] although joined with *Islington* at first instance, was whether there ought to be a different analysis of the availability of restitution for interest rate swaps which have been part-performed and those interest rate swaps which have expired due to full performance. In that case Hobhouse J. chose to make no distinction between such open and closed swaps. However, in the wake of the House of Lords decision in *Islington*, the Court of Appeal in *Guinness Mahon & Co Ltd v. Kensington and Chelsea Royal London Borough Council*[39] was required to consider exactly this point in the context of the availability of restitution for interest rate swaps found to have been void *ab initio*.

---

[33] (1827) 6 B.andC. 651; 108 E.R. 591; 9 Dow. and Ry. 726. Considered at [1994] 4 All E.R. 890 at 924, *per* Hobhouse J.

[34] A concept known to the derivatives community as "cherry-picking".

[35] *Hicks v. Hicks* (1802) 3 East. 16, 102 E.R. 502.

[36] See, for example, *Seddon v. North Eastern Salt Co Ltd* [1905] 1 Ch. 326, [1904–7] All E.R. Rep. 817.

[37] [1994] 4 All E.R. 890 at 924, *per* Hobhouse J.

[38] [1994] 4 All E.R. 890.

[39] [1998] 2 All E.R. 272.

6–24 The council of Kensington and Chelsea ("the authority") bought an interest rate swap from Guinness Mahon ("the bank"). The authority had borrowed £5m from a building society on which it was required to pay a floating rate of interest. At a time of rising interest rates, when local authorities were rate capped in any event, the authority sought to reduce its interest rate cost and protect itself against upward movements in interest rates by contracting interest rate swaps which entitled it to receive a floating rate of interest and pay only a fixed rate. The bank created this arrangement such that the bank paid a floating rate of interest to the authority calculated by reference to a notional £5m, whereas the authority paid a fixed rate to the bank calculated by reference to the same notional amount. All interest payments were made on the same payment dates on a net basis. By the time of the House of Lords' decision in *Hazell*, the interest rate swap had been performed such that the bank had paid £384,409 to the authority on a net basis. Given that the interest rate swap was void *ab initio*, the bank sought restitution of amounts paid to the authority.

6–25 The authority sought to argue that, because the swap was a closed swap (that is, a swap under which all payments had been completed), it ought not to be required to make restitution to the bank. The authority's arguments were twofold: first, that there was no failure of consideration because both parties paid and received what they had bargained for, and, secondly, that the interest rate swap agreement ought to be subjected to the doctrine of apportionment of consideration (or severance) with the result that the transaction should be treated as having expired. The Court of Appeal was unanimous in its decision, although all three judges gave judgments reaching the same destination by different routes.

6–26 The first argument on behalf of the authority was disposed of by Morritt L.J. on the basis that it would be absurd to permit a distinction in the availability of restitution on the basis of whether or not the swap was open or closed. Morritt L.J. held[40] that the underlying purpose for the Court of Appeal's decision was a general policy of supporting the doctrine of *ultra vires*. The doctrine was to be supported on the basis that it existed to protect the public. The second argument on behalf of the authority was rejected on the basis that to have precluded restitution in favour of the bank because the swap was closed would be to give effect to the transaction by covert means once the overt means of enforcement had been precluded by the judgment in *Hazell*: effecting the transaction "by the back door". The underlying thrust of the judgment was summarised by Morritt L.J. as follows:[41]

> "(1) A contract which is *ultra vires* one of the parties to it is and always has been devoid of any legal contractual effect.
>
> (2) Payments made in purported performance thereof are necessarily made for a consideration which has totally failed and are therefore recoverable as money had and received."

Therefore, there was never any valid interest rate swap with the effect that there could be no contractual terms which could have been effected. As a result, none of the payments made between the authority and the bank was enforceable in contract. Robert Walker L.J. agreed in all material respects with Morritt L.J. Similarly, there were no valid terms which could be severed from any other terms—thus permitting allocation of some payments of consideration but not others.

---

[40] [1998] 2 All E.R. 272 at 284.

[41] *ibid.*

6–27 The approach of Waller L.J. was different in that his Lordship considered first the issue raised by Lord Goff in *Islington* as to the proper basis of restitution being sought. The problem was as follows. In *Islington* at first instance Hobhouse J. held that to bring an action in common law for restitution there must be a total absence of consideration, which he found there was not because some payments had been made under the contract. In the alternative, Lord Goff indicated that failure of consideration (as opposed to its total absence) would probably be suitable although his Lordship explained that it was not necessary to dispose of that appeal for him to reach any firm conclusion on the matter.

6–28 Waller L.J. doubted whether a completed contract should necessarily and automatically be unravelled simply on the basis that it had been held to be void *ab initio*. Therefore, it was not necessary to answer directly the problem which had been raised. However, his Lordship held ultimately that, if the authority were not required to make some restitutionary repayment to the bank, the authority would have been unjustly enriched. It should be noted, however, that it is not the principle of "unjust enrichment" advanced in detail by Birks as the foundation of the law of restitution,[42] which his Lordship sought to enforce but rather some more general concern that the authority should not be "'unjustly' enriched".[43] The intended distinction between the two concepts is unclear.

6–29 Waller L.J. agreed with the dicta of Leggatt L.J. in *Islington*[44] where the conviction that the authority be not "unjustly enriched" was made on "policy grounds", as Waller L.J. expressed the matter.[45] It should be noted that Leggatt L.J. held that a finding of a contract having been void *ab initio* required that there be held to have been no contract at any time—precisely the point which led Morritt L.J. to reject the authority's arguments.

6–30 Therefore, the authority failed to resist the bank's claim for restitution of the net balance of money paid under the interest rate swap payment on the basis of complete performance of the agreement. In short, the Court of Appeal held that it was not open to the authority to hold the bank to the effects of a bargain in the situation where that bargain was held to have been void *ab initio*. Unfortunately, the precise scope of the common law claims for restitution based on a defect in consideration remains uncertain. Furthermore, the nature of the emerging doctrine of unjust enrichment is not yet a creature of any identifiable jurisprudence.

6–31 It is submitted that failing to enforce any of the contractual terms is an unfortunate result of the logic of finding the contracts to have been void *ab initio*. What is more important in policy terms is the avoidance of systemic risk in the derivatives markets and the concomitant need to admit a limited application of the doctrine of severance. Severance should not be employed to give effect to the transaction by alternative means, nor as a means of providing a defence to restitution. Rather, severance ought to be permitted to give effect to standard market arrangements such as margin, collateral, set-off and other risk management provisions in interest rate swap contracts which provide that payments are satisfied by payment on a net basis or by recourse to collateral assets supplied to guarantee payment. The approach of the courts has been to ignore all

[42] See generally Birks, *An Introduction to the Law of Restitution* (Oxford, 1989).
[43] [1998] 2 All ER 272 at 288.
[44] [1994] 4 All ER 890 at 967.
[45] [1998] 2 All ER 272 at 288.

of the terms of the interest rate swap contracts, thus increasing the possibility of systemic risk caused by contract failure.[46]

Evaluating the approach

6–32 There is a basic problem of approach with Hobhouse J.'s judgment. At the first level he does not make any distinction between those contracts which had already terminated and those which still had time to run on them.[47] Under the terms of the standard market contracts used between the parties, all contracts should be considered as being a single agreement for the purposes of set-off on insolvency and generally. At this level Hobhouse J., had he taken the point, would have been correct in saying that expired and unexpired contracts should be treated as one for the purposes of legal analysis.[48] Alternatively, this does take account of the mutual debts analysis[49] which would require that each transaction be considered separately, treating those contracts which have been performed as being of no further interest. The drawback of this latter approach is that, where the transactions are simply cash-settled, to achieve equity between the parties it would be necessary to set off all amounts paid and payable on the basis that there was an absence of consideration *ab initio*.

6–33 It is submitted that there is a material difference between the *Islington* and *Sandwell* litigation. In the case where a lump sum has been paid upfront, there is a stronger argument that those moneys should be held on trust for the payer than in the situation where amounts of money were contingently owed on a reciprocal basis over time, where there is no transfer of any capital asset which it would have been possible to identify as separate property capable of being held on trust.[50] The income payments were intended simply to melt into current accounts and were less identifiable as the subject of a tracing claim.[51] Significantly, the income amounts in *Sandwell* discharged an obligation at the moment that they were paid. However, in *Islington* there was a capital sum which was owed contractually back to the payer in any event—being repaid (we are told by Hobhouse J.[52]) during the life of the contract. The latter case concerns a series of mutual debts, or amounts owed reciprocally under an executory contract, which do not involve payments other than income payments. That no point was raised on this distinction, and that no point was taken in the judgment on this distinction, fails to underscore the difference between these derivative contracts.

Restitution and common law

6–34 There appear to be two basic distinctions in the law of restitution: first, awards made on the basis of impost without consideration or, secondly, awards on the basis of compulsion. The swaps cases arise out of voluntary transfers of property which were rendered involuntary by the finding in *Hazell* that the

---

[46] On this see Hudson, *The Law on Financial Derivatives* (2nd ed., London, Sweet and Maxwell, 1998).

[47] As considered immediately above.

[48] As a corollary they should also have been treated as one for the purposes of the final judgment, with amounts owed being set off against amounts owing.

[49] Considered above under *Six Legal Analyses of Financial Derivatives.*

[50] *cf. Re Goldcorp* [1995] 1 A.C. 74.

[51] *Bishopsgate v. Homan* [1995] 1 W.L.R. 31; *Roscoe v. Winder* [1915] 1 Ch. 62.

[52] As set out in the *Repayment Analysis*, considered in Chapter 2.

contracts had been void *ab initio*. The core belief of the High Court and the Court of Appeal was shown in the decision of Leggatt L.J. that the solvency of the authority entitled the bank to recovery "in full". The attitude appears to be that the availability of restitution and of the use of equitable remedies is motivated by the understanding that there was injustice in allowing the authority to use the money without accounting "in full" to the banks. The issue arises whether or not there should be a difference only if insolvency in the manner set out by the restatement of the central principles of restitution by Goff and Jones[53] that there be reversal of unjust enrichment except in cases of insolvency or some other affront to public policy. It is contended that the restitutionary principles applied by the High Court and Court of Appeal do not follow any such rigidly applied principle. Rather, those courts sought to apply conceptions of justice and conscionability. As will be apparent from the following discussion, those principles can be properly identified as equitable rather than restitutionary.

Money had and received

6–35 Hobhouse J. was asked to decide the availability of a restitutionary claim based on the common law action for money had and received.[54] Lord Goff sought to amend the jargon describing claims in this area. Rather than continuing to talk about a claim which, literally at least, seems to make less and less sense, the claim for money had and received[55] is "... what we nowadays call a personal claim in restitution at common law".[56] The principles upon which a restitutionary remedy will be granted are threefold:[57] (1) that some other party or parties have been enriched by the receipt of a benefit; (2) that the benefit has been gained at the claimant's expense; and (3) that the circumstances of their enrichment are such that it would be unjust for them to retain the benefit. Another means of expressing the same principles is to require the claimant to show that an "unjust factor" underlay the circumstances of his payment.[58] At that first level, the three principles would appear to be satisfied where the authority has received the payments on the basis of the validity of a contract which was in fact found to be void.

6–36 Hobhouse J. took the view that there was a prima facie claim in relation to money had and received on the facts in front of him. However, he dealt at the outset with the limitation which he felt had to be placed on the scope of the doctrine of failure of consideration to illustrate that that restitutionary response at common law was not appropriate. Failure of consideration was appropriate only where there had been a total absence of consideration—whereas the interest rate swaps he was asked to consider had been partly performed because some payments had been made before the parties realised that the contract was void *ab initio*. Hobhouse J. was concerned that justice required more than a personal claim

---

[53] Jones ed., *Goff and Jones on the Law of Restitution* (4th ed., London, 1993), p.29.

[54] The High Court considered that a proprietary claim was appropriate to compensate the banks for the loss of their property. The restitutionary response based on a personal claim at common law would have been motivated by the unjust factor of allowing the local authority to retain use of the property during the performance of the void contract.

[55] Less and less understood given the problem of understanding money as property given its nature as records in an electronically-held account, see *The Legal Context of Money* in Chapter 4 and also Smith, "Tracing and Electronic Funds Transfer" in *Restitution and Banking Law* (Rose ed., Mansfield Press, Oxford,1998), p.120.

[56] [1996] 2 All E.R. 961 at 967.

[57] Jones ed., *Goff and Jones on the Law of Restitution* (4th ed., London, 1993), p.16.

[58] Burrows, *The Law of Restitution* (London 1993), p.7, n.7.

which would provide only simple interest. Instead he sought a means by which he could make an order for a proprietary remedy which would include an order for compound interest. Therefore, his Lordship considered that arguments based on restitution would not be appropriate. He indicated a preference for equitable proprietary claims based on a standard of conscionability. In short that it would have been unconscionable for the authority to have had use of the money under a contract which, it transpired, was void without being forced to account to the bank on a proprietary basis. The majority of the House of Lords, as considered below in the *equity approach*, overturned that part of the decision which was based on the availability of equitable proprietary claims and found that a personal action would be satisfactory to dispose of the matter before them in relation to the non-availability of compound interest. Given the focus of Hobhouse J. on equitable remedies, there is therefore only a truncated account of the scope of the action for money had and received in the decision of Hobhouse J.. What his Lordship focused on in greater detail was the restitutionary claim for lack of consideration.

Total failure, or absence, of consideration

6–37 As discussed Hobhouse J. considered the previously understood action of "failure of consideration" to be better reclassified as "absence of consideration". The purpose of the reclassification, on the cases then before him, was to exclude its application in favour of an application of equitable principle. It is instructive to analyse, first, the manner in which that reclassification was carried out and, secondly, the potential application of this new categorisation to swaps contracts. Leggatt L.J. considered that there was no substantive issue to consider on the facts of *Islington* when he held that "The parties believed that they were making an interest rate swaps contract. They were not, because such a contract was *ultra vires* the local authority. So that they made no contract at all." [59] On this basis, the argument proceeds that there was an absence of consideration rather than some failure of consideration. What is not clear is what this idea of "absence", rather than simply "failure", connotes.

How total is "total"?

6–38 The core issue as taken by the court at first instance and by the Court of Appeal, is the precise framing of the action related to a failure of consideration. As Hobhouse J. defined the action:

> "The phrase failure of 'consideration' is one which in its terminology presupposes that there has been at some stage a valid contract which has been partially performed by one party. It is essentially a concept for use in the law of contract and provides a common law remedy governed by rigid rules granted as of right where the contract becomes ineffective through breach or otherwise."[60]

His Lordship therefore saw a failure of consideration as being born out of a valid contract that is not performed. Bound up with this conception is an understanding that the remedy is somehow close to the notion of frustration of contract in that it

[59] [1994] 4 All E.R. 890 at 967.

[60] *ibid.* at 924, *per* Hobhouse J.

deals with the entirety of the consideration, rather than a partial failure in it. As his Lordship continued:

> "The rules that govern the application of the principle include the technical concept of an 'entire' consideration, what amounts in law to a total failure of consideration, and the absence of defences to the action for the recovery of money paid for a consideration which has wholly failed."[61]

6–39 The focus is on a consideration which is absent in its entirety. These cases are to be considered as distinct from a case where the contract is itself found to be invalid, here on grounds of *ultra vires*, and therefore incapable of performance by intervention of law:

> "In the case of *ultra vires* transactions such as those with which I am concerned where there is not and never has been a contract, I prefer to use the phrase 'absence of consideration'. I note that this was the phrase used by the House of Lords in the *Woolwich* case[62] ..."[63]

In this short space, a new tradition in the law of restitution is introduced. There is, in any event, dispute as to the breadth of the proposition that the failure of consideration is required to be "total" let alone an extension of the concept of "totality" via a literal reading that takes "absence" to be its synonym for analytical purposes. The requirement of totality is considered in more detail below in the context of the *restitution approach*,[64] where Lord Goff considered that this reclassification went too far. Hobhouse J. proceeded on the basis that it is necessary to demonstrate that the whole of the consideration failed, rather than simply some part of it.

Where does this idea of totality come from?

6–40 In justifying this approach, Hobhouse J. cited the decision of Viscount Simon in *Fibrosa Spolka Akcyjna v. Fairburn Lawson Combe Barbour Ltd*,[65] where his Lordship held, in the context of the doctrine of failure of consideration, "it is, generally speaking, not the promise which is referred to as the consideration, but the performance of the promise. The money was paid to secure performance and, if performance fails, the inducement which brought about the payment is not fulfilled." These dicta themselves drew on an older tradition that considers the status of a total failure of consideration.[66] The principle of failure of consideration is located in the older authorities with the concentration being on *performance* and not on the *promise*. That is, one does not give consideration as part of the fundamentals of a contract by a promise to perform, but rather by the very performance itself. In the context of simple contracts of sale, the line between promise and performance is a comparatively easy one to draw. However, when considering contracts that have an executory element to them, the line between representation that there will be performance and the incremental performance itself, is a more complicated one.

---

[61] [1994] 4 All E.R. 890 at 924, *per* Hobhouse J.
[62] [1993] A.C. 70.
[63] [1994] 4 All E.R. 890 at 924, *per* Hobhouse J.
[64] Chapter 8.
[65] [1943] A.C. 32 at 48.
[66] *Chandler v. Webster* [1904] 1 K.B. 493.

Where does this idea of totality lead to?

6–41 When considering interest rate swaps, the issue arises again: what constitutes the performance of such an agreement? At the first level, the mutual debts analysis would indicate that each separate payment constitutes a separate performance of a distinct obligation.[67] On that analysis there is not a *total* failure of consideration where individual payments have been made as part of a larger arrangement. Each individual payment would be said to have been perfected once it had been made. On the mutual debts analysis or financial forwards analysis, an interest rate swap analysed as a series of forward transactions is performed each time reciprocal payments required under the contract are performed. In respect of a forward transaction, as discussed above, performance takes place when the contractually due amount of value is transferred by the payer to the payee. Thus, in a mutual debt/financial forward interest rate swap, performance takes place on the appropriate transfer of value referable to each swap payment. In-line with market practice, that is one the payment of a net amount (satisfying two distinct payment obligations) on a given reset date.

6–42 The contrary argument would maintain that performance requires conduct and completion of an entire, single executory contract. To maintain that there is only performance once the entirety of the contract has been performed would be to say that all contracts are voidable until they expire. While there is some superficial attraction in the notion that all legal agreements or undertakings are capable of being made void by the courts or by the parties, that would be to suggest that restitutionary remedies attached to failure of consideration should always be available to the parties to a partially performed contract *throughout the life* of that agreement, rather than being introduced as a remedial event *on the occurrence* of some unjust factor. Therefore, it would be logically uncomfortable for it to be said that there is performance only on expiry of the contract.

6–43 It is submitted that it would be better to consider that restitutionary claims and remedies for failure of consideration can only arise where there has been some defect in the performance of the contract. It cannot be in accordance with principle to say that such claims are always in abeyance from the moment the contract is created, as though some implied but inactive term of the agreement, waiting to be activated. The occurrence of the unjust factor is the event which makes possible *for the first time* the restitutionary possibilities of failure of consideration. As Hobhouse J. put it himself:

> "If the opposite party has at least partially performed his obligations under the contract so as to confer some benefit upon the claimant, then the claimant cannot rely upon the principle."[68]

There is then an "all or nothing" element to the availability of restitutionary remedies to reverse unjust enrichment where there has been alleged failure of consideration. Considering the partial performance of the contract would require minute inspection of nominate and innominate terms of that agreement, where a swaps agreement requires the making of representations and the delivery of credit support documentation, there can be no argument but that that constitutes *at least some part* of the consideration for the counterparty entering into the transaction. However, it could not be in accordance with principle that delivery of an agreement to provide a level of collateral could be said to preclude purely in itself

---

[67] See Chapter 3, above.

[68] [1994] 4 All E.R. 890 at 925, *per* Hobhouse J.

a claim based on failure of consideration to recover moneys paid under an *ultra vires* contract.

Total failure and partial performance

6–44 The tension which Hobhouse J. addresses is how it is that the logic of "absence of consideration" should apply to a situation where one of the Sandwell swaps had been completely performed before the commencement of proceedings. However, there is little analysis of the situation where there have been payments made under the other swaps in both *Islington* and *Sandwell* where those transactions were potentially to be considered as a series of forwards constructed as mutual debts. In considering the two actions before him, Hobhouse J. focused on the third and fourth swaps under which Sandwell had made no payments at all (because the netting arrangements meant that they owed no surplus amount to the bank). In that situation, his Lordship held that there was an absence of consideration. However, with reference to the *Islington* swap and the second *Sandwell* swap, there was partial performance; with complete performance of the first *Sandwell* swap. As his Lordship puts it: "... neither party can, on the contractual approach, say that there was any failure of consideration, let alone any total failure"[69] on the basis that the first *Sandwell* swap had been executed.

6–45 Therefore, Hobhouse J. moved on to consider the position in connection with an *ultra vires* contract where there is an absence of consideration, given the inapplicability of the *Fibrosa* test of total failure of consideration. He held that:

> "... in the absence of some special factor money paid under an *ultra vires* contract can be recovered as money had and received in the same manner as can money paid for a consideration that has totally failed."[70]

These dicta appear in the wake of the decision of Lush J. in *Brougham v. Dwyer*[71] which held that, in relation to the failure of the Birkbeck Building Society:

> "... the defendant had received moneys belonging to the building society under a transaction which had no validity of any sort ... The case appears to me to be on all fours with one in which money has been advanced on something which was thought to be a contract, but as to which it turns out there had been a total failure of consideration ...."[72]

As such, the "ordinary contractual principle" of failure of consideration could not apply where there has been no *total* failure of consideration. In this line of cases are the insurance cases in which policyholders were entitled to recover their premiums on the basis that they would have been recoverable at common law as money had and received.[73] Similarly, in the hire purchase cases where the bill of sale, under which payments were made between the parties, was subsequently held to be void, it was held that sums paid could be recovered as money had and

---

69 [1994] 4 All E.R. 890 at 925.

70 *ibid.* at 926, Hobhouse J.

71 (1913) 108 L.T. 504 at 505.

72 See also *Re Coltman* (1881) 19 Ch.D. 64, CA.

73 *Re Phoenix Life Assurance Co, Hoare's Case* (1862) 2 John and H. 229; 70 E.R. 1041; *Flood v. Irish Provident Assurance Co Ltd* [1912] 2 Ch. 597; see also [1994] 4 All E.R. 890 at 926, *per* Hobhouse J.

received and not on the terms of any general contract formed in the lead-up to the creation of the void bill of sale.[74]

6–46 That the partial performance is considered to be of no importance in the analysis, is made clear in the *Sandwell* swaps. As Hobhouse J. held:

> "... the plaintiffs are entitled to recover from the defendants the net sums claimed in money had and received. ... The fact that the first Sandwell swap 'contract' was fully performed does not make any difference. The payments made had exactly the same status as the other payments the subject matter of these actions."[75]

6–47 Rather than consider the many available analyses of the manner of payments made under a swap transaction, all payments are considered to be the same despite the evident differences between the deep discount structures and the vanilla structure.[76] On the basis of these authorities the central question was whether or not there was something which could be said to constitute consideration on the contract between the parties under the interest swap agreements. In the judgment of Legatt L.J., the issue of whether or not failure of consideration was partial or total was one which could be addressed in a more straightforward manner than had been attempted by the High Court or by counsel before the Court of Appeal:

> "There can have been no consideration under a contract void *ab initio*. So it is fallacious to speak of the failure of consideration having been partial. What is meant is that the parties did, in the belief that the contract was enforceable, part of what they would have been required to do if it had been. As it was, they were not performing the contract even in part: they were making payments that had no legal justification, instead of affording each other mutual consideration for an enforceable contract." [77]

In his view the proper analysis of payments made under a purported contract which has no enforceability at law, are simply not consideration of any sort for the obligations sought to be assumed under that agreement.

Getting what you expected

6–48 The argument for Westdeutsche in this context proceeded by considering whether or not the parties received what they had contracted for. Counsel for the bank sought to rely on cases where there was held to be some consideration where the party involved "got exactly what she contracted to get"[78] and therefore that the bank had not received what it had contracted for.[79] Principally these cases concerned the purchase of goods and securities, and revolved around the issue whether or not the thing acquired under the contract was materially the same as

---

[74] *Davies v. Rees* (1886) 17 Q.B.D. 408; *Bradford Advance Co. Ltd v. Ayers* [1924] W.N. 152, *per* Bailhache J.; *North Central Wagon Finance Co Ltd v. Brailsford* [1962] 1 W.L.R. 1288; [1962] 1 All E.R. 502, *per* Cairns J.

[75] [1994] 4 All E.R. 890 at 936.

[76] See most recently the Court of Appeal in *Guinness Mahon v. Kensington and Chelsea R.L.B.C.* [1998] 2 All E.R. 272.

[77] [1994] 1 W.L.R. 938, 953; [1994] 4 All ER 890 at 969.

[78] *Linz v. Electric Wire Co of Palestine Ltd* [1948] AC 371, where the plaintiff had contracted to buy preference shares that were subsequently held to have been invalidity issued. On a similar basis, the bank relied upon *Rowland v. Divall* [1923] 2 K.B. 500 where the plaintiff had bought a car in which he had not, in fact, been given good title under the sale.

[79] [1994] 4 All E.R. 890 at 928.

the thing which the party had intended to acquire. Hobhouse J. sought to distinguish those authorities on the basis that they were:

> "... very different from the present case where there was in truth no bargain at all and problems of deciding what was the essential part of the bargain do not arise and there can be no question whether the plaintiff's conduct has affected his right to treat the contract as rescinded."[80]

The distinction is an uncomfortable one which is stated rather than explored in the judgment. On similar grounds, in considering the pre-incorporation contract in *Rover International Ltd v. Cannon Film Sales Ltd (No.3)*[81] it was held that moneys paid to the unincorporated entity were recoverable on grounds of mistake of fact. Hobhouse J. distinguished that case on the basis that the Court of Appeal's decision in *Rover* had been based in contract rather than "quasi-contract" or restitution.

6–49 However, it is difficult to distinguish the *Islington* and *Sandwell* cases from the cases cited by *Westdeutsche*. There was every bit as much an agreement in *Sandwell* and *Islington* as there had been in those others, in that the parties had considered their commercial aims and had adopted a large amount of sophisticated risk allocation documentation from standard market practice as well as their own particular requirements. What is beyond question is that, absent the decision of the House of Lords in *Hazell* the parties would have continued to contract perfectly happily. The agreements had been partly performed before it was found that such agreements were without a good basis in law.

Severance

6–50 Given the argument about the total failure of the contract, the question is the role of "severance" here and whether the void commercial terms could be separated from the risk management and credit enhancement provisions which would not have been beyond the *vires* of either party. The possibility of severance arose from Dillon L.J.'s discussion of the decision in *Rugg v. Minett*.[82] That case concerned contracts for the purchase of casks which were to be filled with turpentine. Some of the cases had been filled and others had not. It was held that property had not passed in those casks which had not been filled because it was impossible to identify those casks which would belong to the plaintiff until any such casks had been filled.[83] The issue was therefore whether the remedy could be applied differently in connection with identified and non-identified casks.

6–51 Dillon L.J. summarised the decision in *Rugg v. Minett*[84] as being a case in which the purchaser had been entitled to recover as money had and received the proportion properly attributable to the casks in which the property had not passed when they were destroyed by fire. However, title to the casks that had been filled had passed to the plaintiff. Therefore, it was apparent that there had been no *total* failure of consideration in respect of the whole of the payment in advance on account of the purchases generally, because of the delivery of those casks that had

---

80 [1994] 4 All E.R. 890 at 928.

81 [1989] 1 W.L.R. 912; [1989] 3 All E.R. 413.

82 (1809) 11 East. 210; 103 E.R. 985.

83 This decision should be compared with the decision of the Privy Council in *Re Goldcorp Exchange* [1995] 1 A.C. 74 concerning the need to segregate trust property from other property, as considered below; as contrasted with the decision of the Court of Appeal in *Hunter v. Moss* [1994] 3 All E.R. 215.

84 [1994] 4 All E.R. 890 at 960.

been filled. The court in *Rugg* therefore decided that it had jurisdiction to sever the consideration between filled and unfilled casks. As a result, the court held that the part attributable to the casks which had not been filled had wholly failed.[85] As Dillon L.J. continued:

> "I do not see why a similar process of severance should not be applied where what has happened, in a purely financial matter, is that there has been a payment of money one way and a payment of smaller sums of money the other way. The effect of severance is that there has been a total failure of consideration in respect of the balance of the money which has not come back."[86]

The issue therefore is why severance had not been similarly available with reference to the *Sandwell* litigation where some of the contracts had been performed. The further issue is whether some of the payments made between the parties could be treated as settled (thus supporting a mutual debts analysis) or whether they are to be required as part of a single (executory) contract which had yet to be performed.

6–52 Dillon L.J. did not need to rely exclusively on the doctrine of severance in reaching his decision for the banks. Rather, he decided that the early cases decided under the Grants of Life Annuities Act 1777 justified recovery by the bank under a personal claim in restitution at common law on the basis that the authority would have been unjustly enriched. That unjust enrichment could be said to have arisen on the basis that there was no consideration for the payment by Westdeutsche of the £2.5 million and therefore the balance which has not so far been repaid by Islington could therefore be recovered by Westdeutsche.[87] The argument on behalf of the authority was that there had been partial performance by dint of those payments which had been made under the contract. The implied analysis must be that there is a single executory contract created by the swap agreements.

6–53 Lord Ellenborough's statement in *Hudson v. Robinson* [88] that "an action for money had and received is maintainable whenever the money of one man has, without consideration, got into the pocket of another" is applied by Dillon L.J.[89] It follows from that statement that Westdeutsche was entitled to recover the balance of the £2.5 million from Islington under a personal claim in restitution at common law, or, following Lord Goff in *Lipkin Gorman*[90] "unjust enrichment at the expense of the owner of the money".[91] It should be remembered that, in this context, Dillon L.J. was considering the common law position, rather than the availability of a remedy in equity.[92] Dillon L.J., in considering these dicta of Lord Ellenborough in *Hudson*, held that the payments were not to be considered as purely voluntary because they had been intended to be made for the consideration which had been expressed in the annuity deed. That would be the case with respect to the payments which were made each way in *Islington* on the basis that

[85] The decision in *Rugg v. Minett* is cited with approval by Viscount Simon L.C. in *Fibrosa Spolka Akcyjna v. Fairburn Lawson Combe Barbour Ltd* [1943] A.C. 32 at 32, 48, as well as by Dillon L.J. in the *Islington* litigation.

[86] [1994] 4 All E.R. 890 at 961.

[87] *ibid.*

[88] (1816) 4 M.and S. 475 at 478.

[89] [1994] 4 All E.R. 890 at 962.

[90] [1991] 2 A.C. 548 at 572.

[91] [1994] 4 All E.R. 890 at 962.

[92] See dicta of Clarke J. at [1995] 1 All E.R. 545 at 557.

neither party had intended to make a gift to the other.[93] The issue of severance is pursued in Chapter 12, in the context of the *suitability approach*.

Mistake

6–54 The point which is not given much attention in any of the swaps cases is that the swaps documentation provides expressly for a representation that both parties have the capacity to enter into the contract and to perform all their obligations under the contract.[94] Where this representation fails, the contracts provide that a failure in respect of such a representation is an event of default under the contract, leading to a right in the non-defaulting party to termination. Hobhouse J. was alone among the judges who heard the *Islington* case in addressing the point in the context of the doctrine of mistake between the parties as to the capacity of one of them.[95] He found "[t]here is no evidence or allegation in either case that the relevant bank was mistaken as to any actual fact."[96] However, on balance it does appear that the mistake as to the local authority's capacity to perform under the swaps contracts stemmed from a mistake as to the interpretation of the Local Government Act 1972. The issue of the viability of actions being brought in future cases on grounds of mistake of law was not considered at this stage. However, later in the same judgment, his Lordship held that:

> "There was no consideration for the making of the payment. The fact that the plaintiff's mistake was not a mistake as to any actual matter of fact does not preclude the plaintiff from recovery. The plaintiff's payment does not fall to be categorised as a voluntary payment."[97]

As such it remains at large whether there was a mistake as to law and whether or not this could have precluded a claim for restitution. It is stated on the facts of all of the swaps cases at first instance that the swaps market was aware of the risk of local authority incapacity to perform under swaps agreements some time before the *Hazell*[98] litigation commenced.[99] Further, there was the Audit Commission report and the opinions of many of the legal advisers involved in the market place that these transactions would be held to be valid at law. Therefore, it is not to say that there was a failure to appreciate a risk and therefore no mistake. At some point during the conduct of these transactions and before the creation of further agreements, the parties were in error as to the validity of the contracts that they were purporting to make.

6–55 There is, however, a distinction between an *assumption* that something is the case and a *mistake* as to whether or not something is the case. The view propounded by Hobhouse J. would seem to suggest that this was not a case involving a mistake because the parties were acting on an assumption as to the validity of their contracts. This assumption view suggests that the risk was not considered and therefore was not, in any sense, an active factor that impacted on

---

93 [1994] 4 All E.R. 890 at 962.

94 As discussed above in Chapter 4, this provision is common to the ISDA terms and also to the BBAIRS terms for swaps and OTC derivatives dealings more generally.

95 [1994] 4 All E.R. 890 at 931.

96 *ibid.*

97 [1994] 4 All E.R. 890 at 956.

98 *Hazell v. Hammersmith and Fulham* [1992] 2 A.C. 1; [1991] 2 W.L.R. 372; [1991] 1 All E.R. 545.

99 McKendrick, "Local Authorities and Swaps: Undermining the Market?" in *Making Commercial Law: Essays in Honour of Roy Goode* (Cranston ed., Oxford, 1997).

the parties. However, on the facts there was an assessment of the risks. The standard market contracts purported to deal explicitly with these risks, as set out above. To suggest that there was no operative mistake in the minds of the parties in the creation of some or, in this writer's opinion, all of the contracts is a contention which does not bear any scrutiny of the facts. The mistake that is made is a mistake as to the legal capacity of local authorities in the United Kingdom. As such this is a mistake of law which, in the opinion of the High Court, precludes an action for money had and received.[100] Hobhouse J. came to this conclusion with some reluctance.[101] However, this did not prevent Hobhouse J. from awarding an equitable remedy achieving a restitutionary purpose, as discussed above.[102]

[100] *Lonrho Ltd v. Shell Petroleum Co Ltd* [1982] A.C. 173 at 185; *Bilbie v. Lumley* (1802) 2 East. 469; *Sharp Bros v. Chant* [1917] 1 K.B. 771; *National Pari-Mutuel Association Ltd v. R* (1930) 47 T.L.R. 110; and *per* Hobhouse J. [1994] 4 All E.R. 890 at 931, below.

[101] [1994] 4 All E.R. 890 at 933. The conclusion was after consideration of a number of authorities which advance the proposition that a contract is capable of being set aside on the basis that the parties proceeded on a common mistake where there is a "mutual mistake and misapprehension as to their relative and respective rights": *Cooper v. Phibbs* (1867) LR 2 HL 149, 170. See also *Earl Beauchamp v. Winn* (1873) LR 6 HL 223, esp. 233; *Rover International Ltd v. Cannon Film Sales Ltd (No.3)* [1989] 3 All ER 423 at 440; *Bell v. Lever Bros. Ltd* [1932] AC 161 at 166, *per* Viscount Simon.

[102] However, Lord Goff approaches the question of mistake differently, as considered in the *restitution approach*, below.

Part III

A Question of Ideology: Unjust Enrichment or Equity?

Chapter 7

The conflict between equity and the law of unjust enrichment

The role of equity, not restitution, in the High Court

7–01 The following passage in the judgment of Hobhouse J. is central to his decision and to his analysis of swaps transactions[1]:

> "In my judgment, the correct analysis is that any payments made under a contract which is void *ab initio*, in the way that an *ultra vires* contract is void, are not contractual payments at all. They are payments in which the legal property in the money passes to the recipient, but in equity the property in the money remains with the payer. The recipient holds the money as a fiduciary for the payer and is bound to recognise his equity and repay the money to him ... The principle is the same in both cases: it is unconscionable that the recipient should retain the money. Neither mistake nor the contractual principle of total failure of consideration are the basis for the right of recovery."

What Hobhouse J. was doing in *Islington* and *Sandwell* was rejecting those arguments which did not fit with his underlying conviction as to the conceptual basis of the litigation, to wit: failure of consideration was the wrong premise for this action, it was equity which would be motivated to impose a resulting trust over the value paid away by the bank, on the grounds of the unconscionability of the retention of moneys paid, given that the transaction had been held to be void. It is important to stress that it is the unconscionability of the *retention* that is foremost in the court's mind. It is not concerned that there ought, on principle, to be a proprietary remedy in this type of commercial situation, but rather that it would be wrong to allow that money to remain in the possession of the recipient who is not, *ex post facto*, in conscience entitled to retain it. The ultimate analysis then was far more emotional and far less rigorous than the discussion of restitution which has excluded the application of many of the restitutionary remedies (principally consideration failure and mistake) to the facts before the High Court in *Islington*.

7–02 As will be evident from the analysis of the majority decision in the House of Lords, the focus of Lord Browne-Wilkinson's attention, in reshaping the rules of equity, was to focus on the moment at which conscience should intervene to impose an equitable solution by way of a reinvigorated doctrine of notice. By saying that knowledge of mistaken receipt is the factor which activates equity, Lord Browne-Wilkinson appears to be imposing a remedial constructive trust *de facto* if not *de jure*, as considered below under the *equity approach*. The equitable right is said to arise from the moment the knowledge arises—that is why it is said to be still an institutional constructive trust because it arises by operation of law. However, the constructive trust is imposed to act against the conscience of that

[1] [1994] 4 All E.R. 890 at 929.

knowing recipient—that is why it could be said to remedial because it is cast by the court as a means of providing a remedy for that abuse of good conscience.[2]

7–03 The approach adopted by Hobhouse J. had the effect of saying that: the existing state of affairs is wrong and, because there has been a receipt of money by a party which is considered to be unconscionable in the light of the surrounding circumstances, equity requires that this state of affairs gives rise to an equitable proprietary right on principle. In this way, Hobhouse J. was seeking to grant what was an institutional constructive trust to the banks. In saying that the trust is institutional is meant that it is based on the application of understood principles rather than a bespoke remedy created at the court's discretion, following a principled approach to ownership of the money that was paid by the banks.

7–04 Hobhouse J. found that there ought to be a division between legal and equitable ownership. In the words quoted immediately above he considered that the arrangement consisted of "... payments in which the legal property in the money passes to the recipient, but in equity the property in the money remains with the payer ...". The division between legal and equitable title is not, however, an express one. At no point did the parties, within their extensive negotiations or expansive documentation or otherwise, specify that equitable title in the property passed would remain with the payer. Rather, the court was imposing that analysis on the basis of the "unconscionability" of enabling the payee to retain the benefit of absolute ownership of that value despite there having been some failure of their common intention. It is this analysis which Lord Browne-Wilkinson criticised in his speech in the House of Lords. There ought to be no deemed division of title *ex post facto* as Hobhouse J. suggests, without the occurrence of some factor (such as knowledge of an unconscionable action) which, on principle, would require that equity grant a right in property. In short, there would have to be some event which rise to a need for a division in the beneficial ownership between legal and equitable rights due to an impact on the conscience of the legal owner of that property.[3]

7–05 The conclusions of Lord Browne-Wilkinson aside briefly, it is difficult to see whether or not Hobhouse J. intended to follow the same analysis in *Sandwell* as in *Islington*. *Islington* fits more neatly into the analysis of retention of proprietary rights because it involved a payment of a capital sum to the authority which the authority was later required to return. It is easier to attach proprietary rights to money (represented by capital sums held in electronic bank accounts) than it is to attach them to amorphous mass of small amounts of cash. Beginning with the capital sum, it is possible to extend that principle to the income amounts. This is one of the paradoxes of Hobhouse J.'s decision. There is some accounting for netted income amounts paid between the parties. What is primarily at issue, however, is title to the capital sum and compound interest on that sum. Unconsciously, there is a division between the analyses of the capital asset (the deep discount payment) and the income payments (the interest legs of the structure) just within the *Islington* structure. The analysis would appear to unfortunate not only because Lord Browne-Wilkinson and the majority in the House of Lords consider it to be erroneous in principle, but also because it is

---

[2] Millett, "Restitution: Taking Stock", delivering the Society of Advanced Legal Studies Lecture, Institute of Advanced Legal Studies, London, July 23, 1998, emphasising the continued distinction between institutional and remedial constructive trusts and the need to understand those applications of the constructive trust idea which are really wrongs and not implied trusts—see Chapter 11, below.

[3] It is here that the equity lawyer would seemingly look to knowledge, while the restitution lawyer would look for some unjust factor.

uneven in its application. It is not clear whether restitution of the capital asset is supposed to take effect in the same way as the interest payments.

7–06 For the restitution lawyer, the disappointment focuses on that final quoted sentence above: "Neither mistake nor the contractual principle of total failure of consideration are the basis for the right of recovery."[4] Rather, there was found to be a resulting trust over the deep discount payment. However, as considered below, it is not necessarily an easy matter to decide whether Hobhouse J. himself did intend his decision to be purely equitable or partly restitutionary. The former seems to have a stronger claim in the context of the judgment but there are clear acknowledgements of the role of restitutionary thinking in his Lordship's decision.

The birth of the Repayment Analysis

7–07 The *repayment analysis* has already been considered in some detail above.[5] What is important to say about its role within the decision of Hobhouse J. is that it is an integral part of the single paragraph that states the primacy of the code of equity over the putative rules of restitution in this context. As his Lordship continues from the passage last quoted above[6]:

> "Where payments both ways have been made the correct view is to treat the later payment as, *pro tanto*, a repayment of the earlier sum paid by the other party. The character of the remedy, both in law and equity, is restitution, that is to say putting the parties back into the position in which they were before. Accordingly the remedy is only available to a party on the basis that he gives credit for any benefit which he has received. He must give credit for any payments which have been made by the opposite party to him and, where the court thinks appropriate, pay a quantum meruit or quantum valebat. The same conclusion follows from the application of the principle of unjust enrichment: in so far as the recipient has made cross-payments to the payer, the recipient has ceased to be enriched."

The discussion of the Repayment Analysis set out earlier focused on the opening sentence of this passage. It concentrated on the difficulty of introducing an analysis of the payment structure of a swap which is so completely at odds with the contractual intentions of the parties.[7] However, the role of this analysis is better understood in the context of Hobhouse J.'s discussion of the role of equity.

7–08 The most difficult section of the decision is the following sentence: "Where payments both ways have been made the correct view is to treat the later payment as, *pro tanto*, a repayment of the earlier sum paid by the other party." It is difficult to see how payments made under a netting arrangement could possibly be considered to be repayments. Rather, they are either amounts owed simultaneously which are set-off, or there are two contingent liabilities which are subject to a condition precedent connected to the owing of a surplus amount.[8] Given that the payments *are* simultaneous, the reference to "an earlier amount" would have to be

4 [1994] 4 All E.R. 890 at 929.

5 See *Six Legal Analyses of Derivatives*, Chapter 3.

6 [1994] 4 All E.R. 890 at 929.

7 What is then unfortunate is that it has been taken out of this context by the Court of Appeal in *Kleinwort Benson v. Birmingham City Council* [1996] 4 All E.R. 733 and applied as a generic description of the manner in which a swap operates.

8 This latter analysis looks more like a contract for differences, within the meaning of the Gaming Act, than the former.

a reference to the previous *set* of reciprocal payments. This would clearly be a nonsense and would bear absolutely no relation to the contractual intentions of the parties. Further, the line between executed and non-executed transactions is one which Hobhouse J. chose to blur when he held that: "The fact that the first *Sandwell* swap 'contract' was fully performed does not make any difference. The payments made had exactly the same status as the other payments the subject matter of these actions."[9] So we are left with a core misconception of the payment structure of the interest rate swap—that there are never two payments, indeed there may not be any payment at all if the amounts off-set exactly.

7–09 The remainder of the statement bears closer relation to the contractual intention of the parties. In seeking restitution (in fact, rescission on these facts[10]) the parties are required to give credit that operates on a two-way basis. Amounts received are to be set off against amounts paid. It is important that that does not countenance the return of property paid over initially. Were the contracts formed on the basis of transfers of securities, there would be entitlement only to the net cash value rather than to the return of securities provided at the outset—a personal right and not a proprietary right.

7–10 It would be interesting to see whether or not this thinking would be applied in the case of total return swaps or in the repo[11] markets. With reference to repo's or stock lending,[12] there is an expectation that there is a retention of the proprietary right between the parties. The complication with interest rate swaps is whether or not there is that same expectation of the retention of proprietary rights. The answer from any market participant would be "yes". The proof is in the expectation that there would be compound interest payable to make good the commercial return that would have been obtained in the financial market. This is equivalent to a proprietary right attaching to money which gives the right-holder an entitlement equivalent to the money itself and the profit made on the money.

7–11 The matter can be seen by reference to the Court of Appeal decision in another swaps case *Birmingham*[13] which considered the availability of the defence of "passing on". The plaintiff bank had entered into an interest rate swap agreement with the defendant local authority. In the wake of the House of Lords decision in *Hazell*[14] it transpired that the agreement was void, being *ultra vires* the local authority. The agreement had provided that each party owe amounts of money to one another calculated by reference to a notional amount of money. Usually one payment being a floating rate of interest which has been swapped for the other payment which is a fixed rate of interest.[15]

7–12 The bank contended that the defence of passing on should be available to it on the basis that it had entered into further interest rate swap agreements with

---

[9] [1994] 4 All E.R. 890 at 936.

[10] On some of the difficulties with the application of rescission, see Burrows and McKendrick, *The Law of Restitution* (Oxford, 1997), pp.141–148.

[11] The 'repo' market was not considered in Chapter 2 on the basis that it is not generally considered to be a part of the derivatives family. Repo's are repurchase agreements where investors purchase securities, usually from the government, in return for a rate of interest and/or an undertaking that the security will be re-purchased at some time in the future by the issuer at a calculable rate.

[12] "Stock lending" is similar to a repo structure in that stock is lent to an investor who requires that stock for speculative or collateralisation purposes on the basis that it, or its equivalent is to be restored to the lender at a future date.

[13] [1996] 4 All E.R. 733.

[14] [1992] A.C. 1.

[15] Given that, in many of these swaps cases like *Islington*, a loan was made as part of the agreement and it was by reference to the amount of that loan that payments were calculated.

third parties to "hedge" its risk under the agreement with the local authority. It was this hedge that was said to constitute the passing on. The reason for that was the amount owed to the third party would be the inverse to that owed to or received from the local authority—the value of the hedge would be calculated to move in an opposite and roughly equal way to the value of the main contract. The Court of Appeal held that the hedging agreement was not a part of the main agreement with the local authority and therefore amounts paid under it would not attract the defence of passing on. The decision of the Court of Appeal in *Kleinwort Benson* is predicated on the difficult proposition advanced by Hobhouse J. that, when reciprocal payments are made under an interest rate swap, "the later payment is treated as, *pro tanto*, repayment of the earlier sum paid by the other party."[16]

7–13 For the Court of Appeal to seek a nexus between the agreement with the local authority and the hedging agreement with a third party would necessarily be a difficult task. Tracing any asset through such a mixture would be similarly complicated. However, the proper analysis of an interest rate swap, based on the analysis set out above, might show that it is possibly not a single executory contract in any event. The courts are assuming that there is one single contract (because the point is not being taken before them) and therefore looking for a hedge that operates in the same manner. When the interest rate swap is seen to be what it is, an amalgam of debts which may crystallise or may not, the nexus between the hedge to the original interest rate swap agreement perhaps seems less opaque.

7–14 The better approach might be to assess whether the risk assumed by the bank is one which the bank sought to address through hedging arrangements which were not a requirement of the agreement any more than it was a requirement of the agreement for the local authority to procure further risk management protection. The defence should only be available in those terms where the risk of passing on is within the common intention of the parties. In *Kleinwort Benson*, the plaintiff's hedging strategy was the result of a unilateral decision. The outcome of the Court of Appeal's decision appears to achieve a just result in those terms, but the reasoning behind it appears to open as many issues as it resolves. By restricting itself to the classical discussion of passing on, the Court of Appeal is failing to appreciate the context of modern portfolio theory.

7–15 Hobhouse J., in *Islington* and *Sandwell* is seeking the achieve "restitution" despite coming to it by avowedly equitable means. The most suitable remedy then is "credit for any benefit received". The result, though based on equity,[17] is the same as that which follows from the application of the principle of unjust enrichment. What is still not clear, however, is why it is that one payment must be seen as a "repayment of an earlier payment" to achieve this result. There is no difference in result between this approach and an equitable set-off. All that is happening is that there is a straightforward mathematical exercise. What it does show, interestingly, is that there is a problem of the analysis of the swaps contract which requires some sleight of hand to justify the award on equitable terms via *quantum meruit* or *quantum valebat*.

Is the remedy one in equity or in restitution?

7–16 Hobhouse J. is keen to point out that his judgment rests on a finding of unconscionability in allowing the local authority to retain the money for the life of

[16] [1994] 4 All E.R. 890 at 929, *per* Hobhouse J. and affirmed at [1996] 4 All E.R. 733 at 738, *per* Evans L.J.

[17] As considered above.

the void contract. That money is subject to an implied trust. The office of trusteeship is imposed on the local authority because of the unconscionability of retaining moneys paid under an agreement which was held in *Hazell* to have been void *ab initio*. As considered earlier, the decisions in *Islington* and *Sandwell* are based expressly on the basis of there having been unjust enrichment that it would be unconscionable not to reverse. The remedy appears to bear many of the characteristics of a resulting trust (although that term, nor any other, is used expressly), rather than being a constructive trust. As considered in detail below, a resulting trust is considered by Birks[18] and Chambers[19] to be the most appropriate restitutionary response to a case of unjust enrichment. The issue arises then whether Hobhouse J. intends a solution that is based on equity or on restitutionary principles. There is clearly some elision between the two concepts in his judgment.

Conclusions on the use of equity

7–17 As Hobhouse J. identifies the underlying judicial policy in this regard:

> "The application of the principle [underpinning the law of restitution and unjust enrichment] is subject to the requirement that the courts should not grant a remedy which amounts to the direct or indirect enforcement of a contract which the law requires to be treated as ineffective."[20]

In the case of an interest rate swap, that would require either that the parties receive their speculative return over the remainder of the putative life of the contract (it would be impossible to quantify this accurately unless the parties "wait and see" for the remainder of the 10–year period), or that the buyer of the swap receives a hedge for its interest rate exposure. The aim of the transactions was to receive a cash flow over time. As with building society mortgages, the financial institution securitises bundles of executory mortgage agreements.[21] That is, the institution markets these contracts in groups by selling them as securities to investors whose return is a payment calculated by reference to the value of cash flow received from the many mortgagors.[22] This enables the mortgagees to receive capital sums secured on the performance of their income assets over time. What the financial institutions do not want is for those cash flows to be interrupted.[23]

7–18 The same logic applies to the interest rate swap markets. The parties' intention is to secure a cash flow—that is a periodic payment of money over time. The parties do not want a lump sum equivalent—even if it takes into account the time value of money under the original interest rate swap. The parties are seeking to manage the volatility risks associated with an obligation to pay sums over time. Alternatively, where the transaction is speculative, they are seeking to receive the

---

[18] Birks, "Restitution and Resulting Trusts" in *Equity and Contemporary Legal Developments* (Goldstein ed., Jerusalem, 1992), pp.335, 364–73.

[19] Chambers, *Resulting Trusts* (Oxford, 1997).

[20] [1994] 4 All E.R. 890 at 929.

[21] Wood, *Title Finance, Derivatives, Securitisations, Set-off and Netting* (Sweet & Maxwell, 1995); Haynes, "Asset Securitisation", WG Hart Workshop 1998, Institute of Advanced Legal Studies, London.

[22] This structure is known as "asset securitisation".

[23] Brealey and Myers, *Principles of Corporate Finance* (5th ed., McGraw Hill, 1995); Smith and Walter, *Global Financial Services* (Harper & Row, 1990), which attest to the business school mantra: "cash flow is king".

speculative return on a given indicator over time.[24] The basis for a remedy which enforces the contract must therefore be either rescission or the replacement of the bargain.[25] In either case, there is little likelihood of effective, indirect enforcement of the contract as Hobhouse J. feared, at least not in the manner which the parties had originally intended.[26] Rather, it would be a lump sum, not the cash flow which was the original purpose of the transaction.

7–19 The central point is that any question relating to a payment made under a purported contract which is void *ab initio* is not a question which is capable of being solved by reference to principles of the common law of contract. Rather, it is addressed by equitable principles as to title in that value transferred. Hobhouse J. held that payments made in connection with a contract void *ab initio* leave the equitable title in the value transferred in the hands of the payer. That value is therefore held on trust for the payer. The basis for the repayment of money, as found by Hobhouse J., must therefore be a proprietary one and is therefore not based on a contractual claim. That remedy relies upon a notion of "unconscionability" rather than any doctrine of failure of consideration or mistake. This issue is the core of the decision of the majority in the House of Lords, and it is where that majority reject the decision of Hobhouse J.

7–20 The remainder of the book considers that various approaches taken by the members of the judicial committee of the House of Lords and by a variety of academic commentators, before resolving to advance a thesis of its own.

---

[24] In this situation that return is not capable of being ascertained in a lump-sum damages award because the actual return on that index over time is only capable of being ascertained at the end of that time period.

[25] It could be argued that damages aimed at replacement of the bargain would be an amount which could then be invested to produce the same return, thus producing the same economic result as the bargain. However, it is submitted, that that would not be enforcement of that economic result by the disallowed contract itself. Rather it would be an economically equivalent result achieved by other transactions.

[26] See also *R Leslie Ltd v. Sheill* [1914] 3 K.B. 607 at 613, *per* Lord Sumner.

Chapter 8

The restitution analysis

Lord Goff's restitutionary approach in *Islington*

8–01 The matter was appealed to the House of Lords specifically on the issue of the availability of compound interest. This specific point was broadened out to consider questions of the availability of equitable remedies. The chief proponent of a restitutionary view in the House of Lords was Lord Goff. What his Lordship did not embark upon was a detailed examination of the principles of restitution and their potential application to cases such as the *Islington* appeal. Therefore, this section will confine itself to the discussion of the issues as raised by Lord Goff. Towards its end it will set out the core test for restitution as contained in *The Law of Restitution* by Goff and Jones.[1] The new model approaches to restitution propounded by Birks and others are reserved to the *radical restitution approach*, where the hostile, equity lawyer's approach of Lord Browne-Wilkinson is stacked up against the core argument for the greater understanding of equitable remedies like resulting trust, tracing and subrogation as being means of effecting restitution of unjust enrichment on this new model.

8–02 This book has already identified the appeal in *Islington* as being a battle between equity and restitution. There is no doubt that it constitutes an ideal forum for the end–game in this conflict. That is the attitude which Lord Browne-Wilkinson appeared to take of the matter. However, it is important to note at this point that Lord Goff did not take up arms in such a fight, except to make a few general remarks of approach to a case of this sort. As such, many of his remarks will also be rehearsed in the section entitled the *commercial common sense approach*[2] under which his Lordship sought to keep a clear eye on the outline of, what was otherwise, a very difficult case. The battle is therefore reserved to the attitudes of the radical restitution school and the speech of Lord Browne-Wilkinson.

The core of the approach of Lord Goff

8–03 Whereas the arguments for the parties commenced at the level of personal claims in restitution, Lord Goff did not consider the detail of the claim for money had and received (which he renames the "personal restitutionary claim") because it was not an issue before the House of Lords. However, he did acknowledge that there was a real issue about the doctrine of "absence of consideration" developed by Hobhouse J. at first instance. He referred to a number of articles which have criticised the decision of Hobhouse J.[3]

8–04 Having left the issue of personal restitutionary claims to one side as issues which the House is not required to decide to dispose of the claim arising on the availability of compound interest, Lord Goff then considered the proprietary claim argument. As an introductory point he expressed his inability to see any

---

[1] Albeit, it is acknowledged that the latest edition is authored by Professor Jones.

[2] Discussed in Chapter 10, below.

[3] Birks (1993) 23 UWALR 195; Swadling [1994] R.L.R. 195; and Burrows [1995] R.L.R. 15.

reason why Westdeutsche ought to be entitled to a proprietary interest where they took a commercial risk to contract on the terms that they did. It was clear from the outset of his judgment that he would not seek to propound the award of any property claim on the basis that there was no common sense reason which appealed to his Lordship why it should have been allowed. Rather, it was only the speeches of the House of Lords in *Sinclair*[4] and the equitable jurisdiction to award compound interest which give him pause at all. In Lord Goff's opinion *Sinclair* should not have been overruled. In any event, *Sinclair* would not have provided an answer to the issues which arose in the *Islington* appeal in any event. Rather, the House in *Sinclair* should be considered to have been an example of the House of Lords seeking to provide a just result on the facts before them rather than seeking necessarily to create an iron-clad rules for future cases. Lord Goff considered that the resolution of the various principles in *Sinclair* was "not relevant to the decision in the present case".[5] In fact, he went further, to say that any overruling of *Sinclair* would be *obiter.*[6]

8–05 The central policy point made by his Lordship was that a personal claim in restitution should not be used as a means of enforcing an *ultra vires* contract. In a revealing use of language, his Lordship held that a *lender* must not be left without a remedy. However, the resulting trust would not be available to effect restitution, on the Birks model, on the basis that that would be inconsistent with the core principles of trust law. In such a situation, the role of trustee would be problematic in any event. In his Lordship's opinion, having imposed such a trust it is not clear what the obligations of the trustee would be in dealing with the property held under the resulting trust. The detail of the radical restitutionary approach was rejected as not being an issue before the court and therefore not necessary to determine the availability of compound interest on that appeal.

8–06 The argument ran as follows. In deciding the appeal, there was a need to do justice. The jurisdiction of the court to award remedies should extend as far as doing justice. The availability of an award of compound interest was to be considered to be a remedy based on justice. On the facts of the *Islington* appeal, the common law remedy would have been inadequate and therefore compound interest should have been awarded to achieve a just remedy for the "lender".[7]

8–07 It is clearly necessary to consider these findings in greater detail. At the outset it is useful to identify how the *restitution approach* would analyse the subject matter of the appeal: the interest rate swap. The judicial attitude to the derivative arises from Lord Goff in the House of Lords in *Islington,* for example: "Interest rate swaps can fulfil many purposes, ranging from pure speculation to more useful purposes such as the hedging of liabilities".[8] In accordance with the House of Lords in *Hazell,* there is great suspicion of the derivative. Bound up with it also is a recognition of the ability of the interest rate swap to achieve "useful purposes". As to the structure of the swap, and the preferable analysis of the payment structure, the speech is silent.

---

4 *Sinclair v. Brougham* [1914] A.C. 398.

5 [1996] 2 All E.R. 961 at 972.

6 *ibid.*

7 As considered below, a number of questions arise as to whether or not an award of compound interest is in fact an award of a proprietary interest in considering the use of money in a financial transaction.

8 [1996] 2 All E.R. 961 at 964.

Restitution by rescission

8–08 The form of restitution which Lord Goff favoured was one which returned the parties to the positions which they had occupied originally. This rescission approach would appear to achieve two goals. On general restitutionary grounds, it has a superficial attraction in that it terminates the unjust enrichment which the local authorities enjoyed at the expense of the banks. However, as considered below, it would not necessarily restore to the banks the whole of the loss which they have suffered by entering into the transaction, including the cost of hedging arrangements.[9] The second goal achieved by the rescission approach is the avoidance of seeming to enforce the void contract by an award of lost opportunity cost to the parties. In the case of cash-settled derivatives, any award of damages[10] would be equivalent to performance of the contract.

8–09 As considered above in the *Legal Context of Money*,[11] the central issue is the ability of common law or equitable remedies to restore the parties to the positions which they occupied before they purported to enter into the deep discount swap transaction. Given the nature of the property, all that would be required is a payment of an equal amount of the same currency. As Lord Goff considered the position, " ... in the present case, there ought to be no difficulty about that at all ... because the case is concerned solely with money". [12] The restitution-by-rescission approach simply requires that " ... each party should pay back the money that it has received—or more sensibly strike a balance, and order that the party who has received most should repay the balance ... with an appropriate order for the payment of interest".[13] The most suitable method of achieving the result would be to affect some form of set-off in respect of the moneys which remained outstanding. The irony is, of course, that the parties had already created a mechanism for the set-off of outstanding claims in the event that the purported contracts were terminated before its due expiry date. It is perhaps unfortunate that within Lord Goff's stated intention of "keeping my eyes on the simple outline of the case,"[14] this allocation of risks was ignored.

Absence of consideration

8–10 In analysing Hobhouse J. framing the doctrine of absence of consideration, Lord Goff is mindful that the concerns about the scope of failure of consideration need not be confined as narrowly, as the court at first instance considered, to a requirement of *total* failure of consideration. [15] Lord Goff referred to the academic commentary which was generated in response to the introduction of absence of consideration,[16] and explained that he will be bearing in mind the need to consider the appeal on the basis that failure of consideration may be the

---

[9] See on this the discussion of the defence of passing on in *Kleinwort Benson v. Birmingham C.C.* [1996] 3 All E.R. 741, below.

[10] Providing they are payable in the contract currency.

[11] Chapter 4.

[12] [1996] 2 All E.R. 961 at 966.

[13] *ibid.*

[14] *ibid.*.

[15] [1996] 2 All E.R. 961 at 967.

[16] Birks, "No Consideration: Restitution after Void Contracts" (1993) 23 U.W.A.L.R. 195; Swadling [1994] R.L.R. 73; Burrows, "Swaps and Friction between Common Law and Equity" [1995] R.L.R. 15.

more appropriate ground.[17] What this does not make clear is the precise attitude which Lord Goff was taking to the utility of a doctrine of absence of consideration replacing failure of consideration.

8–11 It is therefore important to see where this doctrine came from and how it fits into the *restitution approach*. The issue of absence of consideration arose in the decision of Lord Thurlow in *Heathcote v. Paignton*[18] in the context of the development of the law on absence of consideration:

> "... if the inadequacy of the consideration is so gross that it shows that the plaintiff did not really understand the transaction, or was so oppressed that he was glad to make it, this will amount to fraud. But if that amounts to fraud, it is simply a roundabout way of saying that gross inadequacy of consideration justifies setting aside a contract."[19]

These dicta highlight the problems of the chancery courts in considering commercial transactions. The first is that it is often only possible for the courts to interfere with freedom to contract where there has been some unconscionable behaviour which amounts to provable fraud. The other is the difficulty of intruding on freedom of contract by replacing the precise terms of the agreement with some standard arrived at by applying principles according to conscionability—for example, by judges fixing the price of the contract.

8–12 Atiyah points out the difficulty of measuring the adequacy of consideration in circumstances concerning speculative transactions, in particular financial derivatives. As he put it: "A person who indulges in a foolish speculation is apt to feel, after the speculation has failed, that it was an unfair arrangement. Of course, the same is true of any transaction which necessarily involves some element of risk, though that is not nearly so obvious to the parties involved".[20] The buyer of a product which generates a loss is likely to argue that there is little probity in the pattern of dealing which led to the creation of the arrangement in the first place. In the seventeenth century, the South Sea Bubble crisis produced a litany of litigation. For example, there were a number of decision which set aside contracts on the basis that they were "against natural justice", in the words of *Stent v. Baillie*.[21] In that case, shares had been sold at a vastly inflated price at the height of speculative fever. Similarly, inflated house prices were not enforced by the courts where the purchaser had lost money after the South Sea Bubble burst, even though he had already contracted for the purchase of the property.[22] The Lord Chancellor held that the property "would appear dear sold and consequently a bargain not fit to be executed by this court."[23] There were cases involving commercial risk which were upheld at this time.[24] As Atiyah saw it, there was a clash of moralities between the "paternal, protective Equity" of the old school and "the newer individualism, stressing risk-taking, free choice, rewards to the

---

[17] He acknowledges, however, that the issue of 'absence of consideration' was not, strictly, within the ambit of the appeal which he was required to consider: [1996] 2 All E.R. 961 at 968.

[18] (1787) 2 Bro. C. C. 167, 29 E.R. 96.

[19] Atiyah, *The Rise and Fall of Freedom of Contract*, (Oxford, 1979), p.174.

[20] *ibid.*

[21] 2 P. Wms. 217, 24 E.R. 596.

[22] *Savile v. Savile* (1721) 1 P. Wms. 745, 24 E.R. 596. Also *Keen v. Stuckley* (1721) Gilb. Rep. 155, 25 E.R. 109.

[23] 2 P. Wms 217 217, 24 E.R. 596 at 597.

[24] See, for example, *City of London v. Richmond* (1701) 2 Vern. 421, 23 E.R. 870; and discussion in Atiyah (1979), pp.175 *et seq.*

enterprising and sharp, and devil take the hindmost".[25] What better summary of the role of equity in the context of the financial derivatives markets?

Failure of consideration

8–13 The genesis of the doctrine of failure of consideration appears to have been in a decision of Holt C.J. in 1691 where he held that "the money was received without any consideration, and consequently was originally received to the plaintiff's use".[26] Atiyah considered this principle to have emerged from an understanding that contract and quasi-contract grew out of an purposive policy behind contracts existing to confer benefits which were to be recompensed.[27] Therefore, on this approach, there would be some ground for saying that the benefits envisaged by the parties in the creation of a contract are the rights that the court should be seeking to enforce. The context of suitability and risk can be seen as impinging on the manner in which restitution should be carried out in the case of commercial contracts. The parties envisaged a commercial state of affairs—the restitutionary response should mould itself in the image of that mutual expectation.

8–14 Of some interest in the context of equitable treatment of commercial agreements, is the old law on usury. In the emerging democracies of central and eastern Europe a law of usury forms a part of the counter-revolutionary commercial codes.[28] Similarly, many Islamic states retain legal prohibitions on the charging of interest on commercial transactions.[29] The eighteenth century approach to usury under English law made illegal contracts that charged unacceptable rates of interest.

8–15 The eighteenth century conception of suitability was orientated, in part, around this measure of reasonableness. The concern was, where the lender would receive his capital back, that a lender would nonetheless charge an unacceptable level of interest. As Atiyah put it:

> "All the accepted methods of borrowing money at rates above the permitted maximum depended ultimately on the concept of risk ... One of the most common procedures, [illustrated by *Chesterfield v. Janssen*[30]] was for the borrower to agree to repay a capital sum exceeding that which he borrowed, but only on the condition that he survived some other party ... The lender thus took the risk of losing all if the borrower died first, and this risk generally justified a rate of interest higher than that normally permitted ... A similar procedure ... was for the borrower to agree to pay an annuity terminable the borrower's death in return for a capital sum ..."[31]

This last alternative begins to look like a swaption or option, or (given the size of the payments) the structure undertaken in *Islington*. The upshot of this discussion would appear to be some notion of what constitutes an unconscionable bargain

[25] Atiyah, *The Rise and Fall of Freedom of Contract* (Oxford 1979), p.176.

[26] *Martin v. Sitwell* (1691) Holt 25, 25; 90 E.R. 912 at 913.

[27] Atiyah, *The Rise and Fall of Freedom of Contract* (Oxford, 1979), p.181.

[28] See, for example, Hudson, "The Counter-Revolutionary Business Code in Hungary", (1992) 18 *Review of Central and East European Law* 301.

[29] For example, Article 76 of the Bahraini Commercial Code permits the payment of interest only at an agreed rate which does not exceed the legal rate. In Saudi Arabia, interpretations of the Shi'a law permit the payment of commissions for rendering services but not the payment or charging of interest.

[30] (1750) 1 Atk. 331; 26 E.R. 211.

[31] Atiyah, *The Rise and Fall of Freedom of Contract* (Oxford, 1979), p.131.

emerging from the law on usury and similar cases as an historical part of the common law of contract and quasi-contract.[32]

On the conflict between equity and restitution

8–16 The development of a law of restitution, begun in no small part by Lord Goff himself,[33] has created a difficulty in defining the role for equity if the developing principle of reversing unjust enrichment is to continue to grow. As Lord Goff acknowledges "Equity lawyers ... have displayed anxiety that the equitable principles underlying these institutions may become illegitimately distorted ... they remain concerned that the trust concept should not be distorted, and also that the practical consequences of its imposition should be fully appreciated".[34]

8–17 While this section considers the *restitution approach*, it should be remembered that Lord Goff does not actively propound a didactically restitutionary view in his speech. Rather, he declared that the role of judicial committee was "simply to decide the questions at issue before it in the present case ...". [35] The question arising before him was defined as being whether there was an equitable proprietary claim available to a party who had paid money to a party under the terms of a contract which was *ultra vires* the other party and so void *ab initio*. Therefore, the issue of the role of equity was perhaps made secondary, although it clearly impinged on the question of the availability of an equitable proprietary claim.

8–18 While that was the restricted ambit of the question asked on appeal, there was still a marked difference of approach between Lord Goff and Lord Browne-Wilkinson. The core notion of restitution is restated by Lord Goff as being founded "upon a principle of justice, being designed to prevent the unjust enrichment of the defendant" in which context his Lordship cross-refers with the decision of the House of Lords in *Lipkin Gorman*.[36] The dissenting judgment on the issue of the availability of compound interest is founded on a principles of justice[37] and therefore it is clear that Lord Goff is applying principles akin to those which underpin restitution even though he is not expressly reaching any opinion on the turf war between restitution and equity.

8–19 The preference for a restitutionary approach appears from the assertion of the scope of the equitable jurisdiction to award compound interest. The *South Tyneside* litigation was a situation where the lack of availability of a proprietary remedy meant that compound interest was unavailable. Lord Goff identified this as being a result of the "technical and unrealistic"[38] nature of the equitable approach. On the equitable approach, despite a finding of personal liability to make restitution both at law and in equity, the court would have no jurisdiction to award compound interest. As Lord Goff put it, "[i]t seems strange indeed that, just because the power to trace property has ceased, the court's jurisdiction to award compound interest should also come to an end".[39]

---

[32] Simpson, *A History of the Common Law of Contract*, pp.113–117, 510–518.

[33] With the publication of the first edition of *The Law of Restitution* with Jones in 1966.

[34] [1996] 2 All E.R. 961 at 969.

[35] *ibid.*

[36] [1991] 2 A.C. 548.

[37] As considered in Chapter 6.

[38] [1996] 2 All E.R. 961 at 978.

Equitable proprietary claims

8–20 It is worth considering the words of Lord Goff in considering whether or not proprietary recovery ought to have been available to the bank. Lord Goff asked himself simply "why should it?" [40] Where the parties had entered into a commercial transaction that was then held to have been void *ab initio*, the suitable remedy would have been one which enabled each party to recover its money. That does not mean that the bank ought to have been given the benefits which flowed from a remedy which grants a secured, proprietary interest in the property. The point did not become acute in the *Islington* appeal because Islington was still solvent.[41] To reiterate the central complaint of this book, his Lordship considered that the bank had taken the risk of the defendant's insolvency without more. Therefore it should be considered to be in the same position as the authority's other creditors.[42]

8–21 Lord Goff would have disposed of the issue of proprietary claims at that point were it not for the decision in *Sinclair v. Brougham* and the nature of the equitable jurisdiction to award compound interest on the authorities.[43] The core question for Lord Goff on the precise appeal before the House was " ... whether that jurisdiction [to award compound interest] should be developed to apply in a commercial context, as in the present case".[44] There is an acceptance that the remedy available on the general law would be insufficient for financial transactions such as interest rate swaps.

8–22 There was no further, detailed discussion of the availability of equitable proprietary claims. To achieve the goal of the *restitution approach*, it was necessary to do justice on the facts of the particular appeal. The appeal related to a situation in which the parties were in disagreement as to the manner of repayment of amounts of money. Therefore, a claim in money would be adequate, provided that it was of the correct amount, whether that claim was based on personal or on proprietary grounds. In the market, the banks would have been able to earn amounts equivalent to compound interest on their money. Therefore, an award of compound interest was appropriate on grounds of justice to effect justice.

Achieving restitution at common law

8–23 His Lordship did turn to consider the appropriate principles affecting restitution at common law. The starting point for Lord Goff was with the speech of Lord Mansfield in *Moses v. Macferlan*,[45] where he said that the "gist of the action for money had and received"[46] is that "the defendant, upon the circumstances of the case, is obliged by the ties of natural justice and equity to refund the money". Thus, in considering whether or not compound interest ought to have been awarded to the bank, Lord Goff felt that it would have been "strange

---

[39] [1996] 2 All E.R. 961.

[40] *ibid.* at 968.

[41] Indeed, as considered above, the authority had made provision for a fund which would meet the whole of the bank's claim.

[42] [1996] 2 All E.R. 961 at 968.

[43] *ibid.*

[44] *ibid.* at 969.

[45] (1760) 2 Burr. 1005 at 1012.

[46] [1996] 2 All E.R. 961 at 980.

indeed if the courts lacked jurisdiction in such a case to ensure that justice could be fully achieved by means of an award of compound interest".[47] Lord Goff considered *Sinclair*, in particular, the speech of Lord Sumner[48] who was concerned that a common law right to restitution, based on what he considered to be "a notional or implied promise to repay", would have had the effect of sanctioning an *ultra vires* borrowing. However, Lord Dunedin was concerned that the absence of a remedy would lead to "the society's shareholders [being] enriched to the extent of some 500 per cent".[49] Lord Goff summed up this intractable problem with the conclusion that "[a]s a matter of practical justice, such a result was obviously unacceptable; and it was to achieve justice that the House had recourse to equity to provide the answer".[50] The point of principle which arose was clearly that there were equitable remedies which had been applied historically by the courts, whereas his Lordship was defining this issue as being a question of restitution.

8–24 There is no reason of principle why a personal claim in restitution should have been refused. In accordance with the prescriptions of the House of Lords in *Sinclair*, permitting such a claim would not have indirectly enforced the *ultra vires* contract, "for such an action would be unaffected by any of the contractual terms governing the borrowing,[51] and moreover would be subject (where appropriate) to any restitutionary defences ...".[52] Further, it achieved Lord Goff's underlying concern that the lender should not be without a remedy.

8–25 To achieve "full restitution"[53] it was deemed necessary to award compound interest, "having regard to the commercial realities of the case".[54] Lord Goff considered that Westdeutsche was entitled to receive what he described as "a complete remedy".[55] What is not clear is what this term means. At one level, a *complete* remedy would seem to require the restoration of Westdeutsche's proprietary rights in the value transferred. On these facts, the suitability of a cash payment by means of settlement would have given Westdeutsche *de facto* the whole of their claim in one judgment order. The *realpolitik* attitude of the courts to this case does appear to have interfered with the form of remedy which was being granted. The understanding that the case is simply about the payment of money avoids the question at law generally of rights in property and the more particular situation of physically-settled contracts. We know that there will not be a proprietary remedy on these facts. What is not clear on the *restitution approach* is "why".

8–26 Lord Goff was prepared to allow an order for the payment of compound interest. The issue, as considered above however, is why it is that the impact of an award of compound interest in relation to cash-settled transactions achieves for the plaintiff precisely the result that an equitable proprietary claim would have achieved in the context of a physically-settled derivative. Westdeutsche would have received a remedy equal in size to a situation where it remained absolute owner of the money that in fact was paid to the authority. What must also be appreciated is that, had there been

---

47 [1996] 2 All E.R. 961 at 980.
48 [1914] A.C. 398 at 452.
49 [1914] A.C. 398 at 436.
50 [1996] 2 All E.R. 961 at 971.
51 Again it is important to note that the language of debt is being used.
52 [1996] 2 All E.R. 961 at 972–3.
53 *ibid.* at 975.
54 [1996] 2 All E.R. 961 at 975.
55 *ibid.*

an order for compound interest, Westdeutsche would have received a remedy equal in *quality* to the situation if it had remained absolute owner of the money which in fact was paid to the authority.[56] In the context of transfers of value held in electronic bank accounts, an award of compound interest is the same as awarding a proprietary claim in respect of the value held in that account.

The availability of compound interest

8–27 Following the preceding discussion of what compound interest really is, it is important to identify the basis on which Lord Goff was prepared to award compound interest. It is submitted that the *restitution approach* informs the dissenting judgment on this point. As Lord Goff held, compound interest had been awarded "regularly" where "justice so demanded". [57] More specifically, those awards were most common "in cases where money had been obtained and retained by fraud, or where it had been withheld or misapplied by a trustee or anyone else in a fiduciary position".[58] There is a link on the authorities cited by his Lordship between awards of compound interest and knowing breach of fiduciary duty. The frequent use of a standard of justice to award compound interest is visible "where the defendant has wrongfully profited … from having the use of another person's money …".[59]

8–28 The issue which arose most specifically on the *Islington* appeal was the exercise of that jurisdiction where receipt of money has been made under an *ultra vires* contract. Whether, in fact, such a claim will obtain under a personal claim in restitution at common law for repayment of the balance of the bank's money on the ground of unjust enrichment.[60] In Lord Goff's opinion it was satisfaction of a principle of justice that was required from the court.

8–29 In this context, it is possible to discern the restriction even of restitutionary remedies in commercial cases to situations where there has been fraud or breach of a fiduciary duty. It is contended that this approach does not take account of other forms of unjust factor which may be appropriate in commercial disputes. For example, it is not clear whether reckless risk-taking or negligent implementation of an unsuitable financial structure should give rise to restitutionary remedies.[61]

8–30 In Lord Goff's dissenting judgment, an equitable remedy can be used to support a common law claim, particularly where the only common law remedy available was inadequate for the purpose.[62] It is submitted that it would have been open to Lord Goff to have decided that compound interest is equivalent to a proprietary claim in respect of cash-settled transactions. Therefore, a proprietary claim should have been awarded to do justice between the parties. As it was, Lord Goff would have awarded something equivalent to a proprietary claim—but called it by another name.

---

[56] It was accepted between the parties that Westdeutsche would have received compound interest on the money paid to the authority had it not paid the money to the authority. It is submitted that it would not have been possible to seek to adduce evidence in any event that the money would have been invested in any form other than retaining it in the currency and the amount in which it was paid to the authority.

[57] [1996] 2 All E.R. 961 at 976.

[58] *ibid.*

[59] [1996] 2 All E.R. 961 at 977.

[60] *ibid.*

[61] *cf. Royal Brunei Airlines v. Tan* [1995] 2 A.C. 378.

[62] [1996] 2 All E.R. 961 at 979.

Defences

8–31 For the sake of completeness, it is useful to remember that there are two main defences to the equitable and restitutionary claims which have been set out above and which are accepted as existing on the authorities, without having been singled out specifically by Lord Goff.

Passing on

8–32 This defence is also known as the defence of windfall gain. Where A pays money to B, B might seek to argue that it is entitled to keep its gain if it has been spent. The counter-argument would be that there is no loss suffered by B in repaying the money. For example, where B has a hedging transaction in place or has not been required to pay money to A, A would say that B suffers no loss in repaying the money. This defence was considered by the Court of Appeal in *Birmingham*[63] where it was held that a hedging transaction was separate from the underlying swap and therefore the question of loss could not be answered by reference to the hedging transaction.

Change of position

8–33 The most commonly argued defence is change of position. Where A pays money to B, and B incurs obligations in reliance on receiving that money, B will argue unfairness in being forced to repay A. The existence of this defence has been established in *Lipkin Gorman v. Karpnale Ltd.*[64] It was discussed in the area of derivatives in *South Tyneside MBC v. Svenska International plc,* [65] where it was similarly held to exist but without being considered applicable on those facts.

Conclusions on the restitutionary approach

8–34 The restitutionary approach then seeks to provide a remedy to a claim based on restitution for unjust enrichment on the basis of "justice". While criticising the narrowness of the equitable approach, the implementation of the restitutionary approach by the majority of the House of Lords would have had, it is submitted, an impact identical to the making of a proprietary award. This is despite identifying from the outset, explicitly, that there was no observable reason why a proprietary claim should be awarded to a payer under an *ultra vires* contract.

8–35 As such, the *restitutionary approach* appears to advance a remedy lying somewhere between a general intent to do justice by reversing an unjust enrichment in respect of money had and received, and the *de facto* award of a remedy *in rem*. It would only have been in the context of insolvency that there would have been a meaningful distinction between a proprietary and a personal claim. Islington's solvency meant that this question did not apply on the facts. On the facts of the *Islington* appeal, there was no prospect of the judgment order not being performed because the respondent was in funds and the appellant was not seeking money and not specific property. Nor, as a matter of principle, would a proprietary award have been made in any event.

---

[63] [1996] 4 All E.R. 733.

[64] [1992] 4 All E.R. 512, HL.

[65] [1995] 1 All E.R. 545.

Chapter 9

The primacy of equity

The equity approach in the House of Lords

9–01 To call this section of the debate the *equity approach* is perhaps to obscure the true nature of the opinions of their Lordships who subscribed to it. Perhaps it appears to bear connotations of an enthusiasm to use equity in commercial situations. That there is a problem with the use of equitable remedies in commercial transactions is beyond question. The words of Lord Lloyd loom large in this context:

> "As one who has in the past attempted to keep open the availability of equitable remedies in commercial disputes, I am now conscious of the strength of the arguments the other way."[1]

The certainty of commercial documentation and of the parties' purported intentions led to the conservative conclusion that it is only in cases of fraud or straightforward breach of fiduciary duty that equity will be invoked in commercial situations. What the majority in the House of Lords is attempting to do is to identify the response which should be made by equity to particular situations. The speech of Lord Browne-Wilkinson relocates equity in that context by spelling out the situations in which the resulting and constructive trust will operate.

9–02 An equitable positivist would prefer to see equity used more proactively. In the local authority swaps cases there was perhaps a greater role for the use of equity than was otherwise the case in some disputes. The introduction of mistake or legal norms as to capacity, clearly alter the context. The issue is whether it is useful for equity to interfere in these commercial contexts at all—particularly when the traditional concerns of equity do not marry exactly with contractual intentions of commercial parties. As has been considered above, the responses of the derivatives community to the decisions of the High Court and of the Court of Appeal in all of the local authority swaps cases has been one of dismay. Apart from the unfortunate termination of a profitable area of swaps business, that community has not been able to take away either a clear analysis of the structures which they use on a daily basis nor have they received a clear pointer in future cases to the situations in which they can expect to be awarded proprietary remedies. In the context of taking collateral and seeking to secure transactions using standard market contracts, there is clearly some potential for the equitable principles expounded in the House of Lords to interfere with the parties' property rights on the happening of bankruptcy or some other event of termination of their agreements.

9–03 It is possible to say that the use of restitutionary principles offers a more certain rationale for the application of equitable *remedies*. Given the problem of setting out more precisely the situations in which an "unjust factor" would be said to arise, there is greater potential flexibility within the scope of restitutionary responses to select the remedies most appropriate to the commercial context.

---

[1] [1996] 2 All E.R. 961 at 1021.

However, that is not to say that restitution has the exact measure of the commercial context. Rather, restitution has grown as a means of explaining or codifying *ex post facto* the application of common law and equitable remedies in given contexts.[2] For restitution to become a useful tool in the analysis of commercial disputes, there needs to be a recontextualisation of its application. On this basis, at the section below on the development of a new model unjust factor based around suitability and risk is potentially a more useful departure.

9–04 The genesis of the *equity approach* came from the weight of authority which ran against the proposal for awarding compound interest on the basis of some abstract notion of conscionability. Lord Lloyd especially expressed himself as having particular difficulty in reconciling an award of compound interest as an equitable remedy being made available in support of the common law claim for money had and received, on the one hand, with the *ratio decidendi* of the House of Lords in *President of India*,[3] on the other.[4]

The speech of Lord Browne-Wilkinson

9–05 The leading speech for the *equity approach* was delivered by Lord Browne-Wilkinson, with whom Lord Lloyd[5] and Lord Slynn[6] concurred. Therefore, it constituted the majority of the House of Lords. His Lordship's thinking can be summed up briefly as holding that: there was no resulting trust because that principle was to be restricted to two distinct categories; that there was no constructive trust because there was no impact on the conscience of the payee given that it had no knowledge of the invalidity of the contract at the time the money was paid to it; that *Sinclair v. Brougham*[7] was probably not to be followed in future; and, finally, that the controversial decision of Goulding J. in *Chase Manhattan Bank v. Israel-British Bank*[8] can be explained better although the result was probably correct.

9-06 The limitations of the *equity approach* were summed up early in his Lordship's speech where he found that "[i]n the absence of fraud the courts of equity have never awarded compound interest except against a trustee or other person owing fiduciary duties who is accountable for profits made from his position".[9] In his Lordship's opinion, the authorities established that in cases where there was no demonstrable fraud, compound interest would only be awarded against a defendant who is "a trustee or otherwise in a fiduciary position". [10] The appropriate response for a court in such a situation would be "recouping ... an improper profit made by him".[11] Two points would appear to

---

[2] See, for example, Morrison, *Jurisprudence—from the Greeks to Postmodernism* (London, Cavendish, 1997), p.353.

[3] *President of India v. La Pintada Cia Navegacion SA* [1985] A.C. 104.

[4] [1996] 2 All E.R. 961 at 1019.

[5] Lord Lloyd delivered a judgment which considered, as discussed above, the commercial context of equity rather than focusing, as Lord Browne-Wilkinson did, on the redrawing of the commonly–used equitable remedies and principles.

[6] Lord Slynn did not deliver a substantive judgment, although he did make some reference to awards of compound interest being available generally on where there has been fraud or some breach of fiduciary duty.

[7] [1914] A.C. 398.

[8] [1981] Ch. 105.

[9] [1996] 2 All E.R. 961 at 984.

[10] *ibid.*

[11] *ibid.* at 985.

arise. First, it is possible to identify the restriction, considered above, of equitable institutions to fairly uncontroversial categories of fraud or breach of fiduciary duty. Secondly, the response advocated by his Lordship is one of recouping a profit made outwith such a duty—a response which smacks of restitutionary purpose[12] as much as equitable operation on the conscience of the defendant.

The nature of the trust

9–07 In broad terms a proprietary constructive trust will be imposed on a person who knows that his actions in respect of specific property are unconscionable. It is important that the trustee has knowledge of the unconscionability of the treatment of that property. This issue is separate from the issue of *in rem* and *in personam* rights. Whether the rights are proprietary or not, being made a trustee under a constructive trust will be dependent on knowledge and unconscionability. Section 53(2) of the Law of Property Act 1925 refers to "implied resulting or constructive trusts" not requiring formalities for their creation. The most important recent statement of the core principles of the areas of implied trusts law was made by Lord Browne-Wilkinson in *Westdeutsche Landesbank v. Islington* where his Lordship went back to basics. The first of his "Relevant Principles of Trust Law" was identified as being that that:

> "(i) Equity operates on the conscience of the owner of the legal interest. In the case of a trust, the conscience of the legal owner requires him to carry out the purposes for which the property was vested in him (express or implied trust) or which the law imposes on him by reason of his unconscionable conduct (constructive trust)."[13]

As a result of the requirement that the conscience of the holder of the legal interest is affected "he cannot be a trustee of the property if and so long as he is ignorant of the facts alleged to affect his conscience". Therefore, he must have knowledge of the factors which are suggested to give rise to the constructive trust.[14] He continued:

> "(ii) Since the equitable jurisdiction to enforce trusts depends upon the conscience of the holder of the legal interest being affected, he cannot be a trustee of the property if and so long as he is ignorant of the facts alleged to affect his conscience, *i.e.* until he is aware that he is intended to hold the property for the benefit of others in the case of an express or implied trust, or, in the case of a constructive trust, of the factors which are alleged to affect his conscience."

9–08 One important issue arises: does the constructive trust take effect by granting proprietary rights over specific property, or does it simply impose a personal obligation on a person who has dealt with property? It is the distinction between a right *in rem* to the property and any increase in value associated with the property, and a right *in personam* being a personal claim against a person for money. There are situations, considered below, which fit into both categories. The third fundamental principles identified by Lord Browne-Wilkinson operates as follows:

---

[12] Birks, *Introduction to the Law of Restitution*, (Oxford, 1989), p.11.

[13] [1996] 2 All E.R. 961 at 988.

[14] *ibid.*

> "(iii) In order to establish a trust there must be identifiable trust property. The only apparent exception to this rule is a constructive trust imposed on a person who dishonestly assists in a breach of trust who may come under fiduciary duties even if he does not receive identifiable trust property."

The constructive trust comes into effect at the date this knowledge is acquired and "as from the date of its establishment the beneficiary has, in equity, a proprietary interest in the trust property". The proprietary interest is then "enforceable in equity against any subsequent holder of the property (whether the original property or substituted property into which it can be traced) other than a purchaser for value of the legal interest without notice".[15]

> "(iv) Once a trust is established, as from the date of its establishment the beneficiary has, in equity, a proprietary interest in the trust property, which proprietary interest will be enforceable in equity against any subsequent holder of the property (whether the original property or substituted property into which it can be traced) other than a purchaser for value of the legal interest without notice."

9–09 Hobhouse J. and the Court of Appeal both held that the defendant should be treated as having held the payment made to it in equity for the plaintiff. It was held that it would have been unjust for the defendant to keep the money without being subject to an equitable proprietary remedy when the contract was found to be void at law. Both courts held that in equity the plaintiff should be considered as having retained the equitable interest in the money paid to the defendant. They preferred this approach to a solution founded on restitution for unjust enrichment on the basis of absence of consideration. The issue was appealed to the House of Lords specifically on the issue whether or not compound interest ought to be paid by the defendant, or simply simple interest. It was argued that compound interest is only available in cases where the recipient has some equitable proprietary interest in the property; otherwise only simple interest is payable.

9–10 The argument on constructive trust for the bank in *Islington* was that it should retain a proprietary interest in the money paid to the defendant and therefore that compound interest ought to have been made available. The majority held that there is no division in title to property where that property was transferred outright beneficially to the defendant. Lord Browne-Wilkinson held that there is no division between legal and equitable title to property of necessity. Rather, there was only such a division between legal and equitable title where an express trust is created (below) or where the absolute owner of that property has knowledge of some factor affecting his knowledge which requires the imposition of a constructive trust. There could be no retention of any rights in the lump sum payment by the plaintiff because both parties intended that there be an outright transfer of that sum to the defendant local authority at a time when neither party knew that the contract was void at law.[16]

9–11 In summary then, the core of the trust concept is identified as equity operating on the conscience of the person who is the owner of the legal interest: the First Principle. There is a confusing distinction made between an "express or implied trust", on the one hand, and a trust imposed "by reason of his unconscionable conduct" which is termed a "constructive trust", on the other

---

[15] [1996] 2 All E.R. 961 at 988

[16] Worthington, *Proprietary Interests in Commercial Transactions* (Oxford, 1996), p.xi.

hand.[17] Given the importance of conscience, a person "cannot be a trustee of the property if, and so long as, he is ignorant of the facts alleged to affect his conscience": the Second Principle.[18] It is on this basis that Islington could not be a constructive trustee because it did not know it was incapable of entering into the swaps contract until after the House of Lords decision in *Hazell.* Where the allegation is that there be a constructive trust imposed, there must be awareness of "the factors which are alleged to affect his conscience".[19]

9–12 The further problem which arises is that the property which is transferred under the deep discount payment has ceased to exist when it is transferred from a bank account which is then overdrawn. This offends against the Third Principle that there must be identifiable trust property.[20] As Lord Browne-Wilkinson held, in reliance on *Re Goldcorp Exchange Ltd (in receivership)*,[21] "[o]nce there ceased to be an identifiable trust fund, the local authority could not become a trustee".

9–13 The Fourth Principle is that a beneficiary acquires an equitable proprietary interest in the trust property from the establishment of the trust.[22] On the facts before him, Lord Browne-Wilkinson held that there was never a coming together of all of these factors before the judgment in *Hazell* was handed down. "There was therefore never a time at which both (a) there was defined trust property and (b) the conscience of the local authority in relation to such defined trust property was affected. The basic requirements of a trust were never satisfied."[23]

9–14 What is important within the redefinition of the principles of the trust is the assertion that property does not have latent within it a legal and an equitable title. Rather, it is only when the four principles are satisfied that a division between legal and equitable title is created. The legal owner of property simply carries "all rights" until a trust is imposed. It is on this basis that the equity established by Hobhouse J. is to be rejected.[24]

> "... to talk about the bank "retaining" its equitable interest [after the deep discount payment is made] is meaningless. The only question is whether the circumstances under which the money was paid were such as, in equity, to impose a trust on the local authority. If so, an equitable interest arose for the first time under that trust."[25]

Lord Browne-Wilkinson referred to a number of authorities on this point.[26] As such, equity would not grant any proprietary remedy to the payer under a void contract unless there had been either some effective, express retention of proprietary rights or some unconscionable act on the part of the recipient which would create a constructive trust.

---

[17] [1996] 2 All E.R. 961 at 988.

[18] *ibid.*

[19] *ibid.*

[20] *ibid.* There is an exception to this principle in the case of personal liability imposed under constructive trust on a person who dishonestly assisted in a breach of trust.

[21] [1995] 1 A.C. 74.

[22] [1996] 2 All E.R. 961 at 988. There is an exception to this principle in the case of a purchaser for value without notice of the beneficiary's rights.

[23] [1996] 2 All E.R. 961 at 988–989.

[24] As considered above.

[25] [1996] 2 All E.R. 961 at 989.

[26] *Re Cook (dec'd), Beck v. Grant* [1948] Ch. 212; *Vandervell v. IRC;* [1967] 2 A.C. 291 at 317, *per* Lord Upjohn and Lord Donovan; *Comr of Stamp Duties v. Livingston;* [1965] A.C. 694 at 712; Underhill and Hayton *Law of Trusts and Trustees* (15th ed., 1995), p.866.

9–15 Further, there is the possibility that even where legal and equitable title are separated by the intervention of some other action, that there will not be a personal liability to account as a trustee on the basis of knowing receipt "… unless he has the requisite degree of knowledge …".[27] This principle is divined from *Re Diplock*[28] and *Re Montagu's Settlement Trusts.*[29] As Lord Browne-Wilkinson expresses it " … innocent receipt of property by X subject to an existing equitable interest does not by itself make X a trustee despite the severance of the legal and equitable titles".[30]

The structure of the equity approach

9–16 It had been conceded in argument by counsel for both sides that there could be no argument on the basis of constructive trust. Rather, the appeal had proceeded on the basis of the restitutionary role of resulting trusts, until their Lordships indicated that they would be amenable to submissions on the correctness of *Sinclair v. Brougham* and the role of the constructive trust.

9–17 The central question to be addressed by the *equity approach* was as follows:

> "Does the recipient of money under a contract subsequently found to be void for mistake or as being *ultra vires* hold the moneys received on trust even where he had no knowledge at any relevant time that the contract was void?"[31]

9–18 There are two issues arising from this understanding of the question. First, whether an unjust factor will cause the imposition of a trust. Secondly, the establishment of "knowledge" as the appropriate yardstick by which the applicability of the trust would be appropriate. In the opinion of Lord Browne-Wilkinson, the imposition of a trust would then lead to two consequences. First, that the recipient would be "personally liable, regardless of fault, for any subsequent payment away of the moneys to third parties even though, at the date of such payment, the 'trustee' was still ignorant of the existence of any trust".[32] The problem is the office of trustee under such an implied trust. Without knowledge that a trust has been imposed, there would be retrospective liability on that recipient under the implied trusteeship.

9–19 Secondly, "as from the date of the establishment of the trust[33] the original payer will have an equitable proprietary interest in the moneys so long as they are traceable into whomsoever's hands they come other than a purchaser for value of the legal interest without notice".[34] The tracing claim open to the claimant would run from the moment of payment. As a result, these equitable rights would bind all recipients of that value. The express exception to that is equity's darling; the implied exception would be someone subject to a defence of change of position or passing on.

---

[27] [1996] 2 All E.R. 961 at 990.

[28] *Re Diplock's Estate, Diplock v. Wintle* [1948] Ch. 465.

[29] [1987] Ch. 264.

[30] [1996] 2 All E.R. 961 at 990; see also Smith, "Tracing and Electronic Funds Transfer" in *Restitution and Banking Law* (Rose ed., Mansfield Press, Oxford, 1998), p.120.

[31] [1996] 2 All E.R. 961 at 986.

[32] His Lordship refers here to Burrows, "Swaps and the Friction between Common Law and Equity" [1995] R.L.R. 15.

[33] This would appear to include the receipt or mixing of the moneys by the "trustee".

[34] [1996] 2 All E.R. 961 at 986.

Creating proprietary rights *de novo*

9–20 The central issue is posed again by Lord Browne-Wilkinson. He identified the same core difficulty as Lord Goff with awarding a proprietary claim to the banks that there is no apparent, common sense reason why they should be entitled to a proprietary claim, regardless of the strict application of principle. Of particular concern is the position of third parties dealing with the recipient of the money who would be disadvantaged if the banks were allowed to exercise a proprietary claim over the authorities. His Lordship maintains that the imposition of the proprietary claims would mean that those third parties would be unfairly disadvantaged in circumstances where they were not being enriched necessarily at the bank's expense. He declared that he "... can see no moral or legal justification for giving such priority to the right of [Westdeutsche]".[35]

9–21 In a rigid application of the equitable view to a hypothetical situation, Lord Browne-Wilkinson held that "[i]f the contract had been valid, [Westdeutsche] would have had purely personal rights against [the authority]. Why should [Westdeutsche] be better off because the contract was void?"[36] However, on the extension of this principle, it could be said that a beneficiary, who had a mixture of proprietary and personal claims against a fiduciary, would have only a personal claim against that fiduciary to perform the terms of its duties. Failure to perform those duties in paying away the trust fund would give rise to a proprietary claim in the beneficiary. It is not clear why it should be so important in Lord Browne-Wilkinson's example to demonstrate that the rights must always have been proprietary in nature when it is possible for rights to alter their quality.

9–22 In *Att-Gen for Hong Kong v. Reid*,[37] the employers of the recipient of bribes were granted a proprietary claim in assets acquired with those bribes despite having had only personal claims against that recipient under the terms of his employment contract before the payments were made.[38] Therefore, it is not impossible for personal rights to be translated into proprietary rights on the happening of a suitable event. The distinction between *Reid* and *Islington* would be said to be, on Lord Browne-Wilkinson's terms, the knowledge Reid had that his receipt of the payments was a breach of the trust held in him by his employers. However, the authority in Islington was similarly aware of the terms of their (void) contract and therefore could be said to have consented to the liability imposed by their swaps contract as to the allocation of risks. What is not clear in the *equity approach* is the nature of the knowledge that is applicable. What the *equity approach* fails to account for is that fact that Westdeutsche had sought to protect their position in the event that property in which they had absolute title (the deep discount payment) was paid away, in a number of circumstances which included the incapacity of the local authority. Therefore, the award of a proprietary claim would be a response which gave rise to a state of affairs which put the parties in a position which was envisaged under their contracts.

---

[35] [1996] 2 All E.R. 961 at 987.

[36] *ibid.*

[37] [1994] 1 A.C. 324; [1994] 1 All E.R. 1.

[38] See also *Boardman v. Phipps* [1967] 2 A.C. 46, where personal rights against the solicitor to the trust fund appear to translate to proprietary claims against profits made by that solicitor derived from information gained while on trust business, despite the trust's inability to make those same investments. The nature of the remedy in *Boardman* is however somewhat problematic, see Hayton, *Underhill & Hayton Law Relating to Trusts and Trustees* (15th ed., Butterworths, 1995), p.356, discussing particularly *Regal v. Gulliver* [1942] 1 All E.R. 378; [1967] 2 A.C. 134n.

9–23 The restitutionary view would have looked at the presence of an unjust factor which made a restitutionary response appropriate. As discussed above, this resulted in a finding on the basis of a need to do justice which provided a quasi-proprietary claim, in the speech of Lord Goff. The difference in approach of the restitutionary views is the need to subtract unjust enrichment from the person who received the benefit of that enrichment at the expense of the plaintiff. The *equity approach* focuses instead on the knowledge of the recipient of the property of some factor which ought to have affected the recipient's conscience. There is no manifest measurement of the justice of that receipt; only of the conscionability attaching to the recipient personally. This constitutes a return in practical terms to the doctrine of notice. The restitution viewpoint concentrates on there having been an enrichment at the expense of the plaintiff. The provision of an equitable proprietary claim is therefore based on a notion of conscionability.

9–24 However, the *equity approach* does look to the broader commercial context of the payments. The impact on third parties and on the certainty of the enforcement of commercial contracts of these agreements as to credit support is dealt with in the following passage which explains why a proprietary right for the banks would be unsuitable on principle:

> "... a businessman who has entered into transactions relating to or dependent upon property rights could find that assets which apparently belong to one person in fact belong to another; that there are off balance sheet liabilities of which he cannot be aware; that these property rights and liabilities arise from circumstances unknown not only to himself but also to anyone else who has been involved in the transactions."[39]

The problems that arise here are numerous. First, it is true to say that swaps were always held off-balance sheet. As had been recognised, there are general problems of systemic certainty with allowing these products to be undeclared in published accounts. Secondly, in relation to specific property, there would be problems with causing property to be pledged to more than one secured interest.

9–25 However, these contentions do not necessarily apply on the facts of the *Islington* litigation. First, given that the deep discount payment was held off-balance sheet, no third party could have relied on its existence for security purposes. Second, Islington was in funds to meet the proprietary obligation in any event although reaching a principled position for all cases appears to be a preferable approach rather than restricting the application of the principles solely to the facts. Thirdly, it is not clear that any third party would have had secured rights over the general purpose bank accounts into which this money was paid.

9–26 In Lord Browne-Wilkinson's view, the upshot of granting a proprietary claim would be that "[a] new area of unmanageable risk will be introduced into commercial dealings".[40] However, the real impact of their Lordship's approach remains the difficulty of asserting a proprietary claim in void commercial contracts at all. The commercial risk could be said to have been created by failing to implement the termination provisions of agreements entered into in good faith and at arm's length.

---

39 [1996] 2 All E.R. 961 at 987.

40 *ibid.*

Risk in equity

9–27 The most interesting recent development in the area of risk and equity is the decision of the Privy Council in *Royal Brunei Airlines v. Tan.*[41] In the leading speech of Lord Nicholls, he holds that a breach of trust by a trustee need not have been a dishonest act *on the part of the trustee*. Rather, it is sufficient that some accessory acted dishonestly for that accessory to be fixed with liability for the breach. The test as set out by Lord Nicholls creates a test of "dishonesty".

9–28 Lord Nicholls held that it is "dishonesty" that is needed to fix a third party to the trust with liability with reference to the beneficiaries under that trust. The trustee's state of mind is unimportant. The scenario is posited that the trustee may be honest but the third party is dishonest. Where the third party is acting dishonestly, that third party will be liable to account. The test for "acting dishonestly, or with a lack of probity, which is synonymous, means simply not acting as an honest person would in the circumstance. This is an objective standard."[42] The interesting notion is that dishonesty can be an *active* state of mind or alternatively a *passive* "lack of probity". It is suggested instead that this *active deceit* is the natural meaning of "dishonesty".

9–29 Lord Nicholls expands his discussion of "dishonesty" to consider the taking of risk. Risk is expressly encompassed within the new test. Lord Nicholls says:

> "All investment involves risk. Imprudence is not dishonesty, although imprudence may be carried recklessly to lengths which call into question the honesty of the person making the decision. This is especially so if the transaction serves another purpose in which that person has an interest of his own."[43]

The basis of liability is that a third party "takes a risk that a clearly unauthorised transaction will not cause loss ... If the risk materialises and causes loss, those who knowingly took the risk will be accountable accordingly."[44] For these purposes it is said that "fraud includes taking a risk to the prejudice of another's rights, which risk is known to be one which there is no right to take".[45]

9–30 The test for "dishonesty", as set out above, goes far further than a natural meaning of the word "dishonesty". It imports a number of notions: dishonesty, recklessness, inappropriate risk-taking, and fraud. Any of these concepts will, of itself, found liability to account as an accessory. These categories are capable of standing alone in conceptual terms. To group them together under the heading "dishonesty" is to create a new standard that fits awkwardly under the scope of the term "dishonesty". Therefore, it cannot be an objection to the use of unconscionability as the test that it "means something different" from dishonesty, as Lord Nicholls suggests. Rather, all of the categories quoted above involve a common notion of unconscionability. The example of an investment advisor who is "dishonest" on this technical meaning while only actually being reckless as the form of the investment, could be described as acting unconscionably, given the nature of his client.

9–31 The test for dishonesty is therefore a level of risk which the court considers to be too great. Therefore, an accessory may be liable where the risk taken, for

---

41 [1995] 2 A.C. 378.

42 *ibid* at 386.

43 *ibid* at 387.

44 *ibid.*

45 *ibid.*

example, an interest rate swap, is done in furtherance of a contractual obligation to invest property and manage its level of risk. The court might consider that risk to be too great. Whereas the market might consider a plain interest rate swap to be standard practice and even advisable in many circumstances. On the basis that it is the court's decision on the level of risk that counts, it is therefore difficult to counsel an investment advisor as to the approach to be taken to the investment of trust property.

9–32 It is not a failure to ascertain whether or not the investment is in breach of trust which is decisive of the matter, but rather whether or not the *level of risk* assumed is in breach of trust. "[H]onesty is an objective standard". Therefore it is for the court to measure the level of risk and, consequently, the honesty of the third party. The outcome would seem to depend upon "the circumstances known to the third party at the time". However, recklessness as to the ability of the trust to invest must similarly be a factor to be taken into account in deciding on the honesty of the third party investment manager.

9–33 The test for "dishonesty" that covers such a context, to use Lord Nicholls's own words, "means something different" from the natural use of "dishonesty". It is submitted that a better approach would be admit that the test is really one of unconscionability in line with the majority of the House of Lords in *Islington*. Therefore, liability in connection with dishonesty and fraud in equity already includes within it the idea of risks taken in a suitable or an unsuitable fashion. The context of risk within the local authority swaps cases is not considered by any of the courts despite the development of the concept in relation to personal liability as a constructive trustee in *Tan*.[46]

Equitable obligations and current portfolio theory

9–34 The courts have begun to accept the need to adapt to the manner in which financial markets and finance professionals operate in the modern context. In this way, principles of equity relating to the investment powers and obligations of trustees have altered. Hoffmann J. in delivering judgment in *Nestle v. National Westminster Bank plc*[47] held that:

> "Modern trustees acting within their investment powers are entitled to be judged by the standards of current portfolio theory, which emphasises the risk level of the entire portfolio rather than the risk attaching to each investment taken in isolation."

In pursuing this point, his Lordship continued to find that a trustee is required to act fairly between all the beneficiaries of the trust fund which he was empowered to invest. However, the reference back to the behaviour of trustees acting in the context of the modern financial markets indicates the appropriateness of trustees balancing their investments between different types of product to even out risk, as well as taking into account the necessary risk required to make the maximum return for the trust.

9–35 The position which the trustee is placed in by equity appears to be a deeply invidious one, without some reference to common market practice. The

---

[46] The issue also arises whether this is properly a wrong or an incidence of trusteeship: Millett, "Restitution: Taking Stock", delivering the Society of Advanced Legal Studies Lecture, Institute of Advanced Legal Studies, London, July 23, 1998.

[47] [1993] 1 W.L.R. 1260; see also Hayton, *Underhill and Hayton, The Law of Trusts and Trustees* (15th ed., Butterworths, 1995), pp.598 *et seq.*

duty to act evenly between different categories of beneficiaries requires a difficult balancing act between generating short-term return and protecting the integrity of the long-term fund. High-risk, short-term investments are necessary to satisfy the requirements of the rule to make the maximum possible return for the trust.[48] However, within that doctrine of maximum gain there is a requirement to act as a prudent person of business would act[49] specifically with reference to someone for whom the trustee felt morally bound to provide (over and above dealings in that person's own affairs). The types of transaction available for the trustee's investment without stricture are similarly limited by statute[50] and by common law.[51]

9–36 The trustee is similarly required to supervise professionals to whom delegation of the investment function is made. The principle in *Learoyd v. Whiteley*[52] indicates that the trustee when investing trust property must not only act as a businessman of ordinary prudence, but must also avoid all investments of a hazardous nature. Whereas in *Bartlett v. Barclays Bank*,[53] a distinction was drawn between a prudent degree of risk and unacceptable hazard: the former would be acceptable whereas the latter would not. Under section 6 of the Trustee Investments Act 1961, there is a statutory duty to consider the suitability of particular investments, especially in the light of the need for diversification.

9–37 This reflection of the current portfolio theory in the 1961 Act underlines the need for the trustee to walk a narrow line between modern practice and long-established equitable obligations. In this field, perhaps as in no other, the particular nature of the trust is illustrated. The trust occupies a place somewhere between rules of property and rules of personal obligation.[54] Whereas equity operates on the property that is held as the trust fund by means of proprietary principles, there are also a raft of personal claims against the trustee in connection with the manner in which the function of minding the trust fund is carried out.[55] There are obligations for making too little profit,[56] making profits for himself which were not open to the trust,[57] and taking risks to make greater profit which then caused loss to the trust.[58]

9–38 The trustee's duty of investment can be summarised as being threefold: to act prudently and safely; to act fairly between beneficiaries; and to do the best for the beneficiaries financially. As Megarry V.-C. held in *Cowan v. Scargill*: "When the purpose of the trust is to provide financial benefits for the beneficiaries, the best interests of the beneficiaries are their best financial interests". Somewhat remarkably, his Lordship also held that: "Trustees may even have to act dishonourably (though not illegally) if the interests of their beneficiaries require it". This is a positive duty to invest regardless of ethics.

---

48 *Cowan v. Scargill* [1985] Ch. 270.

49 *Bartlett v. Barclays Bank Trust Co Ltd.* [1980] Ch. 515.

50 Trustee Investment Act 1961.

51 Aside from the requirement of prudence, there are prohibitions on lending on personal security: *Holmes v. Dring* (1788) 2 Cox. Eq. Cas. 1; *Khoo Tek Keong v. Ch'ng Joo Tuan Neoh* [1934] A.C. 529.

52 (1887) 12 App. Cas. 727.

53 [1980] Ch. 515.

54 See Birks [1996] R.L.R. 3.

55 As to the nature of trusteeship in this context, see Hayton, "The Core Content of Trusteeship" in *Laundering and Tracing* (Birks ed., Oxford, 1996), emphasising the core of the nature of the trust being the ability of the beneficiary to enforce the trust by personal obligations enforceable against the trustee.

56 *Cowan v. Scargill* (*op. cit.*).

57 *Boardman v. Phipps* [1967] 2 A.C. 46.

58 *Bartlett v. Barclays Bank* [1980] Ch. 515.

9–39 An express power on a trustee to make an investment may be general, giving the trustees power to invest in whatever they wish, or limited to specific types of investment. The trustee will nevertheless be subject to certain limitations. Although in *Re Harari's ST*[59] it was held that such a power would not be interpreted restrictively, the case of *Re Power's WT*[60] (distinguishing *Re Wragg*[61]) established that the word "invest" implied a yield of income and, thus, non-income-producing property would not be permissible as an investment.

9–40 In the context of delegating authority to investment, the classic statement of the trustee's obligation is set out in *Speight v. Gaunt*[62] in the decision of Lord Jessel MR: "It seems to me that on general trust principles a trustee ought to conduct the business of the trust in the same manner that an ordinary prudent man of business would conduct his own, and that beyond that there is no liability or obligation on the trustee."

9–41 Exceptionally in *Re Vickery*,[63] where a trustee had given money to a solicitor who absconded with it, Maugham J. considered the central issue to be whether the trustee was negligent in employing the solicitor or permitting money to remain in his hands. It was held that there was no liability on the trustee unless there had been some "wilful default" by him, being something more than a lack of care. This test has come in for much academic criticism,[64] being based on *Re City Equitable Fire Insurance*,[65] a company law case looking at the obligations of fiduciaries in the context of specific articles of association. Jones contends that the better test is one based on "want of reasonable care" rather than "wilful default". The *Re City Equitable Fire Insurance* decision is dismissed as having been decided very much on its own facts and therefore should not have been applied to this area of trustee discretion. The test for trustees ought to be higher. Similarly, Hayton argues that there are problems then with delegation to market makers or to finance professionals who will deal on their own account, as well as providing financial products for their clients. In his suggestion, it would be better to subject this area to control by established market regulators such as Investment Management Regulatory Organisation (IMRO).

9–42 The core issue appears to be whether or not the law should recognise that the beneficiaries (ultimately) have to rely on market professionals to do things which trustees cannot do. Within that recognition must be some recognition of the role of market regulators and the shortcomings of regulation. The requirement of equity that beneficiaries under trusts should be insulated from the risk of market movement and personnel default (whether by trustees or market professionals) in making investment decisions, does not accord with the basis upon which financial professionals are prepared to enter into terms of business. The client is required to accept the risk of loss as well as the possibility of gain. In this context equity must also consider how to balance the need to make best profit against requirement not to lose trust money. One solution might be to grant an automatic trustee indemnity where the trustee is able to obtain an indemnity from the market professional, thus freeing trustees from the need to control that which they cannot control in standard terms of terms of business letters.

---

59 [1949] 1 All E.R. 430.
60 [1951] Ch. 1074.
61 [1919] 2 Ch. 58.
62 (1883) 9 App. Cas. 1.
63 [1931] 1 Ch. 572.
64 Jones (1968) 84 L.Q.R. 474; Hayton, "Investment Management Problems" (1990) L.Q.R. 89–93.
65 [1925] Ch. 407.

9–43 The context of risk is therefore problematic in equity, The courts have imposed near strict liability in the context of fiduciaries.[66] *Tan* indicates a growing acceptance of reckless risk-taking as part of the unconscionable behaviour against which equity will act. However, *Islington* fails to accept the commercial context of risk management as something which ought similarly to be encompassed in granting remedies. The context of equitable proprietary remedies remains outwith the ambit of these developing principles, except for the protection of beneficiaries.

Resulting trust

9–44 In *Vandervell (No. 2),*[67] Megarry J. divided resulting trusts between "automatic" and "presumed" resulting trusts. The basis on which a resulting trust is said to operate, is somewhat controversial still. The correct approach would appear to be that there must be a transfer of the property from S to T, without an intention that T take that property beneficially. Where it appears to have been the intention of the donor that the donee should not take property beneficially, there will be a resulting trust to the donor or the donor's estate.

9–45 However, a different approach was taken by Lord Browne-Wilkinson in *Islington*:

> "Under existing law a resulting trust arises in two sets of circumstances:
> (A) where A m akes a voluntary payment to B or pays (wholly or in part) for the purchase of property which is vested either in B alone or in the joint names of A and B, there is a presumption that A did not intend to make a gift to B: the money or property is held on trust for A (if he is the sole provider of the money) or in the case of a joint purchase by A and B in shares proportionate to their contributions. It is important to stress that this is only a *presumption*, which presumption is easily rebutted either by the counter-presumption of advancement or by direct evidence of A's intention to make an outright transfer.[68]
> (B) Where A transfers property to B *on express trusts*, but the trusts declared do not exhaust the whole beneficial interest.[69] Both types of resulting trust are traditionally regarded as examples of trusts giving effect to the common intention of the parties. A resulting trust is not imposed by law against the intentions of the trustee (as is a constructive trust) but gives effect to his presumed intention.
>
> Megarry J. in *Re Vandervell's Trusts (No.2)*[70] suggests that a resulting trust of type (B) does not depend on intention but operates automatically. I am not convinced that this is right. If the settlor has expressly, or by necessary implication, abandoned any beneficial interest in the trust property, there is

---

[66] See *Bartlett v. Barclays Bank* [1980] Ch. 515; *Nestle v. National Westminster Bank plc* [1993] 1 W.L.R. 1260; [1994] 1 All E.R. 118.

[67] [1974] Ch 269 at 294; [1974] 1 All ER 47 at 64.

[68] See Underhill and Hayton, *Law of Trusts and Trustees* (15th ed., 1995), pp.317 *et seq.*; *White v. Vandervell Trustees Ltd* [1974] Ch. 269 at 288 *et seq.*

[69] See Underhill and Hayton, *Law of Trusts and Trustees* (15th ed., 1995) pp.317 *et seq.*; *White v. Vandervell Trustees Ltd* [1974] Ch 269 at 288 *et seq.*; *Barclays Bank Ltd v. Quistclose Investments Ltd* [1970] A.C. 567.

[70] [1974] Ch. 269.

> in my view no resulting trust: the undisposed-of equitable interest vests in the Crown as *bona vacantia*.[71]"[72]

Therefore, Lord Browne-Wilkinson identified two possible forms of resulting trust existing under the common law. The first form of resulting trust is where a voluntary payment is made towards the purchase of property, whether or not vested in the payer, where there was no intention to make a gift of the asset purchased. The property acquired is then held on trust for the payer and others in proportion to their contributions to the purchase. These assumptions are rebutted by evidence of intention to make an outright transfer.[73]

9–46 The second model of resulting trust arises where property is transferred on express trust in circumstances where the express trust did not exhaust the whole beneficial interest.[74] An example of this form of trust is that in *Vandervell v. IRC*[75] where, on transfer of legal and equitable title in shares to be held on trust for the benefit of a third party, the equitable interest represented by an option to repurchase the shares was unallocated by the trusts. It was therefore held by the House of Lords that that option was held on resulting trust for the settlor. [76] Megarry J. in *Re Vandervell's Trusts (No.2)*[77] considered that this model of resulting trust did not depend on intention but rather operated automatically.

9–47 Both types of resulting trust are described as being "traditionally regarded as examples of trusts giving effect to the common intention of the parties". [78] As Lord Browne-Wilkinson held: [79]

> "A resulting trust is not imposed by law against the intentions of the trustee (as is a constructive trust) but gives effect to his presumed intention ... If the settlor has expressly, or by necessary implication, abandoned any beneficial interest in the trust property, there is in my view no resulting trust: the undisposed-of equitable interest vests in the Crown as *bona vacantia*.[80]"

Therefore, on the facts of the *Islington* appeal any presumption of resulting trust is rebutted since it is demonstrated that the bank paid, and the local authority received, the upfront payment with the intention that the value transferred should become the absolute property of local authority.[81] The claim for a proprietary remedy is therefore lost because of the rebuttal of what remains simply a presumption of resulting trust on the two models set out above. The importance of finding common intention or automatic imposition is therefore important in this context. The argument for the banks would run that there must be an implied intention to retain some interest should the contract turn out to be void; or that it would be just to impose such a trust automatically.

---

[71] See *Re West Sussex Constabulary's Widows, Children and Benevolent (1930) Fund Trusts* [1971] Ch. 1.

[72] [1996] 2 All E.R. 961 at 990–991.

[73] See Underhill and Hayton, *Law of Trusts and Trustees* (15th ed., 1995), pp.317 *et seq.; White v. Vandervell Trustees Ltd* [1974] Ch. 269 at 288 *et seq.*

[74] See Underhill and Hayton, *Law of Trusts and Trustees* (15th ed., 1995), pp.317 *et seq.*; *White v. Vandervell Trustees Ltd* [1974] Ch. 269 at 288 *et seq.*; *Barclays Bank Ltd v. Quistclose Investments Ltd* [1970] A.C. 567.

[75] [1967] 2 A.C. 291.

[76] [1996] 2 All E.R. 961 at 990–991.

[77] [1974] Ch. 269.

[78] [1996] 2 All E.R. 961 at 990–991.

[79] *ibid.*

[80] See *Re West Sussex Constabulary's Widows, Children and Benevolent (1930) Fund Trusts* [1971] Ch. 1.

[81] [1996] 2 All E.R. 961 at 991; see also Swadling, "A new role for resulting trusts?" (1996) 16 LS 110, esp. 113.

9–48 Contrariwise Birks[82] defines a resulting trust "argues from restitutionary principles that the definition should be extended so as to cover a perceived gap in the law of 'subtractive unjust enrichment'[83] so as to give the plaintiff a proprietary remedy when he has transferred value under a mistake or under a contract the consideration for which wholly fails."[84]

9–49 That the deep discount swap clearly intended to pass absolute legal ownership in the money to the authority necessarily precluded any contention of retention of interest on these facts. Lord Browne-Wilkinson was clear that there was no division between legal and equitable title before the creation of a trust or of some impact on the conscience of the defendant that would create a constructive trust. The *radical restitutionary approach* takes a different analysis which would lead to an ill-defined trust in which it would be difficult for the court to establish the terms of the trusteeship.

On the conflict between restitution and equity

9–50 The *equity approach* adopted by Lord Browne-Wilkinson is suspicious of the "... perceived need to strengthen the remedies of a plaintiff claiming in restitution ..." as involving "... a distortion of trust principles."[85] The chief enemy in the conflict is the approach set out by Birks[86] and latterly by Chambers.[87] These latter viewpoints consider the resulting trust to be the ideal mechanism for returning property to its original owner and thereby of affecting restitution.[88] The distortion of trust principles referred to is said to arise from the elision of property rights and "rights in 'the value transferred'".[89] On the basis of the Fourth Principle of trust law set out by Lord Browne-Wilkinson, it is essential that the property to be held on trust be defined. One identified weakness with Birks' approach is that trusteeship would have been imposed without the trust property being defined.[90]

9–51 The second weakness which Lord Browne-Wilkinson identified in Birks' approach is its implication that trusteeship be imposed on a person at a time when he could not know that a trust had arisen. As such it would be problematic for the court to police the duties of trusteeship if there were some breach of the trust from the implied establishment of the trust. On the facts of *Islington*, the authority, as recipient of the transfer of value under a void contract, would be deemed to have been a trustee from the date of its original receipt of money. This would have resulted in the trust arising at a time when the authority could not have known that there would be a total failure of consideration.

9–52 In-line with the First Principle of the *equity approach*, "[t]his result is incompatible with the basic premise on which all trust law is built, *viz*. that the conscience of the trustee is affected. Unless and until the trustee is aware of the factors which give rise to the supposed trust, there is nothing which can affect his

[82] Birks, "Restitution and Resulting Trusts" in *Equity and Contemporary Legal Developments* (Goldstein ed., Jerusalem, 1992), pp.335, 364–73.

[83] Birks, *Introduction to the Law of Restitution*, (Oxford, 1989), p.368.

[84] [1996] 2 All E.R. 961 at 991.

[85] *ibid.* at 992.

[86] Birks, "Restitution and Resulting Trusts" in *Equity and Contemporary Legal Developments* (Goldstein ed., Jerusalem, 1992), pp.335, 364–73.

[87] Chambers, *Resulting Trusts* (Oxford, 1997).

[88] As considered below in the radical restitutionary approach.

[89] [1996] 2 All E.R. 961 at 992.

[90] See Birks, *Introduction to the Law of Restitution*, (Oxford, 1989), p.361.

conscience."[91] This returns, once again, to the attitude which ought to be taken, first, in commercial cases, and secondly, in situations where the recipient has consented to a credit support structure in the creation of the swaps documentation. The result of this approach is that a resulting trust could never be imposed as a restitutionary response to any unjust factor including failure of consideration or mistake.

9–53 The third objection to Birks' approach is the need "to impose on his wider view an arbitrary and admittedly unprincipled modification so as to ensure that a resulting trust does not arise when there has only been a failure to perform a contract, as opposed to total failure of consideration ...".[92] Birks introduces this circumlocution to meet the circumstances where there is an insolvent recipient.[93] Lord Browne-Wilkinson's view of this exclusion is that "[t]he fact that it is necessary to exclude artificially one type of case which would logically fall within the wider concept casts doubt on the validity of the concept"[94] and it should consequently be dismissed as likely to produce greater commercial uncertainty.

9–54 In conclusion, the view of the majority of the House of Lords was that equity should continue to take priority over the emerging doctrine of restitution by reversal of unjust enrichment. The possibilities offered by an approach based on the emerging principle of restitution of unjust enrichment were dismissed. Lord Browne-Wilkinson explains that in his view the development of a proprietary interest based on restitutionary principles would not be based on sound principle and, while it would be put into effect in the name of unjust enrichment, would be "capable of producing most unjust results".[95] Similarly, an extension to the law of resulting trusts in the manner proposed by Birks and Chambers would give a plaintiff a right to recover property from those who have not been unjustly enriched at his expense at all. There would not only be restitution from those who have some nexus with plaintiff but would also cover a section of third parties at whose expense that plaintiff would be able to effect recovery. His Lordship considers as falling within this category a lender whose debt is secured by a floating charge "albeit in all innocence and for value."[96] This would also encompass any creditor who has purchased a mere equitable interest in the same way.

Money had and received

9–55 *Sinclair v. Brougham*[97] had been considered to be a difficult case without a discernible *ratio decidendi*. Its possible uses to support both the restitutionary attitude and the classical equitable approach are evident. Lord Browne-Wilkinson acknowledged that the common law claim for money had and received was based on unjust enrichment and not on implied contract.[98] Thus a positive obligation to repay was created rather than continued reliance on the fiction of an implied

[91] [1996] 2 All E.R. 961 at 992.

[92] *ibid.*

[93] Birks, *Introduction to the Law of Restitution*, (Oxford, 1989), pp.356–359, 362.

[94] [1996] 2 All E.R. 961 at 992.

[95] *ibid.* at 999.

[96] *ibid.*

[97] *Sinclair v. Brougham* [1914] A.C. 398.

[98] "... your Lordships should now unequivocally and finally reject the concept that the claim for moneys had and received is based on an implied contract.": [1996] 2 All E.R. 961 at 992, *per* Lord Browne-Wilkinson.

agreement between the parties to make repayment. [99] The irony in the *Islington* litigation was that there was in fact a purported contractual agreement as to termination set-off between the parties to calculate the size and nature of any necessary repayment of money had and received. Therefore, it would not have been necessary to redress that rule in the circumstances because there would not need to be the judicial fiction of an implied contract to effect restitution.

9–56 Given the difficulty of the implied contract approach to restitution, and its reliance on a judicial fiction,[100] it is not clear what is to be made of the common intention constructive trust which is imposed by equity. As considered below, it would be open to equity to develop a principle based on a common intention evident between the parties. In this instance, there was a common intention evidenced by the void contract between them. It is submitted, as set out below, that to grant a proprietary claim on this basis would not necessarily constitute an indirect validation of the void contract. By acknowledging the parties' intention to allocate the risks between them by contract, the court is able to effect restitution by rescission by returning the bank's property to it. This is considered in detail in Chapter 12.

Executory contract analysis

9–57 In support of the executory contract analysis Lord Browne-Wilkinson identified

> "[t]he essence of the swap agreement is that, *over the whole term of the agreement*, each party thinks he will come out best: the consideration for one party making a payment is an obligation on the other party to make counter-payments *over the whole term of the agreement*."[101]

There is therefore an assumption that there has been a failure of consideration on the basis that an executory contract requires performance of all of the periodic payments before there has been performance of the agreement. The claim for money had and received would therefore be required to take into account the need to effect restitution for unjust enrichment over the life of the entire agreement, rather than by reference to each separate debt owed.

Constructive trusts

The distinction between institutional and remedial constructive trusts

9–58 In considering *Chase Manhattan*,[102] the problem which arose was the use of a seemingly remedial constructive trust with reference to a void contract. Lord Browne-Wilkinson held that English law will only impose an institutional constructive trust. The institutional constructive trust is defined as arising by operation of law without the scope for discretionary application on a case-by-case basis.

---

[99] *Fibrosa etc. v. Fairbairn etc.* [1943] A.C. 32 at 63–64, *per* Lord Wright; *Pavery & Matthews Pty Ltd v. Paul* (1987) 69 A.L.R. 577 at 583, 603; *Lipkin Gorman v. Karpnale* [1991] 2 A.C. 548 at 578; *Woolwich Equitable Building Society v. IRC (No.2)* [1993] A.C. 70.

[100] Birks, *Introduction to the Law of Restitution*, (Oxford, 1989).

[101] [1996] 2 All E.R. 961 at 993.

[102] [1987] Ch. 264.

> "Under an institutional constructive trust, the trust arises by operation of law as from the date of the circumstances which give rise to it: the function of the court is merely to declare that such trust has arisen in the past. The consequences that flow from such trust having arisen ... are also determined by rules of law, not under a discretion." [103]

9–59 However, in *Chase Manhattan*, Goulding J. had sought to provide that there was no distinction between English and New York law, even though New York law would apply a remedial constructive trust in the following way:

> "A remedial constructive trust, as I understand it, is different. It is a judicial remedy giving rise to an enforceable equitable obligation: the extent to which it operates retrospectively to the prejudice of third parties lies in the discretion of the court."[104]

While the institutional constructive trust is found to be the English law approach, it is held possible for the remedial constructive trust to be introduced in future: "Although the resulting trust is an unsuitable basis for developing proprietary restitutionary remedies, the remedial constructive trust, if introduced into English law, may provide a more satisfactory road forward."[105] The future of restitution would therefore appear to lie with a constructive trust imposed by the court, perhaps in similar manner to the doctrine of proprietary estoppel, by means of a remedy which is tailor-made for each case. The resulting trust thesis, at least in the practice of the common law, will not been called in to bat. There are two other views of the result in *Chase Manhattan*. The first is that rescission ought to effect automatic revesting of the property in the plaintiff.[106] The second is that a remedy based on a tracing claim should exist to prevent unjust enrichment.[107] Neither was explored by Lord Browne-Wilkinson.

Equitable proprietary claims

9–60 From the point of view of the commercial or financial lawyer, it is a problematic notion that it is necessary to start an analysis of the availability of proprietary rights to electronically transferred funds with the example of physical possession of tangible chattels. "The stolen bag of coins" is the title which the judgment gave to the opening of this segment of the analysis. There is a theme running through the law of tracing and following which has to do with the conceptualisation of the property involved. Typically property which is not land is considered to be a tangible chattel. The rules on tracing and the deemed disappearance of money when the account in which it is held goes overdrawn embody the underlying principle that money is not value in an electronic bank account, but rather that it is to be considered in the same way as ordinary, tangible chattels.[108] In analysing the possibility of tracing the stolen bag of coins, Lord Browne-Wilkinson agrees that they are traceable in equity. The nature of the

---

103 [1996] 2 All E.R. 961 at 997.

104 *ibid.*

105 [1996] 2 All E.R. 961 at 999.

106 *El Ajou v. Dollar Land Holdings* [1993] 3 All E.R. 717.

107 Goff and Jones, *The Law of Restitution* (4th ed., Sweet & Maxwell, 1993), p.101.

108 Smith, "Tracing and Electronic Funds Transfer", in *Restitution and Banking Law* (Rose ed., Mansfield Press, Oxford, 1998), p.120.

proprietary interest recognised by equity "arises under a constructive, not a resulting, trust."[109]

9–61 In *Chase Manhattan*,[110] Goulding J. saw the issue as one of tracing payments made under a mistake into the assets of the recipient bank. In his judgment the receipt of the money under a mistake, without more, constituted the recipient a trustee of that money. Lord Browne-Wilkinson reacted as follows:

> "First, [the decision of Goulding J.] is based on a concept of retaining an equitable property in money where, prior to the payment to the recipient bank, there was no existing equitable interest ... Chase Manhattan may well have been rightly decided. The defendant bank knew of the mistake made by the paying bank within two days of the receipt of the moneys ... Although the mere receipt of the moneys, in ignorance of the mistake, gives rise to no trust, the retention of the moneys after the recipient bank learned of the mistake may well have given rise to a constructive trust ...".[111]

9–62 As Lord Browne-Wilkinson held, lack of knowledge of the unconscionable receipt of property negates any possible imposition of a constructive trust on equitable principles. Therefore, the equity approach sees the constructive trust as an institutional construct which is imposed in response to the defendant's knowledge of its own unconscionable receipt of property. The imposition of a proprietary remedy based on equitable tracing will be available only where there was some pre-existing fiduciary duty owed by the defendant recipient of the property in question. There is a tension between a knowledge-based test for the imposition of a constructive trust and the requirement on the basis of precedent for there to be a proprietary base to found an equitable tracing claim. If a constructive trust can be imposed where there was not necessarily a pre-existing fiduciary relationship, simply on the basis of an unconscionable act, then it appears possible to elude the requirement for a pre-existing fiduciary relationship to found a tracing claim.[112]

Conclusions on the equity approach

9–63 The role of the equitable doctrines of undue influence, constructive trusts to give effect to the settlor's intentions and of common intention constructive trusts, were not issues raised by Lord Browne-Wilkinson. They will be considered below in the context of the *suitability approach*. In *Barclays Bank v. O'Brien*[113] the House of Lords established the need to take independent advice. The issue arises then: what advice will dispel the undue influence? Further to *Credit Lyonnais v. Burch*,[114] it is not clear whether there is the possibility of undue influence in OTC derivatives market or whether these multinational organisations are simply arm's length parties. The decision in *O'Brien* as to the application of the principle of undue influence in the provision of guarantees in respect of domestic mortgages, could be extended to cases of commercial guarantees or collateral agreements which are obtained in respect of derivatives transactions. It is possible to argue

---

109 [1996] 2 All E.R. 961 at 998.
110 [1987] Ch. 264.
111 [1996] 2 All E.R. 961 at 997.
112 Birks, "Trusts raised to avoid unjust enrichment: the *Westdeutsche* Case" [1996] R.L.R. 3.
113 *Barclays Bank v. O'Brien* [1993] 3 W.L.R. 786.
114 *Credit Lyonnais v. Burch* [1997] 1 All E.R. 144.

that *O'Brien* is a decision which is also about risk allocation. In compiling a test for equity in commercial situations, a test of "commercially acceptable conduct" may be better than "unconscionable conduct". As with *Tan*, there would be an establishment of an objective standard of probity.

9–64 The issue is this: if equity will respond to a fiduciary who takes unacceptable levels of risk with the trust fund, what is it that will lead to a person being made a fiduciary? In commercial cases there are a number of established examples of bankers in relation to their clients. With reference to more sophisticated corporate clients, the test must revolve some notion of *suitability*. That is, suitability of advice given and suitability of the financial product used in any given situation. In the context of derivatives, this standard of suitability is more likely to be of greater importance than with reference to established and comparatively risk-controlled forms of product (such as share issues or bond issues). In arranging a bespoke derivative facility, the client is peculiarly in the hands of the advising institution. Where that institution takes unacceptable risks, that should be considered to be a breach of the duty owed to the client.

9–65 Similarly, any analysis of commercial law and the availability of proprietary claims in equity will have to confront the *Re Goldcorp* issue that there be a segregation of property as a trust fund before a valid trust can be created.[115] There, despite a representation to the contrary in the detail of the contractual agreements, there could not be a proprietary right in any property held by the other contracting party. This approach would appear to be preferable from the point of view of avoiding systemic risk because all losses are netted rather than allowing some unsecured creditors to escape with proprietary rights and thus leaving less in the pot for the remainder of the creditors.

9–66 One issue which arises in this context is whether a test for suitability would give rise to a claim in restitution for a wrong committed by the bank, or to a claim in restitution based on a personal claim in restitution (money had and received), or a proprietary claim in equity. The former claim, related to the commission for a wrong, would arise under negligence, breach of contract or negligent misstatement. The latter claims are the business of the decisions in *Islington*.

[115] *Re Goldcorp* [1995] 1 A.C. 74.

Chapter 10

Alternative commercial approaches

The commercial common sense approach

10–01 This chapter considers a part of the speech delivered by Lord Woolf and takes on board some of the sentiments expressed by Lord Goff. It proceeds with the rough and ready argument that the courts should give commercial people the judgments they want, in the absence of partisan concerns or affronts to public policy. Some support for a commercially sensible approach in situations concerning payment of amounts of money comes from Lord Wilberforce in *General Tire and Rubber Co v. Firestone Tyre and Rubber Co Ltd*:[1] "In a commercial setting, it would be proper to take account of the manner in which and the time at which persons acting honestly and reasonably would pay". In the context of the derivatives market, there is similarly some need to take account of the market's typical modes of taking security, as well as to understand the structure of the products which they use.

10–02 A common-sensical approach was adopted by most of the judges during the swaps litigation. That common sense informs different approaches to the legal analysis. The core attitude to personal claims in restitution was expressed by Leggatt L.J.:

> "In my judgment, the payments made are in those circumstances recoverable by Westdeutsche, in so far as they exceed the payments made by Islington, as money had and received to the use of Westdeutsche, by which Islington have been unjustly enriched."[2]

10–03 In Lord Goff's speech there was an acknowledgement of the concern which the *Hazell* litigation had caused among the commercial community. What is perhaps more problematic is the impact of the *Islington* appeal on that same community. As his Lordship held:

> "... I wish to record that it caused grave concern among financial institutions, and especially foreign banks, which had entered into such transactions with local authorities in good faith, with no idea that a rule as technical as the *ultra vires* doctrine might undermine what they saw as a perfectly legitimate commercial transaction."[3]

This echoes Lord Woolf's own opinion that the expectations of commercial parties should be satisfied by the courts so far as that is possible.

---

[1] [1975] 1 W.L.R. 819 at 836; [1975] 2 All E.R. 173 at 188.

[2] [1994] 1 W.L.R. 938 at 953; [1994] 4 All E.R. 890 at 969.

[3] [1996] 2 All E.R. 961 at 965.

The speech of Lord Woolf

10–04 Lord Woolf emphasised the commercial nature of the contract and of the financial contract at issue in the *Islington* appeal. In particular, he approved Hobhouse J.'s award of compound interest on the basis that compound interest would have been payable on an ordinary loan and therefore is the commercially anticipated rate of interest.[4] The need to provide compound interest is a commercial requirement that grows out of commercial expectation, as well as the concept of justice set out by Lord Goff. His Lordship drew on the decisions in *Wallersteiner v. Moir (No2)*[5] and in *National Bank of Greece SA v. Pinios Shipping Co (No. 1), The Maira*[6] in coming to this conclusion. The proper role of the court is to provide the banks with a remedy which accorded with the commercial value of the property which they had paid to the authority under a misapprehension; "[a]ny other decision would be inconsistent with the court's ability to grant full restitution."[7] As in the speech of Lord Goff, there a concept of "full" or "complete" restitution. It is not clear how far this is concept is intended to stretch.

10–05 Lord Woolf was concerned for the reputation of substantive English commercial law when he held that:

> "It is no secret that [the decision in *Hazell*] caused dismay among some of those concerned with the standing abroad of the commercial law of this country. That concern is likely to be increased if the outcome of this litigation is that this appeal has to be allowed by this House because the courts have no jurisdiction to grant compound interest."[8]

This attitude is at the heart of the commercial common sense approach. Participants in financial markets using English law have different expectations from those who might look to the English laws of trusts and restitution for remedies in connection with their own homes. There is a need to look to the expectation that Westdeutsche had that the value transferred to the authority would have generated compound interest, in the normal business of the financial markets, had it not been used in that way.

10–06 Lord Woolf decided, as is therefore the unanimous opinion of the House of Lords, that the bank is not entitled to an equitable proprietary claim. Without adopting the detailed approach of Lord Browne-Wilkinson, he decided that the authority should not have been regarded as being subject to either the duties of a trustee or fiduciary to the bank.[9] Within this common sense commercial view, the dangers which Lord Browne-Wilkinson "*identifies could flow* [Lord Woolf's emphasis] from the wholesale importation into commercial law of equitable principles"[10] are avoided. Thus there would be no confusion by the application of equitable principle to commercial transaction.

10–07 Lord Woolf was eager to draw the distinction between equitable principles and equitable remedies. "We are concerned not with equitable principles of substantive law but with the possible existence of an equitable

---

[4] It is significant that Lord Woolf seems to be treating the upfront payment as a loan.

[5] [1975] Q.B. 373.

[6] [1990] 1 A.C. 637.

[7] [1996] 2 All E.R. 961at 1002.

[8] *ibid.*

[9] *ibid.*

[10] *ibid.*

remedy."[11] That is, the award of compound interest. On this uncomfortable basis, he reassures himself that he is avoiding the uncertainties of equitable principle while also invoking the attractions of fairness which come with the equitable remedy of an award of compound interest.

> "... equitable interests, mere equities, floating equities and the great doctrines of equity cover most of the field of equity; and they are all concerned to a greater or lesser degree with rights of property ... Equitable remedies, though often used in aid of property rights, are also often used in other cases. The underlying principle is the inadequacy of the common law remedy of damages."[12]

10–08 The problem was that there are no damages available because there is no valid contract. Therefore, the parties will be left without a remedy at common law. The role of equity is to supply a remedy where there is an unconscionable lack of recourse at common law. The question is therefore the manner in which such a remedy will be imposed and the circumstances in which it would be appropriate to impose such a remedy. Therefore, based on the above quoted passage, to achieve the troublesome goal of "full restitution", Lord Woolf considered that it is necessary to award compound interest. The overruling of *Sinclair*[13] means that there is no need to proceed on the basis that the local authority is a fiduciary—rather, the application of general equitable principle would be enough.

10–09 Lord Woolf cited the speech of Lord Wright in the *Fibrosa* case where it is clearly problematic to identify whether the principles of restitution are to be derived from equity or from the common law because there is not a strict distinction on the authorities.[14] For example, the decision of the Court of Appeal in *Wallersteiner v. Moir (No.2)*[15] was that it should be presumed that the company would have made the "most beneficial use open to it" of money wrongly taken by a director and that the money wrongly taken from the company should be restored to it "with compound interest at yearly rests". Lord Woolf pronounced himself "content to assume that the cause of action is one at common law" without needing to resolve this jurisdictional dilemma.[16] The core aim of the remedy is "to disgorge a profit made or presumed to have been made out of a payment of a sum of money which should not have been made ... There would be no difference of principle if the contract was void for mistake."[17] Lord Woolf eluded the stricter interpretation set out by Lord Brandon in *President of India v. La Pintada Cia Navegacion SA*[18], which so troubled Lord Lloyd, on the basis that the House of Lords did not appear to have been addressed by counsel specifically on the issue of the extent of the equitable jurisdiction.[19]

---

[11] [1996] 2 All E.R. 961 at 1003.

[12] *Snell's Equity*, (29th ed., Sweet & Maxwell, 1991), p.26.

[13] In this respect Lord Woolf concurs with Lord Browne-Wilkinson rather than Lord Goff, *infra*.

[14] Lord Macnaghten held that it does not matter "... whether the proceedings be taken in a court of equity or in a court of law ..." for the award to be made: *Johnson v. R.* [1904] A.C. 817 at 821. See also *London, Chatham and Dover Rly Co v. South Eastern Rly Co* [1893] A.C. 429 which Lord Macnaghten considered to be authority for the same proposition.

[15] [1975] Q.B. 373 at 388, *per* Lord Denning M.R.

[16] [1996] 2 All E.R. 961 at 1005.

[17] *ibid.*

[18] [1985] A.C. 104 at 118–121.

[19] [1996] 2 All E.R. 961 at 1008.

10–10 Lord Woolf disagreed with the decision of Hobhouse J. in *South Tyneside*[20] where he held that a "personal equitable right", based on the decision in *Re Diplock*,[21] would be insufficient to ground a claim for compound interest.[22] The basis for this disagreement in the availability of compound interest on general principles, as considered above. Hobhouse J. limited his decision to the facts before him that there was only a personal claim as opposed to an equitable proprietary claim.[23] Similarly, the authorities which he cited in support of his finding that no claim for compound interest would stand were based on claims relating only to statutory interest[24], or where the issue was whether interest was payable at all (rather than the distinction between simple and compound interest),[25] or where payment of compound interest had already been accepted between the parties.[26] In Lord Woolf's view, a proprietary base for the claim to receive compound interest would fail in any event where a right to trace had been lost: "This is inconsistent with the commercial realities to which the judge referred to ...".[27]

A new test?

10–11 The core argument raised by Lord Goff in the context of making proprietary claims available within the *restitution approach* is that there is no reason why the banks should recover their money on the basis of a proprietary remedy. The argument would be extended: had the parties intended to allocate these risks then there would have been some collateralisation or guarantee structure which would have allocated that risk effectively? However, what is not considered at all in any of the swaps cases is the fact that the form of the standard contracts *do allocate these risks*. Both the BBAIRS Agreement and the ISDA Master Agreement do specify that the risk of party A being unable to perform under the contract is to be borne by Party A in effecting the termination provisions under the contract.

10–12 The contracts are clearly considered to be void *and therefore of no further utility*: even though they are the mechanism by which the parties sought to allocate their responsibilities. Further, these contractual provisions constitute standard market terms rather than simply a one-off contractual agreement. The ISDA project has been to introduce informal regulation of the OTC derivatives markets by standardising the terms on which business is conducted. The primary aim has been to ensure that it is possible to net reciprocal payments for capital adequacy purposes and also to ensure that netting will work on close-out of transactions on grounds of insolvency or other causes.

10–13 English law has entered into a triple jeopardy. In the first place, it chose that interest rate swaps were *ultra vires* local authorities. In conscience, this was the only decision which the court could realistically come to on the basis that *Hazell* was taken as the test case. The overuse of swaps by Hammersmith and Fulham (more than all the other local authorities put together) meant that the

---

20 *Kleinwort Benson* v. *South Tyneside M.B.C.* [1994] 4 All E.R. 972, *per* Hobhouse J.

21 *Re Diplock's Estate, Diplock v. Wintle* [1948] Ch. 465.

22 [1996] 2 All E.R. 961 at 1008.

23 This necessary restriction was also criticised by Lord Goff, as considered above.

24 *Woolwich Equitable Building Society v. Inland Revenue Commissioners* [1993] A.C. 70; *BP Exploration Co (Libya) Ltd v. Hunt (No.2)* [1979] 1 W.L.R. 783; [1982] 1 All E.R. 925.

25 *Re Diplock's Estate, Diplock v. Wintle* [1948] Ch. 465.

26 *O'Sullivan v. Management Agency and Music Ltd* [1985] Q.B. 428.

27 [1996] 2 All E.R. 961 at 1010.

House of Lords had to rule them *ultra vires* or risk depopulating the whole of a newly bankrupt borough.

10–14 The second jeopardy was the refusal of compound interest. The operation of complicated English doctrines of common law and equity meant that commercially expected rates of compound interest were not enforceable between commercial parties acting at arm's length.[28] In the opinion of Lord Woolf, at the heart of the commercial common sense approach is the quest for a test which is based on the evaluation of the risks involved, the approach of Lord Woolf in this context is particularly instructive:

> "The modern test should be whether the debtor could reasonably foresee that in the ordinary course of things the loss was likely to occur or was on the cards. Who would refuse to impute such knowledge to a debtor? Who would venture to suggest that a defaulting debtor could not reasonably foresee interest as the creditor's loss flowing from the failure to pay?"[29]

On this basis, it is to be considered again why the terms agreed between the parties as to termination and the allocation of risk were not considered by any court to be worthy of examination.

10–15 The third jeopardy is straightforwardly ignoring the prolonged deliberations of the financial derivatives market generally and of these parties in particularly in allocating their commercial risks expressly in contractual form. For the English legal system and the United Kingdom economy to retain the benefits which Lord Woolf has identified in giving judgment and at other times,[30] there is a need for the law to respond to the commercial context as well as to the application of legal principle.

10–16 It is not a straightforward question to argue that the *result* of the House of Lords' decision is necessarily wrong. What is not clear is how the banks could have asserted that they retained proprietary rights in the assets which they transferred to the local authorities. However, a terminologically exact analysis of that transaction and of other forms of financial derivatives, does mean that all parties to derivatives contracts run the risk of not having proprietary remedies awarded to them even where they have divulged specific assets as part of their payment mechanism. Similarly, they run the risk of not being able to enforce market-level rates of return against their counterparties—even where that is the basis of their transaction.

10–17 The bigger issue than whether or not the decision is correct, is whether or not the courts were approaching the questions in the most appropriate way. By ignoring the express context of risk and of suitability in the swaps arena, the courts failed to analyse the commercial context of the creation, pricing and administration of the products. In the same way, nothing was said about the difference between essentially distinct products and those agreements which had been part-performed as against those which had expired.

10–18 If the modern test should be whether the debtor could reasonably foresee that in the ordinary course of things the loss was likely to occur or was on the

---

[28] The argument might be raised that the local authorities were not arm's length commercial parties as a result of *Hazell*. However, the authorities are every bit as much commercial parties as FTSE-100 companies when they enter into long-term lending and debt management in every other context—there seems no reason to treat them differently in this context.

[29] [1996] 2 All E.R. 961 at 1016; citing, with approval, Mann, "On Interest, Compound Interest and Damages" (1985) 101 L.Q.R. 30..

[30] For example, a lecture delivered at the LSE on November 7, 1996.

cards, why were the terms agreed between the parties as to termination and the allocation of risk were not considered by any court to be worthy of examination. At the level of contractual theory, there is a sound argument for holding that the parties should be left free to reach their own conclusions as to risk and reward. As Atiyah explains the interaction of the market and the use of contract:

> "In the market, parties were expected to calculate rationally the various risks, whether of past or of future events, which might affect the value of the contract. Provided that there was no fraud, and provided that the bargaining process was itself fair, the result must be deemed to be fair. Unexpected events, unknown factors, whether occurring before or after the contract was made, were not to be allowed to upset the resultant bargains. In principle all such risks were capable of being perceived and evaluated; in practice, not everybody succeeded in doing so. Or doing it very well ... The whole point of the free market bargaining approach was to give full rein to the greater skill and knowledge of those who calculated risks better ... He who failed to calculate a risk properly when making a contract would lose by it, and next time would calculate more efficiently."[31]

10–19 The *commercial common–sense approach* has an eye on context. In Atiyah's conception, the purpose of the contract is to evaluate the risks between commercial parties. The award of remedies is made conditional on the application of justice in commercial cases. Where the understanding of commercial participants is that compound interest would be available in respect of money, but for the transfer of that money, then compound interest ought to be ordered in connection with its repayment. Fully operational markets require that the law recognise the commercial context in which they anticipate the operation of legal remedies. Globalised economies require control by modern principles of law or there will simply be recourse to greater use of euro-markets outwith the control of municipal legal systems. The development of transnational norms of private international law have the effect of introducing greater commonality of principle. However, there will remain issues as to which system of law will govern commercial contracts. There is a policy requirement for municipal systems of law to prevent the relocation of commercial contracts outside their jurisdictional boundaries because it becomes difficult to enforce policy requirements of that system of rules.

10–20 This feet on the ground approach leads us into the two concluding chapters which seek to set out new approaches to the local authority swaps cases.

[31] Atiyah, *The Rise and Fall of Freedom of Contract* (Oxford, 1979), p.437.

Part IV

Conclusions

New Approaches

Chapter 11

The emerging principle of unjust enrichment

11–01 This concluding section comes in two parts. The first chapter analyses a school of thought that asserts that the new law of unjust enrichment is the best method for analysing problems like the swaps cases. The work which makes up this body of thought was considered in detail by the House of Lords in *Islington*. The second chapter advances an alternative means of analysing the swaps cases and seeks to assert a future test.

11–02 The *radical restitution approach* is centred on the work of Birks and a group of others including Chambers, Mitchell and Smith. The distinction between the restitution considered by Goff, discussed above, and the approach of Birks is centred on the taxonomy of restitution which Birks and Chambers have attempted to draw out.[1] Their aim has been to set out the intellectual bones for a body of law to draw together actions such as money had and received, *quantum valebat, quantum meruit* and "the other fantastic resemblances of contract".[2] However, this work has gone beyond looking at the categories set out by Goff and Jones into the line between equity and restitution and also tort and restitution. The form of restitution which is principally at issue here is "subtractive unjust enrichment" as opposed to profits from wrongdoing.[3]

Outline of the radical restitutionary approach

11–03 The *radical restitutionary approach*[4] is concerned with a remedy which forces a defendant to give up an enrichment received at the plaintiff's expense. The appropriate remedy is then one which requires the defendant to give up to another an enrichment received at the other's expense or its value in money. Birks declares his central concern to be with "the second sense of 'restitution' ... that is, with gains to be given up, not with losses to be made good."[5] The motive for the use of the radical restitutionary approach is summed up by the following assertion of the utility of civilian principles:

> "Any civilised system of law is bound to provide remedies for cases of what has been called unjust enrichment or unjust benefit, that is to prevent a man

[1] See Birks and Chambers, *Restitution Research Resource*, (Mansfield Press, 1997), pp.1–6.

[2] *ibid.* at 1.

[3] In the discussion of the *suitability approach* there is some discussion of the role of tort and wrongdoing.

[4] See Birks, "Misnomer" in *Restitution, Present and Future: Essays in Honour of Gareth Jones* (Cornish, Nolan, O'Sullivan and Virgo, eds, Hart Publishing, Oxford, 1998), p.1.

[5] Birks, *Introduction to the Law of Restitution* (Oxford, 1989), p.11.

from retaining the money of or some benefit derived from another which it is against conscience that he should keep".[6]

The problem is to decide what is captured within the term "unjust enrichment".[7] Must D be enriched by subtraction from P's wealth, or can D also be caught by being enriched "at the expense of P" but in a way that costs P nothing? In Birks' terms, if D is paid money by A to beat up P, P loses no money but D is enriched in a way that causes harm to P.[8] In the same way in the derivatives context, if D speculates on a warrants market in such a way that investor P loses some speculative potential, P has lost some opportunity, D is enriched by P entering that market, but P has not *lost* any money because P acquired warrants which retain their value. Birks requires the doctrine of unjust enrichment is to be based on subtraction—that is, the reparation for wealth taken from the plaintiff.[9]

11–04 In the definition of "restitution" set out by the *radical restitutionary approach*, restitution is the response which requires one person to give up to another an enrichment received at his expense, or its value in money.[10] The law of restitution creates a new right, rather than giving effect *ex post facto* to a pre-existing right. That right is generated by the receipt of the unjust enrichment with the effect of depriving the defendant of the value received at the plaintiff's expense.[11] In Birks' terms: "Restitution is that active or creative response at the moment of enrichment."[12] Its strength is an understanding of the notion of "value" which is required to be restored, rather than concentration on a particular piece of property. As considered in the *Concept of Money*[13] the problem faced by the House of Lords is establishing the precise nature of the property involved before considering the suitability of a proprietary remedy in that context.

11–05 However, in the context of the swaps cases there is still a need to distinguish between property law claims and restitutionary claims. The restitutionary response is considered to be primarily achieved by the award of personal rights. Birks identifies one of the problems in this area as being the difficulty in compounding restitutionary and property codes. Such an assimilation would require that it be broken down again such that it would be comprehensible. One particular area in which Birks considers that this breakdown would occur would be along the "conceptual line between preserving existing rights, so as to prevent enrichment, and creating new ones, so as to reverse it".[14] So, in considering the availability of proprietary remedies under the radical restitutionary approach, it is important to distinguish between the situation in which those rights are being generated by a pre-existing property right (law of property) and being generated by unjust enrichment (law of

[6] *Fibrosa Spolka Akcyjna v. Fairbairn Lawson Combe Barbour Limited* [1943] A.C. 32, 61, *per* Lord Wright. Cited with approval in *Woolwich Equitable Building Society v. Inland Revenue Commissioners* [1993] A.C. 70, 197, 202; and *Westdeutsche Landesbank Girozentrale v. Islington L.B.C.* [1996] 2 All E.R. 961, 1004, *per* Lord Woolf.

[7] See Burrows, "Understanding the Law of Restitution: A Map through the Thicket", *Understanding the Law of Obligations* (Hart Publishing, Oxford, 1998), pp.45 *et seq.*

[8] Birks, *Introduction to Law of Restitution* (Oxford, 1989), pp.23 *et seq.*

[9] *cf.* Smith, "Tracing and Electronic Funds Transfer" in *Restitution and Banking Law* (Rose ed., Mansfield Press, Oxford, 1998), pp.120.

[10] Birks, *Introduction to the Law of Restitution* (Oxford, 1989), pp.13.

[11] The issue which arises in the context of the swaps cases is whether I am deprived of that value if I have already contracted to give it to you?

[12] Birks, *Introduction to the Law of Restitution* (Oxford, 1989), p.14.

[13] Chapter 4, *Issues of Finance and Law*, above.

[14] Birks, *Introduction to the Law of Restitution* (Oxford, 1989), p.15.

restitution of unjust enrichment). The former would arise out of some reservation of title by contract or the segregation of some interest to be held on trust, in the financial context. The latter would be the restitutionary response to some unjust enrichment which is not reliant on a pre-existing reservation title but which would be reliant on a pre-existing proprietary base.

11–06 The radical restitutionary approach draws lines between the law of restitution, the law of property and the law of obligations. In the context of the swaps cases it is necessary to establish where that line is to be drawn with respect to the taking of risks in commercial contracts and whether unacceptable risks ought to be a matter for a restitutionary response or a matter simply for an analysis of the contractual intentions of the parties. As considered above, the radical restitutionary approach received short shrift from Lord Browne-Wilkinson in *Islington*. Its assertion that the resulting trust should be identified as the primary means of affecting restitution was roundly rejected.[15]

11–07 Birks identifies three approaches to establishing a proprietary claim over property which has passed from the original, absolute owner to another party. The first is a following claim[16] where the original owner is able to identify the specific property and say "that's mine". The second approach is to establish that the defendant has committed a wrong, further to a tort of conversion. The third approach would be to establish some unjust enrichment in the current possessor of that property. On the facts of the swaps cases it is impossible to follow the money transferred to the authorities because it was paid into accounts which subsequently went overdrawn before the money was spent. Similarly, there is no suggestion of any wrong which would ground an action in tort. Therefore, the ensuing discussion will focus on the availability of unjust enrichment in the swaps cases.

11–08 The unjust enrichment would itself divide between, first, "technical enrichment" (whereby you acquire something from me unlawfully, you do not own it in legal terms although you have use of it) and, second, "factual enrichment" (whereby you can be proved to have become enriched by acquiring some title in, the possession and use of my property). The issue of title to property should therefore be divided between situations in which title to the property has been passed and situations in which title to that property has not been passed. As Birks acknowledges, the context of this passing of title after the decision of the House of Lords in *Islington* is subject to the requirement of knowledge in the recipient of the property before any claim will be enforceable. The logic of Birks' position, however, is that title can never leave the original owner of the property, regardless of the knowledge of the recipient, hence the concentration on the resulting trust as a means of allowing that equitable interest to "jump back" to its original owner.

11–09 The specific role for restitution of unjust enrichment is something which remains at large in many jurisdictions. While English law has accepted the existence of the doctrine,[17] it is still unclear how it will develop in the future. One argument is to mirror the Canadian approach to domestic proprietary cases by basing them on a conception of unjust enrichment that appears akin to proprietary estoppel in English property law. In the USA, it is arguable that the doctrine of unjust enrichment is the explanation for the imposition of tortious liability where

[15] As considered in *The Primacy of Equity*, Chapter 9, above.

[16] See on this sub-division of common-law tracing Smith, *The Law of Tracing* (Oxford, 1997) Part II, pp.67–104.

[17] *Lipkin Gorman v. Karpnale* [1991] 2 A.C. 548.

there is a creation of abnormally high risks.[18] The first issue in this context is to consider the availability of proprietary claims under the doctrine of unjust enrichment.

Equitable proprietary claims and unjust enrichment: an introduction

11–10 One of the difficulties with the imposition of equitable remedies in commercial cases is that the two instances in which equity will usually intervene are restricted to situations where there has been fraud or some breach of fiduciary responsibility.[19] The limited applicability of fraud (with its peculiarly strict standard of proof) and the uncertain nature of the concept "fiduciary" is that most commercial situations will not have equitable remedies available to them for want of proof or establishment of the necessary equitable relationship. The importance of recent cases on the scope of equitable remedies such as *Tan*[20] is that they reach beyond palpable or demonstrable fraud, or a standard of dishonesty requiring active deceit, and move into a broader spread of commercial activity—principally risk-taking. Given that there is the possibility of an equitable response beyond active deceit, the further issue is then when equity will impose proprietary remedies for such extended categories of claim.[21]

11–11 Birks suggests that, in the light of the speech of Lord Browne-Wilkinson in *Islington*,[22] there is no need to prove a prior equitable interest in the property.[23] In Birks' terms, there is no need to establish a proprietary base to found an equitable tracing claim. The effect of this apparent change in the law would be to enable the purchaser of a physically-settled option to establish a tracing claim via

[18] Keeton, 72 Harv. L. Rev. 401 (1959).

[19] For academic commentary on criticisms of requirement for equitable interest before a tracing claim see: Birks, *Introduction to the Law of Restitution* (Oxford, 1989), pp.380–4; Goff and Jones, *The Law of Restitution* (4th ed., Sweet & Maxwell, 1993), pp.83–6; Oakley, "The Prerequisites of an Equitable Tracing Claim" (1975) 28 CLP 64; Pearce, "A Tracing Paper" (1976) 40 Conv. 277; Dewar, "The Development of the Remedial Constructive Trust" (1982) 60 Can. B.R. 265 at 273; McKendrick, "Tracing Misdirected Funds" [1991] L.M.C.L.Q. 378 at 386–7; Smith, *The Law of Tracing*, (Oxford, 1997), generally.

[20] *Royal Brunei Airlines v. Tan* [1995] 2 A.C. 378.

[21] For academic commentary on the availability of proprietary remedies arising out of restitution and equity see the following eclectic discussions: Birks, *Introduction to the Law of Restitution* (Oxford, 1989), pp.375–401; Burrows, *The Law of Restitution* (Butterworths, 1993), pp.40–5; Goff and Jones, *The Law of Restitution* (4th ed., Sweet & Maxwell, 1993), Chap. 2; Maddaugh and McCamus, 78–100; Maudsley, "Propietary Remedies for the Recovery of Money" (1959) 75 L.Q.R. 234; Dewar, "The Development of the Remedial Constructive Trust" (1982) 60 Can. B.R. 265; Goode, "Ownership and Obligation in Commercial Transactions" (1987) 103 L.Q.R. 433 at 436–7; Litman, "The Emergence of Unjust Enrichment as a Cause of Action and the Remedy of Constructive Trust" (1988) 26 Alberta L.R. 407; Hayton, "Constructive Trusts: Is the Remedying of Unjust Enrichment a Satisfactory Approach?" in *Equity, Fiduciaries and Trusts* (Youdan ed., Toronto, 1989), Chap. 9; Paciocco, "The Remedial Constructive Trust: A Principled Basis for Priorities over Creditors" (1989) 68 Can. B.R. 315; Sherwin, "Constructive Trusts in Bankruptcy" [1989] Univ. of Illinois L.R. 297; Gummow J., "Unjust Enrichment, Restitution and Proprietary Remedies" in *Essays on Restitution* (P.D. Finn ed., Sydney, 1990), Chap. 3; Elias, *Explaining Constructive Trusts* (Oxford, 1990); Fridman, "The Reach of Restitution" (1991)11 L.S. 304; Glover, "Bankruptcy and Constructive Trusts" (1991) 19 A.B.L.R. 98; Goode, "Property and Unjust Enrichment" in *Essays on Restitution* (Burrows ed., Oxford, 1991) Chap. 9; Annetta, "Priority Rights in Insolvency—The Doctrinal Basis for Equity's Intervention" (1992) 20 A.B.L.R. 311; Rajani, "Equitable Assistance in the Seach for Security" in *Insolvency Law: Theory and Practice* (H. Rajak ed., London, 1993) Chap. 2.

[22] [1996] 2 W.L.R. 802 at 838–839 ('The stolen bag of coins').

[23] Birks, "Trusts to be raised to reverse unjust enrichment: the *Westdeutsche* Case" [1996] R.L.R. 3 at 10.

the assets which are to be physically-settled at some time in the future, even though they have not been allocated to the recipient in advance. Oliver[24] divides the decision in *Islington* between three categories of liability. The first revolves around the speech of Lord Browne-Wilkinson that liability to constructive trust is based on knowledge. The second is orientated around receipt of property impressed with a trust.[25] The receipt-based liability created by *Islington* is categorised as "strict" liability subject to defences.[26] The issue is how strict this liability can be said to be.[27] The third category is the "restitution-based personal claim", which Lord Goff established as standing for the common law category of money had and received. Oliver is, however, uncertain what *Islington* does for equitable tracing claims. Commercial tracing cases are really concerned with establishing title, not with the quotidian concerns of conscience. As in *Islington,* conscience is generally shown as having little part to play *in the outcome* because conscience will generally only appear in cases of fraud, *i.e.* an affront to conscience is usually not found in commercial cases (other than express fraud).

11–12 In the light of Lord Browne-Wilkinson's decision in support of the principle in *Re Goldcorp*[28] that property must be segregated before it can be the subject matter of a trust, there must be some restriction on the ability to found an equitable tracing claim—that is, it is important to know which rights are being traced or which property is being followed. Presuming this conflict with *Goldcorp* to be more apparent than intended, at what point does this right crystallise? Does the right to the equitable tracing claim arise at the date of the unconscionable or fraudulent action, or does it not crystallise on maturity of the option, given that there would not have been any right to the property before maturity if there had not been such unconscionable act. The further question is with reference to a cash-settled derivative, as to whether an equitable proprietary claim will obtain even where there is only a right to receive cash. Finally, it is not clear where an equitable proprietary claim will arise where there is an option which can be physically- or cash-settled at the buyer's election. By contradistinction, it now appears possible that a common law right to trace arises to protect a legal right. *F.C. Jones (a firm) v. Jones*[29] appears to allow tracing at common law into an exchange product, rather than being restricted simply to identification or following of the original property which is the object of that tracing claim.[30]

11–13 Bearing these issues in mind, it is important to look at each form of equitable response which will found a proprietary claim. First resulting trust, then constructive trust and then subrogation.

Resulting trusts

11–14 The core of the resulting trust argument in connection with restitution, and particularly the radical approach, is that the resulting trust is said to constitute

---

[24] KCLJ 8 (1997/98) 147.

[25] Similarly Jones, (1996) 55 C.L.J. 432–435.

[26] Oliver, KCLJ 8 (1997/98) 147.

[27] Millett, "Restitution: Taking Stock", delivering the Society of Advanced Legal Studies Lecture, Institute of Advanced Legal Studies, London, July 23, 1998.

[28] *Re Goldcorp* [1995] 1 A.C. 74.

[29] [1996] 3 W.L.R. 703.

[30] Hanbury and Martin, *Modern Equity* (13th ed., Sweet & Maxwell, 1993), 660; Davern, "Common Law Tracing, Profits and the Doctrine of Relation Back" [1997] R.L.R. 93.

the most efficient method of restoring rights in property to their original owner.[31] As accepted in the High Court in *Islington*, fairness required that the banks be said to have retained equitable title in the property transferred to the local authorities. It is precisely this approach which Lord Browne-Wilkinson seeks to redress in his redrawing of the fundamentals of the law of trusts. It was said that "the law with regard to resulting trusts is not in doubt", by Lord Reid in *Vandervell v. IRC*,[32] ironically in a judgment where Lord Reid was dissenting. In Chambers' opinion, the seeming consensus of understanding of the resulting trusts "mask[s] a widespread uncertainty about the true nature of the resulting trust. There is no consensus on the principle by which the resulting trust operates, including the fundamental question whether it arises by operation of law or depends on the presumed intention to create a trust."[33] The further point raised by Chambers is whether or the resulting trust "properly understood, might not be equity's principal contribution to reversing unjust enrichment".[34]

11–15 Elsewhere Martin has described the resulting trust as "a situation in which a transferee is required by equity to hold property on trust for the transferor; or for the person who provided the purchase money for the transfer".[35] Waters describes the resulting trust as arising whenever legal or equitable title to property is in one party's name, but that party, because he is a fiduciary or gave no value for the property, is under an obligation to return it to the original title owner, or to the person who *did* give value for it.[36] Chambers cites a Canadian interpretation of the resulting trust as containing the essential characteristic[37] that "the person in whose favour the trust arises is the person who provided the property or equitable interest vested in the person bound by the trust".[38]

11–16 The difficulty with the use of resulting trust, is the obligation that is placed on the trustee from the time of receipt of the property impressed with a trust, at a time when that person could not have known of that obligation. "The term 'constructive trustee' is sometimes used to describe someone who holds no property in trust, but has assisted a breach of trust and is under a personal liability to compensate the beneficiary for losses caused thereby. 'Resulting trustee' is never used in this fashion. There must be identifiable assets vested in the resulting trustee capable of being the subject matter of a trust."[39]

How resulting trusts arise

11–17 In Chambers' opinion most resulting trusts arise in one of two situations: (i) where there has been an apparent gift of property; or (ii) where an express trust has failed to dispose of all of the trust property. It is said that in either case the principles of equity assume that the owner was not intended to receive the benefit of the property and raises a resulting trust in favour of the provider of that property.[40] Chambers' understanding of the genesis of resulting trusts is that: "All

---

[31] Birks, *Introduction to the Law of Restitution*, (Oxford, 1989), p.62; Birks "Restitution and Resulting Trusts" in Goldstein, *Equity and Contemporary Legal Developments* (Jerusalem, 1992), 353, at 363–4.

[32] [1967] 2 A.C. 291, 307.

[33] Chambers, *Resulting Trusts* (Oxford, 1997), 1.

[34] *ibid.*

[35] Hanbury and Martin, *Modern Equity* (13th ed., Sweet & Maxwell, 1993), p.233.

[36] Waters (1984), p.300.

[37] Chambers, *Resulting Trusts* (Oxford, 1997), p.1.

[38] *Baird v. Columbia Trust Co.* (1915) 22 D.L.R. 150, 151, B.C.S.C.. *per* Morrison J.

[39] Chambers, *Resulting Trusts* (Oxford, 1997), p.2.

[40] *ibid.* at pp.2 *et seq.*

resulting trusts come into being because the provider of property did not intend to benefit the recipient."[41] As he puts it: "Some have preferred to see the resulting trust as dependent on an implied intention to create a trust,[42] others as a trust arising by operation of law[43] and still others as a bit of both.[44] This has left the resulting trust in a limbo between express and constructive trusts."[45]

11–18 In *Vandervell (No.2)*, Megarry J. concluded that the resulting trust operated on different principles in each of these two situations. The distinction that is made by Megarry J. is between an apparent gift as "presumed" and the resulting trust on the failure of an express trust as "automatic". It was said that the "presumed resulting trust" was based on the presumed intention of the provider of the property to create such a trust. This presumed trust would be capable of rebuttal by evidence to the contrary. The "automatic resulting trust" would arise by operation of law, thus it would be independent of intention and therefore capable of rebuttal.[46]

11–19 The *radical restitutionary approach* sees the distinction between express and resulting trusts as being that express trusts are created by an intention to create a trust, whereas resulting trusts arise because of a lack of intention to benefit the recipient.[47] Chambers' view is that resulting trusts arise by operation of law and that when property has been transferred without the provider of that property intending to benefit the recipient, equity responds by imposing a resulting trust. It is therefore said to be a job for the law of restitution to decide between an intention to create rights expressly by means of trust or contract, and an intention (or lack of intention) which should create rights by operation of law.[48] The issue then is whether a resulting trust is an appropriate remedy in a situation where a contract agreed between commercial parties has failed. The *radical restitutionary approach* suggested that the answer is whether the law will operate to impose a resulting trust, rather than whether there is anything in the parties' agreement to create such a resulting trust. In this sense:

> "The term resulting trust is capable of bearing two meanings. In the first it identifies a feature which has nothing to do with the trust's origin: the trust is resulting (from the Latin *resalire*, to jump back) if the interest arising under it is carried back to the settlor. This can happen however the trust originates, whether by expressed intention, implied intention, presumed intention, or irrespective of intention (constructive). In trusts created in all these ways the beneficial interest can 'jump back'. So the term 'resulting' in this wide sense cuts across other classifications.'[49] As Birks continues, it may be possible to have a trust which is 'constructive in origin' and 'resulting in pattern'."[50]

---

[41] Chambers, *Resulting Trusts* (Oxford, 1997), p2.

[42] Oakley, *The Law of Constructive Trusts*, (Sweet & Maxwell, 1994), p.27 *et seq.*; Swadling "A New Role for Resulting Trusts?"(1996) 16 Leg. St. 110–131.

[43] Ford and Lee, *The Law of Trusts*, para. 21000.

[44] Waters (1984), p.301; Hanbury and Martin, *Modern Equity* (Sweet & Maxwell, 1993), p.70.

[45] Chambers, *Resulting Trusts* (Oxford, 1997), p.3.

[46] *ibid.* at p.2.

[47] Chambers, *Resulting Trusts* (Oxford, 1997); Scott and Fratcher, para.404.1.

[48] Birks, *An Introduction to the Law of Restitution* (Oxford, 1989), p.65.

[49] *ibid.* at p. 20.

[50] *ibid.* at p.62; Birks "Restitution and Resulting Trusts" in *Equity and Contemporary Legal Developments* (Goldstein ed., Jerusalem, 1992), p.353 at pp.363–4.

The approach of this work is that the resulting trust arises to return to the original equitable owner the rights which were not intended to pass beneficially to the current legal owner of the property.

Resulting trust rather than constructive trust

11–20 The constructive trust is used as a restitutionary remedy in the USA and Canada. In Chambers' account this has "not proved to be a trouble-free solution". The remedial constructive trust on the North American model runs the risk of "riding roughshod over the legitimate interests of creditors and other third parties."[51] As discussed above, the restitutionary response is based on a civilian distinction between trusts as generated by consent, wrongs, unjust enrichment or other events, rather than the traditional classification of trusts as express, implied, resulting or constructive trusts. In line with Elias' reconstruction[52] of constructive trusts, trusts aligned with the principle of unjust enrichment will be satisfied by the implementation of resulting trusts. In Chambers' terms, "resulting trusts are the chief contribution of equity to the law of restitution."[53]

11–21 In the context of commercial contracts then, the argument would run that there was a lack of intention to benefit the recipient (had the parties known of the mistake) thus founding a right in trust. The issue remains whether the mistake would be enough to constitute an unjust factor in that context.

Mistake

11–22 Chambers suggests that the imposition of a trust, in cases of mistaken payments, are based on the resulting trust affecting restitution for unjust enrichment. There are instances in which property has been transferred by mistake and the court has declared the recipient to be a trustee for the transferor.[54] Those cases have tended not to be explicit about the nature of the trust in this situation.[55] In two cases, the trust was expressly identified as resulting: *El Ajou v. Dollar Land Holdings*[56] and *Clelland v. Clelland*.'[57] As Millett J. held in *El Ajou*:

> "It would, of course, be an intolerable reproach to our system of jurisprudence if the plaintiff were the only victim who could trace and recover his money. Neither party before suggested that this is the case; and I agree with them. But if the other victims of the fraud can trace their money in equity it must be because, having been induced to purchase the shares by false and fraudulent misrepresentations, they are entitled to rescind the transaction and revest the equitable title to the purchase money in themselves, at least to the extent necessary to support an equitable tracing claim ... But, if this is correct, as I think it is, then the trust which is operating in these cases is not some new model remedial constructive trust, but an old-fashioned institutional resulting trust."[58]

---

[51] Chambers, *Resulting Trusts* (Oxford, 1997), p.5.

[52] Or, arguably, "deconstruction".

[53] Chambers, *Resulting Trusts* (Oxford, 1997), pp.5 *et seq.*

[54] *Chase Manhattan Bank NA v. Israel-British Bank (London) Ltd.* [1981] Ch. 105; *Leuty v. Hillas* (1858) 2 De G. & J. 110; *Craddock Brothers v. Hunt* [1923] 2 Ch. 136, CA; *Blacklocks v. J.B. Developments (Godalming) Ltd.* [1982] Ch. 183.

[55] On this see Chambers, *Resulting Trusts* (Oxford, 1997), p.23.

[56] [1993] 3 All E.R. 717.

[57] [1945] 3 D.L.R. 664, B.C.C.A.

[58] [1993] 3 All E.R. 717 at 734.

His Lordship's opinion supports Birks' view that the resulting trust operates in a restitutionary way and that a situation such as the return of money to a person defrauded of that money is essentially a restitutionary response. The obstruction to this view is the decision of the House of Lords in *Islington*. The difficulty with Lord Browne-Wilkinson's model of the resulting trust is that he sees it as arising on the basis of the *common* intentions of the parties, rather than applying the intentions solely of the original owner of the property rights. Chambers confronts this problem in the following way[59]:

> "In *Westdeutsche Landesbank Girozentrale v. Islington L.B.C.*, Lord Browne-Wilkinson suggested *obiter* that resulting trusts are 'traditionally regarded as examples of trusts giving effect to the common intention of the parties'.[60] This is surprising since it is clear that a common intention is not a requirement for a resulting trust, which can arise even though one of the parties is unaware of the transfer.[61] Lord Browne-Wilkinson's speech in *Tinsley v. Milligan*[62] indicates that he is mixing the requirements for resulting trusts with those for constructive trusts in the context of family home ownership. That case involved a resulting trust based on the common intention of the parties. Both parties had contributed to the purchase of a house and their intentions were relevant as providers. However, his Lordship did not distinguish between the resulting trust based on their contributions and the constructive trust based on a 'common intention acted upon by the parties to their detriment'."[63]

11–23 As considered below in *suitability approach* in relation to the *Rosset*[64] form of common intention constructive trust, what is not clear is the extent to which the courts will seek to give effect to the common intention of the parties. As Chambers points out, it is similarly uncertain whether such common intention can be said to fall properly within a resulting trust arising from the contribution to the acquisition of an asset or from a constructive trust imposed by reference to the knowledge of the defendant of some factor which is said to affect his conscience. The remodelling of the resulting trust by Lord Browne-Wilkinson does appear to capture the common intention trust by encompassing situations in which the parties must be presumed to have intended that the plaintiff would acquire an interest in the applicable property.

Restitution and resulting trusts

11–24 The basis of the radical restitutionary approach in respect of the resulting trust is stated most clearly by Chambers[65] in examining Birks' definition of restitution as requiring the defendant to give up to the plaintiff an enrichment which the defendant has received (or its value in money) at the plaintiff's

---

59 Chambers, *Resulting Trusts* (Oxford, 1997), p.37.

60 [1996] 2 All E.R. 961 at 990, HL.

61 *Ryall v. Ryall* (1739) 1 Atk. 59; *Birch v. Blagrave* (1755) Amb. 264; *Lane v. Dighton* (1762) Amb. 409; *Childers v. Childers* (1857) 1 De G.&J. 482; *Williams v. Williams* (1863) 32 Beav. 370; *Re Vinogradoff* [1935] W.N. 68; *In re Muller* [1953] N.Z.L.R. 879.

62 [1994] 1 A.C. 340.

63 *ibid.* at 371.

64 *Lloyds Bank v. Rossett* [1991] 1 A.C. 107; [1990] 1 All ER 1111; [1990] 2 WLR 867.

65 Chambers, *Resulting Trusts* (Oxford, 1997), p.94.

expense.[66] The elements of this definition are said to fit the resulting trust most closely. Chambers and Birks both acknowledge that these principles will potentially fit a number of different responses, and that closer examination of the resulting trust is therefore necessary. Therefore, Birks requires that two further considerations must be borne in mind. First, the preservation of obligations or property rights which have been created by consent and, secondly, the preservation of the owner's pre-existing title. It is this pattern of exclusion from the ambit of the resulting trust any other factual circumstance, including the rights of an insolvent's creditors, which caused Lord Browne-Wilkinson to reject the restitutionary conception of the resulting trust in *Islington*.[67]

11–25 Resulting trusts are generally considered as belonging to the category of subtractive unjust enrichment—that is, an enrichment unjustly realised as a result of some property being taken from the claimant. On this analysis, it is resulting trusts, rather than constructive trusts, which should be applied in cases of subtractive unjust enrichment because the bulk of those cases concern non-voluntary transfers of property.[68] In the case of the financial derivative, the transfer will tend to be a voluntary transfer as a result of a contract. Non-voluntary transfers would tend to involve mistaken transfers of amounts under a contract or by way of providing security. Therefore, the role of the Court of Appeal and of Hobhouse J. in *Islington* requires closer analysis in this context. There a resulting trust was imposed in circumstances where a payment was made in the absence of consideration. In fact, the *equity approach* adopted was based on knowledge of matters which affected the trustee's conscience rather than restitution. As such, the equitable role of the constructive trust was preferred to a restitutionary model restitutionary response.

11–26 The question arises then what is meant by "resulting trust" as opposed to "constructive trust" or "express trust". Particularly, given the growing elision of categories in the case law, together with the importance of identifying which category is intended to lead to which remedy. As Chambers considers the distinction the "resulting trust" classification tells us that the trust property was provided to the resulting trustee by the trust beneficiary and is being returned because the beneficiary did not intend the trustee to receive it beneficially. In contrast, the "constructive" label tells us only that the trust in question was not expressly created by any person other than the court.[69]

11–27 The utility of the resulting trust has been questioned by others.[70] Those views are predicated on the basis that the resulting trust has arisen from a presumed but vitiated intention to create an express trust. This is opposed to the views of Chambers and Birks, as set out below, that the resulting trust fulfils some restitutionary function not based on prior intention. Whatever the differences in view, the sceptical thesis has now established itself in the wake of the House of Lords decision in *Islington*.

---

[66] Birks, *Introduction to the Law of Restitution* (Oxford, 1989), p.13; also Beatson, *Use and Abuse of Unjust Enrichment* (Oxford, 1991), p.1.

[67] [1996] A.C. 669.

[68] See, for example, Chambers, *Resulting Trusts* (Oxford, 1997), p.225.

[69] Chambers, *Resulting Trusts* (Oxford, 1997), pp.225 *et seq.*

[70] Notably Lord Browne Wilkinson in *Islington* [1996] 2 All E.R. 961 at 999; Swadling "A New Role for Resulting Trusts?" (1996) 16 Leg. St. 110.

11–28 The *radical restitutionary approach* speaks of enrichment, but not *unjust* enrichment, to avoid the tautology (within the terms of Birks' taxonomy of restitution[71]) that "restitution is always and necessarily a response to unjust enrichment".[72] In a somewhat syllogistic approach, Chambers supports Birks' view that:

> "The proof that resulting trusts are restitutionary makes it unnecessary to ask whether they respond to unjust enrichment. If they reverse unjust enrichments, those enrichments are unjust." [73]

Thus, it is said that a resulting trust will reverse unjust enrichment because anything which a resulting trust reverses is unjust. Clearly that is not always the case. In *Vandervell v. IRC,*[74] for example, the resulting trust was not imposed on the basis of justice but rather on an institutional basis arising out of the original equitable owner's to dispose of the whole of the equitable interest, instead leaving an amount of that interest (represented in that case by an option to repurchase the property) to come back to him on resulting trust. Further, it is not clear that "unjust enrichment" is necessarily the most useful term when considering commercials cases. In the taxonomy of restitution it might be that it would be better to talk about "restitution" and seek the reversal of "unjust factors" or even a category of "restitutionary events" with which to seek the restoration of property. The recognition of the contractual allocation of risks in swaps agreements might therefore call for a restitutionary response where it would be against the parties' agreement to retain the property.[75] However, Lord Browne-Wilkinson's establishment of an institutional resulting trust in *Islington* would appear to satisfy the restitution of property in the instance of credit enhancement provisions in documentation.[76]

11–29 In Chambers' view "[m]oney is the very measure of enrichment ... by contrast benefits in kind are less equivocally enriching ...". The basis for this focus on money is the potential for the property to be devalued. His view is extended to say that the existence of a market in that thing (in which it could be said to have value) is not an issue: the question is the subtraction of value from the plaintiff.[77] The nature of the resulting trust is that it affects some property that rests in the defendant's hands. For instance, where the plaintiff is seeking a remedy in connection with specific property that has passed to the defendant, what Smith would identify as a following claim,[78] it is a simple matter of evidence to establish the title of the plaintiff. No question of valuation arises in that sense because the remedy is for recovery of property, regardless of its inherent value.[79] An argument based on lack of value will not obtain, it is said.

---

[71] Birks and Chambers, *Restitution Research Resource* (Mansfield Press, 1997) pp.1–6.

[72] Birks, "Misnomer" in *Restitution, Present and Future: Essays in Honour of Gareth Jones* (Cornish, Nolan, O'Sullivan and Virgo eds., Hart Publishing, Oxford, 1998), p.1; as contrasted, for example, with Birks, *Introduction to the Law of Restitution* (Oxford, 1989), p.19.

[73] Birks, *Introduction to the Law of Restitution* (Oxford, 1989), pp.19 *et seq.*

[74] [1967] 2 A.C. 291, HL.

[75] As considered below in *suitability approach,* the issue is whether it is an unjust factor to refuse to effect the contractual common intention of the parties.

[76] As considered above, this is not to revisit, at this stage, the issue as to whether or not the standard market documentation did enough in the swaps cases to allocate title to the property concerned.

[77] Birks, *Introduction to the Law of Restitution* (Oxford, 1989), p.19.

[78] Smith, *The Law of Tracing* (Oxford, 1997) Part II, pp.67–104.

[79] Burrows, *The Law of Restitution* (Butterworths, 1993), p.7.

11–30 In the case of financial contracts, it is the financial value of those assets in the market place that is the heart of the contracting parties' expectations. However, that is not to say that those assets will never have a value distinct from their market value. With reference to hedging contracts, one aspect of the value of the transaction is clearly that it contains a market price but more importantly that it operates in an inverse manner to the risk being hedged. Thus, the true value of the hedge is the extent of its reduction in the risk rather than its resale value. There will be no resale value because an over-the-counter derivative is executed on a one-off basis between the contracting parties. Therefore, there is a potential for a second level of value that is specific to the buyer of the derivative. To segregate the hedge from the original contract in considering defences to restitutionary claims is therefore in conflict with this restitutionary aim.[80]

An exception to Birks' definition

11–31 It is submitted that a contractual obligation can never be restitutionary. There is not a question of unjust enrichment where parties create a contract in the financial markets and at arm's length and that contract is simply enforced. The means of analysing the enforceability of that contract is by the contract's own propriety and not by means of unjust enrichment at the expense of the other party.[81] The restitutionary model resulting trust then will not intervene to reinforce intention. Rather it operates by operation of law where intention does not deal with all the available equitable interest.

11–32 As set out below in the *suitability approach*, the most appropriate means of enforcing financial contracts might be by means of a common intention constructive trust which underpins the risk management sections of the void contract. This is the line at which restitution could operate. One context in which the Canadians use unjust enrichment is to enforce the rights of parties in the family home. The English law version of this doctrine is the common intention constructive trust: not enforcing a contract but rather giving effect to the parties' mutual understanding while compensating detrimental reliance on that understanding.[82] Therefore, the role of restitution in financial contracts will not be to enforce the contract but rather to prevent an unjust enrichment from its unenforceability. It is therefore equity that would be required to reinforce the contract by means of ensuring observance of the common intention of the parties, as considered in the *suitability approach* below.

Proprietary claims over value

11–33 There is a division in restitution between two different measures in which the plaintiff may recover. The first measure is "value received"; and the second measure is "value surviving".[83] As Chambers delineates the subject:[84]

> "First measure claims to the value received are necessarily personal, whereas second-measure claims to the value surviving are usually, but not

[80] See the discussion of *Kleinwort Benson v. Birmingham C.C.* [1996] 3 All E.R. 75, above.

[81] Chambers, *Resulting Trusts* (Oxford, 1997), p.99; see also Birks, *Introduction to the Law of Restitution* (Oxford, 1989), p.46; and Beatson, *The Use and Abuse of Unjust Enrichment* (Oxford, 1991), p.38.

[82] Always careful not to elide completely the concepts of equitable compensation and restitution of unjust enrichment: Birks, "Misnomer" in *Restitution, Present and Future: Essays in Honour of Gareth Jones* (Cornish, Nolan, O'Sullivan and Virgo, eds., Hart Publishing, Oxford, 1998), pp.1, 25.

[83] Birks, *Introduction to the Law of Restitution* (Oxford, 1989), p.6.

[84] Chambers, *Resulting Trusts* (Oxford, 1997), p.105.

> necessarily, proprietary[85] ... The resulting trust itself always effects restitution in the second measure (of the value surviving), because it can arise 'only in respect of something identified as existing in the defendant's hands'.[86] Like all trusts, it cannot exist unless it is 'possible to identify clearly the property which is subject to the trust.'"[87]

Thus the proprietary claim based on the restitutionary resulting trust is necessarily bound by the established rules of equity as to the identity of property. The issue of founding equitable proprietary claims therefore remains central, in the light of a need for a proprietary base. This discussion returns to the *equity approach* to the availability of proprietary remedies as delineated by Lord Browne-Wilkinson.

Conclusions

11–34 Chambers' assumption is that the resulting trust is motivated by the removal of some unjust enrichment from the recipient of property.[88] While it is possible that the prevention of unjust enrichment could be identified as an unspoken common principle which motivates the manner in which resulting trusts have been imposed in past cases, there is little evidence that unjust enrichment was *the* ratio for any of those decisions. The restitutionary role of the resulting trust is potentially a large one. As discussed above, the resulting trust has many features which make it an appropriate vehicle for achieving restitutionary goals. However, the import of Lord Browne-Wilkinson's decision in *Islington*, as considered above, must be that the operation of the resulting trust is to be considered as greatly limited. Rather, the remedial constructive trust would appear to have acquired the foremost position as the most likely tool of providing restitution in future cases.

11–35 The resulting trust occupies an awkward position in current jurisprudence. While it offers an attractively straightforward ability to restore beneficial interests in property to their original owners, the courts have tended to prefer other solutions that provide greater liberty of both form and remedy. Thus the constructive trust has grown to occupy a position of pre-eminence in many spheres. The area of trusts of homes has seen a bicameral development of constructive trust and proprietary estoppel as the most commonly available remedies for those seeking a declaration of their entitlement to property. The resulting trust occupies some residual role, but is mentioned less and less.[89]

11–36 There are structural similarities between the resulting trust and other forms of claim. As Chambers points out "[t]here is an interesting similarity (but no apparent historical connexion) between the resulting trust and the action for money had and received".[90] The action for money had and received, as considered elsewhere in relation to Hobhouse J.'s decision, developed from an explicit promise to pay arising out of indebtedness to include actions arising *quasi ex contractu*. The resulting trust "began as an implication that a feoffment made with neither consideration (in a broad sense) nor declaration of use was intended

---

[85] See Birks, *Introduction to the Law of Restitution* (Oxford, 1989), p.85.

[86] *ibid.*

[87] Waters (1984), 117; *Cowcher v. Cowcher* [1972] 1 W.L.R. 425 at 430.

[88] Chambers, *Resulting Trusts* (Oxford, 1997), p.222.

[89] The speech of Lord Bridge in *Lloyds Bank v. Rossett* [1991] 1 A.C. 107; [1990] 1 All ER 1111, [1990] 2 WLR 867 is an example of the resulting trust being subsumed into the "common intention constructive trust" concept in terms of contributions to the purchase price of property, as with Lord Browne-Wilkinson in *Islington* restricting the resulting trust to only two categories.

[90] Chambers, *Resulting Trusts* (Oxford, 1997), 222, *et seq.*; Baker (1990), pp. 409, 425.

to be to the feoffor's use. However, it developed to become a direct response to the lack of consideration and declared use ... it did not depend on the implied intention to create a trust and could respond in cases where the implication of that intention would be impossible."[91] However, in *Islington* the "implied trusts" theory of the nature of the resulting trust was resurrected.[92]

11–37 To say that constructive trusts are different from other forms of trust is to ignore the fact that constructive trusts are frequently based on some understanding, albeit mute, between the parties.[93] Although, as Chambers indicates, the intention of a resulting trustee is generally as irrelevant of that of a constructive trustee.[94] In many circumstances, a constructive trust created in a case of mutual wills or secret trust, is based on the intention of the parties also.[95] In family home cases,[96] the constructive trust is used more usually to fulfil some expectation rather than to prevent unjust enrichment.[97] Thus, in the USA, the constructive trust is used primarily to provide interests in homes. The resulting trust has been removed from the jurisprudence as a consequence. There is a dividing line between the U.S. remedial constructive trust in this circumstance and the English common intention constructive trust.[98] The role of the resulting trust is thus withdrawn in both jurisdictions and the concept progressively elided with the common intention that founds a constructive trust in that context. The question also arises whether or not these trusts are really a kind of informal express trust.

11–38 In considering borderlines between different concepts, many theorists have propounded the view that constructive trusts have closer links to contracts than do resulting trusts.[99] This is based on the constructive trust's response to an intention to dispose of property in favour of another and an inducement in that other to behave in a certain manner. This coming together of inducement, reliance and detriment is also true of proprietary estoppel. In some sense the element of consideration is provided by this detriment in the constructive beneficiary. The unjust factors of inducement and detriment is restitution's equivalent to consideration in the law of contract. The question then is whether there ought to be any distinction made on the basis that risk is present where there is intention to take risk and benefit a party on that basis—who takes the risk of the ownership of property once it has been passed between parties to a contract which is subsequently found to be void? These issues are considered below in the *suitability approach.*

Constructive trusts

11–39 In considering the lay-out of constructive trusts, Elias' *Explaining Constructive Trusts* attempts the seemingly impossible task of identifying the full

---

91 Chambers. *Resulting Trusts* (Oxford, 1997), p.223.

92 [1996] 2 All E.R. 961 at 990–1, 993.

93 See, for example, the constructive trust considered by Lord Bridge in *Lloyds Bank v. Rossett* [1991] 1 A.C. 107.

94 Chambers, *Resulting Trusts* (Oxford, 1997), p.224.

95 Elias, *Explaining Constructive Trusts* (Oxford, 1990), pp.56–66; Chambers, *Resulting Trusts* (Oxford, 1997), p.224.

96 As considered below in *suitability approach, common intention constructive trusts* in Chapter 12.

97 Chambers, *Resulting Trusts* (Oxford, 1997),p. 226.

98 Lord Browne-Wilkinson in *Islington.*

99 Elias, *Explaining Constructive Trusts* (Oxford, 1990), pp.56–66; Gardner *An Introduction to the Law of Trusts* (Oxford 1990), pp.225–8, 231–2; Chambers, *Resulting Trusts* (Oxford, 1997), p.224.

range of principles on which the many manifestations of the constructive trust can be said to be imposed and the principles on which it ought to be said to exist. The aim of Elias' book is said to be "rationalisation",[100] whereas no general definition of the constructive trust is possible.[101] Elias sets out five representative rules on constructive trusts.[102] Among the rules that Elias identified is the "fourth rule" which is said to compel one who receives money under mistake of fact to hold the money on trust for the payer.[103] In the light of the decision in *Islington*, this rule cannot be asserted as a rule where there is no knowledge in the recipient that the payment has been made on the basis of a mistake.[104] However, despite the development in the law since the thesis was developed, the conceptualisation is of some interest.

11–40 Elias sets out three theses for the underpinnings of constructive trusts.[105] The first two are descriptive of the positions of others. The third is his own preferred approach. First, is the "sceptical thesis" which maintains that there is no single, rational underpinning for the doctrine of constructive trust; rather, the constructive trust is said to be an amalgamation of a number of policy prescriptions which it is impossible to reconcile. The sceptical thesis is identified in Oakley's position that to attempt a rationalisation of essentially dissimilar cases founded on a principle of restitution is not possible.[106] The sceptical thesis,[107] in that it centres on notions of conscience and the application of the true wishes of the parties, appears to be perpetuated in the speech of Lord Browne-Wilkinson in *Islington*.[108]

11–41 Secondly, the "radical thesis" which asserts that the restitution aim is the core of the constructive trust. The radical thesis is identified as being summed up by to Waters[109] as "... an instrument of restitution—ensuring that gains made through losses to other persons should be given up to those others."[110] This is most in-line with the *radical restitutionary approach*. The North American conception sees the constructive trust as a remedy, whereas express trust and resulting trust are substantive institutions. The radical thesis[111] reflects USA and Canadian experience where it is applied as a remedy to effect restitution,[112] in contradistinction to the English constructive trust which is concerned with the institutional imposition of equitable proprietary rights.[113] Bound up in this question of institutional or remedial trust, on which there is a vast periodical

---

[100] Elias, *Explaining Constructive Trusts* (Oxford, 1990), p.2.

[101] *Explaining Constructive Trusts* (Oxford), p.3.

[102] *ibid.* at p.1.

[103] *Selangor v. Cradock* [1968] 1 W.L.R. 1555.

[104] There is also the third rule which identifies the old rule imposing a constructive trust relating to dishonest assistants to a breach of trust as compelling a stranger who negligently assists in a breach of trust. As discussed above, the decision of the Privy Council in *Tan* now establishes the law in that area.

[105] *Explaining Constructive Trusts* (Oxford, 1990).

[106] See the discussion of the sceptical position below. On Oakley see *Constructive Trusts* (2nd ed. Sweet & Maxwell, 1995); Oakley (1973) 26 C.L.P. 17.

[107] *Explaining Constructive Trusts* (Oxford, 1990), pp.150 *et seq.*

[108] This stream of decisions affecting constructive trust is identifiable from *Cooke v. Head* [1972] 1 W.L.R. 518, 520; *Hussey v. Palmer* [1972] 1 W.L.R. 1286 at 1289–90, "justice and good conscience"; *Tanner v. Tanner* [1975] 1 W.L.R. 1346 at 1351.

[109] *Explaining Constructive Trusts* (Oxford, 1990), p.4.

[110] Waters, *The Constructive Trust* (1964) esp. pp.1–5, Chap. 1, pp.332–338.

[111] *Explaining Constructive Trusts* (Oxford, 1990), pp.155 *et seq.*

[112] *Pettkus v. Becker* (1980) 117 D.L.R. (3rd) 257; [1980] 2 S.C.R. 834; *Sorochan v. Sorochan* [1986] 2 S.C.R. 38.

[113] See the discussion of *Islington* above.

literature,[114] is the issue of retrospectivity:[115] the moment when the right comes into existence will be important—whether it is retrospective or prospective, remedial or institutional will be essential—where the defendant goes bankrupt, for example.

11–42 Thirdly, is the "third thesis" which itself identifies the three "good aims" for constructive trusts: perfection, restitution, and reparation. The three good aims[116] are explained as being, respectively: one who has chosen to dispose of his options in favour of another person who should abide by the choice; one who has made a pecuniary gain through another person's loss gives up the gain to the other person; and one who has caused loss to another repairs the loss. The constructive trust discussed by Elias is one that explicitly speaks in the language of gifts and which is of less use in commercial context.[117]

11–43 The "perfection aim" is identified most clearly in *Re Rose*,[118] on the basis that intentions to do something should be given effect to.[119] The perfection aim concentrates on using the constructive trust as a means of perfecting the choices and contracts that individuals had sought to make but which have been found to be ineffective.[120] It is said that to protect people from their choices and the effects of their choices in particular, infantilises them.[121] There is economic efficiency in binding parties to their choices, in affirming voidable transactions, rather than frustrating the underlying commercial purposes.[122] What the perfection aim misses is the very nature of English contracts—the culture of barter that requires consideration for the creation of a contract rather than simply enforcing promises. The role of the constructive trust is to provide a response in situations where contract is not available or where an equitable proprietary remedy is necessary.[123] What is not established by this understanding is whether that response is restitutionary or an equitable remedy based on knowledge and conscience.[124]

11–44 In Elias' view, the restitution aim is inherently less "harsh" than the perfection aim and the reparation aim because the restitution aim does no more than "remove superfluities in the defendant's hands".[125] This is in-line with Birks' conception of restitution as being centred on gains to be given up and not with losses to be made good.[126] As Elias identifies the problem, the law fails the restitution aim where a "barred [invalid] contract" is denied enforcement.[127] The concept of unjust enrichment has come to replace the older doctrine of quasi

---

[114] Pound, 33 Harv. L. Rev. 420 ; Goode, (1983) 3 LS 283, 292; Hayton, [1988] Conv. 259; Rickett, (1991) 107 LQR 608; Elias, *Explaining Constructive Trusts*, (Oxford, 1990), pp.159–163.

[115] *Explaining Constructive Trusts* (Oxford, 1990), p.161.

[116] *ibid.* at p.4.

[117] *ibid.* at p.14.

[118] *Re Rose* [1952] Ch. 499; [1952] 1 All E.R. 1217.

[119] The issue arises how this analysis would work with reference to collateral contracted for but not actually delivered. For example, in the case of bankruptcy, would a trust be imposed over such collateral. In any event, would that be a constructive trust or a species of express trust?

[120] *Explaining Constructive Trusts* (Oxford, 1990), p.9 n.2; Fried, *Contract as Promise* (Oxford, 1981).

[121] Atiyah, *Essays on Contract* (Oxford, 1988).

[122] As considered below under the *suitability approach*, the argument in favour of this approach would be the maintenance of public policy in avoiding unlawful or impolitic transactions.

[123] *Explaining Constructive Trusts* (Oxford, 1990), p.16.

[124] Martin identifies *Tan* [1995] 2 A.C. 378 as demonstrating that recipient-based liability is restitutionary; *Modern Equity*, 301. See also *Macmillan v. Bishopsgate* (No3) [1996] 1W.L.R. 387 at 407, *per* Auld L.J.; Harpum, 11 L.Q.R. 545.

[125] *Explaining Constructive Trusts* (Oxford, 1990), p.75.

[126] Birks, *Introduction to the Law of Restitution* (Oxford, 1989), p.11.

[127] *Explaining Constructive Trusts* (Oxford, 1990), p.22.

contract, as discussed above. Remedies based on specific recovery of property, including increases in value associated with that property have not become a remedy for unjust enrichment in English law.[128] The importance of the concept of "knowledge" has been important with reference to the old doctrine of notice, the imposition of personal claims for breach of trust and now for equitable proprietary remedies.[129] The approaches in the Commonwealth jurisdictions differ from English law. In particular, in Canada where unjust enrichment has established itself as the underpinning for the imposition of constructive trusts in relation to domestic property.[130]

11–45 The reparation aim has been slightly superseded by the development of the *Lipkin Gorman* defences of change of position and of the defence of passing-on. Therefore, it is not proposed to revisit those issues at this stage. There is some mention of risk in the context of the reparation aim;[131] however, there is little discussion of the issue as to how the reparation aim is to deal with the question whether or not a particular risk is too great. In short, the reparation aim does not allocate risk in that way. Therefore, Hoffmann J.'s standard of current portfolio theory in assessing the liability of trustees to make investment will not assimilate to the reparation aim. Similarly, the extension of dishonesty to cover reckless risk-taking in *Tan*[132] is not dealt with by the discussion of the reparation aim.

11–46 Elias is not decided on whether or not a constructive trust is coterminous with the doctrine of estoppel.[133] Constructive trusts give effect to a pre-existing proprietary right but do not provide remedies in themselves.[134] In Elias' view, "inducement trusts" (or "common intention constructive trusts") are not equivalent to the perfection aim.[135] The common intention constructive trust is activated in English law specifically by reference to family home trusts imposed to protect the rights of those who informally acquired equitable rights in property.

11–47 The constructive trust therefore occupies a complex place in the jurisprudence—being in fact a rag-bag of equitable responses to differing problems which do not conform to any recognisable pattern. All that can be done with the constructive trust is to spot those situations in which they clearly do arise.[136] As a result of the speech of Lord Browne-Wilkinson in *Islington*[137] the availability of proprietary constructive trusts will be based on the following principles. In broad terms a proprietary constructive trust will be imposed on persons who know that their actions in respect of specific property are unconscionable. It is important that the trustee has knowledge of the unconscionability of the treatment of that property. This issue is separate from the issue of *in rem* and *in personam* rights. Whether the rights are

---

[128] *Halifax v. Thomas* [1996] Ch. 217.

[129] *Islington* [1996] A.C. 669.

[130] Birks, (1996) *Trusts Law International* 2; Watts, (1996) 112 L.Q.R. 219; Jaffey, [1996] R.L.R. 92; *Muchinski v. Dodds* (1985) 160 C.L.R. 583; *Powell v. Thompson* [1991] 1 N.Z.L.R. 579 at 615; *Equitcorp v. Hawkins* [1991] 3 N.Z.L.R. 700; *Pettkus v. Becker* (1980) 117 D.L.R. (3rd) 257; [1980] 2 S.C.R. 834; *Sorochan v. Sorochan* [1986] 2 S.C.R. 38; *Lac Minerals v. International Corona* (1989) 61 D.L.R. (4th) 14; Hammond, (1990) 106 L.Q.R. 207; *Rawluk v. Rawluk* (1990) 65 D.L.R. (4th) 161; Rickett, [1991] Conv. 125; Friedman, (1991) 11 L.S. 304; *Peter v. Beblow* (1993) 101 D.L.R. (4th) 621.

[131] Elias, *Explaining Constructive Trusts* (Oxford, 1990), pp.38–39.

[132] *Royal Brunei Airlines v. Tan* [1995] 2 A.C. 378.

[133] *Explaining Constructive Trusts* (Oxford, 1990), p.57, n.2.

[134] *Lonrho v. Al Fayed (No.2)* [1992] 1 W.L.R. 1 at 9.

[135] *Explaining Constructive Trusts* (Oxford, 1990), p.65.

[136] On this sceptical approach see Oakley, *Constructive Trusts* (Sweet & Maxwell, 1997), generally.

[137] [1996] A.C. 669.

proprietary or not, being made a trustee under a constructive trust will be dependent on knowledge and unconscionability.

Subrogation

11–48 One further remedy not considered in detail by the English courts, aside from a passing reference in the High Court, is the availability of subrogation. The question arises whether or not it would be possible for the payer to argue for the recovery of the money paid under a void contract on the basis that the payer is subrogated to the rights of some obligation discharged with the original money.

11–49 Subrogation is literally substitution.[138] "The term is used in the context of English and Commonwealth law to describe a process by which one party is substituted for another so that he may enforce that other's rights against a third party for his own benefit."[139] This right can be conferred by contract or may be enforced by law. One useful starting point is Lord Diplock's statement in *Orakpo v. Manson Investments Ltd*[140] that subrogation is not a remedy of general application but rather that it is available only in specific set of situations:

> "There is no general doctrine of unjust enrichment in English law. What it does is to provide specific remedies in particular cases of what might be classified as unjust enrichment in a legal system that is based upon civil law. There are some circumstances in which the remedy takes the form of 'subrogation', but this expression embraces more than one concept in English law. It is a convenient way of describing the transfer of rights from one person to another, without assignment or assent of the person from whom the rights are transferred and which take place in a whole variety of widely different circumstances ...."

11–50 One writer who has situated subrogation as being part of this developing law relating to restitution is Mitchell.[141] He acknowledges the nascent doctrine of unjust enrichment and the difficulties which are inherent in seeking to apply restitutionary thinking on the radical approach to the established doctrines of subrogation which were clearly not expressly based on that principle. What Mitchell does is to explain the roots of subrogation, the manner in which the subject should be delineated, and a common understanding of the need to reverse unjust factors which are said to be inherent in both doctrines. In the final analysis, Mitchell expresses his own view to be that "... subrogation is best understood as a restitutionary remedy: the cases in which subrogation has been awarded to date can all be explained in restitutionary terms, and the award of subrogation in the future should be guided by reference to the principle of unjust enrichment"[142].

11–51 There are two forms of subrogation in Mitchell's analysis: simple subrogation and reviving subrogation. Simple subrogation operates to transfer "subsisting rights of action from one party to another"[143]. The most straightforward example of this form of action is in an indemnity insurance contract where the insurer is subrogated to the rights of the insured against the

---

138 Mitchell, *The Law of Subrogation* (Oxford, 1994), pp.3.

139 *ibid.*p.3 *supra.*

140 [1978] A.C. 95 at 104, *per* Lord Edmund Davies at 112, *per* Lord Keith of Kinkel at 119.

141 Mitchell, *The Law of Subrogation* (Oxford, 1994).

142 *ibid.* at p.4.

143 *ibid.* at p.5.

tortfeasor who has caused the insured loss.[144] The more complex form of subrogation, reviving subrogation, "works to revive extinguished rights of action and then to transfer them from one party to another"[145]. Reviving subrogation is therefore the more complicated of the forms of subrogation, in that it takes rights which have expired and brings them back to life in favour of a party other than the original right holder. Mitchell categorises the parties as the original right holder (RH), the person who is "primarily liable" to the RH (PL), and the person who is to be subrogated to RH's rights (S). The example Mitchell uses is that of a surety arrangement. When a surety (S) pays a creditor (RH), that creditor's right of action is extinguished as against the debtor (PL). However, section 5 of the Mercantile Law Amendment Act 1856 entitles S to recover the payment to RH from PL, despite the extinction of the rights originally held by RH.[146]

11–52 Mitchell considers subrogation to be a restitutionary concept[147] and therefore that the plaintiff must seek to establish three things[148]:

> "(1) that some other party or parties have been enriched by the receipt of a benefit;
> (2) that the benefit has been gained at the claimant's expense; and
> (3) that the circumstances of their enrichment are such that it would be unjust for them to retain the benefit (another way of putting this is to say that the claimant must show that an 'unjust factor' underlay the circumstances of his payment).[149]"

11–53 Burrows[150] has observed that simple subrogation must be outwith the law of restitution of unjust enrichment because it is a preventative remedy rather than a response imposed after the event to restore property or value to the plaintiff. The concentration of restitution must therefore be on reviving subrogation as a restitutionary response to unjust enrichment arising from the use of property.[151]

11–54 Mitchell objects to reviving subrogation being used to substitute for a more direct remedy, where he finds that "the proper function of reviving subrogation is not to provide S with a disguised action for money paid to PL's use."[152] At the root of reviving subrogation is the isolation of the circumstances in which S should be entitled to acquire RH's extinguished secured rights via reviving subrogation.[153] There is therefore a parallel with identifying the situations in which the law of restitution should be motivated to reverse an unjust enrichment. The difficulty with subrogation in relation to unjust enrichment is that unjust enrichment usually deals with bipartite rather than tripartite relationships.[154]

---

[144] Mitchell, *The Law of Subrogation* (Oxford, 1994), p.6.

[145] *ibid.* at p.5.

[146] The other principle difference in the types of subrogation is that in simple subrogation S cannot pursue those rights in his own name, whereas in the context of reviving subrogation S in entitled to bring the action in his own name.

[147] Mitchell, *The Law of Subrogation* (Oxford, 1994), p.9.

[148] Jones (ed.), *Goff and Jones on the Law of Restitution* (4th ed., London, 1993), p.16.

[149] Burrows, *The Law of Restitution* (Butterworths, 1993), p.7, n.7.

[150] *ibid.* at pp.81, 92.

[151] Mitchell, *The Law of Subrogation* (Oxford, 1994), p.10.

[152] *ibid.* at p.11.

[153] *ibid.* at pp.11 *et seq.*

[154] See Gummow, "Unjust Enrichment, Restitution and Proprietary Remedies" in *Essays in Restitution* (Finn ed., Sydney, 1990), Chap. 3, pp.69–70.

Does discharge of another's debt extinguish that debt?

11–55 The issue arises, where you discharge another's debt, that is presumed to be to the advantage of the debtor—even where the debtor would rather not have that debt paid off.[155] The issue in the derivatives context would arise in relation to a payment made by the floating rate payer in an interest rate swap contract and whether the right held by the floating rate payer (S) could be said to be potentially a subrogation right derived from the fixed rate payer's (PL) original debt to the lending bank (RH).[156] Given the repayament analysis adopted by Hobhouse J. in *Islington*,[157] it is important to understand whether or not subrogation could be said to operate so that one payment under a swap transaction is in discharge of another's debt.

11–56 Burrows takes the view that where a third party makes a payment to the creditor (RH), that debt should be automatically discharged[158] and contends that the motivation behind the courts' refusal of an automatic discharge rule is a desire to protect the debtor from a transfer of his rights to a third party. As Mitchell points out, this motivation is now redundant given the freedom to assign debts generally.[159] As Burrows argues, the better solution to the concern about a "hostile intervener" assuming the rights under the debt, would be that there is no unjust factor in allowing the debtor to rely on the discharge of the debt.[160]

11–57 It is also argued that the denial of an automatic discharge rule is inconsistent with the principle that mistaken performance of another's duty (such as to repair a damaged bridge[161]) discharges that duty. However, once a one-off act has been performed, that is different from the situation where it is a financial obligation which has to be performed. That financial obligation, or chose in action, does not cease to exist in the way that the bridge is no longer in disrepair—the question is whether something intangible remains enforceable or not.

When can a claimant acquire secured rights via subrogation?

11–58 The question when a claimant should be entitled to acquire secured rights via subrogation is related to the restitutionary issue as to the circumstances in which a plaintiff ought to be able to assert any kind of proprietary claim.[162] In Birks' view: "... a claimant should be permitted to assert a proprietary claim only where he can show that he began by owning, and that he thereafter retained some legal or equitable proprietary interest in, the property which he seeks to recover...".[163] The view taken by Goff and Jones is that the key factor in an award to grant restitution is the decision whether the plaintiff should be given priority over the defendant's other creditors:

---

155 See, for example, Kay J. in *Patten v. Bond* (1889) 60 L.T. 583, affirming *Forbes v. Moffatt* (1811) 8 Ves. Jun. 384 and *Burrell v. Lord Egremont* (1844) 7 Beav. 205, that where a mortgage debt is paid off, the court will look to the intention of the parties as to whether or not such payment should discharge the mortgage; see also Mitchell, *op. cit.* at 13.

156 As Mitchell sets the issue out: "The court will assume that a mortgage is not discharged, even though the whole of the debt was paid off to the mortgagee, but considers it to be kept on foot in equity for the benefit of the person who paid ...": *Law of Subrogation*, p.14.

157 [1994] 4 All E.R. 890, *per* Hobhouse J.

158 Burrows, *The Law of Restitution* (Butterworths, 1993), pp.222–227.

159 Mitchell, *The Law of Subrogation* (Oxford, 1994), p.25.

160 Burrows, *The Law of Restitution* (London, Butterworths, 1993).

161 *Macclesfield Corporation v. Great Central Railway* [1911] 2 K.B. 528.

162 Mitchell, *The Law of Subrogation* (Oxford, 1994), p.27.

163 Birks, *Introduction to the Law of Restitution* (Oxford, 1989), p.93.

> "...the courts can in appropriate circumstances retrospectively deem a claimant to have an equitable proprietary interest sufficient to allow him to assert a proprietary claim ... whether the plaintiff has voluntarily assumed the risk of the defendant's insolvency ...."[164]

These disparate approaches have been summarised as follows:

> "In some [instances of awards of proprietary remedies] the dominant factor appears to have been that an equitable interest in moneys was regarded as not having been relinquished and in others it appears to have been unconscionability in retaining moneys against claimants."[165]

In Mitchell's view:

> "... Birks' approach provides the most cogent explanation of many of the cases in which the claimants have been allowed to acquire secured rights via subrogation. However, it must be concluded that his analysis cannot explain all the cases of this kind."[166]

11–59 The *radical restitutionary approach* considers that a plaintiff should only be entitled to a proprietary remedy where he can demonstrate that he has a "proprietary base" to the claim. Birks has also pointed out that the effect of reviving subrogation is the same as allowing S to trace property into a "negative asset" [the obligations formerly owned by RH] in PL's hands.[167] "[reviving subrogation] is only semantically different from the imposition of direct restitutionary obligations."[168] In that instance, it is said that there is a different kind of asset involved, but not a different mode of effecting restitution.[169] Birks' analysis does not apply cleanly in the context of the failure of consideration cases where claimants have been allowed to acquire extinguished secured rights via reviving subrogation, despite the fact that the proprietary rights in the property must "unequivocally have passed away from them at the time when they made their payments, with the result that they cannot be said to have had a proprietary base to their claim."[170] This situation, it would appear, cannot be explained by simple reference to Birks' model.

11–60 For example, Beatson disagrees with Birks where he finds that "... subrogation ... puts the intervener in the creditor's shoes for the purpose of taking over claims previously maintainable by the creditor. This means that, like the assignee, the intervener will be in no better position than the creditor ... It is for this reason that it is not possible to regard restitutionary subrogation as only semantically different from the imposition of direct restitutionary obligations."[171] Thus, the effect of subrogation would be said to be no better than an unsecured creditor in many situations.

---

164 Goff and Jones, *The Law of Restitution* (Sweet & Maxwell, 1993), p.93.

165 *Liggett v. Kensington* [1993] 1 N.Z.L.R. 257 at 281, *per* Gault J.

166 Mitchell, *The Law of Subrogation* (Oxford, 1994), p.28.

167 Birks, *Introduction to the Law of Restitution*, (Oxford, 1989), pp.94–7; see also Mitchell, *The Law of Subrogation* (Oxford, 1994), p.29.

168 Birks, *Introduction to the Law of Restitution*, (Oxford, 1989), p.191.

169 *ibid.* at p.96.

170 Mitchell, *The Law of Subrogation* (Oxford, 1994), p.31.

171 Beatson, *The Use and Abuse of Unjust Enrichment* (Oxford, 1991), p.204.

Reviving extinguished rights

11–61 In the radical restitutionary view, the Court of Appeal's decision in *Re Diplock*[172] was founded on the assumption that:

> "no mechanism exists in English law to revive extinguished rights of action for the benefit of claimants whose money has been paid to the former right-holders ... the next of kin in *Re Diplock*[173] should have been allowed to acquire the securities formerly held by the charities' former creditors by means of reviving subrogation."[174]

Support for this approach comes from *Re Byfield*[175] and also from Birks[176] and Martin[177] especially in connection with the decision in *Boscawen v. Bajwa.*[178] In this context it would be argued that *Boscawen v. Bajwa* and *Roscoe v. Winder*[179] lead to the conclusion that, while there is no right to trace into an overdrawn account, there could be a claim based on reviving subrogation in respect of the contract with the bank. However, a different approach is taken by Hayton[180] in relation to *Re Diplock* where it is argued that no reviving subrogation ought to have been available because it would be inequitable to have ordered a sale of the charities' property in *Re Diplock*. For example, in *McCullough v. Marsden,*[181] where beneficiaries subrogated to the rights of a mortgagee where trustee misappropriated trust property to pay off a mortgage.

11–62 In the latest edition of Goff and Jones, they have altered their view as to the courts' discretion to award proprietary remedies. It is now their view that such remedies should be awarded where this seems just and equitable.[182] Their fundamental concerns with regard to the award of restitutionary remedies are the basis of the plaintiff's claim, the defendant's knowledge of the supporting facts, and the question whether or not the defendant is solvent. Their view of subrogation is that it is an equitable remedy created and imposed by the courts in the same manner as constructive trusts and equitable liens.[183]

11–63 In seeking to establish the role of subrogation claims as a restitutionary response, Mitchell believes that "[a] person who confers a benefit, normally a money payment, under mistake, compulsion, necessity, or in consequence of another's wrongful act or unconscionable conduct will be *deemed* to have retained the equitable title in the money paid."[184] This is clearly not the case after *Islington* in the House of Lords—is it even Lord Goff's dissenting argument on that appeal. Goff and Jones are content that subrogation advances the S's rights over the creditors of the PL "... where it can be shown that the defendant's creditors have, and the claimant has not, voluntarily undertaken the risk of the defendant's

---

172 [1948] Ch. 465.

173 *ibid.*

174 Mitchell, *The Law of Subrogation* (Oxford, 1994), p.31.

175 [1982] 1 Ch. 267 at 272, *per* Goulding J.

176 Birks, *Introduction to the Law of Restitution*, (Oxford, 1989), pp.372–5.

177 Martin, *Hanbury and Martin: Modern Equity* (15th ed., London), p.675.

178 [1996] 1 W.L.R. 328.

179 [1915] 1 Ch. 62.

180 "Constructive Trusts: Is the Remedying of Unjust Enrichment a Satisfactory Approach?" in *Equity, Fiduciaries and Trusts*, (Youdan ed., Toronto, 1989), Chap. 9.

181 (1919) 45 D.L.R. 645.

182 Goff and Jones, *The Law of Restitution* (Sweet & Maxwell, 1993), p.29.

183 *ibid.* at p.91; and Mitchell, *The Law of Subrogation* (Oxford, 1994), p.32.

184 Goff and Jones, *The Law of Restitution* (Sweet & Maxwell, 1993), p.94.

solvency."[185] Mitchell's criticism of the risk approach (drawing on Burrows[186]) is that it cannot be said that the defendant's other creditors will have consciously taken the risk of his insolvency.[187] Rather there is a need to weigh up the respective claims of a defendant's creditors.[188] In the swaps cases, no such concern about the other creditor's of the local authorities arises because the transactions were held off balance sheet in any event.

11–64 Burrows is of the view that where a claimant has advanced money on the basis that his advance should be secured, and the borrower fails to execute the security as agreed, the lender should be entitled to acquire secured rights via subrogation where this serves to give effect to the parties' thwarted common intention that the loan should be secured.[189] In the example of swaps agreements which provide for termination provisions in the case of a misrepresentation as to status and the availability of credit support. One argument might be a claimant in this position has never voluntarily agreed to expose himself to the risk by virtue of having contracted out of it. Alternatively, it could be said that one party to the derivative has induced the counterparty to enter into the transaction on the basis that his participation will be secured. As a result it is submitted, the courts should give effect to this promise in whatever way they can, in the event that the promised security fails to materialise because the agreement between the parties has turned out to be invalid.[190] Therefore, following Burrows' core view, a claimant should have his security or credit enhancement supported by the court where that gives effect to the mutual contractual intention of the parties.[191]

Subrogation in the derivatives context

11–65 The importance of subrogation in the derivatives context could be threefold:

(1) there is a perfecting of security by subrogation where there was no effective security in fact;
(2) it is one analysis of the rights owned by the floating rate payer in an interest rate swap contract; and
(3) it provides a possible means of effecting restitution where there is no payment (or where there is some failure of consideration possibly).

The subrogation remedy might enable the payer under a void swaps contract to seek to be subrogated to the rights of the creditors whose debts were discharged by the used of the payment. As considered above, the primary obstruction to this remedy would be whether or not it would be possible to identify the debt which had been discharged. Alternatively, the remedy would be equivalent to a charge over the general current account of the payee.

---

185 Mitchell, *The Law of Subrogation* (Oxford, 1994), p.33; see also Lord Templeman in *Space Investments Ltd v. Canadian Imperial Bank of Commerce Trust Co (Bahamas) Ltd* [1986] 1 W.L.R. 1072 at 1074; and *Lord Napier and Ettrick v. Hunter* [1993] 1 A.C. 713 at 737.

186 Burrows, *The Law of Restitution* (Butterworths, 1993), p.42; also Tettenborn, [1980] C.L.J. 272 at 324–5.

187 See also Paciocco, "The Remedial Constructive Trust: A Principled Basis for Priorities over Creditors" (1989) 68 Can. B.R. 315.

188 Mitchell, *The Law of Subrogation* (Oxford, 1994), p.33.

189 *ibid.* at p.28; and Burrows, *The Law of Restitution* (Butterworths, 1993).

190 Mitchell, *The Law of Subrogation* (Oxford, 1994), p.34.

191 Burrows, *The Law of Restitution* (Butterworths, 1993), pp.85–7 and 89–90.

Subrogation and tracing

11–66 There is a tendency for the courts to apply tracing rules to situations dealing more specifically with subrogation. This tends to support Birks' analysis that there is a great overlap between tracing rules and subrogation.[192] The Court of Appeal decision in *Barlow Clowes International Ltd (in liquidation) v. Vaughan*[193] is, in Mitchell's terms, a "subrogated claim". Investors in the collapsed Barlow Clowes organisation had their losses met in part by the Department of Trade and Industry. The Secretary of State for Trade and Industry then sought to recover, in effect the amounts paid away to those former investors. In Mitchell's terms, this is the point at which the Secretary of State is subrogated to the claims of the investors against Barlow Clowes. At first instance, Peter Gibson J. found that the rule in *Clayton's Case*[194] should be applied. *Clayton's Case* asserts the rule [as considered elsewhere] that tracing claims into mixed funds in current bank accounts are to be treated as the money first paid into the bank account to be first paid out of the account. The Court of Appeal awarded a *pari passu ex post facto* formula.[195]

Part payments

11–67 The question arises when subrogation rights arise if only part payment has been made. In the context of the *Islington* appeal, the issue would arise whether a right arises when the interest rate swap contract has only been part-performed. Referring back to the structure of an interest rate swap contract, where performance is made over a period of, for example, 10 years, it is difficult to isolate whether that contract is simply part performed after only five years where the contract is discovered to be *ultra vires* one of the parties to it. Is the contract part–performed, or has a segment of an ongoing contractual relationship been completed?

11–68 Mitchell is of the view that "... neither simple nor reviving subrogation will be made available to S until RH has been fully paid in respect of PL's obligation".[196] In the case of insured parties there is authority that this is the case.[197] In more general situations where a surety discharges the obligation of PL in part only, PL's liability will not be completely discharged and therefore reviving subrogation will not be available.[198] Mitchell posits some exceptions to this general rule: for example, where RH agrees that part payment will be treated as full discharge of his rights in respect of PL. One example given is where a surety agrees to guarantee part only of a debt, the surety would then appear to be subrogated to the securities given up by PL in respect of that part of the total debt.[199]

11–69 In the derivatives context, the issue arises whether this would be similar to a central amount of collateral given up to cover an amount which is equivalent to part of a debt. If the U.S. $40 million collateral is provided to provide security for a series of swaps transactions contracted between a number of different parties,

---

[192] See, for example, Mitchell, *The Law of Subrogation* (Oxford, 1994), p.40.

[193] [1992] 4 All E.R. 22.

[194] (1817) 1 Mer. 572.

[195] As referred to by Woolf L.J.

[196] Mitchell, *The Law of Subrogation* (Oxford, 1994), p.41.

[197] *Lord Napier and Ettrick v. Hunter* [1993] A.C. 713.

[198] *Ewart v. Latta* (1865) 4 Macq. 983.

[199] Mitchell, *The Law of Subrogation* (Oxford, 1994), p.42.

and there is then an event of default which calls in a total liability of U.S. $200 million, would there be the possibility of a subrogation claim to the extent of the securities which are given up? Or in this context, would a parent ever sue a subsidiary, for example, a special purpose vehicle, joint venture between a financial institution and an investor creates this liability? Seemingly there would be no right to other securities given with reference to an entirely different debt altogether.

11–70 It does appear that a surety who agrees to a limited amount of liability in respect of a total debt, is entitled to recover a pro rata share of the total liability by way of subrogation.[200] The restriction on this claim would be the rule that the courts have held that a claimant S cannot be allowed to use simple or reviving subrogation to recover from PL a greater amount than the sum which S himself was paid.[201]

Reviving subrogation

11–71 Voluntary assumption of risk reasoning will not operate, for example, "in the case where S and PL have a direct contractual relationship because there is no valid distinction to be drawn between a surety who agrees to pay money on PL's behalf at some time in the future and a lender who agrees to pay PL immediately, when assessing whether they have voluntarily undertaken the risk of PL's bankruptcy".[202] Therefore, the issue arises whether a payer could be said to have undertaken the risk of the payee's bankruptcy by undertaking to provide a cash flow equal to the payee's debt obligations, or whether there is a difference by payment of a lump sum upfront (as in the deep discount structure). There appears to be no reason in principle why there should be a difference between these two factual situations.

11–72 Burrows suggests that the unjust factor underlying the insurer's action for money had and received might alternatively be failure of consideration, in that the insurer pays to indemnify the insured, but the insured is already indemnified for his loss by the third party's payment.[203] In Birks' analysis, with reference to the availability of such a restitutionary response in a case where there has been a mistake, "the mistake must not only have caused the plaintiff to act but also be such that relief will not inexplicably disturb the risks distributed by any bargain between the parties".[204]

Other issues with the radical restitutionary approach

Restitutionary damages

11–73 The preceding discussion has focused on whether the restitutionary award would be personal or proprietary. An alternative approach is suggested by Lord Goff's assertion that the problem is simply one of money and therefore there

---

200 *Semble Bardwell v. Lydal* (1831) 7 Bing. 489; and *Re Fenton* [1931] Ch. 85 at 115, *per* Lawrence L.J.; as cited in Mitchell, *The Law of Subrogation* (Oxford, 1994), p.42.

201 Mitchell, 43; Friedmann and Cohen, *The International Encyclopaedia of Comparative Law* (Lancaster, 1991), p.177, n24.

202 Mitchell, *The Law of Subrogation* (Oxford, 1994), pp.53, *et seq.*

203 Burrows, *The Law of Restitution* (Butterworths, 1993), p.80; Mitchell, *The Law of Subrogation* (Oxford, 1994), p.81, n.63.

204 Birks, (1993) L.Q.R. 164 at 166.

could be a solution based on the calculation of an amount of compensation necessary to undo the unjust enrichment. There is a question as to whether or not "restitutionary damages" can logically be said to exist. McGregor takes the view that they probably do not.[205] In Jaffey's analysis, restitutionary damages arise not as a remedy for unjust enrichment by subtraction but rather as an addition to damages awarded in connection with a wrong.[206] This approach is identified most recently in the case of *Inverguie Investments Ltd. v. Hackett*,[207] where the defendant had wrongly occupied the plaintiff's property for 15 years. The award granted was one by reference to the rental value of the property, rather than by reference to the profit made by the defendant, although the true nature of the remedy is not easily established.[208] On this basis it is said that there is a need for restitution to take into account the need to deal with deliberate wrongdoing.[209]

11–74 It is said that where restitutionary damages do exist, they would arise where the defendant's gain exceeds the plaintiff's loss. For example, if X sells warrants in an emerging market with the intention that X's own stakes in such markets benefit from the resulting volatility, it is questionable whether a buyer of those warrants who suffers loss, would be able to recover restitutionary damages equal to the defendant's gain.[210] Is there a difference between the respective situations of: (i) a house bank; (ii) a bank selling on a one-off transaction; and (iii) a financial institutions acting at arm's length? Are restitutionary damages to be imposed in a way which recognises (or punishes) the seller of the product according to the nature of that person's relationship to the plaintiff? A house bank[211] will generally be relied upon by a corporate client to provide advice and to put into place sophisticated financial structures. It is therefore more likely that such an institution will not have its advice corroborated by independent advisors. There is, therefore, greater scope for liability for misstatement on the *Hedley Byrne v. Heller*[212] principle in this context. The question is restitutionary damages concerning profits made by a house bank out of such an arrangement occupy a different category from contracts which concern financial institutions acting at arm's length where it is more reasonable to suppose that the buyer of the derivative will generally be competent to reach its own conclusions as to the advice extended to it by the seller of that product. In the category of restitutionary remedies, there are possibly two benefits in respect of derivatives: first, ownership of securities, secondly, use of securities. In the context of taking collateral, the issue is who owns and who uses those securities put up as collateral.[213]

---

205 McGregor, "Restitutionary Damages" in *Essays in the Law of Restitution* (Burrows ed., Oxford, 1991).

206 Jaffey, "*Restitutionary Damages and Disgorgement*" [1995] R.L.R. 30.

207 [1995] 1 W.L.R. 713; Mitchell [1995] L.M.C.L.Q. 343.

208 However, see *Jaggard v. Sawyer* [1995] 1 W.L.R. 269.

209 See also Burrows, *Remedies in Contract and Tort*, (Butterworths, 1995), p.416.

210 By the same token, with reference to credit derivatives, where representations as to credit of the underlying entity turn out to be false, it would be question whether the buyer could recover the profits on the instrument made by seller of the derivative.

211 That is, a bank on which a corporate client relies almost exclusively for financial advice and banking services.

212 [1964] A.C. 465.

213 Birks, *Introduction to the Law of Restitution* (Oxford, 1989), p.25.

Election between remedies

11–75 There is a difficulty of election between remedies.[214] To what extent can a restitutionary claim be considered to be separate from the contractual claim in connection with which it arises? In valuing the appropriate restitution, is it possible to reach a valuation without reference to the underlying contract? The conclusion to be drawn from *Tang v. Capacious Investments*[215] is that where a plaintiff is required to choose between alternative remedies, he must make such election at the time when judgment is awarded in his favour. The plaintiff is not to be deemed to have made such an election simply by dint of accepting payment as restitution, unless he was in full cognisance of the options open to him.

---

[214] Burrows [1995] C.L.P. 103, 112–113; Stevens [1996] R.L.R. 117, 121—Election between alternative remedies.
[215] [1996] 1 A.C. 514; [1996] R.L.R. 11.

Chapter 12

The suitability approach

12–01 The *suitability approach* aims to identify a means of addressing the availability of proprietary remedies, and to uphold the efficacy of credit support language in commercial and financial transactions, in a manner which both recognises the commercial intentions of the parties and minimises the problems associated with the application of the restitutionary and equitable responses currently permitted by statute. The term "suitability" is culled from American financial regulatory jurisprudence and has been used by some English commentators.[1] The term itself is designed to encompass a sense of the "appropriateness" of both the manner in which the derivatives product is created and in its correlation to the commercial requirements of its end-user. Suitability finds a basis in the general jurisprudence of equity[2] in the context of those actions which are found to be so contrary to conscience that a proprietary claim or entitlement to compensation will be ordered to compensate the plaintiff. For example, where a seller unduly influences a buyer, or relies on some unjust factor in the creation of the product, which would occasion and equitable claim. The concept of suitability would also capture cases of mis-selling of products by making misrepresentations to the buyer or otherwise exerting unacceptable pressure or selling an inappropriate product: in either case, invoking principles of the law of contract or the law of tort.

12–02 The following section aims to set out the core principles which ought to be applied in relation to arm's length commercial transactions when considering the claims available to the parties. This discussion incorporates a discussion of those principles which have not been discussed in the local authority swaps cases but which, it is submitted, ought to form a part of the *suitability approach* to claims and remedies in financial transactions. The motivation behind the *suitability approach* is the need to develop claims and remedies which recognise the commercial intentions of the parties to financial derivatives transactions.[3] The aim is to use general equitable principles from other contexts to meet the specific needs of commercial life.[4] Conscience, as a general principle advanced by Lord Browne-Wilkinson, would appear to apply to commercial situations only in cases where there is fraud or breach of fiduciary duty. On existing authority, there is no explicit suggestion that common intention manifested in void commercial

---

[1] See, for example, Hudson, *The Law of Financial Derivatives* (2nd ed., 1998), Chap. 5.

[2] Or in the language of restitution in the context of those unjust factors which will give rise to a claim for some equitable response.

[3] It is not suggested that there be a code of rules specifically for one kind of financial product. Rather, it is said that there are common features to all commercial transactions that take them outwith the ordinary run of equitable and restitutionary situations.

[4] For example, the common intention constructive trusts considered below, have been created specifically by reference to family situations where there is no commercial allocation of the risks of a bargain. Similarly, as considered above, the application of a test of "knowledge" and "conscience" does not transfer straightforwardly to the commercial context.

contracts ought to create some equity requiring performance in accordance with the allocation of risks under those agreements. Further, there is no analysis in the decided cases as to whether or not the factors affecting the conscience of the seller of a derivative product, thus able to found a constructive trust, would include the creation of an unsuitable financial product for a client. However, it is these issues which reflect most closely the substantive issues raised by the swaps cases and which will be explored in the *suitability approach*.

12–03 The *radical restitutionary approach* could similarly provide the basis for the award of a restitutionary response in circumstances where a payer loses the use of property or suffers some subtraction, to the benefit of the payee, which might be said to constitute an unjust enrichment. There is perhaps a further question, in the financial context, concerning other principles that might be deployed to reflect the parties' allocation of risks and consensual purpose—in short, the suitability of the product for its purpose.

12–04 What is not being suggested in the following section is that a proprietary right ought necessarily to be made available in all commercial cases in the manner that some trading floors might like to see it. It is not even the suggestion of the following section that the banks ought necessarily to have recovered proprietary rights in money paid to the authorities where it is clear that they allocated risks but not clear that they sought to retain proprietary title in the property transferred to the local authorities. In this regard, it is contended that the standard market documentation is defective in that it provides for the payment of termination amounts but not for the preservation of equitable title in property transferred under swaps contracts. However, as discussed above with reference to *Problems of Credit and Security*,[5] it is contended that *even if those contracts had provided for the preservation of title, such provisions would not have been effective.*

12–05 What is contended in the following section is that commercial situations constitute a different case from domestic and family home situations in that the parties are acting at arm's length as commercial people and ought to be bound by the agreements which they form. To fail to hold the parties to their agreements is to create an unacceptable level of commercial uncertainty. In line with the developing concretisation of the principles of equity in recent cases, equity ought to be able to develop principles which accept the allocation of commercial risks and which are capable of even application without introducing further commercial uncertainty. Alternatively, it is said, that principles of the law of restitution ought to be capable of adaptation to meet the requirements of commercial transactions.

12–06 There is reserved within the scope of this suitability response scope for the courts to apply mandatory rules, such as the *ultra vires* principle, to those commercial actions which ought not to be supported by law. It is suggested however, that, unless the provision of credit support is itself found to be contrary to law, the efficacy of the intentions of the parties as to their proprietary and other rights ought to remain binding.

I. Severance: an approach based on the law of contract

12–07 The following discussion of principles of equity and the ensuing discussion based on restitution of unjust enrichment both consider the refusal of the House of Lords in *Islington* to deal with the terms of the standard market

[5] Chapter 4, *Issues of Finance and Law*.

contract. In defence of the *suitability approach* that is set out here, it is submitted that even in the case of contracts which are found to be void *ab initio* with reference to their core commercial purpose, it is open to the court to seek to apply the risk management provisions of those agreements in spite of the avoidance of the remainder of the contract. This approach is based on the application of the basis of severance. In short, the application of this doctrine would permit enable the application of principles of equity or of restitution to reduce systemic risk in commercial contracts by giving effect to those prudent elements of contractual agreements[6] which do not offend against public policy or the other caveats set out below.

12–08 The doctrine of severance was considered above in *Equity and Modern Financial Techniques*.[7] The doctrine provides that, where a contract is held to void on grounds that it offends public policy or is illegal, the offending part of the agreement can be severed from those elements which do not offend against lawfulness or public policy. This severance has the effect of ensuring the validity of those parts of the contract which are maintained. The issue arises then whether any part of the agreements entered into in the swaps cases would have been capable of severance in the manner considered by Dillon L.J. The offensive parts of the swap agreements, as considered by Lord Templeman in *Hazell*, were the elements relating to the *ultra vires* borrowing. The issue remains whether *Hazell* constitutes a case motivated by the desire to rectify the potentially enormous obligations which would have been visited on the ratepayers of Hammersmith and Fulham. Debt management with speculative financial products is the objection identified by the House of Lords.

12–09 The classic statement of the doctrine of severance is that: "where you cannot sever the illegal from the legal part of a covenant, the contract is altogether void; but, where you can sever them, whether the illegality can be created by statute or by common law, you may reject the bad part and retain the good".[8] The decision of Megarry J. in *Spector v. Ageda* [9] held that the whole of the contract must be considered to be void even where a part only of the agreement had been found to be illegal by operation of statute. The policy identified in this decision was to prevent parties to illegal contracts from putting themselves into further harm by enforcing other contracts. Similarly, in *Esso Petroleum v. Harper's Garage (Stourport) Ltd.* [10] it was held that where covenants in a contract are so closely connected that they can be deemed to stand or fall together, the whole contract will fail even though some sections may appear to be severable.

12–10 It is submitted, however, that the risk management features of standard market financial documents introduce greater certainty and lessen the cash amounts required to be paid between market participants. Therefore, the identified policy of precluding the parties from entering into further damaging transactions does not apply in the context of a provision, such as a netting clause on termination, which reduces the net amount of the parties' exposure to one

---

6 Whether negotiated on a bespoke basis or founded on standard market contracts.

7 Chapter 5.

8 *Pickering v. Ilfracombe Railway* (1868) L.R. 3 C.P. 235 at 250; *Payne v. Brecon Corporation* (1858) 3 H. & N. 572; *Royal Exchange Assurance Corporation v. Siforsakrings Aktiebolaget Vega* [1901] 2 K.B. 567 at 573; *Chitty on Contracts* (27th ed., Sweet & Maxwell, 1994), paras 16–165.

9 [1973] Ch. 30.

10 [1968] A.C. 269 at 314, 321.

another. The validity of an instrument need not be compromised because some element of it is held to unenforceable.[11]

12–11 The purpose of the interest rate swap is the creation of two streams of cash flows related to a notional amount of money, with the underlying purpose of acquiring some speculative return or hedging a financial risk. The conservative argument would provide that, where those functions are held to be *ultra vires ab initio*, there is no possibility of upholding any part of the agreement. However, those elements of the agreements which relate to the termination of those agreements and the calculation of termination amounts to settle all outstanding obligations and to deal with the reallocation of property, do not appear to fall into the same category as the active provisions of the swap agreements which provide for the economic terms of the contracts. Therefore, it is submitted, that as part of the *suitability approach*, it would have been possible for the courts to have segregated the economic provisions that created the interest rate swaps, from those risk management provisions which seek to provide for termination and risk allocation.

12–12 It is settled law that the court will not rewrite the contract as part of severance.[12] The court will not therefore blue-pencil any part of the agreement such that there is an effect that is materially different from that which the parties had agreed to originally. However, it is not clear that the effect of enforcing the termination provisions of a financial agreement, where they regulate the manner in which termination takes effect and the rights of the parties to property, would effect a materially different agreement.

12–13 The problem with the application of this principle is the basic assertion by the courts that the entire contract was void *ab initio*, even though the courts did not consider the range of terms contained in the master agreements.[13] It is this ground of public policy that would appear to militate most strongly against application of the credit support or termination provisions.[14] The central question is, therefore, as to the appropriate basis for public policy in this area. It is submitted that the most appropriate policy is to respect the market practice of controlling risks through standard contracts and to recognise the impact these provisions have on lowering systemic risk in relation to financial derivatives contracts.

12–14 The doctrine of severance might also apply with reference to the distinction between executed and non-executed transactions. It could be submitted that, where the parties have acted consensually, and without any other unjust factor such as fraud or undue influence, there is no injustice in requiring the parties to observe their agreement.

12–15 A further issue arises where one type of derivative only is found to be inefficacious or void. The question would arise whether a credit support document, such as an agreement to provide collateral, in support of a range of derivative transactions, would be held to be partly valid to the extent that it covered the valid transaction. The all-or-nothing approach of the courts in the swaps cases does little to appreciate the habitual commercial usage of the credit support structure across a range of transactions potentially in different jurisdictions.

---

[11] *Gaskell v. King* (1809) 11 East. 165; *Gibbons v. Harper* (1831) 2 B. & Ad. 734.

[12] *Goldsoll v. Goldman* [1914] 2 Ch. 603, [1915] 1 Ch. 192; *Ronbar v. Green* [1954] 1 W.L.R. 815; *Scorer v. Seymour Jones* [1966] 1 W.L.R. 1419.

[13] Alternatively, the issue arises whether any credit support documentation, being collateral to the void contract, could be effective against the defaulting party. The doctrine of severance would suggest that any collateral credit support documentation could be made effective against the counterparty.

[14] *Kuenigl v. Donnersmarck* [1955] 1 Q.B. 515; *Hyland v. Barker* [1985] I.C.R. 861 at 863.

12–16 The correct approach would appear to be that the credit support document would continue in full force and effect in relation to those transactions which have not been declared to be void. That does not answer the question whether or not it should be applicable even though the agreement to which it is collateral has been held to be void. It is submitted that the credit support document should be upheld on the grounds that it lowers the financial risk at large between the parties without impacting on third–party creditors who must have proceeded on the basis that such agreements were valid until they were declared to be void by a court.

Contracts void *ab initio*

12–17 Contrary to the sentiments of the English courts in *Islington*, it is not an immutable rule at English law that a contract void *ab initio* is necessarily completely inefficacious in any event. Further to the availability of the doctrine of severance, it has been held, primarily in the context of insurance and shipping contracts, that contracts void *ab initio* can nevertheless be held to be valid to the extent of jurisdiction clauses and arbitration clauses. In the case of *FAI General Insurance v. Ocean Marine Mutual*[15] a contract of reinsurance was held to have been void *ab initio*. The reinsurer sought to commence proceedings in the New South Wales court while the reinsured sought to commence proceedings in the English court. The purported contract of reinsurance had specified that English courts were to have jurisdiction in the event of any dispute. The issue arose as to the efficacy of such jurisdiction provision.

12–18 The court found that simply because a contract was held to have been void *ab initio* did not necessarily preclude the efficacy of jurisdiction clauses and arbitration clauses. There was nothing on the terms of the contract to suggest that the exclusive jurisdiction clause should not apply. In deciding to exercise the jurisdiction of the English court, it was held that the reinsurer should be held to its bargain. This decision was based on broad principles of English commercial law as to the severability of terms of contracts otherwise held to have been void.[16] Similarly, there is a general principle that the parties should be held to their bargain in the first instance,[17] which it is contended ought to include the risk management provisions of a financial derivatives contract.

II. Equity and suitability

12–19 There is a problem in isolating the line between law and regulation in the context of financial transactions. Within the financial community itself the personnel who deal with legal issues and those who deal with regulatory issues tend to be different. There is usually a distinction between "legal", "documentation" and "compliance" departments as a result. The concept of

---

[15] [1998] Lloyd's Rep. I.R. 24.

[16] *Mackender v. Feldia AG* [1967] 2 Q.B. 590; *Woolworths Ltd v. McMillan* (Rogers J., February 29, 1988, unreported; *Harbour Assurance Co (UK) Ltd v. Kansa General International Insurance Co Ltd* [1992] 1 Lloyd's Rep. 81.

[17] *Huddart Parker Ltd v. The Ship "Mill Hill"* (1950) 81 C.L.R. 502; *Oceanic Sun Line Special Shipping Co Inc v. Fay* (1988) 165 C.L.R. 197; *Akai PtyLtd v. Peoples Insurance Co Ltd* (1995) 8 ANZ Ins. Cas. 161; *The Eleftheria* [1970] P. 94; *The El Amria* [1981] Lloyd's Rep. 521; *Citi-March Ltd v. Neptune Orient Lines Ltd* [1996] 1 W.L.R. 1367; [1996] 2 All E.R. 545; *FAI v. Ocean Marine* [1998] Lloyd's Rep. 24.

"suitability" is culled from notions of regulation and, more specifically, whether or not the mixture of clients and products is a suitable one. It is submitted that the approach of equity to financial market contracts should import some notions of suitability to the extent that they chime in with understood equitable principles. For example, the benefits of enforcing standard market contracts to reduce the level of systemic risk is considered below as fitting in with the understood doctrine of common intention constructive trusts from the area of traditional family trusts of homes. As observed earlier from the speech of Lord Browne-Wilkinson in *Target Holdings* there is a need for a parallel understanding of equity in the context of commercial situations which is different from principles of equity and trusts as traditionally understood.

The development of an equitable model for financial agreements

12–20 In considering commercial situations, the appropriate rules of equity should be centred around a central principle: to enforce prudential risk management provisions of the contract between the parties except where that would be contrary to some mandatory principle of equity or contrary to public policy.

Proprietary remedies

12–21 The first issue is to consider those situations in which an equitable remedy should be a proprietary remedy. On the *suitability approach* such an award ought to be made where the contractual agreement between the parties allocates title to the property transferred under the transaction.[18] As part of a contractual agreement, the law should recognise the understanding between those parties as to the allocation of title in property. As an extension of the constructive trust, it is inequitable for one party to represent by purported written contract with a counterparty that the counterparty will acquire title in property, only for that property to be lost and replaced only by a personal claim. It is submitted that this can be achieved either by straightforward application of the principle set out by Lord Browne-Wilkinson in *Islington* for an institutional constructive trust, by means of a development of the remedial constructive trust canvassed by Lord Browne-Wilkinson or by extension of common intention constructive trust and proprietary estoppel principles.

12–22 Equity understands the typical situations in which such a reallocation or transfer of proprietary rights ought not to be effected. For example, in the derivatives markets the regulatory concern is frequently that inappropriate products are being sold to inappropriate clients. As a result there is some unsuitability in the derivatives business. It is contended that the equitable doctrine of undue influence is capable of dealing with exactly such a situation. There might be a different issue where the parties are of unequal bargaining strength as a result of their seller and retail-buyer status in respect of a complex derivative product. As such it could be said that the product or service provided by the stronger party was provided in a context where the buyer would normally rely on the advice of the seller and there was some undue influence in the creation of that product. Consequently, the correct analysis according to the *suitability approach* would be to decide whether or not the buyer of the product had been unduly influenced into

[18] This would not have happened in *Islington* because the contracts did not contain specific retention of title provisions.

purchasing property. As such that person ought to receive a proprietary remedy over property passed to the seller under some undue influence.[19]

12–23 The role of equity after the acceptance of the doctrine of unjust enrichment by the House of Lords in *Lipkin Gorman v. Karpnale*[20] has led some commentators to include a test of unjust enrichment as part of their statement of the availability of proprietary equitable interests.[21] Therefore, it is submitted that there is a requirement that Equity recognise the role of the doctrine of unjust enrichment in the application of equitable doctrines. With this in mind it is contended that, if a risk was allocated between the parties, where as a result of some unjust factor, the either party was caused to be unjustly enriched by the acquisition of some property of the plaintiff at the expense of the other party, Equity should impose a proprietary equitable interest to restore that property to the plaintiff.[22] Such an interest would be required to be a constructive trust, in the wake of Lord Browne-Wilkinson's leading speech in *Islington* on the unsuitability of resulting trusts to achieve restitution. Therefore, where the seller of a derivative product seeks to rely upon the efficacy of that product in circumstances where there had been some duress or misrepresentation, it is contended that unjust enrichment ought to found a proprietary claim in equity over property transferred as part of that transaction.

12–24 As considered above in *The Structure of Financial Derivatives Products*,[23] there is a need to draw a distinction between those derivatives which are cash-settled and those which are physically-settled. The cash-settled products will, generally, not require security in respect of any particular property. The usual mechanisms for credit support in cash-settled transactions are the provision of collateral or margin by deposit of a threshold level of cash or securities in a specified account. However, many derivatives will require delivery of a specific form of security, commodity or other asset to fulfil a further financial obligation owed by the recipient. In such situations it would be desirable for the contractual documentation to manifest such a commercial purpose—lamentably many of the standard market documents do not provide for such opening recitals of intention. In circumstances where a transaction is terminated, if rescission is the appropriate remedy under a physically-settled transaction, where the traceable proceeds of the original transfer remain in the hands of the recipient, it is submitted that an equitable proprietary remedy would be appropriate to give effect to the intentions of the parties.

12–25 As considered below in greater detail, the further factual circumstance in which it is contended that the award of a proprietary remedy would be appropriate is where the allocation of proprietary rights would be where it accords with the common intention of the parties. This common intention would be capable of support where it is set out in a severable part of the agreement between the parties which remains lawful in se and which is not contrary to public policy.

Personal claims

12–26 The House of Lords in *Islington* was unanimous in finding that there was no reason for the award of a proprietary remedy in favour of the bank. As

---

[19] This should be compared with the torts of misrepresentation, etc., as considered below.

[20] *Lipkin Gorman v. Karpnale* [1991] 2 A.C. 548, and also *Woolwich Equitable Building Society v. IRC (No.2)* [1993] A.C. 573; [1992] 3 W.L.R. 366; [1992] 3 All E.R. 737.

[21] See Hayton, *Underhill and Hayton on the Law of Trusts and Trustees* (Butterworths, 1995).

[22] Smith, "Tracing and Electronic Funds Transfer" in *Restitution and Banking Law* (Rose ed., Mansfield Press, Oxford ,1998), p.120.

[23] Chapter 2.

considered above, this did not take account of the terms of the contracts entered into between the parties. However, it is submitted that there will be a number of situations in which it would not be appropriate to provide for proprietary remedies in the context of financial transactions. It is not the intention of this book to suggest that parties ought to be awarded proprietary rights on the basis that, *ex post facto*, the plaintiff would like a proprietary remedy. Rather, it is important to isolate in commercial disputes the situations in which she ought to be entitled to such a remedy. The following sections considers those situations in which it is submitted that a remedy by means of equitable compensation or by imposition of personal liability under constructive trust should be made available to a party where a transaction is caused to be terminated.

12–27 In cases where a particular risk has not been allocated to either party under the terms of their contract, where as a result of some unjust factor either party was caused to be unjustly enriched at the expense of the other party. However, if a risk was assumed by either party, that risk was a reckless risk for that party to have taken in that context, personal liability to account for the loss suffered by that other party should be imposed in line with the decision of the Privy Council in *Royal Brunei Airlines v. Tan.*[24] In circumstances where the parties were of unequal bargaining strength, and the product or service provided by the stronger party was not suitable for the purposes of the weaker party in the context of that transaction, the stronger party should bear personal liability to account to the other party.

12–28 It is suggested that in the case of both cash-settled and physically-settled transactions, rescission is the appropriate equitable response. The nature of the liability to account would be the payment necessary to reverse a cash-settled transaction including any necessary costs associated with the loss of bargain. A similar calculation to reverse the commercial effect of the transaction should be made where the risk taken, or the context in which the risk was taken, contravened some principle of public policy or of statute or of some other mandatory rule of law or equity.

Common intention constructive trusts

12–29 The common intention constructive trust is a creature of equity used with reference to the allocation of rights in domestic homes. The development of this particular principle can be traced to the work of Professor Hayton and to the speech of Lord Bridge in *Lloyds Bank v. Rosset.*[25] So it is to be conceded from the outset that the basis for the equitable principle which is to be advanced for the resolution of disputes in commercial contracts is founded on the law relating to domestic homes. Beyond an understanding of generic equitable principles, this area does not appear to have been extended outside the specific context of "trusts of land". Indeed, it would appear that the rigid application of the decision of the test for the generation of equitable interests in real property created by House of Lords in *Rosset.*[26]

12–30 This section will set out the reason why there is a similarity of purpose and utility of the common intention constructive trust in the contexts both of real property and commercial contracts. It will then consider some of the conceptual

[24] *Royal Brunei Airlines v. Tan* [1995] 2 A.C. 378.

[25] *Lloyds Bank v. Rossett* [1991] 1 A.C. 107; [1990] 1 All ER 1111; [1990] 2 W.L.R. 867.

[26] See, for example, the decision of the Court of Appeal in *Midland Bank v. Cooke* [1995] 4 All E.R. 562 (especially in the judgment of Waite L.J.).

weaknesses of that construct in relation to real property, explaining why those deficiencies do not obtain in relation to commercial contracts.

12–31 The common intention constructive trust aims to impose the office of trusteeship on a person who seeks to use property in a manner which runs contrary to some agreement between the parties as to the allocation of interests in that property or the manner in which it was understood that that property was to be dealt with. In the context of the family home this enables the court to isolate an agreement or arrangement between co-owners as to the allocation of equitable interests in their home (or homes). Where such an agreement, or course of conduct indicating an implied agreement, can be found, the court will order that the property be dealt with in accordance with the existence of such beneficial interests. Typically, under section 14 of the Trusts of Land and Appointment of Trustees Act 1996,[27] this results in an order for sale of the property or an order that one or other party be entitled to reside in the property with the children from such relationship. However, a party who has not been identified as a legal owner of the property, can acquire proprietary rights in the home by virtue of the "common intention".

12–32 In the context of a commercial contract it is clear that there must be common intention as to some parts of the interaction of the parties. In a perfect world a contract would evidence the entirety of the intentions of the parties in relation to their respective obligations, credit support issues and rights in any property transferred between them. Where there is no such agreement as to any of these questions, there could be no constructive trust based on a common intention unless that could be implied from their mutual conduct. Where there is an express agreement between the parties as to the legal and/or equitable interest in property, that contract will be decisive as to that issue. The problem is where the contract is explicit as to title in property and so forth but the contract itself is unenforceable because it has been held to have been void *ab initio*.

12–33 The common intention constructive trust does not require that there have been anything amounting to a binding contract to be imposed on the parties. In part this is because ordinary people unversed in the niceties of the law relating to real property are not expected to have observed the formalities of creating contracts in respect of land.[28] Therefore, this thinking need not be extended to commercial parties who have failed to reached agreement in any contractual form as to their respective proprietary and other rights. However, it is submitted that, where contractual parties have formed detailed contracts borne out of a standard market form, and it is only the technicality of the *ultra vires* rule which has led to performance of their contract being unenforceable either at law or equity, collateral issues of credit support and proprietary rights in property ought to be governed in equity in accordance with their common intention.

12–34 It is submitted that the contracting parties can have no objection to being bound by the terms of their agreement. In situations where the formation of the agreement is said to be founded on some unjust factor, misrepresentation or undue influence, then there would be no valid common intention to form an agreement such that the constructive trust could not be enforced. Alternatively, it cannot be said that there is any hardship to creditors of one of the contracting parties. In the event that the party is insolvent, the creditors receive a windfall in

---

[27] Formerly section 30 of the Law of Property Act 1925.

[28] For example, the requirement under section 2 of the Law of Property (Miscellaneous Provisions) Act 1989 that contracts in relation to land must be in writing.

the event that the contract is found to be unenforceable. The House of Lords in *Islington* were unanimous in their desire to protect ordinary creditors of an insolvent party in a bankruptcy. However, it is contended that there is no reason to protect ordinary creditors beyond ensuring that one category of unsecured creditors does not gain an unjustified advantage[29] over the other unsecured creditors. There is no reason, however, why ordinary creditors should obtain preference over parties who have sought to protect themselves by retaining some proprietary interest. The predeliction for the protection of those who have not acquired proprietary protection for themselves simply fails to recognise that it is the market economy that is at fault in creating inequalities of bargaining power.[30] The weakness of the *Islington* decision is that it precludes the contracting parties from seeking to allocate responsibility and proprietary rights. The strength of the model based on the common intention constructive trust is that it observes the freedom of the parties to contract and thus restricts the scope for systemic risk as set out above.

12–35 The criticism of the common intention constructive trust has been based primarily on its reliance on an implied agreement where no such agreement has never existed. The English concepts of Equity have a use for legal fictions. For example, the mutual conduct common intention constructive trust is simply self-contradictory. Where there is no express agreement of any kind between the parties, the court has given itself the power to assume from the behaviour of the parties that they would have reached a particular agreement had they been appraised of the legal context. Therefore, they are treated as having created an agreement where there was none. A legal fiction. There are other complaints which are specific to the context of the family home and purchase trusts: for example, the necessity that there have been some direct contribution to the mortgage repayments or purchase price[31] rather than any more general contribution to familial expenses.[32]

Proprietary estoppel and the remedial constructive trust

12–36 The doctrine of proprietary estoppel offers a substantive claim[33] which some commentators have considered to be closer to the remedial model constructive trust used in North American jurisdictions than the English institutional constructive trust.[34] It is useful therefore to consider the similarities and differences between the two doctrines to understand better the model of common intention constructive trust which the *suitability approach* would apply to commercial and financial market transactions.

12–37 There is a basic, conceptual distinction to be made between the common intention constructive trust and the doctrine of proprietary estoppel. The common intention constructive trust operates on the basis of a bilateral understanding between two cohabitees as to the nature and allocation of the

---

29 Beyond what is preserved by statute.

30 The writer has argued elsewhere that it is the role of government to intervene in situations where it is considered that such inequalities of bargaining power are insupportable: see *The Law on Financial Derivatives* (Sweet & Maxwell, 1996), pp.199 *et seq.*

31 *Lloyds Bank v. Rosset* [1990] 1 All E.R. 1111 at 1119, *per* Lord Bridge.

32 *Burns v. Burns* [1984] Ch. 317.

33 In contradistinction to the shield of promissory estoppel: *Hughes v. Metropolitan Railway* (1877) 2 App. Cas. 439; *Central London Property Trust Ltd. v. High Trees House Ltd.* [1947] K.B. 130.

34 Hayton (1993) L.Q.R. 485.

interests of each in the property which they co-inhabit.[35] On the other hand, the doctrine of proprietary estoppel operates on the unilateral conduct of one party who represents to the other party that that other will acquire some interest in real property, in reliance upon which that other acts to her detriment.[36] The attitudinal differences between the two doctrines[37] is exemplified by a need to plead each in a distinct way rather than to rely on a common pleading to establish either doctrine inter-changeably. Indeed, the test for proprietary estoppel on the "three–stage basis"[38] set out in cases like *Re Basham*[39] is somewhat more certain than the operation of the general constructive trust set out by Lord Browne-Wilkinson in *Islington* as discussed above.

12–38 The basis of the doctrine of proprietary estoppel is not entirely clear. There appear to be a number of theoretical underpinnings arising from the cases which allow us to choose between: providing a cause of action in equity where the common law will not allow one; preventing the legal owner from relying on legal rights in circumstances where that would be contrary to conscience; simply "raising an equity"; perfecting imperfect gifts where the representation is read as an intention to make a gift; and a simple restitutionary response based on preventing unconscionable conduct.

12–39 The common, modern form of proprietary estoppel has three basic requirements: representation, reliance, and detriment. The term "representation" is most commonly found in the cases although some writers prefer to use the term "assurance".[40] This representation or assurance can be an implied representation.[41] While some cases have identified unconscionable conduct as being at the heart of the doctrine, the representation itself need not be based on any unconscionable conduct.[42] As to the specificity of the rights to be acquired and the precision of the property, it appears from decided case law that a promise as vague as the provision of a "roof over your head" is insufficient. Therefore there is a need to be precise despite the largesse of the legal fiction at the heart of the allocation of rights in homes by the courts.[43] The representation can be manifested by words or deeds, as illustrated by *Pascoe v. Turner*[44] or even by silent acquiescence of the representor with conduct of the representee where the former knows that the latter understands that she will acquire an equitable interest in property by virtue of her conduct.[45]

12–40 Reliance is generally taken to be a matter of evidence and may be assumed (on an evidentiary basis) where there has been a representation.[46] The further question is what form of conduct will constitute "detriment". There are two possibilities: first, expenditure of money on improvements, or secondly, some more general personal disadvantage. At one level it is said that any form of

---

[35] *Gissing v. Gissing* [1971] A.C. 886; *Midland Bank v. Dobson* [1986] 1 F.L.R. 171.

[36] *Pascoe v. Turner* [1979] 2 All E.R. 945; *Re Basham* [1986] 1 W.L.R. 1498; *Wayling v. Jones* (1995) P. & C.R. 170.

[37] See on this Hayton, "Equitable Rights of Cohabitees" in *Equity and Contemporary Legal Developments* (Goldstein ed., Jerusalem, 1992).

[38] As opposed to the "five probanda" test set out in *Coombes v. Smith* [1986] 1 W.L.R. 808.

[39] [1986] 1 W.L.R. 1498.

[40] See Pawlowski, *The Doctrine of Proprietary Estoppel* (Sweet & Maxwell, 1996), pp.22 *et seq.*

[41] *Crabb v. Arun DC* [1976] Ch. 179, *per* Lord Denning.

[42] *Lim v. Ang* [1992] 1 W.L.R. 113.

[43] *Coombes v. Smith* [1986] 1 W.L.R. 808.

[44] [1979] 2 All E.R. 945.

[45] *Ramsden v. Dyson* (1866) L.R. 1 at 129, HL.

[46] *Lim v. Ang* [1992] 1 W.L.R. 113; *Grant v. Edwards* [1986] Ch. 638.

detriment, including personal disadvantage ought to be included.[47] However, the contrary view is that detriment must be directed at the purchase of the property or at the acquisition of rights directly in the property.[48] The scope of the available remedies is orientated around the nature of the loss that is to be compensated: whether that is simply the reversal of the detriment or compensation for the expectation loss. The general approach of English law has been to deal with the expectation of the party who has suffered some detriment.[49] Those jurisdictions which have based their test on "unconscionable conduct" have identified compensation valued by reference to "detriment loss" as the better remedy to deal with that conduct.[50] What is clearer is that the extent of the remedy will be that necessary to do the minimum equity necessary.[51] This has led to the award of the fee simple of one property,[52] whereas at the other end of the scale the Commonwealth jurisdictions have begun to develop the use of equitable compensation in some circumstances.[53]

12–41 As such, the doctrine of proprietary estoppel has established its own specific jurisprudence. Its own core terms have been developed, in English law at any rate, in a specific context outwith the understanding of the constructive trust or the common intention constructive trust. The speech of Lord Bridge in *Rosset*[54] fanned the flames of the debate as to the need or desirability of keeping the common intention constructive trust and the doctrine of proprietary estoppel distinct. Lord Bridge frequently used the expression "constructive trust or proprietary estoppel" as a composite which implied that the two doctrines should be considered to be synonymous. Many commentators have applauded the possibility of using the flexibility of the doctrine of proprietary estoppel to create a remedial constructive trust[55] for family home situations.[56] Other commentators and authorities have argued that the two doctrines should be kept distinct on the basis of their separate conceptual foundations.[57]

12–42 In the context of commercial agreements the substantive claim based on proprietary estoppel is not, it is submitted, a suitable foundation on which equity should build. The discretion that is given to the courts, which Hayton considers to be such a boon in the area of family home trusts,[58] is too great a discretion in situations where the parties seek remedies in connection with detailed commercial

---

47 Browne-Wilkinson L.J. in *Grant v. Edwards* [1986] Ch. 638. See also *Re Basham* [1986] 1 W.L.R. 1498.

48 Jonathan Parker Q.C. in *Coombes v. Smith* [1986] 1 W.L.R. 808.

49 *Pascoe v. Turner* [1979] 2 All E.R. 945; *Greasley v. Cooke* [1980] 1 W.L.R. 1306; *Re Basham* [1986] 1 W.L.R. 1498.

50 *Commonwealth of Australia v. Verwayen* (1990) 64 A.J.L.R. 540; *Walton Stores v. Maher* (1988) 62 A.J.L.R. 110; 164 C.L.R. 387.

51 *Crabb v. Arun D.C.* [1976] Ch. 179; *Pascoe v. Turner* [1979] 2 All E.R. 945.

52 *Pascoe v. Turner* [1979] 2 All E.R. 945.

53 *Palachik v. Kiss* (1983) 146 D.L.R. (3rd) 385; *Novick Estate v. Lachuk Estate* (1989) 58 D.L.R. (4th) 185; *MacDonald v. MacKenzie* (1990) 60 D.L.R. (4th) 476; *Gillies v. Keogh* [1989] 2 N.Z.L.R. 327.

54 *Lloyds Bank v. Rossett* [1991] 1 A.C. 107; [1990] 1 All ER 1111; [1990] 2 W.L..R 867.

55 This description of the manner of constructive trust imposed as a result of a claim based on proprietary estoppel was adopted by the Court of Appeal in *Metall und Rohstoff AG v. Donaldson Lufkin & Jenrette Inc.* [1990] 1 Q.B. 391, 479; *Lac Minerals Ltd. v. International Corona Resources Ltd.* (1989) 61 D.L.R. (4th) 14, esp. 51 where the court refers to the prospective remedy imposed once the claim had been made out.

56 See Hayton [1993] L.Q.R. 485.

57 Nourse L.J. in *Stokes v. Anderson* [1991] 1 F.L.R. 391; Ferguson (1993) 109 L.Q.R. 114; Oakley *Constructive Trusts* (Sweet & Maxwell, 1997), pp.64–84.

58 Hayton [1990] Conv. 370; [1993] L.Q.R. 485.

undertakings. It is better to enforce in equity their common intention as expressed by their contracts so that commercial certainty is upheld.

The availability of equitable proprietary remedies

12–43 Lord Browne-Wilkinson held that there could be no retention of any rights in the deep discount payment by the bank because both parties intended that there be an outright transfer of that sum to the authority. The argument for the imposition of a resulting trust would be that there was no intention to make a voluntary and outright transfer of the property in circumstances where the contract is found to be void *ab initio*.[59] The radical restitutionary approach, effecting restitution as a remedy for unjust enrichment by subtraction of that enrichment, was considered expressly by their Lordships. For the most part the radical approach fairs badly before the House of Lords. Birks suggests that the role of the resulting trust is primarily restitutionary and that this form of resulting trust should be imposed in cases of mistaken payment or failure of consideration to reverse unjust enrichment.[60] However, it is submitted that these suggestions fall into the trap that Lord Browne-Wilkinson has identified: any intention to create a resulting trust is to be rebutted by the intention at the time of the transfer to make an outright transfer. As his Lordship held, there is a difficulty with establishing the role of the resulting trustee from the moment of receipt of the property at a time when there was no knowledge of the trusteeship.

12–44 The better approach, not addressed expressly by any of the courts in *Islington*, would be to extend the common intention constructive trust to commercial situations. Whereas this idea has been restricted to family home trusts, among the competing claims to resulting trusts, unjust enrichment and proprietary estoppel in that context, it is an idea which would appear to sit most comfortably in commercial situations. The weakness of the common intention constructive trust, as with all rules governing trusts of co-owned domestic land, is that it rests on a fiction. The fiction is that there has been some agreement between the parties, or some conduct tantamount to an agreement, which ought to form an institutional constructive trust (that is, one founded on the application of principle rather than being a discretionary remedy provided by the court). As a result of this fiction, a constructive trust is imposed to set out the parties' entitlements to the equitable interest in the land. This form of trust is imposed particularly where it is considered inequitable not to do so.

12–45 In the context of commercial contracts there *is* an agreement between the parties. In seeking to establish the equitable title to property passed under a void contract, it is submitted that the court ought to consider the common intention formed between the parties as to the title to that property. Given Lord Browne-Wilkinson's determination to recognise the intentions of the parties in refuting the possibility of a resulting trust, it would appear appropriate to recognise those intentions when considering the possibility of a constructive trust. This would also appear to address the concerns of Lord Goff and Lord Woolf that justice must be seen to be done and that the confidence of commercial people in the utility of English law must be promoted.

12–46 Lord Browne-Wilkinson rejected the possibility of a proprietary interest based on constructive trust on the basis that the English model of constructive

[59] In this regard, see Worthington, *Proprietary Interests in Commercial Transactions* (Oxford, 1996), p.xi.

[60] See Birks, "Restitution and Resulting trusts" in *Equity and Contemporary Legal Problems* (S. Goldstein ed., Jerusalem, 1992), p.335.

trust is institutional in nature, operating in response to the trustee's knowledge of some factor which ought to impact on his conscience sufficiently to warrant the imposition of such a constructive trust. On the facts of *Islington* it was found that the authority did not have knowledge of the status of the contract until it was declared to be *ultra vires* by the courts.

12–47 However, at that point there is another impact on the authority's conscience: it had already agreed with the bank that it would be bound by the termination provisions in its swap agreement (including calculation of interest and netting of transactions). It is submitted that this prior agreement ought to be sufficient to cause the authority to be bound by those terms of the swap contract with regard to the amount owed under the agreement. Similarly, such common intention as to termination and proprietary rights in assets transferred by arm's length market participants should be enforced by equity through the common intention constructive trust. In the event, the weakness of the market standard contracts for over-the-counter derivatives is that they do not cater sufficiently for retention of title in property. There is clearly an issue for ISDA and for the BBA to redraw its standard contracts to take account of this deficiency in counterparty protection. This is particularly so in the case of physically-settled transactions and transactions annexed to deep discount payments where title to the specific property transferred is of greater importance than receipt of its cash equivalent in a designated currency.

12–48 The issue which arises is: how can a void contract be given effect to in part? More specifically, if the swap contract is held to have been void *ab initio*, how can the termination provisions or retention of title clauses be effective still. There are two arguments on this basis. First, it is clear from *Re Goldcorp*[61] that if a contract is avoided by election of the parties, and property transferred under that contract can still be identified, a constructive trust will be imposed over that identifiable property. Therefore, there is a difference between the enforceability of a voidable contract and a void contract as a result of *Islington*.[62]

12–49 Secondly, it is submitted that it would be possible to sever the termination provisions from the economic provisions of the swap contract, as considered above. The risk management features of standard market financial documents introduce greater certainty and lessen the cash amounts required to be paid between market participants. Therefore, the identified policy of precluding the parties from entering into further damaging transactions does not apply in the context of a provision, such as a netting clause on termination, which reduces the net amount of the parties' exposure to one another. The validity of an instrument need not be compromised because some element of it is held to unenforceable.[63]

Undue influence

12–50 The issue of "suitability" clearly imports notions of unconscionable behaviour on the part of the seller of financial derivatives. As has been considered, the relationship of banker and client will not necessarily import a fiduciary relationship, although there are a number of situations in which a fiduciary relationship will arise: where the bank induces business by agreeing to become

---

[61] [1995] A.C. 74; also Worthington , *Proprietary Interests in Commercial Transactions* (Oxford, 1996).

[62] It is accepted that in *Islington* the property was no longer identifiable because the bank account into which the property had been paid had subsequently been run overdrawn on a number of occasions.

[63] *Gaskell v. King* (1809) 11 East. 165; *Gibbons v. Harper* (1831) 2 B. & Ad. 734.

financial advisor[64]; where the bank advises a customer to enter into a transaction[65]; and where the bank advises a person to enter into a transaction which is to his financial disadvantage without ensuring that he has taken independent advice.[66]

12–51 In the case of derivatives, liability potentially arises for advice given to a client with respect to selling financial derivatives. Where the client is reliant on the expertise of the adviser, there is a liability for the adviser not to exert undue influence over that client by selling him products which are to his financial detriment in situations where he has reposed trust in the adviser. The application of this principle in the recent mortgage cases has revolved around the relationship of "special tenderness" between husband and wife in securing borrowings over the family home. In those circumstances, the bank has been held to have a responsibility to ensure that the spouse who is acting to his or her financial disadvantage (as surety or co-mortgagor) must have received independent advice.

12–52 There is a different relationship between parties in the OTC derivatives market. The clients are sophisticated corporate entities or financial institutions, rather than ordinary members of the public.[67] Therefore, the clients are expected to be able to procure their own legal and accountancy advice. The advice given by the seller of the derivative is likely to be the only advice received by the buyer; either because the seller is the "house bank" to the buyer or is a specialist in the particular product sold. In either case, the client can properly rely on the advice that is given to him.

12–53 There is an overlap here with the tort of misstatement and the principle in *Hedley Byrne v. Heller*.[68] However, tortious remedies will not extend claims *in rem* where the plaintiff is seeking to recovery specific property provided as part of the transaction. This desire for a proprietary claim may arise in respect of a physically-settled transaction or a transaction in which securities are provided as a premium or fixed rate payment, or where compound interest is sought in respect of cash-settled transactions.

12–54 The finding of undue influence would provide a further unjust factor to found a claim in restitution. Where the seller profits from some unconscionable pressure on the client, those profits would constitute an unjust enrichment at the expense of the buyer, remediable by some restitutionary response. The appropriate response to remedy the enrichment would be a proprietary claim to recover the full amount of gain made and the full, potential loss to the buyer connected with the seller's use of the property.

12–55 It is submitted that another possible claim under the umbrella of suitability would arise where there was some undue influence on this model. The appropriate form of remedy would be the imposition of a constructive trust in line with the unconscionable nature of the transaction. Whether there is sufficient knowledge in the seller may not be apparent from the assertion as to whether or not the product sold was considered to be suitable at the time when it was sold. It is possible that the creation of a product which negligently exposed the buyer to

---

64 *Woods v. Martins Bank Ltd.* [1959] 1 Q.B. 55; *Standard Investments Ltd. v. Canadian Imperial Bank of Commerce* (1985) 22 D.L.R. (4th) 410.

65 *Lloyds Bank v. Bundy* [1975] Q.B. 326; *Royal Bank of Canada v. Hinds* (1978) 88 D.L.R. (3rd) 428.

66 *National Westminster Bank plc v. Morgan* [1985] A.C. 686; *Barclay's Bank v. O'Brien* [1993] 3 W.L.R. 786; *CIBC v. Pitt* [1993] 3 W.L.R. 786.

67 With the exception of some occasional retail business done with the private clients of investment banks.

68 *Hedley Byrne v. Heller* [1964] A.C. 465.

an unforeseen risk, would be an unsuitable product. Where the seller had advised the use of that structure and had prepared a pricing model and a risk model in connection with the transaction, it is submitted that that would be sufficient to constitute undue influence in circumstances where the client would naturally rely on the advice given to him by the seller.

Enforceability of illegal contracts

12–56 The local authority swaps cases revolve around the core finding of *ultra vires* in *Hazell*, but the issue may arise in other contexts where contracts are found to be void or unenforceable, such as the supervening illegality of the contract.[69] The long-established principles of equity in this context were redrawn by the House of Lords in the case of *Tinsley v. Milligan*.[70] The appeal concerned a lesbian couple who had concocted a fraudulent scheme to ensure that one of them would receive state benefits to which she would not otherwise have been entitled. M and T used the house as a lodging house that they ran as a joint business venture. This business provided the bulk of both parties' income. The property was registered in the sole name of T although both parties accepted that the property was owned jointly in equity. The purpose for the registration in T's sole name was to enable M to claim state benefits with T's full knowledge and assent. The relationship broke down and T moved out. T claimed absolute title to the house. M claimed that the house was held on trust for the parties in equal shares. T argued that M would be required to rely on her illegal conduct to establish this claim and that equity should not therefore operate to give M the benefits of her wrongdoing. The statement made by Lord Browne-Wilkinson in that case indicated that contracts are capable of being enforceable in part despite being intrinsically unlawful.

12–57 Lord Browne-Wilkinson held that:

> "(1) Property in chattels and land can pass under a contract which is illegal and therefore would have been unenforceable as a contract.
>
> (2) A plaintiff can at law enforce property rights so acquired provided that he does not need to rely on the illegal contract for any purpose other than providing the basis of his claim to a property right.
>
> (3) It is irrelevant that the illegality of the underlying agreement was either pleaded or emerged in evidence: if the plaintiff has acquired legal title under the illegal contract that is enough."

He considered the long-standing principle of Lord Eldon in *Muckleston v. Brown*[71] that in cases where the plaintiff seeks to rely on illegality to establish a trust, the proper response is to say "let the estate lie, where it falls" with the owner at common law rather than holding it on resulting trust. However, his Lordship found that the earlier cases also showed that the plaintiff ought to be entitled to rely on a resulting trust where she did not have to rely on her illegality to prove it. Relying on principles of trusts of homes set out in *Gissing v. Gissing*[72] and *Lloyds Bank v. Rosset*,[73] M was able to argue that she had acquired an equitable interest

[69] The emerging regulation of derivatives in the global context does mean that regulation, criminalisation and prohibition of are factors which emerge after market counterparties have begun to contract those derivatives products.

[70] [1993] 3 All E.R. 65; [1993] 3 W.L.R. 36.

[71] (1801) 6 Ves. 52 at 68–69.

[72] [1971] A.C. 886.

[73] [1991] 1 A.C. 107; [1990] 1 All E.R. 1111; [1990] 2 W.L.R. 867.

in the property. The illegality was raised by T in seeking to rebut M's claim. M did not have to rely on her own illegality because she was entitled to an equitable share in the property in any event.

12–58 Lord Browne-Wilkinson does describe the cases on trusts of homes as establishing the "creation of such an equitable interest does not depend upon a contractual obligation but on a common intention acted upon by the parties to their detriment". The form of trust that his Lordship appears to have in mind is a common intention constructive trust rather than a resulting trust as normally understood. It is submitted that the appropriate form of trust on the facts was a purchase price resulting trust arising from M's contribution to the acquisition of the property. To return to the earlier discussion of the nature of resulting trusts, it does appear that his Lordship is seeking to develop a resulting trust based on 'the common intention of the parties' rather than one which, *strictu sensu*, gives effect to the intention of the settlor. The whole drift of the law on resulting trust is therefore moving towards the establishment of remedial and discretionary principles rather than straightforward operation of law. On extending this thinking, it is not clear why the common intention of the parties evidenced by their *ultra vires* contract, cannot be effected to the extent that it is not *ultra vires*. In accordance with the doctrine of severance, as considered above, there appear to be equitable grounds for giving partial effect to contracts which are unenforceable *in toto*.

12–59 The dissenting speech of Lord Goff in *Tinsley* cites a number of authorities including *Tinker v. Tinker*[74] and *Re Emery*[75] as establishing the proposition that equity will not assist someone who transfer property to another in furtherance of a fraudulent or illegal design to establish an interest in the property disposed of. This approach is founded primarily on the ancient equitable maxim that he who comes to equity must come with clean hands and the fear that an extension of principle propounded by Lord Browne-Wilkinson would "open the door to far more unmeritorious cases". While there is a moral attraction to this approach, it does not deal with the fundamental property law issue "who else can assert title to the property?".

Conclusion

12–60 In considering commercial situations, the appropriate rules of equity should be a remedy by means of an equitable proprietary remedy should be made available to a party where the contractual agreement between the parties allocates title to the property transferred under the transaction, or the award of a proprietary remedy would accord with the common intention of the parties set out in agreement between the parties. It is similarly arguable that such a remedy ought to be available where there was some undue influence in the creation of the financial product, or either party was caused to be unjustly enriched at the expense of the other party, or where rescission is the appropriate remedy under a physically-settled transaction.

12–61 It is suggested that the usual defences of change of position and passing on would still obtain. Similarly, public policy would constitute an exception in such circumstances. A remedy by means of equitable compensation or by imposition of personal liability under constructive trust should be made available

---

[74] [1970] P. 136; [1970] 1 All E.R. 540.

[75] [1959] Ch. 410.

in cases of reckless risk-taking; or where the product was unsuitable; or if rescission is the appropriate remedy under a cash-settled transaction[76]; or if the risk taken, or the context in which the risk was taken, contravened some principle of public policy or of statute or of some other mandatory rule of law or equity. The courts' failure to enforce the credit enhancement and risk allocation provisions of the contracts and standard form agreements between the commercial parties to the swaps contracts, produces inequitable results between those parties, circumscribes the efficacy of English law in the context of financial agreements, and introduces further risk to financial markets by rendering otiose the terms of those standard form agreements.

12–62 The use of standard market contracts, particularly in the area of financial derivatives, sought to remove uncertainty and to control systemic risk by standardising the terms of over-the-counter agreements. Among these terms are provisions for the termination of contracts in a manner that reduces systemic risk while also reducing the immediate financial pressure on the parties to a contract on the happening of a termination event. The English courts have chosen to consider these contracts to be unenforceable. As a result, the markets' attempts to introduce effective, consensual, ad hoc regulation of the derivatives markets have been rendered ineffective.

12–63 What is not supportable is the dismay in the commercial community outside the United Kingdom which relies on English law. Lord Woolf referred to the need for a "modern test" in financial transactions based on foreseeability of loss.[77] As Lord Browne-Wilkinson found in *Target Holdings*[78] there is a need to break from the application of traditional rules of Equity to commercial situations and consider the commercial context for equity. Lord Nicholls has accepted the need to recognise inappropriate risk-taking by a fiduciary as a ground for a claim in equity.[79] In the context of financial contracts, equity must accept the need to account for risk and suitability of product. As a corollary to this, it must enforce the common intention of the parties as to the termination of financial contracts.

III. Restitutionary claims based on suitability

12–64 As considered above, there are cross-overs between the appropriate use of radical restitutionary techniques to reverse unjust enrichment and well-established equitable responses in situations where commercial transactions are terminated before their ordinary expiry. The swaps cases proceeded on the basis of claims both in restitution and in equity. The following outline of the suitability approach aims to consider those problems set out immediately above but from the standpoint of the restitution lawyer.

Restitution model

12–65 It is submitted that restitution by means of a personal remedy or by means of equitable compensation should be made available to a party where a transaction is caused to be terminated as a result of some event which occurred

[76] Absent any remedy identified as a proprietary remedy above.

[77] *Islington* [1996] A.C. 669; [1996] 2 All E.R. 961 at 1016; citing, with approval, Mann, "On Interest, Compound Interest and Damages" (1985) 101 L.Q.R. 30.

[78] [1996] 1 A.C. 421.

[79] *Royal Brunei Airlines v. Tan* [1995] 2 A.C. 378.

outwith the risks allocated expressly by the parties as part of their transacting, where the non-allocation of that risk can be identified as being the fault of one contracting party in the following circumstances. Restitution of unjust enrichment ought to be ordered where a risk was not allocated between the parties by means of their contract and, as a result of some unjust factor, either party was caused to be unjustly enriched at the expense of the other party. Alternatively, where a risk was taken by the defaulting party, that risk was a reckless risk for that defaulting party to have taken in that context, a personal claim for restitution should be ordered.

12–66 Two further situations in which a personal claim in restitution should be ordered where the parties were of unequal bargaining strength, the product or service provided by the stronger party was not suitable for the contractually-identified purposes of the weaker party in the context of that transaction; or if the risk taken, or the context in which the risk was taken, contravened some principle of public policy or of statute or of some other mandatory rule of law or equity.

12–67 The following sections consider aspects of the laws of restitution, contract and principles of equity which were not considered in the swaps cases but which, it is submitted, would be of potential importance in financial derivatives litigation in future.

Mispredictions

12–68 The business of financial derivatives revolves around predictions as to future market movements. In considering the suitability of products, and the potentially available remedies, a further question arises as to the more general liability for 'mispredictions'. This issue can arise in a number of guises. At one level it concerns the availability of torts of misrepresentation and misstatement. At a second level it concerns issue of the enforceability of contractual liabilities based on misrepresentation. The third is the area of the possibility of restitution in situations where there has been a misprediction which would lead to an unjust enrichment or some actionable claim for a restitutionary response. The fourth category would arise out of estoppel. There is not the space here to consider the scope of the torts or strictly contractual categories.

12–69 The restitutionary issue is perhaps interesting. A misprediction in this area can be described as a misjudgment as to what will happen in the future. The availability of a restitutionary category of misprediction is illustrated by Birks by reference to the case of *Barder v. Caluori*[80] where a wife killed her children and herself by destroying the home which was to be passed to her former husband as part of their divorce settlement. As part of the settlement, an amount had been set for the value of the property. The question arose whether there was a remedy based on restitution available for misprediction of the value and condition of property in these circumstances.

12–70 Birks' general view is based on the principle that a claim for restitution cannot be founded on a misprediction. However, he refines the general principle such that it applies strictly in cases of mistake.[81] Where the misprediction arises in the situation where an advisor specifies the circumstances in which it is anticipated that certain events will take place and Birks contends that an action based on failure of consideration is more likely but that the claim should be founded on

---

[80] [1988] A.C. 20.

[81] Birks, *Introduction to the Law of Restitution* (Oxford, 1989), p.451.

failure of basis.[82] As Birks provides, this restriction is important "otherwise it would be difficult to explain to anyone why restitution should not always follow when any risk turns out badly".[83]

12–71 In the example of *Barder*, Birks considers that the basis of the transaction relating to the house within the context of the divorce settlement was built on the condition of the house. It is difficult why, in principle, this approach should differ from advice given by a financial institution with reference to the utility of a derivative product. The uncertainty that forms the basis for the transaction is the movement of rates creating a risk which the purchaser seeks to manage. The claim in restitution would be based on the understanding of the risks which was communicated between the parties in setting up the transaction. There are two potential categories of issue: resultant loss caused by unanticipated movements in market rates (*failure of model*) and loss caused by a reckless level of risk being taken by the buyer on the advice of the seller (*suitability failure*).[84]

12–72 In the context of "model failure", the allocation of risks lies with the adviser in seeking to match market volatility with the forecasts and assessments set out in the pricing model. Failure to anticipate all of the resultant movements may stem from negligence and thereby be actionable in tort. The issue would arise as to the foreseeability of the loss actually suffered. Alternatively, the buyer could seek restitution on the basis of a failure of basis: that is, the perpetuation of anticipated market conditions. In reference to options on equity markets, for example, it would be advantageous to the commercial parties to specify a maximum volatility that they anticipate in the market, such that excess volatility (outside their expectations or common intentions) would be discounted. It is submitted that volatility outwith those boundaries would give rise to a claim founded on failure of basis.

12–73 The claim based on "suitability failure" would arise where the risk which the buyer sought to manage was not met by the risk inherent in the product bought. For example, the use of an interest rate swap which did not pay an interest rate to the buyer equivalent to the size of risk inherent in its existing debt portfolio (a rate equal to x), but rather one which contained an element of speculation (thus specifying a rate equal to $x+y$). The element that equalled y would be unnecessary for the purposes of debt management. The factor to be proved by the buyer claiming suitability failure would be that the element y constituted an unsuitable addition of risk that went beyond the basis upon which the transaction was created. It may be that the element y arises from market disruption that the parties had not foreseen but which was not covered by the contract. Alternatively, y might be an element which was knowingly added to the transaction but which constituted an unacceptable increase in the risk incumbent on the buyer.[85]

12–74 Restitution on a ground similar to this was illustrated in *Muschinski v. Dodds*.[86] That appeal concerned a joint venture between a man and a woman to build a house on a plot of land. The woman was to provide the money for the purchase. The

---

[82] Birks, *Introduction to the Law of Restitution* (Oxford, 1989) at p.219.

[83] *ibid.* at p.451.

[84] At this level there is a potential claim, as considered above with reference to reckless risk-taking.

[85] It was this latter, factual category which founded Proctor and Gamble's claim against Bankers Trust in relation to a claim for a loss of approximately U.S.$160 million caused by the selling of "high octane swaps" for the corporate party's debt management which had an in-built exposure to speculative movements in the underlying markets. The corporate party brought the action on the basis of the bank's allegedly negligent advice in selling the product without recognising its unsuitability both for the purpose and the particular buyer.

[86] (1986) 60 A.L.J.R. 55.

man was to provide some value by dint of his work on the property. He would also put forward some money to the project when his divorce was settled. The venture failed when planning permission for construction on the site was refused. The ensuing strain brought an end to the joint venturers' personal relationship.

12–75 The majority saw the case as one of failure of basis. The dissenting judges (Brennan and Dawson JJ.) considered the case to be one of constructive trust in which property should be distributed according to the agreed shares between the parties. The former approach is based on the restitutionary response to the change of anticipated circumstances. The latter approach mirrors the English courts' development of common intention constructive trusts, considered below.

12–76 On failure of basis, the High Court of Australia in *Muschinski v. Dodds*[87] Deane J. held that:

> "The circumstances giving rise to the operation of the principle were broadly identified by Lord Cairns, L.C., speaking for the Court of Appeal in Chancery, in *Atwood v. Maude*[88] : where 'the case is one in which, using the words of Lord Cottenham in *Hirst v. Tolson* [89] a payment has been made by anticipation of something afterwards to be enjoyed [and] where ... circumstances arise so that the future enjoyment is denied.'[90] Those circumstances can be more precisely defined by saying that *the principle operates in a case where the substratum of a joint relationship or endeavour is removed without attributable blame* and where the benefit of money or other property contributed by one party on the basis and for the purposes of the relationship or endeavour would otherwise be enjoyed by the other party in the circumstances on which it was not specifically intended or specially provided that the other party should enjoy it. The content of the principle is that, in such a case, equity will not permit that other party to assert or retain the benefit of the relevant property to the extent that it would be unconscionable for him to do so."[91]

It is interesting to note that the principle is stated to be without attributable blame, whereas its application in the financial context is as likely to be in cases where the contention is based on the fault of the seller rather than redressing the impact on the buyer.

12–77 However, where the financial institution realises a substantial profit under the transaction, by analogy that profit would be restored to the buyer where it would be unconscionable to retain it. In accordance with the discussion [above, suitability as unjust factor], it is submitted that the better ground for this approach in commercial cases would be where the product created by the seller is unsuitable for the purpose desired by the buyer and communicated to the seller. It is on this basis that unsuitability of product, extended in circumstances where there is a failure of basis, should give rise to a restitutionary response.

12–78 There is no proprietary claim against a dishonest assistant, *i.e.* one who does not receive trust property.[92] Therefore, a personal liability to account as a constructive trustee would attach to a financial institution, in connection with a

---

[87] (1986) 60 A.L.J.R. 55 at 67.

[88] (1868) 3 Ch. App. 369 at 375.

[89] (1850) 2 Mac. & G. 134; 42 E.R. 52.

[90] In *Atwood* the court allowed an order for repayment of a proportionate part of premium where the plaintiff had paid towards the establishment of a partnership which was then dissolved without the fault of either partner.

[91] (1986) 60 A.L.J.R. 55 at 67.

misprediction that was held to be "dishonest", which arranges or brokers a derivatives product without acquiring any of the property. Thus, in the context of a credit derivatives or some warrant issues or swaps embedded in bond issues, there would be liability on the broker for taking "reckless risks" even where that person does not receive any of the underlying property.[93]

IV. General tort claims relating to suitability

12–79 The preceding discussion relates to the availability of proprietary remedies resulting from equitable claims or restitutionary claims, as well as personal remedies based on both of those codes. The following brief section considers the available common law claims based on wrongs rather than on restitutionary or equitable motivations. There is a narrow line in commercial reality between a wrong caused by one party arising out of negligence and a wrong caused by a party arising out of dishonest assistance in a breach of trust. The former is classified as a tort whereas the latter is classified as an action giving rise to a personal remedy under constructive trust.[94] The following remedies are available in situations where the torts referred to have been committed. The reason for dealing with these remedies separately is to evaluate, albeit briefly, the contexts in which the law of tort would ordinarily deal with the termination of transactions, rather than the equitable and restitutionary issues considered thus far.

12–80 It is contended that the expectations of commercial participants in the derivatives markets would usually require more than damages equivalent to out-of-pocket loss where that measure would not incorporate the full loss occasioned by the loss of proprietary rights in property, or of the profits that would otherwise have been made had the property tied up in the void transaction been available for other investment. The issue of physically-settled transactions has been discussed. To some extent, tortious damages will deal with the loss that is suffered from not having possession of the goods which were required under the transaction as had been agreed to. However, with reference to transactions settled "either way",[95] or transactions where a hedging position is lost because of the failure of the commercial effects of the transaction,[96] the tortious damages approach will not necessarily equate with the contractual expectation of rights in property or damages which include, for example, compound interest to reflect the expectation of the increased profit secured by a right in property. Where the contract is not enforced by the courts, this common intention would be frustrated, leaving only restitutionary claims or claims in tort.

---

92 Hanbury and Martin, *Modern Equity* (13th ed., Sweet & Maxwell, 1993), p.666; Oakley (1995) 54 C.L.J. 377, at 383.

93 This liability is different from the liability of a trustee in a eurobond transaction, for example: see Tennekoon, *Legal Aspect of International Finance* (Butterworths, 1992).

94 The latter could also be explained as giving a remedy based on unjust enrichment. That it is said to be a remedy in truth and not an institutional trust device is based on the fact that the award is purely personal in nature and ordered to reverse the wrong that has been done.

95 That is, transactions which are capable of being translated into either cash-settled or physically-settled transactions at the option of the buyer.

96 Which would not appear to satisfy the test for proximity arising out of the decision of the Court of Appeal in *Kleinwort Benson v. Birmingham C.C.* [1996] 4 All E.R. 75.

Wrongs in selling swaps

The Dharmala case

12–81 Perhaps the leading case in this area is the decision of Mance J. in the case of *Dharmala*.[97] This case summarises precisely the issues which are specific to the selling of financial derivatives in general and interest rate swaps in particular.[98] It is therefore proposed to consider the range of claims and factual issues that arose in that litigation before referring them to the specific discussions of each form of contractual, tortious, equitable and restitutionary liability considered below.

12–82 Bankers Trust (BT) sold two forms of interest rate swap to Dharmala (DSS) on which DSS lost money. The litigation centres on BT's attempts to recover money owed to it under the transactions and DSS's concomitant attempts to deny any liability for amounts owed under the transactions. DSS argued most of the range of tortious and contractual claims considered in this *suitability* section: the concept of the unsuitability of the products sold appears in their basic contentions. DSS contended that BT were liable for negligent misrepresentation, deceit in the course of selling the products, and breach of contract.

12–83 DSS was an Indonesian entity with whom BT had had dealings before. On the facts ultimately Mance J. found that the employees of DSS involved in the transaction had received sufficient attention and advice from BT. Furthermore, however, it was found that in DSS, BT had a counterparty who could be expected to have some experience of the financial derivatives markets, being a financial institution, despite the complexity of the products which BT were designing. Importantly, it could be anticipated that DSS would be able to undertake their own evaluation of the products which were suggested to them by BT. However, Mance J. highlights the need to consider the specific relationship between buyer and seller before reaching a decision on the precise nature and extent of the obligations owed.

The nature of the claims

12–84 In response to BT's action for money owed, DSS counter-claimed a long series of common law actions which revolve around the common theme of the suitability of the products sold and the manner in which they were sold and manufactured.[99]

12–85 The claims based on consent, as that term is defined for the purposes of this discussion, were as follows. First, that BT misrepresented the terms of Swap 1. DSS claimed in particular that it had been led to believe that the products had a low likelihood of generating a loss for DSS. DSS also contended misrepresentation on the basis that it understood that complete and accurate economic information had been supplied by BT which induced DSS to enter into the transactions. DSS also relied on alleged representations that BT would replace the transactions at no cost if there were some loss to DSS. The same arguments

---

[97] *Bankers Trust International PLC v. PT Dharmala Sakti Sejahtera* [1996] C.L.C. 518; see also Picarda, "Interest Rate Swap Agreements in the Courts" [1996] B.J.I.B.F.L. 170.

[98] For a particularly useful summary of the decision, see the Financial Law Panel's "*Bankers Trust v. PT Dharmala Sakti Sejahtera*: Case Summary" (London, Financial Law Panel, January 1996).

[99] As a matter of Indonesian law, DSS also claimed that it did not have the capacity to enter into these transactions. It is not proposed to consider this point of Indonesian law in the following discussion.

related to Swap 2 with the addition of an argument that BT had represented that Swap 2 would be better for DSS than Swap 1.

12–86 Secondly, DSS argued that there had been deceit on the part of a specific employee of BT. On these facts DSS alleged that BT had represented that there could only be profit under the transactions, whereas correspondence and marketing material made little or no mention of the risks involved. Thirdly, it was contended that BT's alleged representation that the transactions would be replaced at no cost constituted a collateral contract, if not a term of the contract itself. The claim on behalf of the buyer is this supported by allegations relating to conversations and communications passed between its agents and the seller's agents. In circumstances where there is little or not documentation[100] it becomes more difficult for the seller to establish the full extent of the obligations which were agreed between the parties. Reliance solely on tape recorded evidence of conversations and the buyer's understanding of those issues which must have formed part of its necessary understanding of the effectiveness of the contract, make it difficult for the seller to demonstrate that its liability was to be restricted to particular express contractual terms only.

12–87 Fourthly, breach of duty culminating in negligence. DSS contended that BT were experienced dealers in the products at issue in a way that DSS were not. Consequently, DSS sought to fix BT with a duty in negligence to establish the level of competence that DSS had, to explain all risks to DSS, to consider the particular objectives of DSS, and to ensure DSS took independent advice. The further argument raised by DSS revolved then around a presumed positive obligation on the part of the seller to consider the particular objectives of DSS, and in particular whether or not there were other products or methods which DSS could have used to achieve the risk management requirements it had. The final argument that BT ought to have ensured that DSS took independent advice strays close to undue influence without raising an argument that DSS has necessarily been unduly influenced in a way that ought to have required independent advice.[101]

Judging suitability

12–88 Mance J. held that in respect of the claim for misrepresentation most of DSS's contentions were simply not supported by the facts. His Lordship was critical of BT because the seller's marketing material tended to emphasise the likelihood of gain rather than the risks of the loss, and further that that material might have given a misleading impression of the effect of the product. First, Mance J. found expressly that such a transaction would have founded liability for the tort of misrepresentation in respect of an inexperienced counterparty. On the facts, however, DSS appeared to be suitably experienced and diligent to form its own, independent assessment of the effect and risk of the swaps proposed by BT. Mance J. thus emphasises the relativity involved in assessing potential liability in this context. A counterparty which was demonstrably incapable of ascertaining the risks involved, or a counterparty which had not been as proactive as DSS in

[100] An issue which did not arise in *Dharmala*.

[101] Similar perhaps to the obligations set out in *Barclays Bank v. O'Brien* [1994] 1 A.C. 180, although that obligation to ensure taking of independent advice is strictly linked to the avoidance of constructive notice of the undue influence or misrepresentation of another person in relation to mortgages and similar surety arrangements.

pursuing these particular structures and relying more on the seller, would appear to have good grounds for a claim based on misrepresentation.

12–89 Secondly, in relation to deceit it was held on the facts that the particular employee of BT in question was honest at all times and had no intention to deceive DSS, nor had he been reckless as to whether or not he deceived DSS. Liability is therefore possible but subject to the buyer's claim coming up to proof. Thirdly, as to the enforceability of the alleged representation of replacement of the transaction at no cost, Mance J. found that it was implausible to suggest that BT had offered to replace the transaction. On the facts, it appeared that BT might have offered a restructuring package if the swap ultimately proved to be unprofitable for DSS.

12–90 Fourthly, as to the general claim based on "breach of duty", Mance J. found that many of DSS's requirements for the swaps had not been communicated fully to BT to the extent that the were alleged by DSS to have existed in any event. Further, economists' predictions of the future movement of the U.S. economy which had been supplied by BT were reasonably made and based on detailed research. As such, it was held, BT ought to have no liability based on the outcome of those economic predictions that had not, in themselves, caused DSS to enter into the transactions.

12–91 Importantly, in general terms, there was no duty on BT to act as general adviser to DSS. Furthermore, Mance J. was explicit in his finding that the courts should not assume such duties in all cases. A duty of care, under any of the heads sought be DSS, should be inferred only where it was justified on the particular facts. DSS were experienced in financial matters and as such should be expected to understand the partially speculative nature of the transactions. On these facts, it was held, there was no reason for BT to be saddled with a responsibility to advise DSS generally in the manner suggested by DSS's counter-claim.

12–92 Similarly, in *Morgan Stanley UK Group v. Puglisi Cosentino*[102] the plaintiff bank, MS, sold a principal exchange rate linked security (PERL) to the defendant, P. The PERL was made up of a U.S. $-denominated bond which would increase in value against redemption where specified hard currencies depreciated in value, whereas soft currencies appreciated. It was a part of the agreement between the parties that P would repurchase the security at specified reset dates in the future and it was understood that MS would in fact roll over the security at those times. In the event, devaluation of the Italian lira and the Spanish peseta meant that MS did not roll over as expected. MS then sought U.S.$ 6.6 million from P when the PERL was sold at a loss. P claimed damages in similar amount under section 62 of the Financial Services Act 1986 on the basis that MS had breached TSA rules.

12–93 It was found that the selling bank had been in breach of TSA rule 980.01 in advising P to enter into the transaction as a private customer. The PERL constituted a contract for differences within paragraph 9 of Schedule 1 of the Financial Services Act 1986. The contracts therefore fell within rule 1300.02 of the TSA Rules as being margined transactions in a derivative instrument. Further MS was in breach of rule 730 on the basis that the instruments were not suitable transactions for P. It was a sufficient defence to the bank's claim for P to show that P would not have entered into the transactions if it had received proper advice from MS, including an appropriate risk warning. There was, however, no evidence of undue pressure having been put on P.

---

[102] [1998] C.L.C. 481.

Comparison with the USA

12–94 The main litigation in the USA[103] has concerned large corporate entities claiming exploitation by financial institutions, *Gibson Greetings v. Bankers Trust Co.*[104] and *Proctor and Gamble v. Bankers Trust Co.*,[105] or in relation to the powers of local authorities, *Orange County Investment Pool v. Merrill Lynch & Co.*,[106] and *State of West Virginia v. Morgan Stanley & Co. Inc.*,[107] among others.[108] Where there is an interesting overlap to observe is in the emergence of suitability as a concept within SFA regulation in the United Kingdom[109] akin to the concept of suitability within U.S. regulatory regimes.[110] In the U.S. litigation, "suitability" emerged as a concept by which the liability of the seller could be measured. Therefore, it crossed into substantive legal claims rather than remaining solely applicable to regulatory rules.

12–95 The suitability claim in this context is said to fall into two forms: the *pure suitability* claim and the *disclosure suitability* claim.[111] The former relates to some contumelious failure by the seller to deal with integrity and fairness; the latter refers to a failure on the part of the seller to explain a material risk to an unsophisticated buyer. These potential claims stem from the provisions of NYSE[112] and NASD[113] rule-books which create suitability requirements. While it is not clear whether or not the courts would enforce these rules as private law claims, the specific suitability requirements are said to constitute bases on which the courts' understanding of the nature of those claims should be based. Contrary to the risks associated with mis-selling derivatives, there are the personal risks taken by the officers of the buyer in entering into these products. In one decided U.S. case, directors have been held liable by shareholders for failing to protect the company against market movements by means of hedging derivatives.[114] Alternatively, those directors also run the risk of litigation where their use of derivatives causes loss to the company.[115]

---

[103] See, for example, Henderson, "Derivatives Litigation in the United States" in *Swaps and Off-Exchange Derivatives Trading: Law and Regulation* (Bettelheim, Parry and Rees eds, FT Law and Tax, 1996), p.211.

[104] Civil Action No. C-1-94-620 (S.D. Ohio, filed September 12, 1994).

[105] Civil Action No. C-1-94-735 (S.D. Ohio, filed February 6, 1995).

[106] Ch. 9 Case No. SA 94-22272-JR, Adv. No. SA 94-1045-JR (C.D.BR. Cal., filed January 12, 1995).

[107] Civil Action No. 89-C-3700 (Cir. Ct. Kanawha Co.).

[108] *Chemical Bank v. Washington Power System* 99 Wash. 2d 772 (1983); *Lehman Bros. v. Minmetals* 94 Civ. 8301 (S.D.N.Y.); *Lehman Bros. v. China International* 94 Civ. 8304 (S.D.N.Y.).

[109] Rule 5-31, SFA Rules, considered in *Financial Regulation* below.

[110] See for example, Craig and Hume, "Nightmare 2—Customers: recent litigation between derivatives dealers and their customers involving issues of fraud, breach of fiduciary duty, suitability, etc. and regulator and industry response" (1995) *Columbia Law Review* 167.

[111] Scott, "Liability of Derivatives Dealers" (Oditah ed., Oxford, Clarendon Press, 1996), pp.271, 277.

[112] New York Stock Exchange "Know Your Customer Rule", CCH NYSE Guide, sec. 2405.

[113] National Association of Securities Dealers' Suitability Rule, CCH NASD Manual, sec. 2152 (Art. III, sec. 2).

[114] *Brane v. Roth* 590 NE 2d 587 (Ind App 1 dist 1992).

[115] See Henderson, *op. cit*, who explains that shareholders in Proctor and Gamble brought litigation against directors of that company in the wake of litigation with Bankers Trust: *Elaine Drage et al v. Proctor & Gamble et al*, Court of Common Pleas, Hamilton County, April 1994.

Tort of negligent misrepresentation

12–96 In order to recover damages based on the tort of negligent misrepresentation, the plaintiff must establish that the defendant owed him a duty of care not to cause loss or damage of the kind caused by breach of that duty. Three criteria for the imposition of a duty of care in a particular situation: foreseeability of damage, proximity of relationship and reasonableness.[116]

12–97 The first criterion is proximity. That is, the closeness and directness of the relationship between the parties is particularly important. In evaluating proximity in the context of claims arising from inaccurate statements or advice, three factors are critical: purpose, knowledge and reliance: meaning the purpose for which the statement was made and communicated, the knowledge of the maker of the statement, and reliance by its recipient. The position was expressed as follows by Lord Oliver in *Caparo Industries plc v. Dickman*:[117]

> "What can be deduced from the *Hedley Byrne*[118] case, therefore, is that the necessary relationship between the maker of a statement or giver of advice (the adviser) and the recipient who acts in reliance on it (the advisee) may typically be held to exist where (1) the advice is required for a purpose, whether particularly specified or generally described, which is made known, either actually or inferentially, to the adviser at the time when the advice is given, (2) the adviser knows, either actually or inferentially, that his advice will be communicated to the advisee, either specifically or as a member of an ascertainable class, in order that it should be used by the advisee for that purpose, (3) it is known, either actually or inferentially, that the advice so communicated is likely to be acted upon by the advisee for that purpose without independent inquiry and (4) it is so acted on by the advisee to his detriment. That is not, of course, to suggest that these conditions are either conclusive or exclusive, but merely that the actual decision in the case does not warrant any broader propositions."

The burden of proving each ingredient of this cause of action is upon the plaintiff. The measure of damages is that appropriate to a claim in tort. The context of misrepresentation is important for the seller of a derivative product who also gives advice on which the other party reasonably relies. Particularly in new markets such as that for credit derivatives where the buyer of the product is acquiring it to effect some form of insurance for an exposure to a parties' credit, or to speculate on that same credit, the buyer will rely on the minutiae of the advice that is given by the seller. Typically, this advice will be a mixture of fact, matter which is asserted to be fact, and opinion. Where markets move unexpectedly, there will be a question as to whether or not the seller asserted that the product would provide cover for those particular market movements. Similarly, there will be the issue as to whether or not the seller made the buyer aware that those particular risks were being taken. The issue of the "closer relationship" will also depend on whether the advice was taken at arm's length in the market or whether the buyer was used to relying completely on the advice given to it by seller: for example, where the seller is the house lending bank to the seller.

---

[116] See *Smith v. Bush* [1990] 1 A.C. 861, HL at 865, *per* Lord Griffiths and also *Caparo Industries plc v. Dickman* [1990] 2 A.C. 605.

[117] [1990] 2 A.C. 605.

[118] [1964] A.C. 465.

12–98 It is contended that each of these factual situations may move closer to equity or restitution. For example, where the seller is the house bank to the buyer, it might be that there is some undue influence that could be said to result from the nature of the relationship between those parties. For the seller to make profit and acquire property from the buyer as a result of an abuse of position, would seem to require some restitutionary response if the reliance could properly be classified as an "abuse". There is nothing new in the assertion that the edges of the lines between wrongs, obligations and equity or unjust enrichment are potentially blurred. The aim of the suitability approach is to place the appropriate tests in context such that the courts would have the flexibility to put the parties in the position which they would have wished to occupy and which equity thinks it appropriate for them to occupy.

Tort of negligent misstatement

12–99 All that is said above with reference to the tort of negligent misrepresentation in the context of financial transactions, will hold true for negligent misstatement. In a number of recently decided decisions, tort has expanded into the finance field with the effect of broadening the potential liability of those selling financial products or making representations as to the effect or suitability of such products. Important in this regard was the decision in *Possfund Custodian Trustee Ltd v. Victor Derek Diamond*[119] *per* Lightman J., a case which concerned the liability of those preparing share prospectuses for capital issues to those persons buying the shares in the secondary market, who would not have been specifically within the contemplation of the person preparing the prospectus, although they could have been expected to have relied on the information contained in it. The test set out in this context drew on the principle in *Hedley Byrne v. Heller*, [120] when Lightman J. held that[121]:

> "It is clearly established that in a case such as the present, where the defendants have put a document into more or less general circulation and there is no special relationship alleged between the plaintiffs and the defendants, forseeability by the defendants that the plaintiffs would rely on the prospects for the purpose of deciding whether to make after-market purchases is not sufficient to impose upon the defendants a duty of care to the plaintiffs in respect of such purchases (see *Caparo Industries plc v. Dickman*[122]). The imposition of a duty of care in such a situation requires a closer relationship between representor and representee, and its imposition must be fair, just and reasonable."

There is some resonance of equitable principle in the application of the award here. That the award must be "fair, just and reasonable" moves closer to the tests of unconscionability which Lord Nicholls was astute to deny as a general test in *Royal Brunei Airlines v. Tan.*[123] The suitability approach requires that inequitable wrongdoing is capable of generating personal or proprietary remedies as appropriate. Evidently, there will be overlaps between compensation or personal liability awards under equity and damages awards under tortious principles. The

[119] [1996] 2 All E.R. 774.

[120] [1964] 2 A.C. 465.

[121] In *Possfund Custodian Trustee Ltd v. Victor Derek Diamond* [1996] 2 All E.R. 782.

[122] [1990] A.C. 605.

[123] [1995] 2 A.C. 378.

primary distinction between the two codes will be the availability of proprietary awards and awards such as compound interest.

Damages for breach of contract

12–100 Failure of the contract may, of course, arise in a number of contexts. Roughly those contexts could be divided in a straightforward failure to perform the contract where performance would be possible in legal terms, and cases in which the contract is not performed because its performance is prohibited by law or by some court order. In principle, a statement in a document selling a derivative product or in some conversation between the trader and the counterparty may become incorporated as a term of the contract between the counterparties. Where that term is material to the transaction and the parties' mutual intentions. It is submitted that the failure to perform such a term may constitute a breach of the contract or may be bound up in some larger issue of the efficacy of the contract. This latter option is over and above general damages for breach of contract. It is not proposed to spend much time on breach of contract damages other than to make the point that the test for suitability set out in this section is concerned with the application of restitutionary and equitable principles to cases where financial transactions cease to be operative. It is submitted that failure to perform a contract ought to give rise to damages for breach of contract in the ordinary way. The situation considered in the *Islington* appeal was one of absence or failure of consideration rather than a failure by one of the parties to perform out of some contumelious intent. It is only the situation of lack of capacity or of ability to perform that is meant to be covered by this test of suitability.

V. A new test of suitability

12–101 The following principles are prepared on the basis of analysis of the preceding discussion of cases in equity and in restitution. They do not purport to be a straightforward crystallisation of the principles as set out in those cases. However, they do purport to be a feasible application of those principles to the context of the termination of commercial transactions and the allocation of personal or restitutionary claims as a result. The section immediately following the statement of principles seeks to demonstrate how those principles should be applied in cases relating to financial derivatives to reach the most equitable solutions to those legal issues which arose in the swaps cases.

(1) Equity Model

12–102 In considering commercial situations, the appropriate *rules of equity* should be:

(a) remedy by means of an equitable proprietary remedy should be made available to a party where:

- the contractual agreement between the parties allocates title to the property transferred under the transaction; or
- if the parties were of unequal bargaining strength, the product or service provided by the stronger party was provided in a context where the buyer would normally rely on the advice of the seller and there was some undue influence in the creation of that product; or
- if a risk was allocated between the parties, where as a result of some un-

just factor, the either party was caused to be unjustly enriched at the expense of the other party; or

- if rescission is the appropriate remedy under a physically-settled transaction, where the traceable proceeds of the original transfer remain in the hands of the recipient; or
- the award of a proprietary remedy would accord with the common intention of the parties set out in agreement between the parties.

(b) remedy by means of equitable compensation or by imposition of personal liability under constructive trust should be made available to a party where a transaction is caused to be terminated where:

- if a risk was not assumed by either party, where as a result of some unjust factor either party was caused to be unjustly enriched at the expense of the other party; or
- if a risk was taken by either party, that risk was a reckless risk for that party to have taken in that context; or
- if the parties were of unequal bargaining strength, the product or service provided by the stronger party was not suitable for the purposes of the weaker party in the context of that transaction; or
- if rescission is the appropriate remedy under a cash-settled transaction; or
- if the risk taken, or the context in which the risk was taken, contravened some principle of public policy or of statute or of some other mandatory rule of law or equity.

(2) Restitution Model

12–103 Restitution by means of a personal remedy or by means of equitable compensation should be made available to a party where a transaction is caused to be terminated as a result of some event which *occurred outwith the risks allocated expressly by the parties as part of their transacting*, where the non-allocation of that risk can be identified as being the fault of one contracting party, particularly:

- if such risk was not assumed by either party, where as a result of some unjust factor either party was caused to be unjustly enriched at the expense of the other party; or
- if a risk was taken by the defaulting party, that risk was a reckless risk for that defaulting party to have taken in that context; or
- if the parties were of unequal bargaining strength, the product or service provided by the stronger party was not suitable for the contractually-identified purposes of the weaker party in the context of that transaction; or
- if the risk taken, or the context in which the risk was taken, contravened some principle of public policy or of statute or of some other mandatory rule of law or equity.

Applying the suitability approach

12–104 The preceding outlines of the test follow on from the previous discussion of the availability of equitable and restitutionary responses to the treatment of financial transactions. In line with the discussion that opened this book it is appropriate to revisit the themes and concerns which have brought us to this stage.

12–105 The *Islington* litigation has generated enormous concern among commercial people. At one level that concern is simply grounded in the fact that the banks did not get what they wanted. On another level the concern is based on a concern that the technical rules surrounding compound interest precluded the parties from terminating their transaction on payment of the amounts which commercial people would have expected to have become due. There are larger concerns as to the efficacy of standard market agreements, totally ignored by the English courts in the local authority swaps cases, which were framed by market users as an ad hoc regulation of systemic risk in the derivatives market. This failure to apply the terms of those contracts raises problems generally of the way in which proprietary rights could be asserted in financial contracts in future in a way which guards against the failure of the contract itself, and also of the ability of globalised marketplaces to rely on English law to assist them in standardising risk by means of documentation and thus controlling it.

12–106 There are a plethora of fascinating questions for the legal technician arising from that same litigation. First is the conflict between equity and restitution. Restitution of unjust enrichment is championed by a group of academics who see it as a means of balancing out the laws of obligations and wrongs with a third code that prevents cases of injustice slipping between the cracks in the common law and statute. The equity lawyers see that as their preserve. As such, Lord Browne-Wilkinson went to great lengths in *Islington* to dismiss the applicability or utility of Birks' model of the resulting trust motivated by restitution and to set out the fundamental principles of the law of trusts which were to deal with the issue instead.[124]

12–107 The scope of the argument in the House of Lords was between the generations of restitution lawyers (typified by Lord Goff), the traditional trusts lawyers (the majority in the House of Lords in *Islington*) and the realpolitik commercial lawyers (typified by Lord Woolf). Within these ranks are the new restitution lawyers such as Birks who are motivated by more technically-focused analyses of property rules and unjust enrichment than Lord Goff's desire to achieve 'justice' through an award of compound interest. Similarly, Lord Browne-Wilkinson is identified as a 'traditional' trusts lawyer in this work despite countenancing a need for equity to develop in commercial situations and move away rules which were originally founded to deal with family trust situations.[125] Similarly, Hayton has argued for the introduction of a form of constructive trust which gives the judges greater freedom to frame appropriate remedies for the facts in front of them.[126] This book has drawn on Hayton's example to frame a form of common intention constructive trust that would be suitable for equity to examine financial and commercial transactions.

12–108 Secondly, among the interesting features of *Islington* is the role of risk in commercial equity. While the courts in the swaps cases were quick to dismiss any argument based on risk allocation (despite the terms of the contracts effected between the parties), there are a number of recent cases dealing with equitable institutions and remedies which have concentrated as risk as a litmus test for the availability of the equitable response sought. For example, the test for dishonest assistance expressly incorporates reckless risk-taking as being among its definition of "dishonest". Similarly, the allocation of risks in current portfolio theory has

---

[124] Chapter 9.

[125] *Target Holdings v. Redferns* [1996] 1 A.C. 421; [1995] 3 W.L.R. 352; [1995] 3 All E.R. 785.

[126] Hayton [1990] Conv. 370; [1993] L.Q.R. 485.

played a part in understanding the duties of trustees in respect of the investment of trust funds. The question is then the role of risk in deciding the allocation of proprietary and personal rights in equity and restitution. There may be situations in which the parties have sought to allocate risks and thereby rights in specific property or to amounts of money. In such cases, the allocation should be protected as manifesting the common intention of the parties. Alternatively, there may be situations where a party is forced to take a risk which it did not intend to take. In such circumstances, the forced taking of the risk ought to be remedied by a proprietary remedy which would place the wronged party in the position it would have occupied but for that risk.[127]

12–109 Thirdly, the concept of money itself continues to be difficult in English law. Apart from the difficulty of seeing money as a physical chattel in all cases, there is a problem with understanding the intangible nature of the property with which financial institutions are concerned. In contracting a financial derivative, obligations are made and undertaken to transfer amounts of value between electronic accounts. Therefore, there is a need for English law to understand the nature of that value in property law terms. As discussed in *The Concept of Money*[128] there are difficult jurisprudential questions of the precise nature of the property envisaged by English law when granting rights *in rem.*

12–110 It is contended that contracts surrounding money held in electronic bank accounts ought to consider property rights in terms of rights between individuals rather than as full rights *in rem.*[129] The money in the electronic bank accounts is "virtual money". That is, there is no money that has ever been deposited as notes and coins in a bank which is equal to the amounts involved in those transactions. Rather the counterparties are trading value held in bank accounts. That value is created in the form of debts with the institution holding the account or loans that constitute permissions to pledge virtual money up to a certain amount. It is difficult to see how there could ever be a right *in rem* in respect of something that has never existed. There has never been "a thing" which could be the object of that right. Rather there is only ever an obligation to pay or receive amounts of value by reference to a further chose in action—the bank account.

12–111 While such choses in action are themselves considered to be money, they are not chattels in the manner which Lord Browne-Wilkinson considers them. Rather, they are intangibles, promises to pay. They are "virtual" money contracted in the virtual reality of the financial markets. Therefore, in deciding whether or not a proprietary remedy is appropriate, what is at stake is the size of the return which is to be awarded in respect of value of that nature and that size. The issue for a proprietary remedy is the nature of the obligation to pay. As considered by Lords Goff and Woolf, the justice of the situation was that compound interest ought to be paid even though a proprietary remedy was expressly disavowed by their Lordships. That is the error, it is submitted, of the two partially dissenting speeches in *Islington*. An award of compound interest in a situation where value calculated in a particular currency is paid and owed, would be an award based on continued ownership of that value throughout the life of the transaction. On the facts in *Islington* that value had been transferred outright to

[127] The other party would simply need to reprice the transaction to absorb its own potential liability.

[128] Chapter 4.

[129] An issue explored in Eleftheriadis, "The Analysis of Property Rights" (1996) O.J.L.S. 31; discussing the ideas of Hohfeld, *Fundamental Legal Conceptions As Applied in Judicial Reasoning* (Cook ed., 1923).

the authority. Therefore, when Lords Goff and Woolf refused a proprietary award but yet contend that compound interest ought to be paid, they were granting a proprietary remedy in fact. The logical leap in their reasoning was not accounting for the nature of the property. The property was value held in an electronic bank account—an obligation to pay money. This fits more closely with Hohfeld's analysis of property rules as being obligations between persons rather than being "rights in a thing".

12–112 Fourthly, following on from the discussion of the nature of "money", is the problem of reserving proprietary rights over such property or ensuring some means of credit support. This cuts to the heart of the use that commercial markets make of English property law. Failure to support the common intentions of commercial people to rights in property, or awards tantamount to such rights, weaken the confidence of all users in that code. On the agreements before the courts in the swaps cases there must be some doubt as to the efficacy of the proprietary claims made by the banks. The BBAIRS agreement[130] and the ISDA agreement[131] simply did not protect the participants in the manner they would have wanted. However, that does not satisfy a need for the courts to examine the extent of those shortcomings and to give some clue as to the future. It is contended that the suitability approach, specifically through the use of common intention constructive trusts and the doctrine of undue influence, ought to be able to regulate the availability of proprietary rights and security for commercial transactions.

12–113 Fifthly, the approach of equity to commercial cases in decisions involving and contemporaneous to the swaps cases demonstrates a significant undercurrent of change in the form of its principles. The test for a constructive and resulting trust in *Islington*,[132] the test for dishonesty in *Tan*[133] and the drift of common intention constructive trusts cases like *Lloyds Bank v. Rosset*[134] in the speech of Lord Bridge, have seen a solidifying of the techniques of equity into hard and fast rules. While common law appears to loosening itself in the torts discussed above, equity is moving in the opposite direction. As such it is proposed that the suitability approach outlined above constitutes a part of this reformulation of equity in response to changing subject matter.

12–114 Sixthly, the question remains: what is a swap? This book has sought to explain in a little more detail than the swaps cases did the breadth of the derivatives firmament and also to consider the different impacts of the various possible analyses of similar transactions. The core of this analysis is based on swaps pricing models and credit risk models, both of which are central to the formation of a derivative. Rather than viewing a swap as a transaction which is always the same as the one before and the one after, it is important to construe financial derivatives in the same way that other commercial and shipping contracts are typically construed in detail. To achieve this construction it is important to look at the commercial purpose of the transaction. That commercial purpose (be it hedging, speculation or otherwise) will indicate the appropriate analysis of the transaction. Consequently, the appropriate equitable or restitutionary response will emerge.

---

130 British Bankers' Association, *BBAIRS Agreement for Interest Rate Swaps* (London, BBA, 1987).

131 ISDA, ISDA Multicurrency Master Agreement (ISDA, 1992).

132 [1996] A.C. 669.

133 [1995] 2 A.C. 378.

134 [1991] 1 A.C. 107.

12–115 The approach of this book has been to analyse complex legal material in the context of a changing and ever more complex world. The sociology of late twentieth century western economies has changed rapidly over the last two decades. The establishment of a globalised economy, increased use of supra-national entities such as the EU and the UN, a growth in supra-national regulation, the entrenchment of mass unemployment in most economies, demographic shifts towards a population which is living longer with a shrinking number of people paying tax, and the growth of information technology all offer a very new context for the courts in considering commercial transactions.

12–116 While this book has argued for a different approach from the courts to complex financial and commercial transactions, it has not sought to protect those markets mindlessly or even to argue that the swaps cases were wrongly decided on their facts given the shortcomings of the standard market contracts used at the time. The broader understanding which informs this book is that the world is becoming a more complex place in which it is less possible for the courts to rely on the breadth of arcane equitable principles such as "he who comes to equity must come with clean hands" in situations where commercial people are creating contracts born out of complex mathematical understandings of the world. For the autopoietic theorists this is a situation in which different social systems have failed to meet and communicate. The legal system has not been able to translate the operations of the global financial system in a way that enables one to understand the complexities of the other. The result is a continuation of the doctrinal conflicts within the English legal system and a problem for the financial world to ensure that their transactions are properly secured.

12–117 For the sociologists like Giddens globalisation is something broader than the operation of financial markets across geographic boundaries.[135] Globalisation refers to a systematic change in social relations. While it incorporates the growth of international and supra-national control of government, administration, regulation and economics, it also refers to a centralisation of governmental power away from local authorities while at the same time requiring the individual to make more decisions which would otherwise have been made for them. At one level, this arises from the deconstruction of economies built around heavy industry together with the broadening of economic opportunity. The range of options produced creates problems for the individual in a way which a lack of choice never did.[136] The financial derivatives market is an illustration both of the growth of international possibilities for action with a greater range of choices for actors. The ability to speculate through derivatives without needing to enter into a market physically is one manifestation of this globalisation, as is the ability to restructure contractual loan obligations through interest rate swaps. The techniques, in the best postmodern tradition, are both simple and very complex. The swaps cases have shown English law to be caught between very simple, intuitive ideas and subject matter too complex to analyse closely. The role of restitution and of equity is to address itself to that form of social realignment: to provide justice in a more difficult and more complicated world than the one that produced them originally.

---

[135] Giddens, *Beyond Left and Right*, (Polity Press, 1994).

[136] Giddens, *Modernity and Self-Identity*, (Polity Press, 1991).

Bibliography

Allen, "Bribes and Constructive Trusts: *A-G Hong Kong v. Reid*" (1995) 58 M.L.R. 87.

American Law Institute, *Restatement of the Law of Restitution* (St Paul, 1937).

Annetta, "Priority Rights in Insolvency—The Doctrinal Basis for Equity''s Intervention" (1992) 20 A.B.L.R. 311.

Arora, "The Bank's Liability as a Constructive Trustee" [1990] J.B.L. 217.

Arrowsmith, "Ineffective Transactions and Unjust Enrichment: a Framework for Analysis" (1989) 9 L.S. 121.

Atiyah, *The Rise and Fall of Freedom of Contract* (Oxford, 1979).

Atiyah, *Essays on Contract* (Oxford, 1986).

Austin, "Constructive Trusts" in *Essays In Equity* (Finn ed., 1985), p. 196.

Baker and Langan, *Snell's Principles of Equity* (29th ed., Sweet & Maxwell, London, 1990).

Bamforth, "Unconscionability as a Vitiating Factor" [1995] L.M.C.L.Q. 538.

Banks, *The Credit Risk of Complex Derivatives* (Macmillan, 1994).

Beatson, "Restitutionary Remedies for Void and Ineffective Contracts" (1989) 105 L.Q.R. 179.

Beatson, *Use and Abuse of Unjust Enrichment* (Oxford, 1991).

Beatson, "The Relationship between Regulations Governing the Financial Services Industry and Fiduciary Duties under the General Law" in *Commercial Aspects of Trusts and Fiduciary Obligations* (McKendrick ed., Oxford, 1992), p. 55.

Benjamin, *The Law of Global Custody* (Sweet & Maxwell, London, 1996).

Birks, *Introduction to the Law of Restitution* (Oxford, 1989).

Birks, "Misdirected Funds" (1989) 105 L.Q.R. 258.

Birks, "Misdirected Funds Again" (1989) 105 L.Q.R. 528.

Birks, "Misdirected Funds; Restitution from the Recipient" [1989] L.M.C.L.Q. 296.

Birks, *Restitution—the Future* (Sydney, 1992).

Birks, "Restitution and Resulting Trusts" in *Equity: Contemporary Legal Developments* (Goldstein ed., Jerusalem, 1992), p. 335.

Birks, "Trusts in the Recovery of Misapplied Assets: Tracing, Trusts and Restitution" in *Commercial Aspects of Trusts and Fiduciary Obligations* (McKendrick, Oxford, 1992).

Birks, "No Consideration: Restitution after Void Contracts" (1993) 23 U.W.A.L.R. 195.

Birks, "Establishing a proprietary base" [1995] R.L.R. 83.

Birks ed., *Laundering and Tracing* (Oxford, 1995).

Birks, "Overview: Tracing, Claiming and Defences" in *Laundering and Tracing* (Birks ed. Oxford, 1995), p. 289.

Birks, "Equity in the Modern Law: An Exercise in Taxonomy" (1996) 26 U.W.A.L.R. 1.

Birks, "Trusts raised to avoid unjust enrichment: the *Westdeutsche* Case" [1996] R.L.R. 3.

Birks, "Tracing, Subrogation and Change of Position" (1996) *Trusts Law International* 2.

Birks and Chambers, *Restitution Research Resource* (Mansfield Press, 1997), p. 1-6.

Birks, "The Burden on the Bank" in *Restitution and Banking Law* (Rose ed., Mansfield Press, 1998), p. 189.

Birks, "Misnomer" in *Restitution, Present and Future: Essays in Honour of Gareth Jones* (Cornish, Nolan, O'Sullivan and Virgo, eds., Hart Publishing, Oxford, 1998), p. 1

BIS, *International Convergence of Capital Measurement and Capital Standards*; BIS (1988).

Black, *Rules and Regulators* (Oxford, 1997).

Brealey and Myers, *Principles of Corporate Finance* (5th ed., McGraw Hill, 1995).

British Bankers Association, *British Bankers Association Interest Rate Swap Terms* (London, BBA, 1987).

Burns, Cheshire and Burns, *The Law of Real Property* (15th ed., Butterworths, London, 1994).

Burrows, ed., *Essays in the Law of Restitution* (Oxford, 1991).

Burrows, "Public Authorities, *Ultra Vires* and Restitution" in *Essays in the Law of Restitution* (Burrows ed., Oxford, 1991).

Burrows, *The Law of Restitution* (Butterworths, London, 1993).

Burrows, "Swaps and Friction between Common Law and Equity" [1995] R.L.R. 15.

Burrows, *Remedies in Contract and Tort* (2nd ed., Butterworths, London, 1994).

Burrows and McKendrick, *The Law of Restitution* (Oxford, 1997).

Burrows, "Understanding the Law of Restitution: A Map through the Thicket" in *Understanding the Law of Obligations* (Hart Publishing, Oxford, 1998), pp. 45 *et seq*.

Chambers, *Resulting Trusts* (Oxford, 1997).

Chambers, "Restitution, Trusts and Compound Interest" (1996) 20 Mel. U.L. Rev. 848.

Cheshire and Burns, *The Law of Real Property*, (15th ed., Butterworths, London, 1994).

Chitty on Contracts (27th ed., Sweet & Maxwell, London, 1994).

Collins, *Dicey and Morris on the Conflict of Laws* (12th ed., Sweet & Maxwell, 1993).

Copeland and Weston, *Financial Theory and Corporate Policy* (3rd ed., Addison Wesley, 1988).

Cowan, "Banks, Swaps, Restitution and Equity" [1993] L.M.C.L.Q. 300.

Cranston, *Principles of Banking Law* (Oxford, 1997).

Das, *Swaps and Derivative Financing* (2nd ed., Irwin, 1994).

Dewar, "The Development of the Remedial Constructive Trust" (1982) 60 Can. B.R. 265.

Eleftheriadis, "The Analysis of Property Rights" (1996) O.J.L.S. 31.

Elias, *Explaining Constructive Trusts* (Oxford, 1990).

Ferguson (1993) 109 L.Q.R. 114.

Finn, ed., *Fiduciary Obligations* (Sydney, 1977).

Finn, ed., *Essays in Equity* (Sydney, 1985).

Finn, ed., *Equity and Commercial Relationships* (Sydney, 1985).

Finn, ed., *Essays on Restitution* (Sydney, 1990).

Finn, "Fiduciary Law in the Modern Commercial World" in *Commercial Aspects of Trusts and Fiduciary Obligations* (McKendrick, Oxford, 1992).

Ford and Lee, *The Law of Trusts* (3rd ed., Sydney, 1996).

Fridman, "The Reach of Restitution" (1991) 11 L.S. 304.

Fried, *Contract as Promise* (Oxford, 1981).

Friedmann and Cohen, *The International Encyclopaedia of Comparative Law* (Lancaster, 1991), 24n., p. 177.
Friedmann (1991) 11 L.S. 304.
Giddens, *Beyond Left and Right* (Polity Press, 1994).
Giddens, *Modernity and Self-Identity* (Polity Press, 1991).
Glover, "Bankruptcy and Constructive Trusts" (1991) 19 A.B.L.R. 98.
Goff & Jones, *The Law of Restitution* (Sweet & Maxwell, 1993).
Golden, "*OTC Derivatives, the Legal and Regulatory Challenge*", May 31, 1997, London (IBC U.K. Conferences).
Goode, (1983) 3 L.S. 283.
Goode, "Ownership and Obligation in Commercial Transactions" (1987) 103 L.Q.R. 433.
Goode, "Property and Unjust Enrichment", in *Essays on Restitution* (Burrows ed., Oxford, 1991), Chap. 9.
Goode, *Principles of Corporate Insolvency Law* (2nd ed., Sweet & Maxwell, 1997).
Goudling [1992] Conv. 367.
Grantham, "Doctrinal Bases for the Recognition of Proprietary Rights" (1996) O.J.L.S. 561.
Grantham, "Restitution, Property and Ignorance—a Reply to Mr Swadling" [1996] L.M.C.L.Q. 463.
Gray, *Elements of Land Law* (2nd ed., Butterworths, 1993).
Gummow J., "Unjust Enrichment, Restitution and Proprietary Remedies" in *Essays on Restitution* (P.D. Finn ed., Sydney, 1990) Chap. 3.
Hammond (1990) 106 L.Q.R. 207.
Hanbury and Martin, *Modern Equity* (13th ed., Sweet & Maxwell, London, 1993).
Harpum, 50 C.L.J. 409.
Harpum, 11 L.Q.R. 545.
Haynes, "Asset Securitisation", WG Hart Workshop 1998, Institute of Advanced Legal Studies, London.
Hayton [1988] Conv. 259.
Hayton, "Constructive Trusts: Is the Remedying of Unjust Enrichment a Satisfactory Approach?" in *Equity, Fiduciaries and Trusts* (Youdan ,ed., Toronto, 1989), Chap. 9.
Hayton, "Investment Management Problems" (1990) L.Q.R. 89-93.
Hayton [1990] Conv. 370; (1993) L.Q.R. 485.
Hayton, "Equitable Rights of Cohabitees" in *Equity and Contemporary Legal Developments* (Goldstein, ed., Jerusalem, 1992).
Hayton, Underhill and Hayton, *Law of Trusts and Trustees* (Butterworths, 1995).
Hayton and Marshall, *Cases and Commentary on the Law of Trusts and Equitable Obligations* (Sweet & Maxwell, London, 1996).
Hedley, "Unjust Enrichment as the Basis of Restitution—an Overworked Concept" (1985) 5 L.S. 56.
Henderson and Price, *Understanding Swaps* (London, 1990).
Henderson, *Legal, Accounting and Control Challenges of Credit Derivatives*, IBC.
Hohfeld, *Fundamental Legal Conceptions As Applied in Judicial Reasoning* (Cook ed., 1923).
Hudson, "The Counter-Revolutionary Business Code in Hungary", (1992) 18 *Review of Central and East European Law* 301.
Hudson, *The Law on Financial Derivatives* (1st ed., Sweet & Maxwell, London, 1996; 2nd ed., Sweet & Maxwell, London, 1998).

Hudson, "The Legal Aspect of Financial Derivatives", *Business Law Review*, October 1996, 199, 199-201.

Hudson, *Amicus Curiae*, November 1997, Vol. 2, p.27.

International Swaps and Derivatives Association, *ISDA Multicurrency Master Agreement 1992* (New York & London, ISDA, 1992).

International Swaps and Derivatives Association ("ISDA"), *ISDA News*, December 1997.

Jaffey, "*Restitutionary Damages and Disgorgement*", [1995] R.L.R. 30.

Jaffey [1996] R.L.R. 92.

Jones (1968) 84 L.Q.R. 474.

Jones, "Remedies for the Recovery of Money Paid by Mistake" (1980) 39 C.L.J. 275.

Jones, *Restitution in Public and Private Law* (London, 1991).

Jones, Goff & Jones, *The Law of Restitution* (Sweet & Maxwell, London, 1993).

Jones (1996) 55 C.L.J. 432-435.

Keeton, 72 Harv. L. Rev. 401 (1959).

Konoshi and Dattatreya, *Derivative Instruments* (revised ed., Konoshi & Dattatreya, ed., Irwin, 1996), pp. 1-19.

Law Comm., *Fiduciary Duties and Regulatory Rules* (1992, LCCP 124).

Law Comm., *Restitution: Mistakes of Law and Ultra Vires Public Authority Receipts and Payments* (1994, Law Com. No. 227).

Law Comm., *Fiduciary Duties and Regulatory Rules* (1995, Law Com. No. 236).

Litman, "The Emergence of Unjust Enrichment as a Cause of Action and the Remedy of Constructive Trust" (1988) 26 Alberta L.R. 407.

Little, "An Overview of Regulation in the U.K.", in *Swaps and Off-Exchange Derivatives Trading* (Bettelheim, Parry and Rees eds., FT Law and Tax, London, 1996), pp. 15 *et seq*.

Lomnicka, *Modern Banking Law* (2nd ed., Oxford, 199).

Mann, "On Interest, Compound Interest and Damages" (1985) 101 L.Q.R. 30.

Mann, *The Legal Aspect of Money* (5th ed., Oxford, 1992).

Mason, K.C.L.J. 8 (1997/98), 1.

Maudsley, "Propietary Remedies for the Recovery of Money" (1959) 75 L.Q.R. 234.

Mann, "On Interest, Compound Interest and Damages" (1985) 101 L.Q.R. 30.

Martin, Hanbury and Martin, *Modern Equity* (13th ed., Sweet & Maxwell, London, 1993).

Martin, "Tracing, Fraud and *Ultra Vires*" [1993] Conv. 370.

McCormack, "Assisting in a Breach of Trust: Principles of Accessory Liability" (1995) T.L.I. 102.

McCormack, "Mistaken Payment and Proprietary Claims" [1996] Conv. 86.

McCormack, "The Eye of Equity: Identification Principles and Equitable Tracing" [1996] J.B.L. 225.

McKendrick, "Tracing Misdirected Funds" [1991] L.M.C.L.Q. 378.

McKendrick, *Commercial Aspects of Trusts and Fiduciary Obligations* (Oxford, 1992).

McKendrick, "Local Authorities and Swaps: Undermining the Market?" in *Making Commercial Law: Essays in Honour of Roy Goode* (Cranston ed., Oxford, 1997).

Merton Miller, *Merton Miller on Derivatives* (Wiley Investment, 1997).

Millett (1991) 107 L.Q.R. 71.

Millett, "Restitution: Taking Stock", delivering the Society of Advanced Legal Studies Lecture, Institute of Advanced Legal Studies, London, July 23, 1998.
Mitchell, *The Law of Subrogation* (Oxford, 1994).
Moriarty, "Tracing, Mixing and Laundering", in *Laundering and Tracing* (Birks ed., Oxford, 1995), p. 73.
Morrison, *Jurisprudence—from the Greeks to Postmodernism* (Cavendish, London, 1997).
Oakley, "The Prerequisites of an Equitable Tracing Claim" (1975) 28 C.L.P. 64.
Oakley (1995) 54 C.L.J. 377.
Oakley, *Constructive Trusts* (Sweet & Maxwell, London, 1997).
Oliver (1997/98) KCLJ 8 147.
Paciocco, "The Remedial Constructive Trust: A Principled Basis for Priorities over Creditors" (1989) 68 Can. BR 315.
Pawlowski, *The Doctrine of Proprietary Estoppel* (Sweet & Maxwell, London, 1996).
Pearce, "A Tracing Paper" (1976) 40 Conv. 277.
Pound, 33 Harv. L. Rev. 420.
Rajani, "Equitable Assistance in the Seach for Security", in *Insolvency Law: Theory and Practice* (H. Rajak ed., London, 1993), Chap. 2.
Rickett (1991) 107 L.Q.R. 608.
Rickett [1991] Conv. 125.
Rider, "The Fiduciary and the frying pan" [1978] Conv. 114.
Rider, Abrams and Ashe, *Guide to Financial Services Regulation*, (3rd ed., CCH, Oxford, 1997).
Rose, ed., *Restitution and Banking Law* (Mansfield Press, Oxford, 1998).
Sherwin, "Constructive Trusts in Bankruptcy" [1989] Univ. of Illinois LR 297.
Simpson, *A History of the Common Law of Contract.*
SIB, *SIB Consultative Paper 89* (SIB, August 1995)
SIB, *SIB Guidance Note 1/96.*
Smith, "Tracing into the Payment of a Debt" (1995) 54 C.L.J. 290.
Smith, *The Law of Tracing* (Oxford, 1997).
Smith, "Tracing and Electronic Funds Transfer", in *Restitution and Banking Law* (Rose ed., Mansfield Press, Oxford, 1998), p. 120.
Smith and Walter, *Global Financial Services* (Harper & Row, 1990).
Stevens, "Election between alternative remedies" [1996] R.L.R. 117.
Swadling [1994] All E.R. Rev. 259.
Swadling [1994] R.L.R. 195.
Swadling, "A New Role for Resulting Trusts?", (1996) 16 L.S. 110, esp. 124-125, considering.
Swamy, *Derivative Instruments* (revised ed., Konoshi & Dattatreya, eds., Irwin, 1996), p. 47.
Tennekoon, *Legal Aspect of International Finance* (Butterworths, London, 1992).
Tettenborn [1980] C.L.J. 272.
Tettenborn, *The Law of Restitution in England and Ireland* (2nd ed., Cavendish, London, 1997).
Tettenborn, "Misnomer: A Response", in *Restitution, Present and Future: Essays in Honour of Gareth Jones* (Cornish, Nolan, O'Sullivan and Virgo, eds., Hart Publishing, Oxford, 1998), p. 31.
Teubner, *Law as an Autopoietic System* (Oxford, 1994).
Walker, "Financial Derivatives—Global Regulatory Developments" [1996] J.B.L. 66.
Waters, *The Constructive Trust* (1964).

Watts (1996) 112 L.Q.R. 219.

Whittaker and Kumar, "Credit Derivatives—A Primer" in *Derivative Instruments* (revised ed., Konoshi & Dattatreya eds., Irwin, 1996).

Wood, *Title Finance, Derivatives, Securitisations, Set-off and Netting* (Sweet & Maxwell, London, 1995).

Worthington, *Proprietary Interests in Commercial Transactions* (Oxford, 1996).

Youdan, ed., *Equity, Fiduciaries and Trusts* (Toronto, 1989).

Zimmerman, *The Law of Obligations: Roman Foundations of the Civilian Tradition* (Oxford, 1996).

Index